Trout Streams of Pennsylvania

An Angler's Guide

by Dwight Landis

HEMPSTEAD - LYNDELL
BELLEFONTE, PENNSYLVANIA

Trout Streams of Pennsylvania: An Angler's Guide

Copyright 1991 by Dwight Landis

Manufactured in the United States

Library of Congress Catalog Card Number: 90-86247
ISBN: 1-879475-00-6

Printing   94 93   8 7 6 5 4 3

Published by Hempstead-Lyndell
P.O. Box 69
Bellefonte, PA 16823

Photos and maps are by the author unless credited otherwise.
Cover design by Steve Kress

Additions or Corrections?
    Conditions are constantly changing along our trout streams.
If you would like to suggest additions or corrections to help update
future editions of this guide, please write to Dwight Landis, c/o
Hempstead-Lyndell, P.O. Box 69, Bellefonte, PA 16823. All letters
are welcome.

Cover photo: Hunts Run, Cameron County

Acknowledgments

It would have been impossible to complete this book without the generous assistance of many wonderful people. I am very grateful to everyone who contributed. I would like to thank especially the following:

My brothers and sisters for their support, suggestions, and help with all aspects of the book. Special thanks to Marv Klassen-Landis for spending many hours at the unenviable task of editing and proofreading the manuscript.

The many members of the Pennsylvania Fish Commission, including fisheries managers, fisheries technicians, biologists, office-of-information personnel, and Waterways Conservation Officers, all of whom were very helpful in providing trout stream information.

Rome Hanks for sharing his time and expertise of computers and laser printers.

Gretchen Hanks, a librarian at the Centre County Library in Bellefonte, for locating many books used in my research, including some rather obscure angling titles.

Dave Dibiase for his sharing his knowledge of map design and map production techniques.

The cheerful staff of the Maps Room at Penn State University's Pattee Library for locating (and refiling) the seemingly endless reference maps needed for this project.

The many anglers and tackle shop proprietors who shared information about their local streams.

Jere White and Rick Landis for introducing me to trout fishing and teaching me the basic skills of fly fishing and fly tying many years ago.

Table of Contents

Pennsylvania Regions

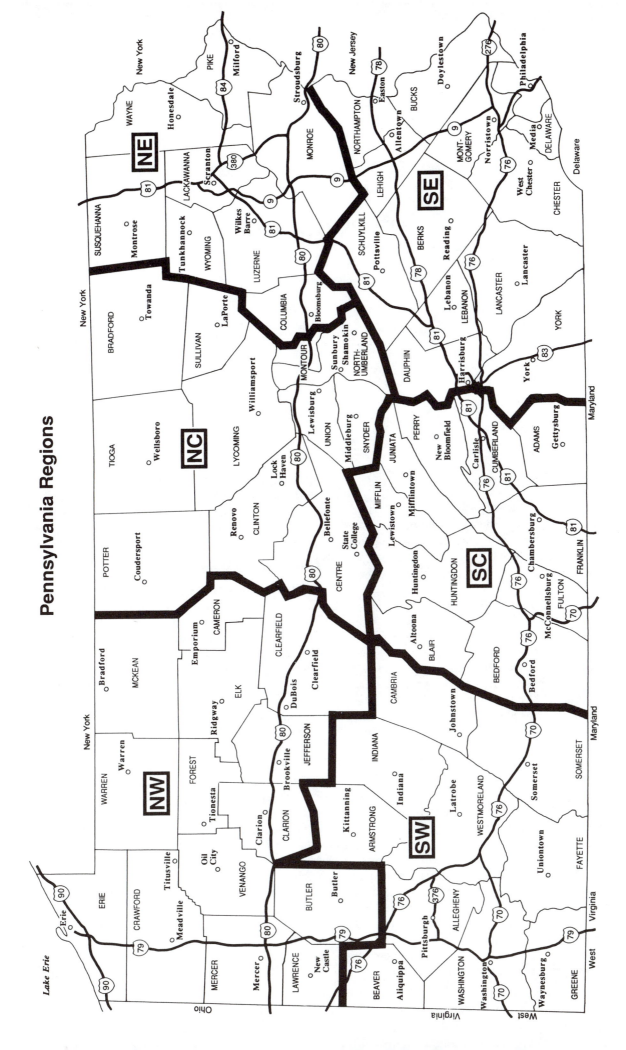

Introduction

The Streams

Pennsylvania has a great wealth of trout streams, ranging in size from tiny mountain brooks to large rivers such as the Delaware and the Youghiogheny. Throughout the state you can find good fishing for both wild, stream-bred trout and stocked, hatchery-reared trout.

Pennsylvania's streams flow through a variety of landscapes. Many flow through little-developed woodlands, often within the boundaries of state forests, state game lands, or the Allegheny National Forest. Other streams flow through rural farming valleys. Some flow through suburban areas or even right through the middle of cities and towns.

In this book I have tried to include a good sampling of the diversity of trout water found in the state: big streams and small, limestone and freestone streams, wild trout streams and stocked trout streams, streams under general regulations and streams with special regulations areas. I also selected streams from each region of the state. Scenic surroundings, fly hatches, and absence of posted property were also considered.

Many streams with good wild trout populations were chosen because anglers can fish these streams at any time during the season with the confidence that they hold trout. I also chose many streams with special regulations areas. On stocked trout streams, the special regulations limit the kill of trout and maintain good numbers of hatchery fish through mid-June on most streams and through the summer and into the fall on some streams. Special regulations on wild trout streams have often led to increases in the numbers and size of trout found in those streams. The special regulations areas also have the advantage of being open to fishing year around.

Freestone Streams

Trout streams are often classified into two broad categories: freestone streams and limestone streams. Most trout streams are considered freestone streams. These streams originate as small hillside trickles, which join to form brooks, which in turn join to form medium-sized streams, eventually forming large rivers such as the Lehigh and the Allegheny.

Freestone streams collect their waters by surface drainage, and their flow fluctuates greatly with changes in rainfall. Melting snow and heavy rains often combine to produce high water in the early spring. As spring turns to summer, water levels drop, and by July and August, most freestone streams flow at a fraction of their spring volume. The larger freestone streams often become too warm in midsummer to provide good fishing. As water temperatures climb into the 70's, trout move to the mouths of cool tributary streams and many also migrate up into these tributary streams.

Freestone streams are less fertile than the limestone streams, but their fertility varies considerably from stream to stream, depending on the minerals found in the soil and rocks of the watershed and also on the amount of nutrients entering the stream from fertilizers, livestock waste, sewage effluent, and other sources. Some freestone streams have tremendous insect hatches and excellent wild trout populations; others seem to be nearly barren of trout and insects. Some of the most infertile freestone streams have had their trout and aquatic insect populations greatly reduced by the ravages of acid rain.

Limestone Streams

Limestone streams are fed by large springs, which provide a consistent flow of cool, fertile water throughout the year. These streams are characterized by their mineral-rich, alkaline water chemistries and their abundance of trout food. Most of the limestone streams in Pennsylvania are found in the southeast region, southcentral region, and the southern part of the northcentral region (from Williamsport south).

The limestone spring creeks in southcentral Pennsylvania near Carlisle and Chambersburg, such as the Letort, Big Spring, and Falling Spring, have been written about a great deal and are often considered the "typical" Pennsylvania limestone streams. Because these streams receive virtually all of their water from springs, their flow is fairly constant in volume and temperature throughout the year. They are often called meadow spring creeks because they flow slowly through meadows and fields, their smooth surfaces only occasionally broken by gentle riffles.

These meadow streams have silt bottoms along much of their lengths, anchored by extensive weedbeds of elodea and watercress, which provide shelter for the trout and the insects and crustaceans that the trout feed upon. The crustaceans commonly called cress bugs, which include sowbugs (Isopods) and scuds (Amphipods), are very abundant on such streams and make up the bulk of the trout's diet. The main mayfly hatches on the meadow streams are Blue-winged Olives, Sulphurs, and Tricos.

Not all of the limestone streams in Pennsylvania fit the meadow stream mold, however. Many large limestone streams, such as the Yellow Breeches, Penns Creek, Fishing Creek (Clinton County), Kishacoquillas Creek, Little Juniata River, and Yellow Creek, have the rich, alkaline water chemistries characteristic of all limestone streams, but they have rocky bottoms and the sequences of riffles and pools often found on freestone streams. Because these streams are fed by freestone tributaries as well as by limestone springs, their volumes and temperatures

West Branch Delaware River.

vary more during the year than those streams that are entirely spring fed.

These rocky-bottomed limestone streams do not have the extensive weed-beds of the meadow streams, and while sowbugs and scuds may be present, they are usually not abundant. These streams usually have not only the typical limestone stream mayflies mentioned above, but also a great variety of other mayflies, caddis, and stoneflies.

Many streams in the ridge-and-valley region of Pennsylvania originate as small freestone streams flowing out of the hills and mountains and become limestone streams when they reach the wider farming valleys. Some streams are converted into limestone streams by the influx of large springs; other streams sink into the ground and flow underground through limestone aquifers for some distance before emerging again as limestone spring creeks.

Tailwaters

Tailwater trout fisheries are created by cold water releases from large dams. In the summer months, water near the bottoms of deep lakes and reservoirs remains very cold. Dams equipped with special gates can draw this water from the depths and release it to the stream or river below. Tailwater trout streams in Pennsylvania include the upper Delaware River, Youghiogheny River, Tulpehocken Creek, Allegheny River below Kinzua Dam, East Branch Clarion River, and Codorus Creek.

Stream and Map Organization

The stream descriptions in this book are organized into six geographical regions. At the front of the book, there is a Pennsylvania map showing the six regions and the major cities and highways of the state.

At the beginning of each regional chapter, you will find a map of that region. These regional maps show the areas covered by the stream maps and the page numbers where they can be found.

The stream maps accompany the written descriptions of the streams. At the beginning of each stream description you will find the page number for the map of that stream. At the end of each regional chapter, there are descriptions of several "other streams," for which no maps were included.

The easiest way to find the description of a particular stream is to look up the name of the stream in the index at the back of the book.

The Trout

Brook Trout

Brook trout, or "brookies," as they are often called, are the only native salmonids in Pennsylvania streams. Both brown and rainbow trout have been introduced from other places. Biologists classify brook trout as members of the char family, rather than as true trout.

In Pennsylvania's early days, brook trout were found in large numbers, not only in the small mountain streams where they are usually found today, but also far downstream in the larger streams such as Loyalsock Creek, Kettle Creek, Pine Creek, and the Lehigh River. Water temperatures remained much cooler in the summer then because of the deep shade cast by the stands of tall trees that covered most of the state. Writings from the 1880's describe catches of 50 or 70 or even 200 brook trout per day, including fish up to 18 inches and "broad as a bass."

Brook trout were also native to the limestone spring creeks, including such well-known "brown trout streams" as the Letort and Spring Creek. Brown trout have replaced native brook trout in most of the limestone streams, but some brook trout remain in limestone streams such as Fishing Creek (Clinton County), Elk Creek (Centre County), and Big Spring Creek (Cumberland County).

Wild brook trout are now found mostly in the upper reaches of mountain freestone streams. They seldom grow to large size in these small, infertile streams. Because brook trout are gullible creatures, eager to strike at the angler's offerings, they are usually caught soon after they reach the legal length of 7 inches. Brook trout of 4 to 7 inches in length are the usual catch, and a 10-inch brookie is considered quite a good fish. Native brook trout over 12 inches in length are caught occasionally, but they are rare.

Brook trout are easier to catch than brown trout and do not leap as spectacularly as the rainbow trout, but many anglers have a special affection for the native brook trout. Their vivid colors make them among the most beautiful of fish, and they are often found in the wildest, most scenic places in Penn's Woods.

Hatchery brook trout are stocked in many streams, but they are very different in appearance from the native brook trout. The hatchery brook trout are even more easily caught than the wild brook trout, and where fishing pressure is high, few of them remain in the stream very long after stocking.

Brown Trout

Brown trout were introduced to Pennsylvania in the early 1900's from Germany and Britain, and they have adapted well to both freestone and limestone streams. Brown trout are a hardier fish than the brook trout and better able to withstand some of the rigors imposed by civilization, such as warmer water temperatures, reduced water quality, and heavy fishing pressure. Brown trout have established wild, naturally reproducing populations all through the

Hawk Falls is located on a small tributary to Carbon County's Mud Run.

state and are found not only in the lower and middle stretches of streams, but also far up into the headwaters, where they often coexist with the brook trout.

Wild brown trout are challenging quarry. Anglers accustomed to fishing for hatchery trout should realize that fishing for wild brown trout is quite a different game. Wild browns are easily spooked and must be carefully approached. In slow, clear water, browns are particularly difficult to catch. They can be caught, though, and acquiring the skills necessary to catch them regularly is what makes wild brown trout fishing so interesting and satisfying.

Brown trout can grow to a very large size, and although you may fish for years without catching one of the big ones, the possibility of hooking into a really large fish adds a lot of spice to fishing on brown trout streams. I think many people would be surprised at the number of brown trout over 20 inches long that are caught in Pennsylvania each year. These big brown trout are usually caught by the specialists who spend countless hours seeking them out, and many of the biggest fish are caught at night, but sometimes a typical weekend angler lucks into one.

Hatchery brown trout seem to be a wilder, warier strain of fish than either the hatchery rainbow or the hatchery brook trout. They are more difficult to catch than those fish, and fair numbers of hatchery browns survive through the summer. Though usually rather pale when first stocked, they begin to take on the deeper tones of the wild trout in several weeks. The fins become reddish-orange, and the brown spots and smaller red spots become more pronounced.

Hatchery brown trout that survive through the winter and into the following season are referred to as holdover trout. These trout sometimes retain bent or frayed fins from their hatchery origins, but often they look very much like wild brown trout. Biologists often must resort to using scale samples to distinguish wild browns from holdover browns.

Rainbow Trout

Rainbow trout were introduced into Pennsylvania from California. Only a very few streams in Pennsylvania hold wild rainbow trout. The upper Delaware River has a good population of wild rainbows, as does Falling Spring Branch, a small limestone spring creek near Chambersburg. Several tributaries to the Allegheny Reservoir (behind Kinzua Dam) hold fair numbers of wild rainbows, which result from the spawning of trout running up from the reservoir. Several other streams in mountainous areas of northwestern and northeastern Pennsylvania hold wild rainbows, but only in very limited numbers.

Hatchery rainbow trout are much more easily caught by anglers than hatchery brown trout. Fish Commission creel surveys indicate that on some hard-fished streams nearly 100% of the rainbow trout stocked are caught within a few weeks of stocking.

Trout Stocking

Pennsylvania has an extensive trout stocking program. Over 4 million legal-size trout are stocked annually by the Fish Commission. Approximately 1 million more are stocked by sportsmen's groups who raise Fish Commission-provided fingerlings to legal size in cooperative hatcheries. Trout are stocked in 886 streams over a length of approximately 5,000 stream miles. Trout are also stocked in 124 lakes and ponds. Roughly equal numbers of brook trout, brown trout, and rainbow trout are stocked. Hatchery trout average 9 to 10 inches in length and 1/2 pound in weight, but sometimes much larger fish are stocked.

The opening day of trout season in Pennsylvania falls on the first Saturday following April 11. From March 1 up to opening day, Fish Commission personnel stock streams throughout the state in what are referred to as preseason stockings. Some streams receive only this one stocking per year, but most receive one or several additional stockings after the opening of the season. These inseason stockings continue through the end of May and into the first week of June.

Most of the stocked trout are gone from the streams by mid-June, except where special regulations limit their harvest. Trout stocking attracts heavy fishing pressure, and freshly stocked hatchery trout are much easier to catch than wild trout. On some streams more than half the stocked trout are caught on the opening day of the season.

Trout are stocked in every county in the state, including metropolitan counties such as Philadelphia County and Allegheny County (Pittsburgh). The booklet that comes with your fishing license lists all of the streams that are stocked by the Fish Commission. An inseason stocking schedule, which lists the weeks each stream will be stocked, can be ordered from the Pennsylvania Fish Commission, P.O. Box 1673, Harrisburg, PA 17105-1673. The cost is $1.00.

Early season anglers pursue stocked trout with spinners, worms, minnows, salmon eggs, cheese, and corn. Fly fishers usually do not catch as many trout during the opening-day frenzy as those using bait, particularly if they insist on using dry flies. Good fly patterns for freshly stocked trout include White Marabou streamers, Muskrat Nymphs, chartreuse Glo-Bugs, and Wooly Buggers.

The Fish Commission stocks fingerling trout in some stream sections that have good water quality but limited spawning habitat. Many of these stream sections are below dams. The fingerlings feed and grow in the stream and soon take on the appearance and behavior of wild trout. Fingerling stocking is not an extensive program in Pennsylvania, but in some cases it has achieved good results.

Wild Trout Streams

Beginning in 1976, the Fish Commission surveyed most of the state's trout streams to identify the streams that hold good wild trout populations. Stream sections that held at least 36 pounds per acre of brown trout, or 36 pounds per acre of mixed brown and brook trout, or 27 pounds per acre of brook trout were classified as class A wild trout waters. The few stream sections in the state that held at least 2 pounds per acre of wild rainbow trout were also classified as wild trout waters.

Stocking was ended on these stream sections to protect the wild trout populations from competition with hatchery trout and from overharvest caused by heavy fishing pressure. About 107 streams in 36 counties, involving 388 miles of stream length, were included in the program. Trout numbers have increased on many of these streams since stocking ended and fishing pressure has decreased.

The Fish Commission has unfortunately received a lot of criticism for ending stocking on these streams. If you appreciate these efforts to protect our wild trout populations, show your support by sending a letter to the Pennsylvania Fish Commission, 450 Robinson Lane, Bellefonte, PA 16823.

Wild trout are found in good numbers not only in these class A streams, but also in many other stocked and unstocked streams across the state. Many of the better wild trout streams are included in this book, but there are also many others. Part of the fun of fishing is exploring new streams. I found out about one stream in southcentral Pennsylvania just by asking a gas station attendant if he knew any good trout streams in the area. He directed me to a small, shallow stream where I caught a beautiful 15-inch wild brown trout and had strikes from several other fish. This stream is not stocked and is not classified as a wild trout stream by the Fish Commission. Very few people fish it.

No one really knows for sure how many small brook trout streams there are in the mountainous, wooded parts of the state. According to Fish Commission estimates, there are roughly 1,000 of these streams that have been named. Some of the smallest brook trout streams appear as thin blue lines on topographical maps and have never been named.

As these tiny freestone streams gather to form slightly larger streams, you'll often find mixed populations of brown and brook trout. As the streams further increase in size, brown trout become dominant.

The lower stretches of many large freestone streams become too warm in midsummer to hold many wild trout, but often trout can survive year around in deep pools and where springs and tributary streams flow into the mainstream. Such places often produce large brown trout.

Many of the limestone streams in Pennsylvania have very good wild brown trout populations. These streams are rich in food and sometimes produce very large trout. Because these fish are so well fed, they are often more difficult to catch than the trout in freestone streams.

You can do your part to maintain and improve Pennsylvania's wild trout populations by releasing most of the wild trout you catch. You can usually tell which trout are wild by their bright colors and well-formed fins.

Special Regulations Areas

Many trout streams in Pennsylvania have sections managed under special regulations. These areas produce good fishing because the restrictions limit the number of fish killed, helping to ensure a reliable supply of trout. Below you'll find just a brief description of the different special regulation areas. You should check the Summary of Fishing Regulations and Laws booklet, which comes with your fishing license, for a detailed explanation of the rules governing trout fishing.

Fly Fishing Only Projects

Only artificial flies and fly tackle may be used. Open to fishing year around. No night fishing. Daily creel limit is three fish per day. Minimum size is 9 inches. No fish may be killed from March 1 to the opening day of the regular trout season.

Delayed Harvest, Fly Fishing Only

Only artificial flies and fly tackle may be used. Open to fishing year around. No night fishing. No fish may be killed from March 1 through June 14. From June 15 through the last day of February, the daily limit is three fish per day. Minimum size is 9 inches.

No Harvest, Fly Fishing Only

Only artificial flies and fly tackle may be used. Barbless hooks are required. Open to fishing year around. No night fishing. No trout may be killed. Wading is prohibited.

Catch and Release

Only artificial lures or flies may be used. Barbless hooks are required. Spinning tackle or fly tackle is permitted. Open to fishing year around. No night fishing. No trout may be killed.

Delayed Harvest, Artificial Lures Only

Only artificial lures or flies may be used. Fly tackle or spinning tackle is permitted. Open to fishing year around. No night fishing. No fish may be killed from March 1 through June 14. From June 15 through the last day of February, the daily limit is three fish per day. Minimum size is 9 inches.

Trophy Trout Projects

Only artificial lures or flies may be used. Fly tackle or spinning tackle is permitted. Open to fishing year around. No night fishing. Daily creel limit is two fish per day. Minimum size is 14 inches. No trout may be killed from March 1 to opening day of the regular trout season.

Limestone Springs Wild Trout Waters

The same regulations apply as under "No Harvest Fly Fishing Only."

Fly Fishing

In the following pages, you will find information on fly hatches that occur on Pennsylvania streams and fly patterns to match these hatches. A basic knowledge of fly fishing techniques is assumed. Many very good instructional books have been written about fly fishing and fly tying. You might start off with some of the following.

A good introductory book is *Fly Fishing For Trout* by Richard Talleur. George Harvey's *Techniques of Trout Fishing and Fly Tying* contains valuable information on fly tying, tackle, and fishing techniques. Good books on fly tying include *Art Flick's Master Fly Tying Guide, The Complete Book of Fly Tying* by Eric Leiser, and *Poul Jorgensen's Book of Fly Tying*. A good book on mayfly hatches and their imitations is *Hatches II* by Al Caucci and Bob Nastasi. *Naturals* by Gary Borger and *Dave Whitlock's Guide to Aquatic Trout Foods* are good guides to the various creatures trout eat and flies to match them. *Trout Tactics* by Joe Humphries is an excellent book covering very practical on-the-stream fishing techniques.

Of course, the best way to learn about fly tying and fly fishing is from personal instruction. Many fly fishers are glad to instruct newcomers to the sport, and Trout Unlimited chapters, other fishing clubs, and fly shops often offer fly tying classes.

The Hatches

The number of different aquatic insect species found in Pennsylvania streams run far into the hundreds. Following are descriptions of the some of the most common mayflies and caddisflies. You may notice that the starting dates given for some of the hatches on the emergence chart are earlier than those given in many well-known fly fishing books, such as *Matching the Hatch*, *Selective Trout*, or *Hatches*. The reason is that much of the material in those books was based on information from New York and Michigan, which have a colder climate than Pennsylvania. Because Pennsylvania has a somewhat milder climate than those states, water temperatures warm more quickly in the spring, and the hatches begin earlier.

Picking a starting date for fly hatches is never very exact, of course. Unusually cold or warm water temperatures can advance or retard hatches by a week or even two weeks from the expected hatching period. Spring weather in Pennsylvania is very unpredictable. In some years, the weather on opening day in mid-April is sunny with temperatures reaching the 70's. In other years you'll experience cold winds, freezing rain, and even snow flurries.

Because insect hatching dates vary with water temperatures, hatches begin earlier in the southern part of the state and on large streams with little shading. Hatches begin latest on small mountain streams in the northern half of the state.

Blue-winged Olives
Baetis and *Ephemerella* species – sizes 16 and 18

Blue-winged Olives can be found hatching at virtually any time of the year. They appear on both limestone and freestone streams. I have seen good hatches as early as mid-March and as late as the first week in November. Many streams have good hatches in June. Fur nymphs tied with dark olive-brown dubbing are effective before and during the hatch.

During the hatch, try dressing an unweighted fur nymph with dry fly floatant and presenting it to rising trout. Blue-winged Olive dry flies are available from many fly shops, and if you don't have a specific imitation, try one of these patterns: Adams, Red Quill, Blue Quill, Blue Dun, or Dun Variant.

Blue Quills
Paraleptophlebia adoptiva – sizes 16 and 18

Blue Quills are similar in size and appearance to Blue-winged Olives and are often mistaken for them. Specific Blue Quill patterns are sold by some fly shops. A favorite old pattern, the Red Quill, is a good imitation of this insect. Other suitable patterns include Dun Variant, Blue Dun, Blue-winged Olive, and Adams. Blue Quills are abundant on many small to medium-sized freestone streams and also on some rocky limestone streams, such as Fishing Creek (Clinton County).

Quill Gordons
Epeorus pleuralis – sizes 12 and 14

Quill Gordons are not as common as they once were, probably because of their requirement for clean, cold water, which is also not as common as it once was. Some clean, rocky streams in northcentral and northeastern Pennsylvania still have fair hatches.

The old classic Quill Gordon pattern is a good imitation, but other patterns, such as Red Quill, Dun Variant, Adams, and Blue Dun, will also work. Quill Gordon or Hare's Ear wet flies will often take more fish than the dry flies.

Grannoms
Brachycentrus species – sizes 14 and 16

These dark caddis flies hatch in tremendous numbers on Penns Creek and Fishing Creek (Clinton County), and they are also found on the Delaware River, Pine Creek and many other streams. Grannoms have mottled grey-brown wings and bodies that range in color from dark olive-brown to black. An Elk Hair Caddis with a black fur body works well when the trout are taking the adult caddis on the surface. The female Grannoms have bright green egg sacs and some anglers imitate these with a ball of green dubbing at the rear of their dry flies.

Most of the feeding on the Grannoms takes place under the surface on the emerging pupae. My best luck has been with this pupae pattern: *body* – dark green dubbing, *head* – dark brown fur, *wing cases* – strands of dark brown fur tied low along sides. Some anglers report having good success with the traditional Hare's Ear and Leadwing Coachman wet flies.

Hendricksons
Ephemerella subvaria – sizes 12 and 14

Hendricksons are the favorite spring mayfly hatch of many fly fishers. These mayflies are widely distributed across the northern half of Pennsylvania. The Hendrickson and the Red Quill are the traditional and still very popular dry fly patterns for this hatch. Many anglers also use Hendrickson imitations tied in the compara-dun style. Nymph and emerger patterns also work well.

In years with mild spring weather and low water levels, heavy hatches can occur as early as the opening weekend of trout season in mid-April. In cooler years, the last week in April and the first week of May are the most reliable time to catch the hatch. On small mountain streams in northern Pennsylvania, Hendricksons can often be found hatching into the second week of May.

Insect Emergence Chart

COMMON NAMES / Hook Size	Approximate Emergence Date						LATIN NAMES
	APRIL	MAY	JUNE	JULY	AUGUST	SEPT.	
Blue-winged Olives #16–18							Baetis and Ephemerella sp.
Blue Quills #16–18							Paraleptophlebia adoptiva
Quill Gordons #12–14							Epeorus pleuralis
Grannom (caddis) #14–16							Brachycentrus species
Hendricksons #14							Ephemerella subvaria
Olive Caddis (Green Caddis) #14–16							Rhyacophila and Hydropsychidae species
Sulphurs #14–16							Ephemerella invaria, rotunda & dorothea
Tan Caddis #14–16							Hydropsyche species
March Browns #12							Stenonema vicarium
Grey Foxes #12–14							Stenonema fuscum
Green Drakes #8–10							Ephemera guttulata
Brown Drakes #10–12							Ephemera simulans
Dun Caddis #14							Psilotreta species
Light Cahills #14							Stenonema & Stenacron species
Slate Drakes #12–14							Isonychia species
Tricos #22–24							Tricorythodes species
White Mayflies #14							Ephoron leukon

Olive Caddis

Rhyacophila and Hydropsychidae species – sizes 14 and 16

The terms Olive Caddis and Green Caddis are used by anglers to refer to a great number of different species of caddis that have green-colored bodies. These caddis are very widely distributed in both limestone and freestone streams throughout the state. If you want to explore the identification of caddis in detail, you should consult the books *Caddisflies* by Gary LaFontaine and *The Caddis and the Angler* by Larry Solomon and Eric Leiser.

The Green Caddis Larva, tied with an olive or green dubbed body and a head of dark brown dubbing, is a good pattern throughout the year. The body colors of the larvae vary from pale yellow-olive to bright green to dark olive tinged with grey or brown.

During the emergence, a wet fly tied with an olive body and a few turns of grouse or partridge hackle works well. An Elk Hair Caddis with a body of olive dubbing is a good imitation of the adults. The bodies of the adult caddis also vary greatly in color, covering a wide range of greens and olives.

Sulphurs

Ephemerella invaria, rotunda, and *dorothea* – sizes 14 to 18

The term "Sulphur" is used by anglers to refer to several different species of mayflies with yellow bodies and pale blue-grey wings. The Sulphurs appear on virtually all of the limestone streams and are the most prolific hatch of the year on many of them. They are also found on some freestone streams.

Most fly fishing books list the Sulphur hatch as beginning around May 15, but I've seen fair hatches as early as April 29 and heavy hatches as early as May 3. These early Sulphurs often hatch around 2:00 to 4:30 in the afternoon, and they seem to hatch most heavily on cloudy, rainy days. On clear, warm days they hatch later in the day—from about 4:30 p.m. to 7:00 p.m. Some of the early Sulphurs are fairly large flies and are best imitated by size 14 patterns.

The Sulphurs that hatch from around May 15 into June are smaller, best imitated by size 16 and 18 patterns, and they usually appear most heavily at dusk. Although the heaviest hatching tapers off around the second week in June, Sulphurs continue to hatch sporadically all through the summer. I have seen them on the water as late as September 1.

Size 16 is the best all-around hook size for Sulphur imitations. There are many Sulphur patterns. The cut-wing, thorax-style patterns are probably the best imitations of the Sulphur duns.

Fur nymphs tied with a mixture of brown Hare's Ear fur and yellow fur often work very well before and also during the hatch. Emerger patterns, which can be fished below the surface or dressed with floatant and cast to rising trout, also work very well at times. Try these two emerger patterns:

(1) *body* – light brown fur, *wing* – grey muskrat fur, *tails* – light ginger hackle fibers.
(2) *body* – pale yellow fur, *wing* – grey muskrat fur, *tails* – light ginger hackle fibers.

The Sulphur spinners, with their bright yellow-orange egg sacs, usually return to the stream in the evening, and the trout often feed heavily on them just as it gets too dark to see your fly on the water.

Tan Caddis

Hydropsyche species – sizes 14 and 16

According to entomologists, these are the most widely distributed and most numerous caddis in Pennsylvania. They are found in both limestone and freestone streams. The heaviest hatches occur during the month of May, but Tan Caddis also appear sporadically all through the season.

The larvae are usually greyish-green in color, with a dark brown head. These larvae are probably partly responsible for the effectiveness of the popular Muskrat Nymph.

During the emergence, use a wet fly tied with a body of tan fur and a few turns of grouse or partridge hackle. In recent years, Emergent Pupa patterns tied with Antron yarn, which were originated by Gary LaFontaine, have become popular for fishing caddis hatches, and many fly shops now sell these flies. An Elk Hair Caddis with a tan body works well for imitating the adults. This is also a very good general dry fly pattern and it often catches trout even when no caddis are apparent on the water.

March Browns

Stenonema vicarium – size 12

These large mayflies seldom hatch in great numbers, but they often hatch sporadically throughout the day, and trout take them readily. Specific March Brown dry flies are available in many fly shops, and these standard patterns will also take fish when the March Browns are hatching: Grey Fox, Grey Fox Variant, and Ginger Quill.

Grey Foxes

Stenonema fuscum – sizes 12 and 14

Grey Foxes are similar in appearance to the March Browns, but they are slightly smaller and lighter in color. The Grey Fox, Grey Fox Variant, Ginger Quill, and Light Cahill are all good imitations.

Green Drakes

Ephemera guttalata – sizes 8 and 10

The Green Drake hatch is one of the high points of the fly fishing season. These large mayflies often attract the feeding of large trout. Most anglers associate the Green Drake hatch with the big limestone streams of central Pennsylvania, such as Penns Creek and Fishing Creek (Clinton County), but good hatches are also found on many freestone streams, especially in the northern half of the state.

The Delaware River, Pine Creek, Kettle Creek, First Fork Sinnemahoning Creek, Driftwood Branch Sinnemahoning Creek, and many other freestone streams have good hatches. The Green Drakes are slightly smaller and darker in color on the freestone streams than on the limestone streams.

Green Drakes are not found on most of the slow-moving limestone streams, such as Spring Creek, Big Spring Creek, the Letort, Falling Spring, and Little Lehigh Creek.

The Green Drakes can begin hatching as early as the third week in May, but usually the hatching begins in earnest around Memorial Day and continues most heavily during the first week of June.

Most fly shops carry specific imitations of both the Green Drake (dun) and the Coffin Fly (spinner). Alternative patterns include a Grey Fox Variant to suggest the dun and a White Wulff to suggest the spinner. Green Drake nymphs have a light tan body with dark brown wingcases. Some anglers have reported very good success before and during the hatch with nymph imitations.

Brown Drakes
Ephemera simulans – sizes 10 and 12

Brown Drakes usually hatch at the same time as the Green Drakes or slightly later. They are not as widely distributed as the other insects on this list and the hatch usually lasts only about three days on any particular stream. Good hatches are found in the canyon of Pine Creek (Tioga County). The spinner falls at dusk can be very heavy there.

Brown Drakes are also found on the Delaware River, Kettle Creek, Driftwood Branch, First Fork Sinnemahoning Creek, and Neshannock Creek. Few fly shops sell specific Brown Drake patterns, but patterns such as the Grey Fox Variant and the Ginger Quill suggest the naturals.

Dun Caddis
Psilotreta species – size 14

The dun caddis hatch may not be as important in Pennsylvania as it is in the Catskills of New York, where it is a very heavy hatch, but these insects are found on Pennsylvania streams such as Pine Creek, Kettle Creek, Penns Creek, Delaware River, and Dyberry Creek.

During the emergence, try a wet fly tied with a body of chocolate brown fur and several turns of grouse or partridge hackle. An Elk Hair Caddis with a body of chocolate brown fur and a wing of grey elk or deer hair imitates the adult.

Light Cahills
Stenonema and *Stenacron* species – size 14

The name Light Cahill is used to describe several species of pale, straw-colored mayflies that hatch from late May into July. They hatch sporadically rather than in great numbers, but they are widely distributed and trout take their imitations readily. The Light Cahill is an excellent pattern, both for matching this hatch and as a general purpose dry fly.

Slate Drakes
Isonychia species – sizes 12 and 14

These mayflies are also known as Leadwing Coachmans, Mahogany Duns, and White-Gloved Howdys. Slate Drakes are common in freestone streams and rocky limestone streams throughout the state. Hatching is from late May through the summer and into early fall. You will often see their dark nymph cases on rocks along the stream.

The Zug-Bug and the Leadwing Coachman are popular wet fly imitations. Nymphs tied with dark reddish-brown fur also work well. The Dun Variant, Red Quill, and Quill Gordon patterns are all good dry fly imitations.

Tricos
Tricorythodes species – sizes 22 and 24

These tiny mayflies appear on many streams virtually every morning from early July to the end of October. Most limestone streams have Trico hatches, and some freestone streams do also. Tricos usually appear on the water between 7:00 and 11:00 in the morning. They appear early in the morning when the weather is hot and late in the morning when the weather is cool.

The spinners are the most important stage of the Trico hatch; most anglers do not bother with nymph or dun imitations. The following Trico spinner pattern works well: *tail* – blue dun fibers, *body* – pale olive tying thread, *thorax* – black dubbing, *wings* – white polypropylene yarn fibers, tied spent.

On streams such as Falling Spring Branch, where the Trico hatch attracts many anglers, the trout become very selective and difficult to fool. On most streams, though, few anglers fish the Trico hatch and the trout are somewhat easier to catch.

White Mayflies
Ephoron leukon – size 14

White Mayflies are not found on very many trout streams, but they appear in great numbers on Yellow Breeches Creek and the Little Juniata River. They also appear on Yellow Creek (Bedford County) and the

Delaware River. The hatch usually appears in late August and early September and most of the action takes place at dusk and after dark. Popular dry fly patterns include White Wulffs, Cream Variants, and Cream Cahills.

Spin Fishing

This book deals mostly with fly fishing, but spin fishing is also an enjoyable and productive way to pursue trout. In recent years, the excellent fishing found in the delayed-harvest, artificial-lures-only areas and trophy trout projects has increased the popularity of catch-and-release fishing among spin fishers. The survival rate of trout caught and released on artificial lures is very good and essentially the same as for trout caught on flies. Trout caught on bait, however, are often hooked too deeply to survive.

Artificial lures usually come equipped with barbed treble hooks, which make releasing trout a clumsy, difficult procedure. Pinching down the barbs and cutting off one or two of the treble hooks makes releasing trout much easier. Needle-nosed pliers will do the job. An even better solution is to replace the treble hooks with a single hook.

Spinners are surprisingly effective, even for wild brown trout in the low, clear water of midsummer. Mepps, Rooster Tails, and Panther Martins are proven brands of spinners, and there are also many effective spinners offered by smaller manufacturers. Brass and black are two of the best finish colors for spinners.

Conservation Organizations

The following non-profit organizations have been good friends of trout anglers and deserve our support:

Trout Unlimited   501 Church Street NE, Vienna, Virginia 22180. Tel: (703) 281-1100.

Trout Unlimited is a large organization of conservation-minded trout anglers, with local chapters throughout Pennsylvania, the United States, and in other countries.

Federation of Flyfishers   P.O. Box 1088, West Yellowstone, Montana 59758. Tel: (406) 646-9541.

FFF is most active in the western states, but there are several affiliated chapters in Pennsylvania and neighboring states.

Western Pennsylvania Conservancy   316 Fourth Avenue, Pittsburgh, PA 15222.

This group has purchased over 100,000 acres of land in Pennsylvania for state parks, forests, and game lands. These purchases have helped protect and ensure public access to many miles of streams. Examples include McConnells Mill State Park (Slippery Rock Creek), Ohiopyle State Park (Youghiogheny River), State Game Land No. 295 (Cherry Run), and Oil Creek State Park (Oil Creek).

Pennsylvania Environmental Defense Foundation   P.O. Box 774, Mechanicsburg, PA 17055.

This small but effective organization uses the courts to pursue the enforcement of environmental laws. They have won some important water quality decisions involving trout streams.

Additional Maps and Information

The *Pennsylvania Atlas and Gazetteer* contains maps of the entire state in one convenient atlas. Topographic features, streams, roads (including forest roads), and even some jeep and hiking trails are shown in as much detail as you're likely to need. This publication costs $14.95 and it's available at many tackle shops, bookstores, and newstands. These maps are simply excellent. I used them constantly while researching this book. The publisher is DeLorme Mapping Company, P.O. Box 298, Freeport, Maine 04032. Tel: (207) 865-4171.

The *Stream Map of Pennsylvania* by Howard Higbee is a large, 3 feet by 5 feet map that shows virtually every stream in the state, including the very small brook trout tributaries. It's not only a great reference to Pennsylvania's streams, it's also a superb example of the mapmakers craft. Mr. Higbee spent years painstakingly handscribing the thousands of streams. Rolled or folded maps cost $19.95. The laminated, rolled version costs $39.95. The *Stream Map* is published by Vivid Publishing, 347 Rural Avenue, Williamsport, PA 17701. Tel: 1-800-326-9694.

The *Pennsylvania Recreational Guide* is a good general highway map that shows the major roads and also publicly owned lands, such as state forests, state parks, and state game lands. The back of the map describes camping facilities available in these areas. This map provides a good overview of the state, which is useful for planning long drives and extensive trout fishing trips. The map is available at no cost from the Bureau of State Parks, P.O. Box 1467, Harrisburg, PA 17120. Tel: (717) 787-8800.

Maps of individual state parks are available from the same source. Most of the state parks are not large enough to encompass significant stream mileages, but the following state parks do, and their maps are very useful:

Lehigh Gorge State Park Map – shows the Lehigh River and its tributaries.

Hickory Run State Park Map – also shows the Lehigh River and its tributaries.

McConnels Mill State Park Map – shows access to much of Slippery Rock Creek.

Ohiopyle State Park Map – includes most of the Youghiogheny River.

A superb *Allegheny National Forest Map* is available, at the cost of $2.00, from the Supervisor's Office, Allegheny National Forest, 222 Liberty Street, P.O. Box 847, Warren, PA 16365. This large map covers the Allegheny Reservoir (Kinzua Dam), Tionesta Creek drainage, Clarion River drainage, and some tributaries to the Allegheny River, such as East Hickory Creek, West Hickory Creek, and Thompson Run.

State forest public use maps are available at no cost from the Department of Environmental Resources, Bureau of Forestry, P.O. Box 1467, Harrisburg, PA 17120. Ask for maps of the particular forest or forests you need. Here are some particularly useful state forest maps and the trout streams they cover:

Wyoming State Forest Map – upper Lycoming and Loyalsock Creeks and their many tributaries.

Tiadaghton State Forest Map – the lower Loyalsock drainage, the entire Lycoming Creek drainage, the lower Pine Creek drainage, Little Pine Creek, and Slate Run.

Tioga State Forest Map – the middle stretch of Pine Creek, including Pine Creek Gorge, Slate Run, Cedar Run, and many smaller tributaries.

Susquehannock State Forest Map – upper Pine Creek (from Galeton upstream), the Kettle Creek drainage, most of First Fork Sinnemahoning Creek, upper Allegheny River, and Genesee River.

Sproul State Forest Map – Young Womans Creek, Hyner Run, lower Kettle Creek, and many unstocked native brook trout streams.

Forbes State Forest Map – Laurel Hill Creek and Youghiogheny River.

Bald Eagle State Forest Map – Fishing Creek (Clinton County), Penns Creek, Elk Creek, and White Deer Creek.

Topographic quadrangle maps (1: 24,000 scale) are the most detailed and accurate maps available. The disadvantage of these maps is that they cover only a small area, requiring the purchase of numerous maps to show the length of even a medium-sized stream. They are useful, though, for hiking into small headwater streams in rugged, remote country.

The maps cost $2.50 each and they are available from some sporting goods stores or from the Distribution Branch, U.S. Geological Survey, Box 25286, Federal Center, Building 41, Denver, Colorado 80225. Their toll-free number is 1-800-USA-MAPS. A free index map of Pennsylvania, available from the same address, will enable you to locate the maps you need. Topographic maps at the scale of 1: 100,000 cover larger areas, but at less detail.

The following informative publications are available at no cost from the Pennsylvania Fish Commission, Publications Section, P.O. Box 1673, Harrisburg, PA 17105-1673:

Stream Fishing and Boating Map – The front is a good general highway map, essentially identical to the *Pennsylvania Recreational Guide* map already described, and the back has information on lakes, stream access areas, and fish hatcheries.

Wild Trout Fishing in Pennsylvania – This pamphlet includes a map of the major watersheds in the state and a listing of the unstocked wild trout streams in each watershed.

Trout Fishing in Pennsylvania – This pamphlet includes a map of the major watersheds in the state and a listing of the "approved trout waters" (stocked streams and lakes) in each watershed.

Limestone Streams – This pamphlet provides information about trout fishing on the limestone spring creeks of Pennsylvania.

Lake Erie, Pennsylvania's Great Lake – This pamphlet includes a map of the Lake Erie shore and tributary streams. It also includes the regulations affecting salmon and steelhead fishing.

Acid Precipitation – This publication outlines the damage already done to Pennsylvania's trout streams by acid precipitation (acid rain and snow) and explains how we may lose many more miles of trout habitat if acid-producing air pollutants are not reduced.

Northeast Pennsylvania

The Lehigh River downstream from White Haven.

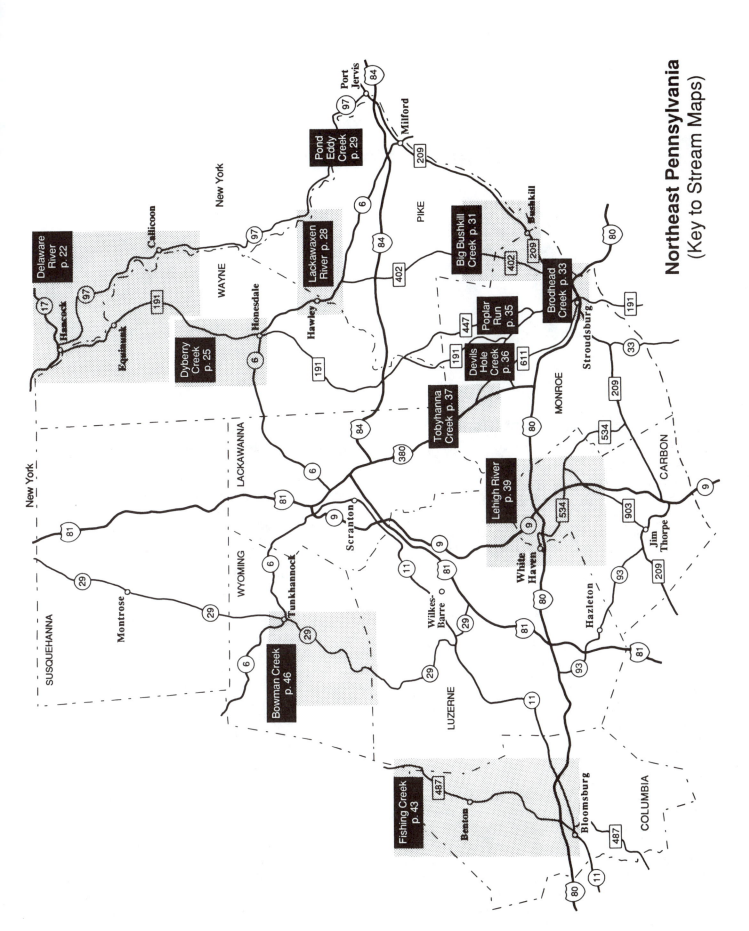

Northeast Pennsylvania
(Key to Stream Maps)

Northeast Pennsylvania

Delaware River and West Branch - Wayne County
(map: page 22)

The upper Delaware River was at one time a famous smallmouth bass fishery, but cold water releases from New York City water supply reservoirs constructed on the East and West Branches of the Delaware have turned the upper Delaware into a large trout river. Wild browns and rainbows are found in the West Branch and in the main stem of the Delaware downstream as far as Callicoon. Trout are also caught below Callicoon, sometimes even as far downriver as New Hope, but the farther downstream you go from the source of the cold water, the more marginal summer water temperatures become, so the trout population becomes increasingly sparse.

The main stem of the Delaware and the lower stretch of the West Branch form the border between New York and Pennsylvania. Possession of a New York or a Pennsylvania fishing license allows you to fish from either shore.

Trout Population

The Delaware's trout population is maintained mostly by spawning in several small tributaries scattered along the length of the river. The fisheries agencies of both Pennsylvania and New York also stock fingerlings. No adult trout are currently stocked in the main branch or in the section of the West Branch that borders Pennsylvania. Brown trout predominate in the West Branch and in the upper part of the main branch, and wild rainbow trout increase in numbers from Lordville downstream. Trout grow large in the Delaware River; 14- to 15-inch fish are common, and fish up to 20 inches are caught regularly.

Just how many trout are actually in the Delaware River is the subject of much debate. Fishery biologists from New York and Pennsylvania have tried to measure the trout population, but they agree that accurate sampling is nearly impossible in the rocky riffs and deep eddies, where most of the trout are found. Anglers who have had some good days on the river, when the bugs were hatching and the trout were rising, will tell you that the Delaware is the best trout water in the eastern United States. Anglers who have spent too many frustrating days on the river, when the water level was too high or too low, or when the water temperature was too warm or cold, will tell you that the Delaware is greatly overrated. Many anglers believe the trout population is not as good now as it was in the late 1970's.

In the summer months, trout survival depends on cold water releases from the upstream dams, and in drought years the flow has been cut back to a mere trickle. High water temperatures caused a minor fish kill in the summer of 1981 and a major fish kill in August of 1985. Since these fish kills, water authorities have promised to increase summer flows, but low flows still occur each year. Another problem affecting the river is fishing pressure. Regulations limit the daily kill to three fish per day, but the river is fished hard, and more stringent regulations would probably increase the wild trout population and make the stocking of hatchery fingerlings unnecessary.

Water Levels

Because of the erratic water releases from the upstream dams, the Delaware often flows very high or very low. It is difficult to catch the river at a nice, moderate level. When it is running high, wading is dangerous and fishing is difficult, and when water levels are low, much of the river is reduced to ankle-deep flats. Many Pennsylvania anglers travel to the Delaware River in hopes of finding good conditions, but if the water level is very high or low, they just drive east on New York Route 17 to Roscoe, New York, and fish the Beaverkill and Willowemac. During the month of May and the first week of June, you have the best chance of finding moderate flows on the Delaware River, and this is also the peak time for fly hatches.

Even though water levels can change quickly on the Delaware, you can increase your chances of finding moderate flows by calling to find out what the present water levels are before driving a long distance to the river. There are two gages on the upper Delaware that measure water levels: the Hale Eddy gage on the West Branch and the Callicoon gage on the main branch. Water levels are given as gage height, measured in feet, and discharge, measured in cubic feet per second (cfs).

The National Park Service hotline, (914) 252-7100, provides a prerecorded message that gives the gage height and water temperature at Callicoon. Information on the gage height and discharge at the Callicoon and Hale Eddy gages is available from offices of the U.S. Weather Bureau. Call the Harrisburg office at (717) 234-6812 or the Philadelphia office at (215) 627-5575.

The gage height and discharge numbers may at first seem meaningless, but the following tables will give you a very general idea of what to expect at different water levels, and if you fish the Delaware regularly, you will soon find what water levels you prefer.

Hale Eddy Gage (West Branch)

Gage Height	Discharge	Description
1.4 feet	70 cfs	lowest flow in a typical year
2.2 feet	260 cfs	a good fishing level
2.7 feet	460 cfs	swift, wading becomes difficult
3.1 feet	665 cfs	very swift, wading very difficult
3.2 feet	720 cfs	average flow in a typical year
9.1 feet	8,000 cfs	highest flow in a typical year

Callicoon Gage (Main Branch)

Gage Height	Discharge	Description
2.4 feet	470 cfs	lowest flow in a typical year
2.9 feet	1,135 cfs	a good fishing level
3.3 feet	1,950 cfs	wading becomes difficult
3.5 feet	2,480 cfs	average flow in a typical year
9.7 feet	36,000 cfs	highest flow in a typical year

Fly Hatches

The Delaware River has a variety of fly hatches, including Blue-winged Olives, Hendricksons, Grannoms, Sulphurs, Olive Caddis, March Browns, Grey Foxes, Green Drakes, Brown Drakes, Isonychia, Light Cahills, Tricos, and White Mayflies.

When no flies are hatching, try drifting weighted nymphs through the deep riffs and runs. When flies are hatching, but the trout aren't rising, try drifting a trio of nymphs, emergers, or soft hackle wet flies. Big, chunky flies like Wooly Buggers or Marabou Muddlers sometimes work well when the water is high. In late spring and during the summer, fishing will be sometimes be slow during the day, but often the fish feed heavily right at dusk. In the summer months, night fishing can be productive.

The Hendrickson hatch is one of the most eagerly awaited hatches on the Delaware, and it usually reaches its peak during the first week of May. The Green Drake hatch is not as heavy on the Delaware as on many other streams, and it usually lasts only three or four days, but anglers who have hit the hatch at the right time reported having excellent fishing.

Many anglers enjoy fishing for shad, which move up the Delaware on their spawning runs. These strong, swift fish are found in the upper Delaware during the month of May. Shad can be caught on flies, spinners, and spoons, but shad darts are generally considered to be the most effective lures. Most anglers use spin gear to cast shad darts, but others lob these lead-headed little missiles with fly gear, using a technique that's sometimes called chuck-and-duck.

Getting access to the Delaware is tricky. Most of the land along the river is privately owned, and much of it is posted. Between Hancock and Callicoon, there are several old abandoned bridges, but no bridges that are open to vehicles. The river itself is public property. Once you get to the water, you can boat or wade all you please, but it's the getting to the water's edge that is sometimes difficult. Canoeing or rafting the river will take you to areas seldom reached by other anglers.

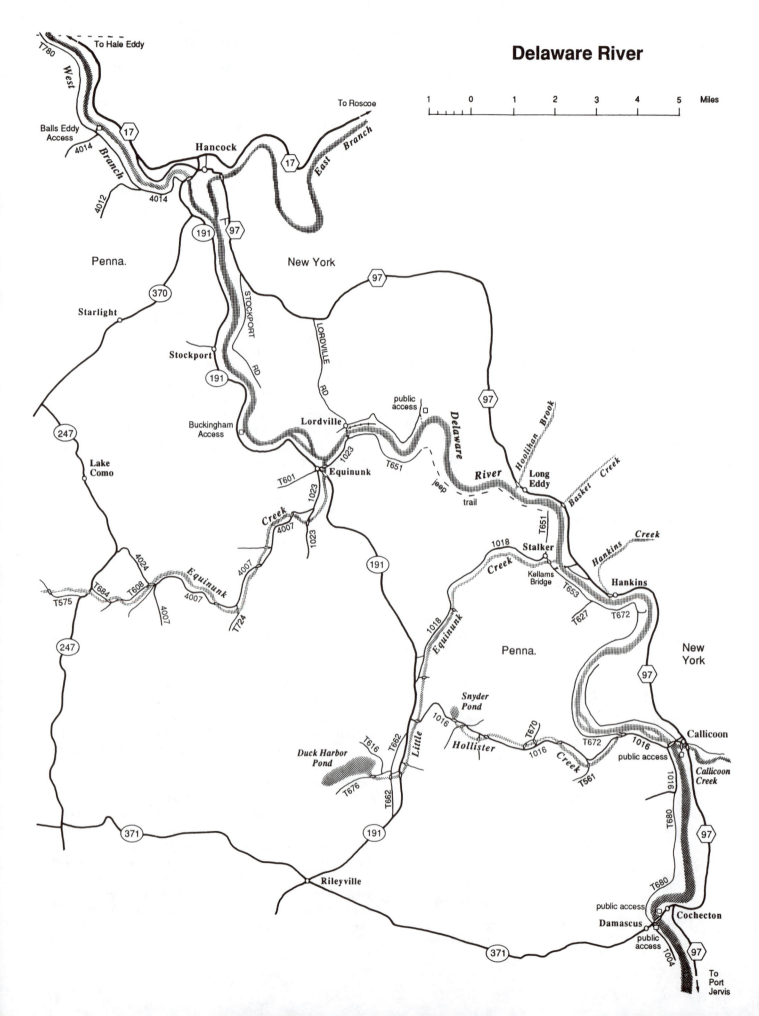

Delaware River

Access Points

Some access points to the Delaware, starting upstream on the West Branch and moving downstream, include the following:

1) Hale Eddy, N.Y. This access site on the West Branch is north of the area shown on the map. It can be reached by driving north on T780, or from a side road off N.Y. Route 17. The bridge at Hale Eddy is a good spot to put in a canoe or raft on the West Branch and float down to Hancock or Lordville. A parking area is located on the east bank.

The riffs and large pool just below the Hale Eddy bridge are popular with anglers, but a New York fishing license is required here because the river is bordered on both sides by New York state. The West Branch begins to border Pennsylvania about 1 mile below Hale Eddy. Downstream from this point, on the West Branch and on the main stem of the Delaware, a New York or a Pennsylvania fishing license allows the angler to fish the river from either bank.

2) Balls Eddy Access. This Pennsylvania Fish Commission site is a good spot to launch a canoe on the West Branch and a very good fishing spot.

3) New York Route 17 parallels the West Branch upstream from Hancock, and there are several places to pull off and scramble down the bank to the river.

4) The Route 191 bridge at Hancock is a good canoe access site and also a popular fishing spot.

5) Junction Pool, where the East and West Branches meet near Hancock, is a productive fishing spot. Drive into Hancock and drive south on Route 97. You'll cross a bridge over the East Branch and 0.9 miles past the bridge you'll see a road to the right that leads to a Bard-Parker factory. The Bard-Parker property is posted against trespassing. Turn left at the factory entrance and park along the road near the entrance to a sewage treatment plant. A path follows along the sewage plant's fence to the river. From here you can walk upstream to Junction Pool, and there is some productive water along the way.

If you fish this stretch in the summer, it's a good idea to check water temperatures. Usually the West Branch flows much colder than the East Branch, and since the water doesn't mix immediately, the fishing is often better along the western shore (Pennsylvania side) for a considerable distance downstream.

6) Route 191 parallels the Pennsylvania side of the Delaware River from Hancock downstream to Equinunk. Much of the land along the road is posted, but there are a few open stretches. Look for small pulloffs along the road and anglers' paths leading down the steep banks.

7) The Buckingham Access is a Pennsylvania Fish Commission boat ramp located north of Equinunk. The river flows too slowly to provide good fishing here, but this is a good place to put in or take out a canoe.

8) At Equinunk you can park near the SR 1023 bridge over Equinunk Creek and walk down the creek to the Delaware. Here the river flows through a swift, narrow chute, past some scenic rock formations, and into a deep pool. A road (numbered SR 1023 and T651) follows the river downstream from Equinunk, but it soon deteriorates into a rough jeep trail. Most of the land on the Pennsylvania side of the river from Equinunk down to Callicoon is posted.

9) Stockport Road turns off New York Route 97 south of Hancock and parallels the river downstream, but most of the land along this road is posted.

10) The Lordville bridge. Drive south from Hancock on Route 97 about 4.5 miles, turn right on Lordville Road, and follow it to where it ends at the site of the old Lordville bridge. Little remains of the bridge now, but there is a nice riff and pool here that offer good fishing. Another good riff is located downstream about another 0.7 miles, and some anglers reach this by driving down the railroad service road that parallels the south side (river side) of the tracks.

11) A New York state public access site can be reached from Lordville by following a dirt road that follows the north side of the railroad tracks past some cabins. The beginning of the road is marked in Lordville with a dead end sign. After 3 miles, the road arrives at a large parking lot. From here you can walk along a rough dirt track to the river.

12) About 0.7 miles south of Long Eddy, Route 97 crosses a high bridge over Basket Creek. You can park on the shoulder of the road, north of the bridge, and hike down the steep bank on a path that begins right beside the bridge. There is a large pool where Basket Creek meets the Delaware and some heavy rapids just downstream.

13) About 0.8 mile north of Hankins, a dirt road turns off from Route 97 and follows the river a short distance.

14) In Hankins, the proprietors of the Red Barn Campgrounds allow canoe launching or takeout for a small fee.

15) At Callicoon a New York public access site is located a short distance below the mouth of Callicoon Creek. The riff below the Callicoon bridge is a popular fishing spot. Callicoon Creek is a good trout stream, but a New York fishing license is required to fish it.

16) The roads that parallel the Pennsylvania side from Callicoon up past Stalker are mostly single-lane dirt roads and they offer very little access to the river because most of the land along here is posted.

The Delaware River downstream about a quarter-mile from the junction of the East and West Branches.

Equinunk Creek - Wayne County
(map: page 22)

Equinunk Creek is a clear, shallow stream with a fishery supported almost entirely by hatchery fish. The Fish Commission stocks the lower part of the creek, from the mouth on the Delaware River upstream to T724, preseason and once inseason. Above T724, Equinunk Creek is stocked prior to opening day only because the stream is small in its upper reaches and because of scattered posting. Fishing pressure is heavy early in the season.

Little Equinunk Creek - Wayne County
(map: page 22)

Little Equinunk Creek is a small, shallow tributary to the Delaware River. The Fish Commission stocks trout preseason only, and the stream holds few wild trout, so fishing is best early in the season. Trout are also stocked in Duck Harbor Pond, which is located at the headwaters of Little Equinunk Creek.

Hollister Creek - Wayne County
(map: page 22)

Hollister Creek is a very small tributary to the Delaware River. Trout are stocked preseason only, from the T670 bridge downstream to the T561 bridge.

Dyberry Creek - Wayne County
(delayed harvest, fly fishing only, 0.8 mile)
(map: page 25)

Dyberry Creek offers good fishing for stocked trout from the early season to about the middle of June. After that its waters become too warm and few fish remain. Because of its easy accessibility, the creek is stocked heavily and it's fished hard in the early weeks of the season. The Fish Commission stocks trout preseason and also twice inseason. Trout are stocked from Tanner's Falls, where Dyberry Creek is formed by the junction of its East and West Branches, downstream 6 miles to the Schoonover Cemetery, which is north of Honesdale.

Dyberry Creek is a medium-sized stream, about 50 feet wide, that flows over a moderate gradient. Gentle riffles separate its quiet pools, but there is no really swift water. Most of the stream is open enough to allow easy casting.

The delayed-harvest, fly-fishing-only area, which begins about a mile below Tanners Falls and extends downstream 0.8 mile to a bridge on SR 4009, offers the most consistent fishing because the regulations prohibit the harvest of fish until after June 15. Many trout can still be found there even after the trout have been thinned out by heavy fishing in other parts of the creek.

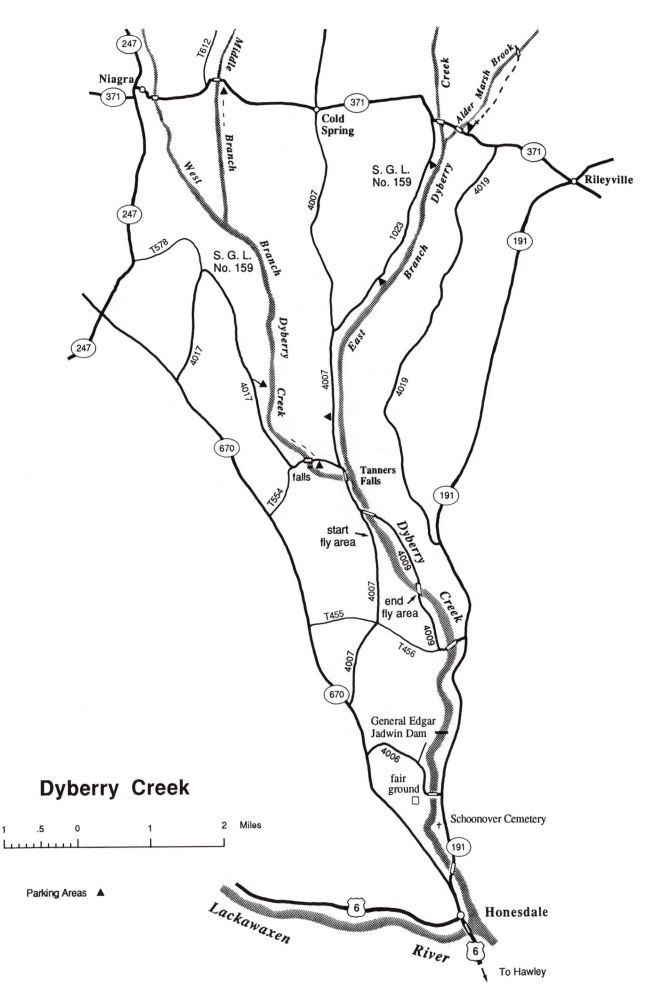

Dyberry Creek

Parking Areas ▲

From the origin of Dyberry Creek down to the fly area, the banks are mostly wooded with medium-sized hardwoods. Within the fly area, grassland and shrubs line the stream, and some big, old willow trees provide partial shade. About a half-mile below the fly area, near the intersection of SR 4009 and T456, there are several large sand and gravel pits along the stream.

On the lower part of the creek, anglers can park their cars at the county fairgrounds and near the General Edgar Jadwin Dam. This dam was built for flood control and ordinarily does not back up any water behind it. Downstream from the fairgrounds, the many houses and businesses scattered along Route 191 make finding access difficult.

Fly hatches on Dyberry Creek include Hendricksons, Sulphurs, March Browns, Grey Foxes, and Dun Caddis. Terrestrial patterns are also useful.

During the dog days of July and August, Dyberry Creek becomes low and warm and fishing is poor. Stream surveys in mid-August found few trout remaining, even in the fly area.

Dyberry Creek's tributaries (East Branch Dyberry Creek, West Branch Dyberry Creek, Middle Branch Dyberry Creek, and Alder Marsh Brook) are smaller, brushier streams that flow for much of their lengths through State Game Land No. 159.

East Branch Dyberry Creek - Wayne County
(map: page 25)

The East Branch is the most easily accessible of Dyberry Creek's tributaries because most of the stream is paralleled by paved roads and because there are several State Game Land parking areas distributed along the length of the stream. The first half-mile of the stream below the Route 371 bridge is posted, but most of the rest of the stream is open to fishing.

The East Branch is rocky-bottomed and clear, and it flows faster than either the West Branch or the main stem of Dyberry Creek. Its width is 15 to 20 feet and much of the stream consists of shallow riffles. There are few deep pools. A mixed hardwood-evergreen forest provides good shade along most of the creek. The lower stretch is more open, with grassy and brushy areas along the banks.

The East Branch is stocked preseason and three times inseason, with the last stocking coming in mid-May. The East Branch also holds scattered wild brown and brook trout, particularly in its upper reaches. Although summer fishing is tough anywhere in the Dyberry watershed, fair numbers of anglers fish the East Branch into mid-July.

Alder Marsh Brook, a small, unstocked tributary to the upper East Branch, holds some native brook

Falls on West Branch Dyberry Creek.

trout. Just east of the Route 371 bridge, a road goes north about 100 yards to a State Game Land parking lot. Near the parking lot, and on downstream to the mouth, Alder Marsh Brook is a typical rocky little freestone stream, about 6 to 12 feet wide. Farther upstream the flow is slowed by beaver dams and marshy areas, and the streambed is heavily silted. A gated access road follows the stream up from the parking lot.

West Branch Dyberry Creek - Wayne County
(map: page 25)

Anglers who like fishing in the woods, away from traffic and houses, will enjoy West Branch Dyberry Creek. Most of the stream flows through the forests of State Game Land No. 159, and road access is limited.

You can reach the lower stretch of the stream by parking near the SR 4007 bridge at Tanners Falls, which was once a village but now only a name on the map. SR 4017, a rough gravel and dirt road, parallels the stream up from Tanners Falls, but it travels high on a hillside above the creek.

Just below the old iron bridge where SR 4017 crosses the West Branch, there is a beautiful waterfall and a large plunge pool beneath it. It's surprising that many people pay admission to see the commercialized waterfalls in northeastern Pennsylvania, when there are so many attractive falls on public lands in the region.

From the falls downstream to near the mouth, the West Branch is fast flowing and rocky, but upstream from the falls the stream flows slowly, with only gentle riffles breaking its quiet surface. You can park next to the iron bridge near the falls and walk up along a gated Game Land access road that follows the east bank of the stream.

At its intersection with T554, SR 4017 turns north and parallels the West Branch, but at a fair distance from the creek. This section of SR 4017 is passable to ordinary cars, but it is narrow, and numerous potholes and rocks make the going rough. About 1.2 miles north from the intersection with T554, near a bridge over a small tributary stream, a dirt road leads a short distance to a Game Land parking lot near the streambank. This is a good place to park because north of this point SR 4017 turns away from the stream and posting signs appear along the road. From this parking lot, you can fish upstream for about another 4 miles in State Game Land No. 159 before you encounter private property.

The Route 371 bridge provides no access to the West Branch because the land on either side of the bridge is posted.

The Fish Commission stocks the West Branch before opening day and also once inseason, with the last stocking coming in late April. Some wild brown and brook trout are found in the upper and middle sections of the West Branch.

Middle Branch Dyberry Creek is a small, unstocked tributary of the West Branch that holds some native brook trout. A State Game Land parking lot is located a short distance below the Route 371 bridge. From this parking lot downstream to the mouth, the Middle Branch flows through forested land in State Game Land No. 159. Above the Route 371 bridge, the stream is posted.

Lackawaxen River - Pike County
(map: page 28)

The Lackawaxen River has several sections that are stocked with trout, but the most enjoyable part of the river to fish is the swift, rocky lower stretch. Trout stocking in this lower section begins at the confluence of Middle Creek at Hawley and continues downstream 15 miles to the mouth on the Delaware river. The stream flows here through a narrow valley that is still mostly wooded, with the exception of some vacation homes scattered along the banks and the small village of Rowland.

Just above Kimbles a PP&L power plant releases water into the Lackawaxen. This water is piped in an aqueduct from Lake Wallenpaupack and is released during times of peak electric power demand. The water releases are not completely predictable, but they often take place on weekday mornings. When the releases begin, the Lackawaxen rises very high and very fast, and wading anglers are advised to get out of the stream. There aren't many bridge crossings, so try not to get stuck on the bank away from your car. Wading is also made hazardous by flat layers of shale, which offer slippery footing on the streambed.

The Lackawaxen is very popular with both spin fishers and fly fishers from opening day into early June. The Fish Commission stocks trout preseason and twice inseason, with the last stocking coming in mid-May. There are very few wild trout found in the Lackawaxen River.

In the spring the lower Lackawaxen is a big, brawling stream, but in the summer it becomes low and warm. Not many people fish here in midsummer or fall, but some regulars on the Lackawaxen say they catch big holdover brown trout in the summer by fishing at the mouths of tributaries.

Although the land along the lower Lackawaxen is still relatively undeveloped compared with most other areas in the Poconos, this situation may soon change. A large housing project has been planned for a site along the river about 2 miles downstream from Kimbles. Even now, finding a place to park near the river is difficult on some stretches of the lower Lackawaxen because of posting along the roadside.

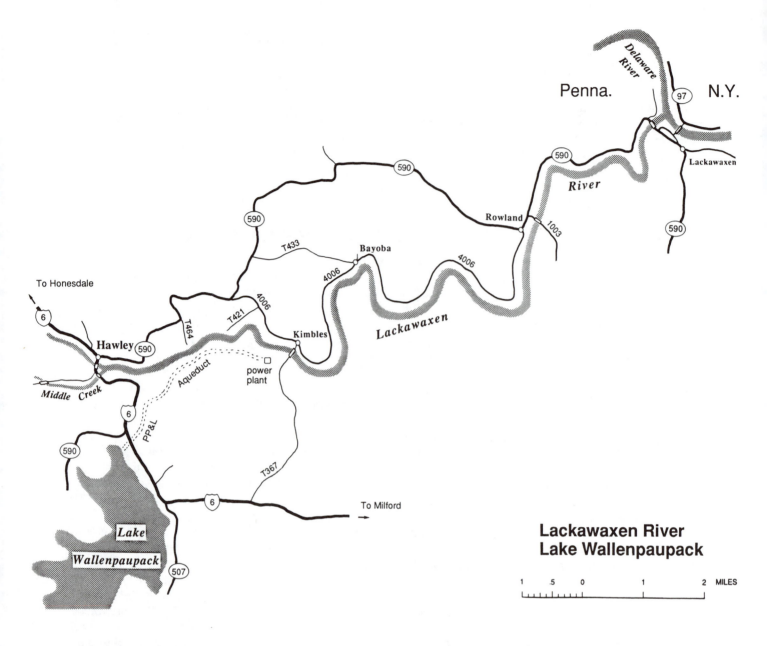

Lackawaxen River
Lake Wallenpaupack

1   .5   0   1   2   MILES

Lake Wallenpaupack - Wayne and Pike Counties
(map: page 28)

This is primarily a book on trout streams, not lakes, but Lake Wallenpaupack deserves mention here because of its gigantic brown trout. On April 27, 1988, the previous Pennsylvania state brown trout record was broken by the catch of a trout from Lake Wallenpaupack that measured 32.5 inches and weighed 17 pounds, 7 ounces. The girth of this monster was 19 3/4 inches. Brown trout weighing from 8 to 10 pounds are caught here annually. The lake also holds stripers, walleye, pickerel, bass, and panfish.

Big browns are sometimes caught in Wallenpaupack Creek (not shown on the map) when they move up from the lake to spawn in October and early November. Much of this creek is posted against trespassing, however.

Pond Eddy Creek - Pike County
(map: page 29)

This small, out-of-the-way creek flows through State Game Land No. 209 for about 2 miles before flowing into the Delaware River. No trout are stocked in Pond Eddy Creek, but it holds a good population of wild brown and brook trout. The creek tumbles through a steep-sided ravine, and it is well shaded by the hardwood and evergreen trees that line its banks.

At the village of Pond Eddy, New York, turn off from New York Route 97 and cross a bridge over the Delaware River. After crossing the bridge, turn right and continue about a half-mile, to a fork in the road. The road to the right leads upstream along the Delaware River to some summer homes, then ends without providing any access to Pond Eddy Creek. So, take the road to the left and follow it over the railroad tracks. This road leads past a house on the right, then

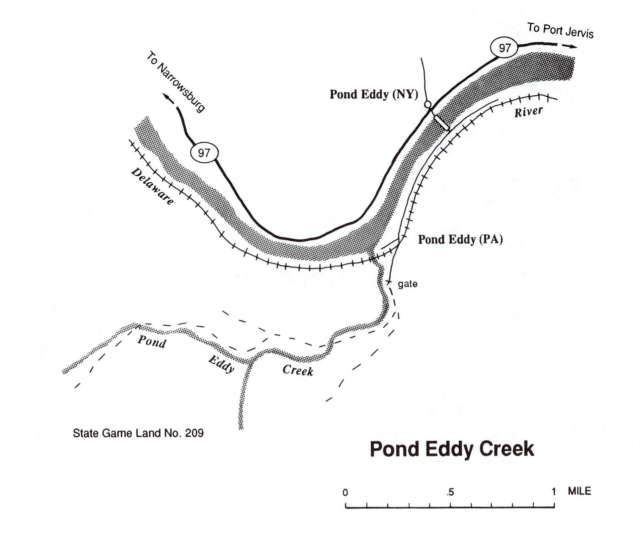

State Game Land No. 209

Pond Eddy Creek

```
0              .5              1  MILE
```

a cabin on the left, then ends at a State Game Land parking area about 100 yards past the cabin. This last stretch of road is rather rough. From the parking area, you can follow a trail up along the stream.

Big Bushkill Creek - Monroe and Pike Counties

(fly fishing only, 6.1 miles)

(map: page 31)

Many trout streams in the Poconos have been posted against public fishing, but the lower 12 miles of Big Bushkill Creek are still open and offer fishing on a very scenic stream. The Big Bushkill flows swiftly over rock ledges and it is large enough to require some care in wading. Its waters are brown from tannic acid, which comes from decaying leaves and plants in swampy areas drained by the headwaters. This brown-tinted water is common in many streams in the Poconos, the Adirondacks, and Maine.

The most popular stretch of Big Bushkill Creek is the 6.1-mile fly-fishing-only area at Resica Falls Scout Camp. The creek flows here through a rock-walled gorge with numerous rapids and several waterfalls. A canopy of evergreens shades the creek.

To reach this stretch, take Route 209 north from Stroudsburg to the village of Marshalls Creek. Turn left onto Route 402 and in about 5 to 6 miles you will cross the creek. Just after the bridge, there is a drive to the right, which goes into the scout camp. On the left you will see a store. The scout camp management requests that, before fishing on their stretch of the creek, you stop at the store and get an annual permit. A donation of $15 is requested. A sportsmen's parking lot is located a short distance past the store. From here you can follow a path down to the creek. A beautiful waterfall is located just below the Route 402 bridge. A short stretch above and below the falls is closed to fishing.

To reach the upper part of the fly area, drive back across the Route 402 bridge and take the first right, onto Firestone Road. In 1.5 miles you will see a gated fire road to the right. Park here without blocking the fire road and walk down to the creek. Just upstream

Big Bushkill Creek. This spectacular falls is located off Firestone Road, about 1.5 miles upstream from the Route 402 bridge.   (Marv Klassen-Landis photo)

is a spectacular waterfall. About 0.4 miles farther up on Firestone Road, there is a sportsmen's parking lot on the right and another trail leading to the creek.

The lower part of the stream is wider and less shaded than the Resica Falls stretch. To reach the lower stretch of the Big Bushkill, take Route 209 north from Marshalls Creek until you cross the creek just before the traffic light at the village of Bushkill. Immediately after the bridge, turn left onto Creek Road, which follows the Big Bushkill upstream for about 2 miles. A parking area is located at the mouth of Little Bushkill Creek, which is also a good trout stream. If you continue up along Creek Road, you will come out to a T intersection on Winona Falls Road. Turn left over the creek and park in the large pulloff on the left. Above this bridge, a private road follows the creek upstream. This road is closed to vehicles, but walk-in fishing is permitted.

The Fish Commission stocks trout preseason and once inseason. Fishing is good in the early season, but by early June the creek begins to warm and fishing slows. The Big Bushkill is definitely not worth fishing in July and August. Because of the warm summer water temperatures, there are few wild or holdover

trout in the Big Bushkill. Twenty to thirty years ago the stream ran cooler in the summer, and large browns were often caught. The warmer summer temperatures were probably caused by changes in water drainage due to extensive vacation home development in the upper Big Bushkill watershed.

Big Bushkill Creek has hatches of Blue Quills, Quill Gordons, Olive Caddis, and March Browns. Streamers such as Wooly Buggers and Marabou Muddlers are often effective.

Little Bushkill Creek - Pike County
(map: page 31)

Little Bushkill Creek is a small, scenic woodland stream that flows into Big Bushkill Creek near the village of Bushkill. The stream is open to fishing from the mouth upstream about 2 miles, then there is a long stretch of posted property. The lower 2 miles of the creek are swift-flowing, and the water is cooled by several small tributaries and by the deep shade cast by tall trees along the banks. Parking is available at the bridges on Creek Road and Sugar Mountain Road. Some stocked trout, and even a few wild trout,

Big Bushkill Creek
Little Bushkill Creek
Toms Creek

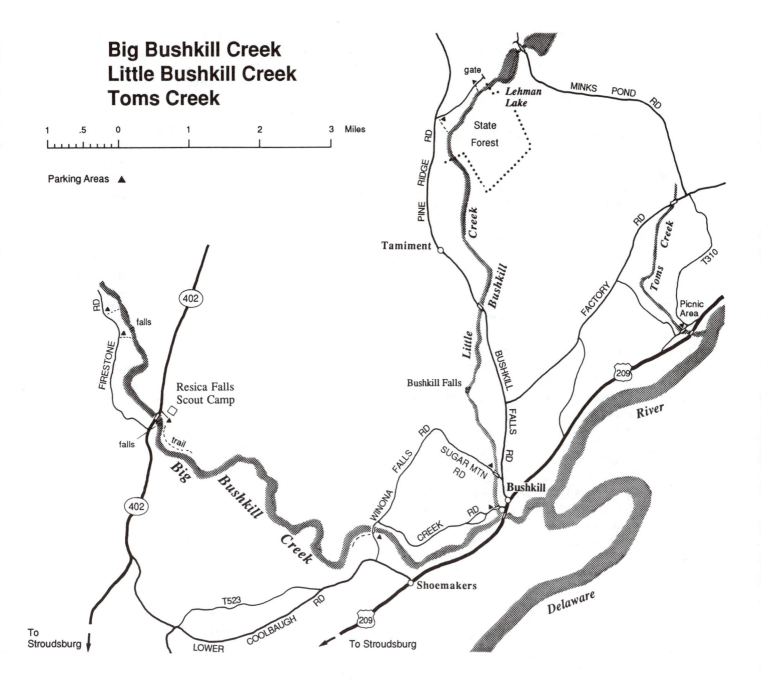

Parking Areas ▲

can be found in this lower stretch of Little Bushkill Creek into the summer and fall, but fishing is best from the season opener through about mid-June.

Another stocked stretch, about 1.2 miles long, is located on Delaware State Forest land. To reach this stretch, begin at the village of Bushkill and drive north on Bushkill Falls Road. Two miles after passing the entrance to the Tamiment resort, turn right onto an unmarked gravel road. This road continues for 0.7 miles before ending at a chain flanked by no-trespassing signs. You can park at several places along this road and walk down along some cabin lanes to the creek. The upper and lower boundaries of the state forest land along the creek are well marked with no-trespassing signs, which are an integral part of the Poconos landscape. This upper stretch of Little Bushkill Creek becomes warm in the summer months because it flows out of a series of lakes, and few trout are found here in the summer and fall.

Toms Creek - Pike County
(map: page 31)

Toms Creek is an attractive, tumbling brook that flows into the Delaware River about 3 miles north of the village of Bushkill. The lower 2 miles of the stream are within the Delaware Water Gap National Recreation Area, so public access is assured. The Toms Creek Picnic Area is a good place to park your car while fishing and a good place to have lunch.

Toms Creek is not stocked with trout, but it has a good population of browns from 5 to 10 inches long and a few larger ones. Brook trout are found in the upper part of the creek. Above the picnic area, Toms Creek is deeply shaded by large trees.

Brodhead Creek - Monroe County
(map: page 33)

Brodhead Creek was an early center of fly fishing in the United States. Fishing clubs were active here when the Catskill Mountains of New York were still remote wilderness. After the railroads improved access to the Catskills, the streams there became the hub of the fly fishing scene. Some of the fishing clubs that originated on the Brodhead moved to new water in the Catskills.

James Leisenring was considered one of the best fishermen on the Brodhead in the early days. He preferred wet flies tied without wings and used soft hackles from chickens, grouse, partridges, starlings, and other birds to give his flies life-like movement. This type of fly fell out of favor for many years, replaced by the more popular dry flies and nymphs, but in recent years there has been a revival of these versatile flies, which are now often called soft-hackle wet flies or flymphs.

The Leisenring lift is a wet fly technique that has also been revived. The angler casts upstream of a trout and allows the fly to sink in a dead drift, then stops the rod, allowing the line to tighten and raise the fly towards the surface. The idea is to imitate an emerging insect as it rises toward the surface. If all goes according to plan, the trout reacts by promptly taking the fly.

Most of Brodhead Creek above Analomink is posted, but decent fishing remains in the lower water, which is still open to the public. Trout are stocked from the SR 1002 bridge, just above Analomink, downstream 8 miles through Stroudsburg to the lower I-80 bridge, which is located about 1 mile above the mouth on the Delaware River. The Fish Commission stocks trout preseason and three times inseason, with the last stocking coming in late May.

Analomink to Stroudsburg

The very top of the stocked stretch, from the SR 1002 bridge down to near Analomink, has some good riffles and runs and several large, deep pools. This upper stretch holds fair numbers of trout year around. The best place to park is along SR 1002, near the bridge.

Below Analomink there is a straight, channelized stretch about 1.2 miles long. Some of this stretch is above the Route 191 bridge and some below. This part of the creek was channelized after a hurricane in 1955 produced severe flooding in Stroudsburg. This stretch is not great trout habitat, but the Brodhead

Chapter of Trout Unlimited has been doing stream work to improve cover. There is a large pulloff along Route 191, about 0.2 mile north of the Route 191 bridge, that provides parking. You can follow the railroad tracks up or downstream from here.

Below the channelized stretch, there is some nice water downstream to Stokes Avenue. There is not much parking available at the Stokes Avenue bridge, perhaps two or three spaces. Better parking is found by turning off Stokes Avenue onto Crowe Road. Drive back Crowe Road until you reach an entrance to a factory, then turn left and park near a baseball field. From here you can walk through an open field to the stream.

Some good runs and pools are found downstream from Stokes Avenue also, but as the stream nears Stroudsburg the banks become increasingly lined with houses and businesses. A long stretch of the creek through Stroudsburg and East Stroudsburg is channelized. This stretch is also stocked with trout, but it's not very attractive.

Pocono Creek and McMichaels Creek add their flows in Stroudsburg and greatly increase the size of the Brodhead. These streams are stocked with trout, and they also hold some wild trout, but trying to find access to these streams, and figuring out which stretches are open and which are posted is very frustrating, so they are best left to the local anglers.

The Gorge

Below East Stroudsburg, the Brodhead flows through a rugged, narrow gorge with steep hillsides rising up from the water's edge. There are heavy rapids here, interspersed with deep pools. The wading can be treacherous. White water canoeists find this an exciting place to mash their boats up against rocks. To reach this stretch, take Lincoln Avenue in East Stroudsburg past the Pocono Plaza Shopping Plaza, and park along the road just before the entrance to a sewage plant. Walk along the road until you are under the I-80 overpass, then walk along the railroad tracks that follow the creek through the gorge. In many places it's a steep, brushy hike from the tracks down to the water. Look for anglers' trails that lead down in the easier places. It's about a 2-mile hike down through the gorge to the lower I-80 bridge and a paper mill.

Recently the Fish Commission, with the help of local anglers, has begun float stocking the gorge. Even before this stretch was stocked, there was fair fishing for wild browns. There have been some water quality problems from sewage effluent and industrial pollution in this part of Brodhead Creek, but the water quality is good enough to allow trout survival year around. Browns from 15 to 18 inches are sometimes caught in the gorge.

Access to the lower end of the gorge is limited. Some anglers park near the intersection of Route 209

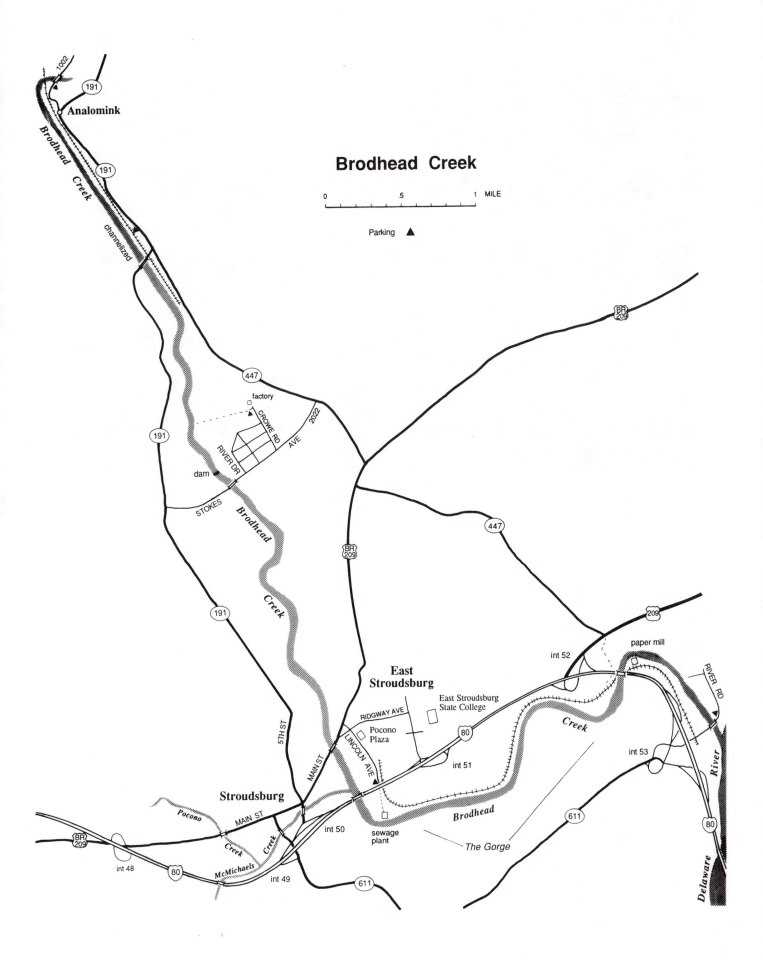

Brodhead Creek

Brodhead Creek in the gorge downstream from East Stroudsburg.

and Route 447 and walk down along an old road that leads to the stream near the I-80 bridge. You must be careful parking here, though, because the traffic on Route 209 can be horrendous.

To reach the lower water on Brodhead Creek, take Route 80 east from Stroudsburg and get off at exit 53, the Delaware Water Gap Exit. As you get off the ramp, take the first left, onto River Road. You will soon cross a bridge over the Brodhead. Park just after the bridge at the pulloff on the left. There are some swift runs near the bridge, but farther downstream the Brodhead slows as it approaches the Delaware. From the River Road bridge up towards the paper mill, there are some deep, fast runs that are difficult to fish because the water is almost too deep to wade, and the banks here are lined with thick brush. A short section of the creek at the paper mill is closed to fishing.

Fly Hatches

The Brodhead has good fly hatches, including Blue-winged Olives, Quill Gordons, Hendricksons, Olive Caddis, Slate Drakes, and Light Cahills. Caddis hatches are very common in the gorge downstream

from East Stroudsburg. In the summer months, the lower Brodhead gets pretty warm and fishing slows. Fishing then is best early in the morning, at dusk, or at night. Some anglers have reported catching large rainbow trout in the the winter months in the lower part of the Brodhead. Apparently these fish move up from the Delaware River.

Tackle and fishing information can be found in Stroudsburg at Dunkelberger's Sporting Outfitter at Sixth and Main Street, and at Windsor Fly Shop at 348 N. Ninth Street.

Poplar Run - Monroe County
(map: page 35)

Poplar Run is a small brook that flows through Delaware State Forest. It isn't stocked, but it holds fair numbers of wild brown and brook trout. From Analomink, drive north on Route 191, then turn right onto Route 447. Route 447 crosses Poplar Run about 3.5 miles farther north. About 0.2 mile before the bridge, Laurel Run Road, a forest road, leads to the right and soon crosses Poplar Run. The State Forest boundary is near this bridge. From the bridge down

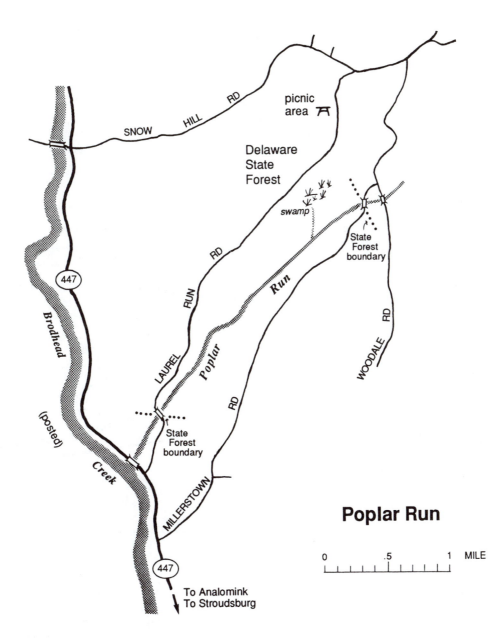

Poplar Run

0   .5   1   MILE

to the mouth, the creek flows through private property. For about 2.5 miles upstream of the bridge, to near Millerstown Road, Poplar Run flows through state forest land and is open to fishing. Poplar Run is a tributary to Brodhead Creek. Unfortunately, Brodhead Creek is mostly posted in this area.

Devils Hole Creek - Monroe County
(map: page 36)

Devils Hole Creek is a small forest stream that flows through State Game Land No. 221. No trout are stocked in this stream, but it holds a good population of wild brown and brook trout.

From Mount Pocono, travel east 2.4 miles on Route 940, then turn left on Devils Hole Road. In another 1.2 miles you will cross a railroad grade. You can park here and follow the trail that leads down to the creek, or you can drive 0.2 miles past the railroad tracks and park at the State Game Land parking lot on the right. A trail also leads from this parking lot down to the creek. Once you get on the stream, fish upstream or downstream until you encounter posting. About 1.5 miles of the stream lies within State Game Land No. 221.

In State Game Land No. 221, Devils Hole Creek flows through a narrow, wooded ravine, with no roads, houses or other distractions in sight. This is a fine place for a walk in the woods, even for those who don't fish.

Brown trout are common in the lower water, and wild brook trout predominate farther upstream. The stream gets quite small as you move upstream, and some short stretches actually disappear under the

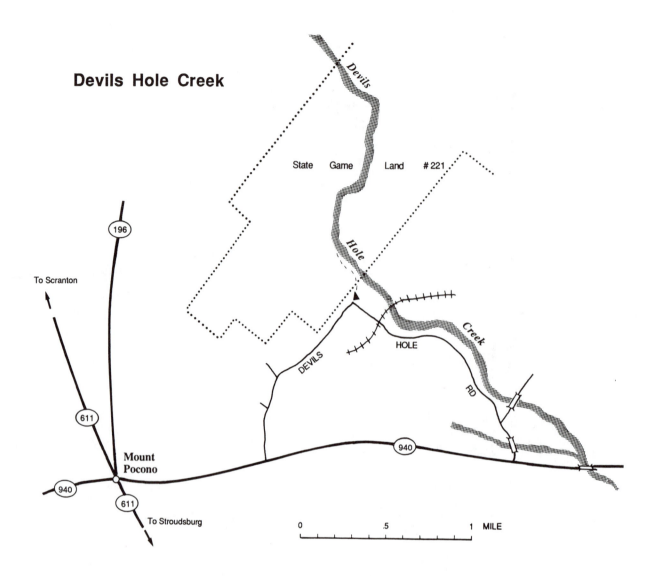

Devils Hole Creek

State   Game   Land   # 221

196

To Scranton

611

DEVILS

HOLE

RD

Creek

Mount
Pocono

940

611

940

To Stroudsburg

0   .5   1   MILE

rocks when water levels are low. It may seem as though you have reached the upper limit of Devils Hole Creek, but if you continue hiking upstream, you will find water flowing on the surface again and little brookies darting around in the pools.

Tobyhanna Creek - Monroe County
(delayed harvest, artificial lures only, 1 mile)
(map: page 37)

Tobyhanna Creek is stocked with trout from the outflow of Tobyhanna Lake downstream 7 miles to a PP&L service road bridge in State Game Land No. 127. This is a medium-sized trout stream, with the brownish, tannic water common in the Poconos region. Camping and picnic areas are located next to Tobyhanna Lake in Tobyhanna State Park.

The upper part of the stocked stretch, from the lake downstream to the village of Tobyhanna, is the "civilized" portion of Tobyhanna Creek; there is easy road access and fair numbers of houses near the stream here. Singer Run, a small stream with a good

brook trout population, flows in about a mile below Tobyhanna Lake.

South of the village of Tobyhanna, Tobyhanna Creek flows for several miles through the woods and swamps of State Game Land No. 127. Route 423 follows this part of the Tobyhanna, but there are long stretches that can only be reached by walking.

A 1-mile delayed-harvest, artificials-only stretch extends from Stillswamp Run downstream to the PP&L service road bridge. Because of the special regulations, many trout remain in this stretch when the trout in other parts of the creek have been thinned out.

Tobyhanna Creek is a wide, low-gradient stream with few swift riffles or deep pools. Brushy swamps adjoin much of the stream. Because of summer warming and the acidity of the water, the Tobyhanna does not support a wild trout population, and the fishing is dependent on stocked trout.

The Fish Commission stocks trout preseason and twice inseason, with the last stocking coming in early or mid-May. When the water gets very warm in July

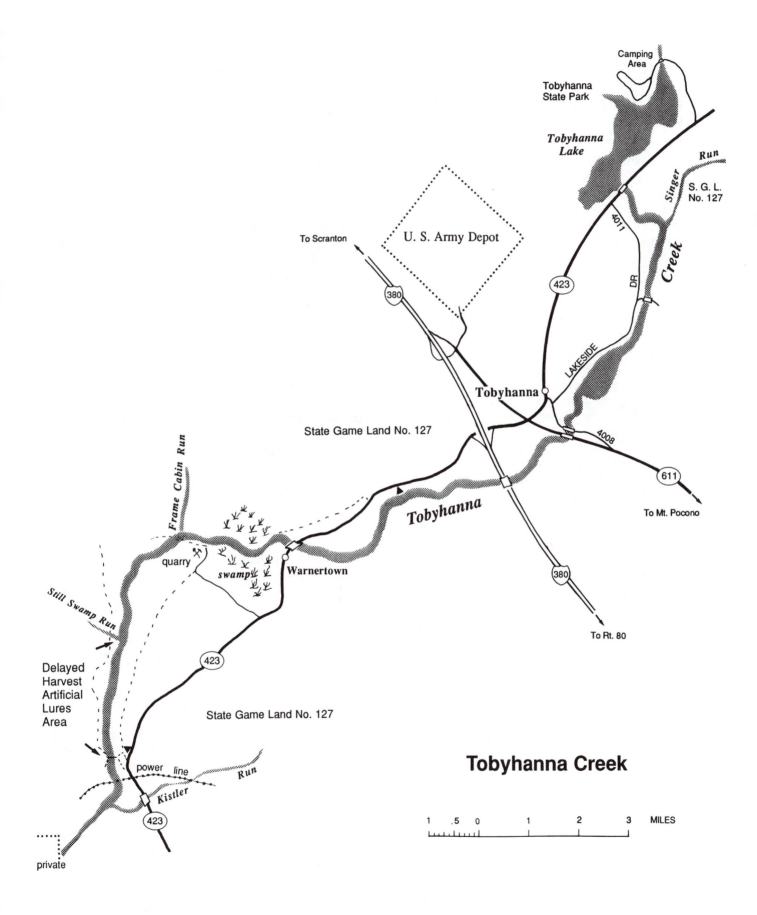

Camping Area

Tobyhanna State Park

Tobyhanna Lake

Singer *Run*

S. G. L. No. 127

Creek

4011

To Scranton

U. S. Army Depot

380

423

DR

LAKESIDE

Tobyhanna

4008

611

To Mt. Pocono

State Game Land No. 127

Frame Cabin Run

Tobyhanna

380

To Rt. 80

quarry

swamp

Warnertown

Still Swamp Run

Delayed Harvest Artificial Lures Area

423

State Game Land No. 127

power line

Run

Tobyhanna Creek

Kistler

423

private

1   .5   0   1   2   3   MILES

and August, fishing is poor on Tobyhanna Creek, even in the delayed-harvest area.

Frame Cabin Run and Kistler Run are two small, unstocked tributaries that are worth a try for native brookies and the stocked trout that move up from Tobyhanna Creek.

Lehigh River - Carbon and Luzerne Counties
(map: page 39)

The Lehigh River is one of the best known white water boating rivers in Pennsylvania, and it is also gaining a reputation as a fairly good trout river. The upper Lehigh, above Francis E. Walter Dam, is stocked in some places and holds some wild browns and brook trout, but there is a lot of posted property. The best place to fish the upper river is in State Game Land No. 127 near Clifton (not shown on the map). This Game Land is located south of the Gouldsboro exit of Route 380.

Because of the access problems in the upper river, I'll concentrate here on the Lehigh River downstream from the dam. The Lehigh River is not as large as the Delaware River or the Youghiogheny, but it is much larger than most Pennsylvania trout streams. It is about 50 to 60 feet wide below the dam and well over 100 feet wide below White Haven. It is also swift and rocky, and wading is a challenge. Wading the big water below White Haven and down through the Lehigh Gorge can be particularly hazardous. In many places you are clambering over large, slick boulders. You can be standing knee-deep in water, take one step and plunge in over your head. The wading in the Lehigh Gorge is the among the most difficult I have encountered in Pennsylvania. Only the Youghiogheny River presents more brutal wading conditions. During low-water periods, the wading is not quite so tough.

The Fish Commission stocks the Lehigh for opening day and once inseason, in late April or early May. In addition to stocking the usual adult trout, the Fish Commission has stocked fingerling trout in the fall. Only the stretch from the Francis E. Walter Dam down to Sandy Run is stocked, but trout are also found the whole way downstream through the Lehigh Gorge. Despite the great number of rafters that float the Lehigh River, fishing pressure in the gorge is very light, except at the upper part of the gorge near Lehigh Tannery and the mouth of Black Creek.

At the lower end of the gorge, upstream from the town of Jim Thorpe, Nesquehoning Creek adds a lot of mine acid to the river, and trout fishing is spotty below this. (This lower section is not shown on the map.) I have talked to anglers, though, who have caught trout near Jim Thorpe and even as far downstream as Allentown. The trout fishery in the gorge results from spawning in several tributaries, as well as from hatchery trout that drift down from the stocked stretch and from stocked tributary streams.

The Lehigh River has had some water quality problems in the past, particularly with acid mine drainage, but water quality has improved in recent years, and both trout and aquatic insects are making a comeback. Water levels can be high around opening day, and the best fly fishing usually takes place from late April through early June. The major hatches include Hendricksons, March Browns, Light Cahills, Isonychia, and numerous caddis. Big stonefly nymphs and bulky flies such as Marabou Muddlers and Wooly Buggers are also effective, especially when the water is high. In July and August, the river warms and fishing slows. Fishing is good again in the fall, but very few people take advantage of it.

On spring weekends, for as long as water levels remain high, the river from White Haven down through the gorge is crowded with rafts and kayaks. It is pretty difficult to fish with all the boats going by, and you will be asked the eternal question, "Catching any?" about once every 30 seconds. Since most of the rafters start out in White Haven, you can avoid the boat traffic by fishing the water above White Haven.

If you would prefer to fish in the gorge below White Haven, you can avoid most of the boat traffic by fishing early in the morning or in the evening. In the summer and fall, water levels are usually too low for white water boating, except for on several weekends when special water releases are made from Francis E. Walter Dam.

Access Points

Some access points to the Lehigh, starting upriver and proceeding downriver, include the following:

1) Francis E. Walter dam. There is a parking area right beside the dam, and you can walk up over the dam to the outlet hole, a favorite fishing spot. A picnic area is located 0.4 mile west of the dam, and here a dirt road turns off the main road and leads down to the river. This road is open to vehicles from the opening day of trout season through Labor Day. The reservoir behind the dam is also stocked with trout.

2) White Haven Poconos. Some anglers drive through this housing development and follow a dirt road to a parking area by the river.

3) Just south of the entrance to White Haven Poconos, a paved road (T422) leads past a tavern. Some anglers park here and walk down a trail to the river, but this access is questionable because of some no-trespassing signs in the area.

4) White Haven. There is no good access right at the Route 940 bridge. Just before the bridge, turn north onto a street that goes past several several restaurants and shops. After a few blocks, the street turns sharply to the left at an old brick building. Turn

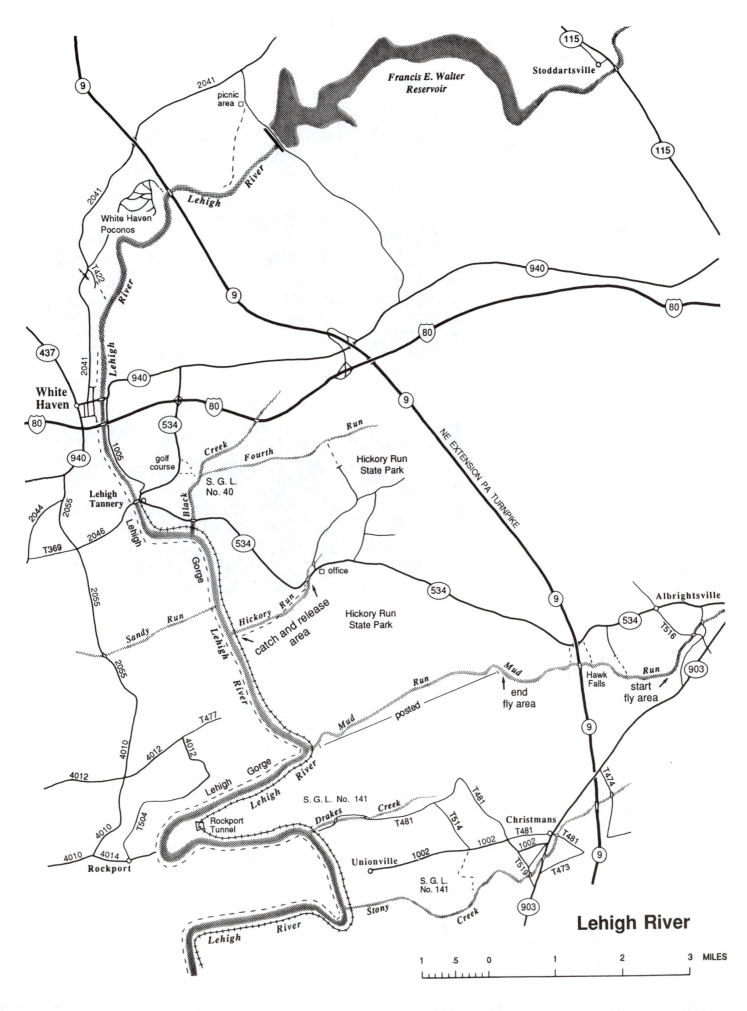

Lehigh River

to the right here onto a dirt track, which soon ends at a parking area. A trail follows the river upstream.

5) Beside the Thriftway grocery store in White Haven, a gravel lane leads to a parking area under the I-80 bridge. This is the put-in point for most white water boaters. An old railroad grade, which has been converted to an excellent walking path, follows the river downstream.

6) Lehigh Tannery. At the small village of Lehigh Tannery, you'll find the A. A. Pro Shop, where you can purchase fly fishing gear. The bridge at Lehigh Tannery is a popular fishing access point. On the west side of the bridge, you can get access to the old railroad grade, now a great walking path, that follows the river for miles down through the Lehigh Gorge. This rugged and remote area is protected by the Lehigh Gorge State Park. Motorized vehicles are prohibited on the path. The path offers access to anglers, but in many places it's a steep, rugged hike down to the river.

7) Black Creek. One mile south of Lehigh Tannery, on Route 534, there is a bridge over Black Creek (often called Hayes Creek). Next to the bridge there is a parking area and from here you can follow the creek down to the river. The wide, flat pools on this part of the Lehigh often produce good dry fly fishing.

The Lehigh River at the mouth of Black Creek.

8) Hickory Run. A hiking trail follows Hickory Run from Route 534 to the river. From here anglers follow the railroad tracks up or downstream along the river, but use caution because this is an active rail line. In most places it's a steep, rugged hike from the tracks down to the water.

9) Rockport. The Lehigh Gorge State Park office is located here, and a parking area provides good access to the lower end of the gorge and to the walking path along the river. Many rafters use Rockport as their takeout point.

10) Drakes Run. A very narrow, rough road follows Drake Run down to its mouth on the Lehigh. High clearance vehicles are recommended. If you are headed down the road and a busload of rafters is driving up, you may have to back up a long way on a rocky, muddy road. It happened to me. Most trout caught in the Lehigh Gorge are brown trout, so I was

surprised to catch a plump, red-streaked, 12-inch rainbow just below Drakes Run in early September.

Black Creek (Hayes Creek) - Carbon County
(map: page 39)

The Fish Commission and most maps name this Lehigh River tributary Black Creek, but most local residents know it as Hayes Creek. Whatever you call it, this is a pretty, woodland stream with a good population of wild brown trout and also a few brookies.

Black Creek is in the Fish Commission's wild trout program, and no trout are stocked. Much of the stream lies within State Game Land No. 40. Black Creek has a nice mix of riffles, pockets, and small pools. Hardwood trees and brush line the banks. The stream is about 25 feet wide in its lower stretch and much narrower above the confluence of Fourth Run.

There is a parking area at the Route 534 bridge about 1 mile southeast of the village of Lehigh Tannery. The mouth on the Lehigh River is just a short distance below this bridge. If you would rather start farther upstream, drive north from Lehigh Tannery on Route 534 until the road bends to the left and a golf course appears on the left. Along the right side of the road, there are two game land parking lots and trails leading to the creek.

Fourth Run - Carbon County
(map: page 39)

Fourth Run is a small, rocky stream that flows through Hickory Run State Park and State Game Land No. 40 before joining Black Creek (Hayes Creek). There is no direct road access to Fourth Run. You can reach the mouth of the stream while fishing on Black Creek, or you can reach the upper stretch by walking about a half-mile on a trail in Hickory Run State Park. Stop at the park office for a map and specific directions to this trail. The upper part of the creek is only 6 to 8 feet wide and it flows through a narrow tunnel of mountain laurel that nearly chokes the stream off in places.

The Fish Commission stocks trout for opening day and once in-season, in mid-May. Fourth Run holds fair numbers of wild brown and brook trout.

Hickory Run - Carbon County

(catch and release, artificials only, 1.5 miles)
(map: page 39)

Hickory Run is a small free-stone stream that holds a good wild brown trout population and also a few brook trout. The Fish Commission manages it as a wild trout stream and no longer does any stocking. West of the bridge on Route 534, there is a parking area and a sign for Hickory Run Trail, which follows down along the stream. From the Route 534 bridge to the mouth on the Lehigh River, a distance of about 1.5 miles, Hickory Run is managed under catch-and-release, artificials-only regulations.

Most of the stream has a gentle gradient with shallow riffles and pockets, but it flows more swiftly as it nears the Lehigh. Surrounding trees keep the stream well shaded. Hickory Run is quite small, but browns of 12 to 14 inches are sometimes caught.

Above Route 534, Hickory Run is infertile, suffers from acid rain, and holds few trout. The effluent from the sewage treatment plant at Hickory Run State Park buffers the acidity and increases the nutrients in the water below Route 534. Odd as it may seem, trout numbers are increased here by the addition of sewage effluent.

Mud Run - Carbon County

(fly fishing only, 2.5 miles)
(map: page 39)

Mud Run is a scenic stream with waterfalls, large boulders, and pools carved out of solid rock. The name Mud Run doesn't do it justice. Much of the stream is posted, but a 2.5-mile stretch within Hickory Run State Park is open to the public under fly-fishing-only

Mud Run in Hickory Run State Park.

regulations. Mud Run flows here through a secluded wooded area with no direct road access.

Along Route 534, just west of the turnpike overpass, you will find a parking area marked with a fly-fishing-only sign and a trail leading to Mud Run. Just east of the turnpike overpass, there is another parking area and a trail leading down to Hawk Falls. This beautiful falls is located on a small tributary stream, just upstream of its confluence with Mud Run. A little farther east on Route 534, a gravel road marked by a group-camping-area sign turns to the right. Follow this road until it ends at a gate. From here it's about a half-mile hike to the stream.

Mud Run is stocked by the Fish Commission for opening day and once inseason, in mid-May. Even though Mud Run is an infertile and somewhat acidic stream, it holds a fair population of wild brown trout and also a few brook trout. The water has the tannic brownish color common in Pocono streams. The fly area holds good numbers of wild and hatchery fish through the summer and into the fall, and summer water temperatures remain cooler in Mud Run than on larger streams such as the Lehigh River.

From the lower boundary of the fly area downstream to near the mouth on the Lehigh River, Mud Run is privately owned and posted against trespassing. A stretch about 200 yards long at the very mouth is open to public fishing.

Drakes Creek - Carbon County
(map: page 39)

Drakes Creek is stocked with trout from near the intersection of T514 and T481 downstream to the mouth on the Lehigh River, skipping a posted stretch in the middle. The Fish Commission stocks this small, shallow, woodland stream preseason and once again in mid-May. Drakes Creek also holds some wild browns and brookies, but not very many. T481 follows Drakes Run to its mouth. The lower part of this road is very narrow and rough.

Stony Creek - Carbon County
(map: page 39)

Only the upper part of Stony Creek is stocked with trout, from T474 downstream to T519. Below this the stream flows through a steep, narrow gorge on its way to the Lehigh River. In this remote, wooded area, Stony Creek has a good population of wild brown and brook trout. About half of the land bordering the creek is in State Game Land No. 141, and about half is privately owned.

Access to the top of this stretch is made difficult by posting on the downstream side of the T519 bridge. The middle stretch can be reached by walking in from SR 1002. A gated dirt road next to a power line leads down to the stream. Do not block the gate.

There is a place to park on the opposite side of SR 1002. The mouth of Stony Creek can be reached by taking a long walk along the railroad tracks from the mouth of Drakes Run.

Fishing Creek - Columbia County
(catch and release, artificials only, 1.1 mile)
(map: page 43)

Pennsylvania has many Fishing Creeks, perhaps the best known being the limestoner in Clinton County. Columbia County's Fishing Creek is a freestone stream that begins with the junction of its East and West Branches near Grassmere Park, then winds 32 miles past farmlands, woods, and small towns before meeting the North Branch of the Susquehanna River near Bloomsburg.

The Fish Commission stocks trout along 23 miles of the stream, from its origin downstream to the bridge at Lightstreet. Trout are stocked prior to opening day and three times inseason, with the last stocking coming in late May. Fishing pressure is heavy in the early season, but it drops off after mid-June, except in the catch-and-release area.

The catch-and-release area begins at the junction of the East and West Branches and continues downstream 1.1 mile. Plenty of wild and stocked trout inhabit this stretch year around. Just west of the Route 118 bridge at Grassmere Park, turn south onto Schoolhouse Road, which crosses the creek and leads to a small parking area near a covered bridge.

The catch-and-release area gets most of the fishing pressure in the summer and fall because it holds more trout than other parts of the creek, but fair numbers of wild browns can be found all along the creek, at least as far down as the Route 487 bridge near Orangeville.

In the summer months, Fishing Creek gets low and clear, but water temperatures remain surprisingly cool. Many parts of the creek become quite shallow, and most of the trout drop into the deeper pools. There is a lot of stream to explore here, and some of the places away from the road are scenic and seldom fished after the opening weeks of the season.

Access Points

Some access points to Fishing Creek, starting downstream and going north on Route 487, include the following:

1) The Route 487 bridge just north of Orangeville. The bridge pool is a popular fishing spot and there are some good runs farther downstream.

2) At the village of Forks, Huntington Creek joins Fishing Creek, adding greatly to its volume. There is a large, slow pool where the two streams meet and some good riffles and pools downstream from the junction.

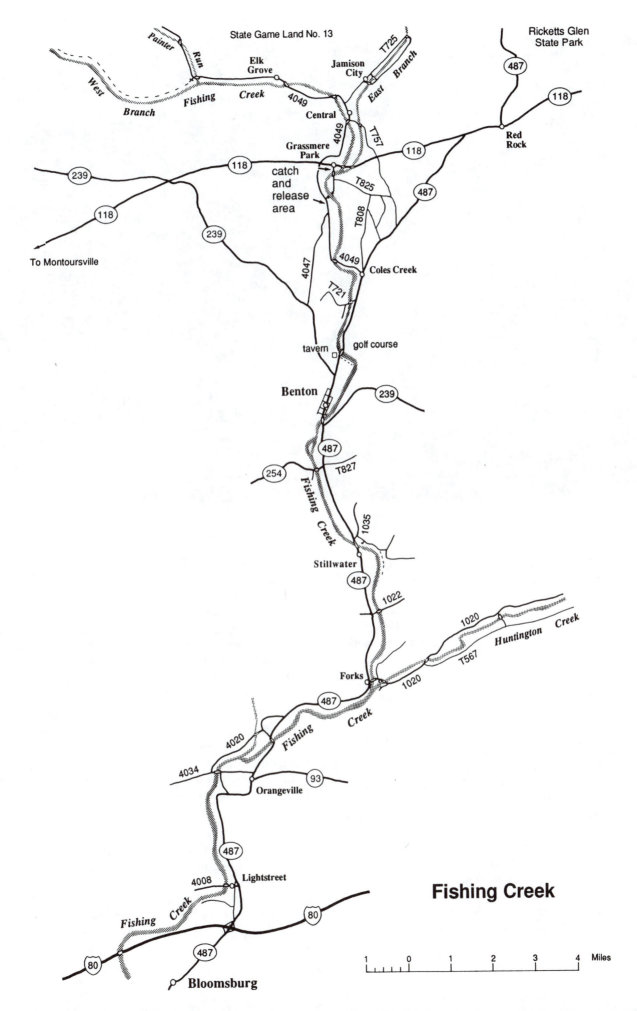

Fishing Creek

Fishing Creek at an old dam north of Benton.

Huntington Creek is not stocked, and most of it is posted, but if you can persuade a landowner to allow you to fish, you may find some good fishing. This stream has a fair population of wild browns in its lower reaches and quite a good population of wild browns and brookies in the middle and upper parts of the creek.

3) About 1.5 miles north of Forks, SR 1022 crosses the stream. Good parking and fishing are found near this bridge.

4) At Stillwater, Route 487 crosses the creek, and just past the bridge SR 1035 goes to the right. Turn here, then turn right again, and park near a covered bridge. Good fishing is found up or downstream from this covered bridge.

If you follow the road past the covered bridge and continue past a barn and farmhouse, you will soon come to an old quarry site on the left. From here an old railroad grade, which is now used as a hiking path, follows downstream along the creek. There are deep, narrow runs here, well shaded by overhanging trees. Farther down along the railroad grade, you will encounter a posted stretch of stream.

5) About 1 mile north of Benton, Route 487 crosses the stream again. Just before the bridge is a tavern. Park here and walk downstream along a gravel road. The road is marked with a sign that reads, "fishing permitted, walk in only." At the end of the road is an attractive pool with rock ledges rising above the opposite bank. A long stretch of Fishing Creek below this pool is separated from immediate road access by a wide field.

6) About 1.5 miles north of the Route 487 bridge, turn left onto T721 (Hackett Road). This road turns off from Route 487 just before a large dairy farm. Immediately above the T721 bridge there is a long, shallow stretch, but if you continue walking upstream you'll find a large pool in a wooded area.

Fly Hatches

Fishing Creek has good fly hatches, which include Blue Quills, Hendricksons, Grannoms, Sulphurs, March Browns, and Grey Foxes. Terrestrial patterns are effective in the summer months. Fly fishing tackle can be found at Beckie's Fishing Creek Outfitters. Look for their sign on the east side of Route 487 about 2 miles north of the village of Benton.

Camping

Campsites are available about 7 miles northeast of Fishing Creek's catch-and-release area at Ricketts Glen State Park. Be sure to allow time to hike the trails in the park that follow along Kitchen Creek and its branches. If you own a camera, bring it along; this is a favorite location of outdoor photographers.

Ricketts Glen State Park is one of the most beautiful places in Pennsylvania. Its streams tumble over numerous waterfalls, the highest of which is the 94-foot Ganoga Falls. Most of the falls are much smaller, but no less scenic. Giant pines, oaks, and hemlocks tower over the stream banks. The falls are best seen when water levels are moderate to high; during dry summers Kitchen Creek slows to a trickle.

West Branch Fishing Creek - Columbia County
(map: page 43)

The West Branch of Fishing Creek is not stocked, but it holds many wild brown and brook trout. From Grassmere Park, near the catch-and-release stretch on Fishing Creek, take SR 4049 up along the West Branch and through the villages of Central and Elk Grove. The stream holds trout near these villages, but there are many cottages and cabins along the banks.

Farther upstream you will enter heavily forested State Game Land No. 13. After crossing tiny Painter Run, the main road turns away from the West Branch, so park your vehicle here and walk up along the gated forest road that follows the stream towards its headwaters.

West Branch Fishing Creek is small and rocky, and you aren't likely to catch any trophies, but the near-wilderness surroundings are a great place to enjoy Penn's Woods. Many of the miniscule tributaries to the West Branch also hold native brook trout.

East Branch Fishing Creek - Columbia County
(map: page 43)

The East Branch of Fishing Creek is not as good a trout stream as the West Branch because trout populations are limited by acidity from acid precipitation and swamp drainage, but it does hold some wild brown and brook trout. No trout are stocked. Follow T725 up along the creek from Jamison City to a parking lot in State Game Land No. 13.

Bowman Creek in the fly area.

Bowman Creek

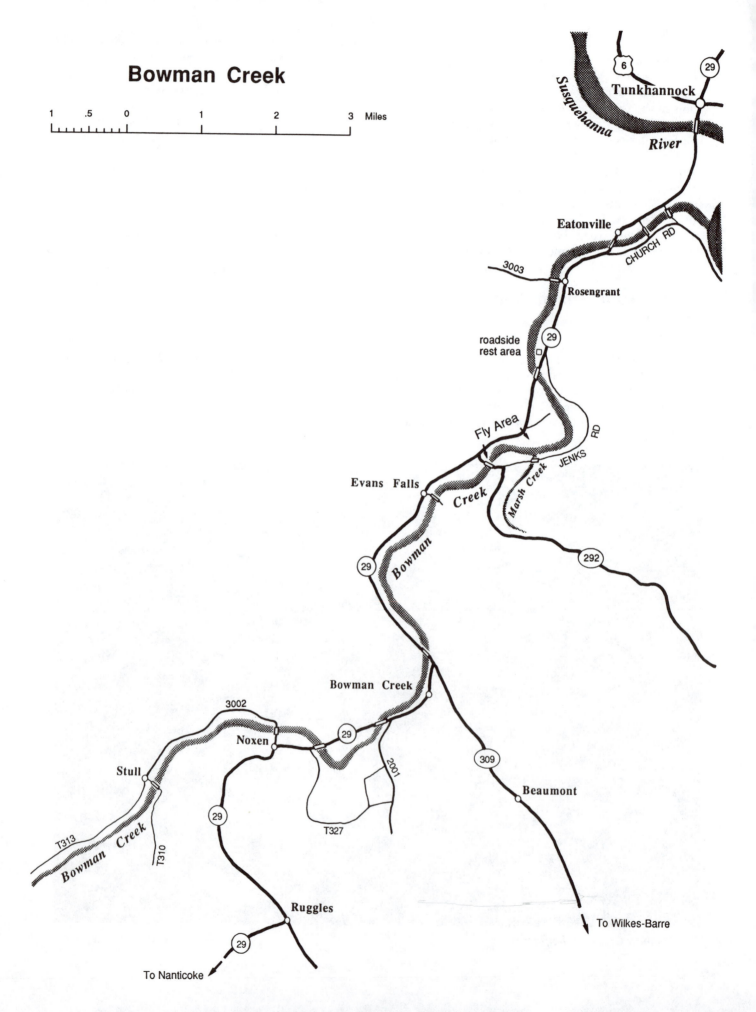

Bowman Creek - Wyoming and Luzerne Counties

(delayed harvest, fly fishing only, 1 mile)
(map: page 46)

Bowman Creek is very popular with anglers from the Scranton/Wilkes-Barre area, and the mile-long delayed-harvest, fly-fishing-only area is particularly popular. Stocking begins about 3.5 miles upstream of Stull, at the border of Luzerne and Wyoming Counties, and continues downstream 18 miles, almost to the mouth on the Susquehanna River. The Fish Commission stocks trout prior to opening day and twice inseason, with the last stocking coming in mid-May.

From the headwaters downstream to Stull, Bowman Creek flows through a patchwork of privately owned woodlands and State Game Land No. 57. Much of the private land is posted against trespassing. In the remote headwaters upstream from the Luzerne/Wyoming County line, no trout are stocked because of seasonal acidity problems, but fair numbers of wild brook trout are found. A gravel road follows the stream from Stull into the headwaters.

From Stull, which consists of just a few cabins, downstream to near Noxen, Bowman Creek is still mostly wooded. The stream reaches medium size by this point, being about 40 to 60 feet wide.

From Noxen downstream to the mouth, Bowman Creek flows past woods, farms, and small towns. Houses scattered along the stream and paralleling roads, as well as several posted stretches make finding access tricky in some places.

Plenty of parking is available at the first Route 29 bridge downstream from Noxen. Parking is also available at the Route 292 bridge. From here you can fish downstream into the delayed-harvest, fly-fishing-only area. Parking is available near the lower end of the fly area at a pulloff next to the bridge where Jenks Road crosses Marsh Creek. The fly area begins at the mouth of Marsh Creek and extends upstream 1 mile. The fly area gets most of the fishing pressure in the summer because the regulations keep higher numbers of trout here than in other parts of the creek.

A roadside rest area provides a good fishing access point on the lower part of the creek, and the lawns and shade trees here make this a pleasant spot to stop and eat lunch.

Bowman Creek gets very low and clear in the summer months, and parts of the stream have been channelized, but fair numbers of wild trout and stocked trout remain into the summer and fall. Above Stull brook trout predominate, from Stull to Noxen brook and brown trout are mixed about equally, and below Noxen you'll find mostly brown trout. A small population of rainbows exists in the lower half of the creek as a result of natural reproduction and escapement from a private hatchery.

Other Northeast PA Streams

(no maps)

No maps were included for the following streams and the descriptions were kept brief, but these streams are also well worth fishing.

Pohopoco Creek - Carbon and Monroe Counties

Trout are stocked in Pohopoco Creek in the tailwaters downstream from the Beltzville Reservoir. This stretch is mostly shallow except for the large pool directly below the dam. The discharge from the dam keeps water temperatures low, so many trout remain throughout the summer. Big browns are sometimes washed down from the reservoir into the creek, and browns up to 28 inches long and weighing 8 pounds have been caught in the reservoir. The reservoir is stocked with trout once each year, prior to opening day.

A 2-mile section from the backwaters of the reservoir upstream to the Route 209 bridge near Kresgeville is open to fishing, but not stocked with trout. This stretch holds fair numbers of wild browns and a few brook trout. All trout must be released here.

Several miles of Pohopoco Creek are stocked upstream from Kresgeville, but this stretch of stream is slow moving and muddy, and there are few places to park your car.

Dotters Creek flows into Pohopoco Creek near Kresgeville. This small stream is stocked for several miles and it also holds some wild brown trout. There are some posted stretches that make finding access difficult.

Butternut Creek - Wayne County

Butternut Creek flows into Wallenpaupack Creek a short distance upstream of where that stream flows into the backwaters of Lake Wallenpaupack. A fly-fishing-only area extends from the mouth upstream 2.5 miles to SR 3002. Route 191 crosses the stream near the middle of the fly stretch, and secondary roads cross the stream near the top and bottom of the fly stretch.

There have been some access problems on the fly area. When I visited the stream there was no posting, but I was told by a local resident that fishing was prohibited in the stretch above and below the bridge on SR 3002. Butternut Creek holds fair numbers of wild brown and brook trout in its upper stretches.

Harveys Creek and Harveys Lake - Luzerne County

Harveys Creek is the most heavily stocked and heavily fished stream in Luzerne County. The stream flows approximately 13 miles from Harveys Lake downstream to the mouth at West Nanticoke. Much of the land along the creek is owned by the Pennsylvania Gas and Water Company or by the state, so access problems are minimal. The fishing on Harveys Creek is mostly put-and-take, but fair numbers of trout carry over into the summer months.

Harveys Lake produces some big trout. An overnight gill net survey conducted by the Fish Commission captured five landlocked salmon from 18.5 to 23 inches long and eight brown trout ranging from 23 to 27 inches long.

Pike County Streams

There are many small streams in the Poconos that hold wild brown and brook trout, but fishing can be frustrating because so much stream mileage is posted. The best bet is to explore streams that flow through public lands.

Saw Creek is paralleled by Route 402 between Resica Falls and Porters Lake. A Delaware State Forest map will help you to find access and to separate out which sections of the stream are privately owned and which are within the state forest. A 3-mile section from the Porter Lake Property downstream to the Saw Creek Club property is stocked with hatchery trout, and Saw Creek also holds wild brown and brook trout.

A stretch of Bushkill Creek (a different Bushkill Creek than covered elsewhere in this book) flows through a section of the Delaware State Forest near the village of Millrift, which is north of Matamoras. This stretch can be reached only by walking, and it's swampy and brushy, but it holds a good population of wild brook trout.

The Delaware National Recreation area is a long strip of land along the Delaware River where public access is assured. The small streams flowing through this area and into the Delaware River are worth a try for wild trout, and they are easily reached from Route 209. Dingmans Run and Adams Creek are two of the better ones.

Southeast Pennsylvania

An old mill dam on Ridley Creek in Ridley Creek State Park.

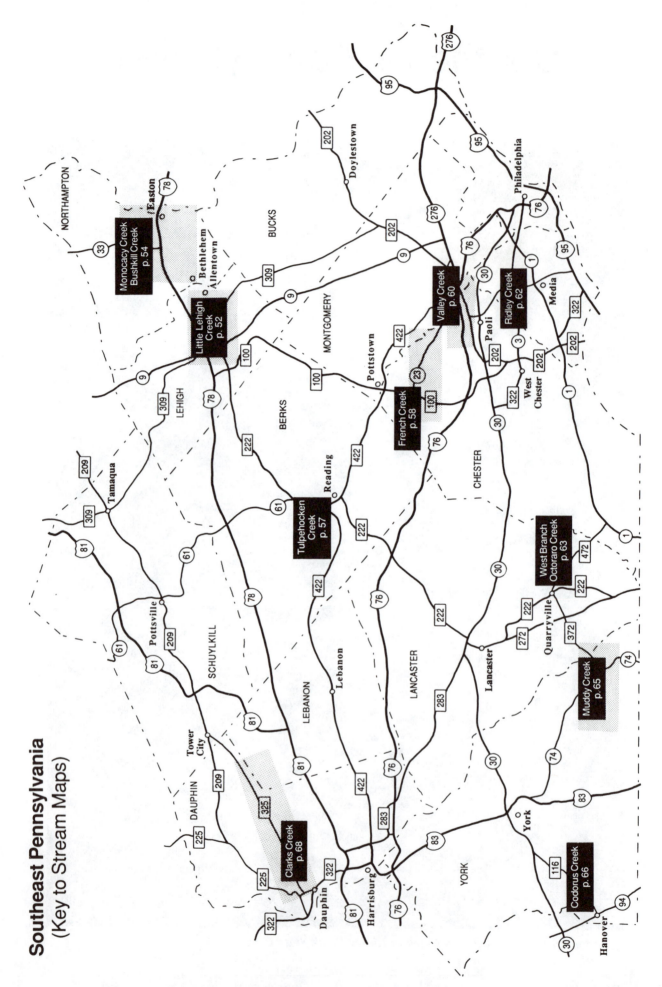

Southeast Pennsylvania
(Key to Stream Maps)

Monocacy Creek
Bushkill Creek
p. 54

Little Lehigh
Creek
p. 52

Valley Creek
p. 60

Ridley Creek
p. 62

French Creek
p. 58

Tulpehocken
Creek
p. 57

West Branch
Octoraro Creek
p. 63

Muddy Creek
p. 65

Clarks Creek
p. 68

Codorus Creek
p. 66

NORTHAMPTON

/Easton

Bethlehem
Allentown

Doylestown

Philadelphia

Media

BUCKS

MONTGOMERY

Pottstown

Paoli

West
Chester

LEHIGH

BERKS

CHESTER

Reading

Tamaqua

Pottsville

SCHUYLKILL

LEBANON

Lebanon

LANCASTER

Lancaster

Quarryville

Tower
City

DAUPHIN

Dauphin

Harrisburg

York

YORK

Hanover

Southeast Pennsylvania

Little Lehigh Creek - Lehigh County
(fly fishing only, 1.4 miles)
(no harvest, fly fishing only, 1 mile)
(map: page 52)

There aren't many places where you can enjoy good trout fishing in the middle of a city, but the stretch of Little Lehigh Creek that lies within the city limits of Allentown is a notable exception. Cold limestone springs, special regulations, and the protection of the city parks that form a greenbelt along the creek make this possible.

The Little Lehigh is stocked from near Mertztown in Berks County downstream to its mouth on the Lehigh River in Allentown. (The upper stretch of the creek is not shown on the map.) Most of the stream is open to fishing, but a few areas are posted. In Berks County and in the upper water in Lehigh County, siltation and summer warming limit the wild trout population, so fishing is generally slow after the early weeks of the season.

A fly-fishing-only area begins at T508 (Wild Cherry Lane) and extends downstream 1.4 miles to Lauderslager's Mill Dam. A few wild browns are found here, and the special regulations maintain good numbers of stocked trout. Not many years ago, this stretch of Little Lehigh Creek ran through a rural farming area, but now housing developments are springing up rapidly near the stream.

Downstream from Cedar Crest Boulevard (Route 29), the Little Lehigh flows through the golf course of the Lehigh Country Club. Fishing is prohibited here.

A short distance above the iron bridge (Keck's Bridge) on Keystone Road, the Little Lehigh flows out of the country club and into the Allentown Park system. This is where you will find the best fishing. The park's trees and wide lawns buffer the creek from the surrounding city, providing a great place to picnic, bicycle, throw frisbee, and fish for trout. The stream is about 40 to 60 feet wide here, and several limestone springs keep a good supply of water flowing through the summer months.

A no-harvest, fly-fishing-only area begins at the bridge on Hatchery Road and extends downstream 1 mile to near the 24th Street (Oxford Drive) bridge. A large parking area is located just above the Hatchery Road bridge. A mixture of stocked trout, wild trout, and escaped fish from a small, city-owned hatchery keeps a high density of trout in the no-harvest stretch, especially in the upper part of the stretch, near the hatchery. You will often find a high density of anglers in this area also.

To escape the crowds, fish upstream or downstream from the no-harvest stretch. Fishing pressure is heavy in these areas early in the season, but light the rest of the year. Below the no-harvest stretch, the stream continues through Allentown's park system, and good numbers of stocked and wild trout can be found downstream at least as far as the mouth of Cedar Creek. Below the mouth of Cedar Creek, traffic and industry increase along the banks of the Little Lehigh, but some anglers report catching trout year around almost as far downstream as the mouth on the Lehigh River.

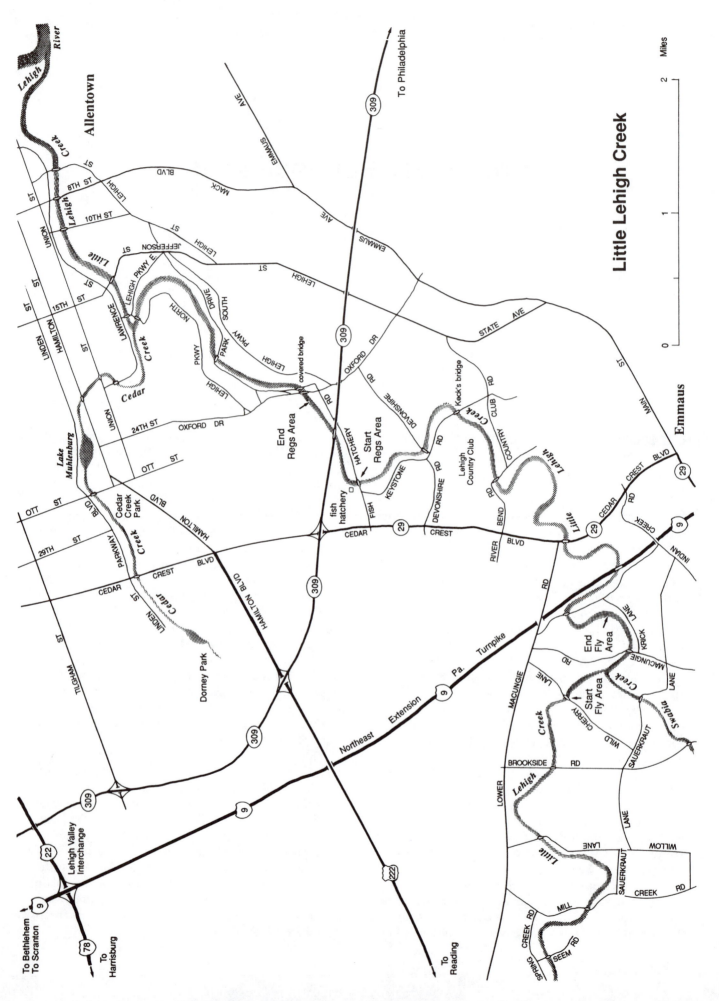

Little Lehigh Creek

Little Lehigh Creek flows through a greenbelt of parks in the middle of Allentown.

The major fly hatches on the Little Lehigh are the limestone creek favorites: Blue-winged Olives, Sulphurs and Tricos. The two special regulation areas are good places for fly fishing early in the year. They are open to fishing year around, and Blue-winged Olives often begin hatching around the third week in March.

Swabia Creek - Lehigh County
(map: page 52)

Swabia Creek is a small tributary that flows into Little Lehigh Creek's fly area. The Fish Commission stocks 5 miles of the stream with trout, skipping over some posted areas. Swabia Creek holds few wild trout and is best fished early in the season.

Cedar Creek - Lehigh County
(map: page 52)

Cedar Creek is a tiny limestone spring creek that flows through park land in the city of Allentown. If you are in the Allentown area to fish Little Lehigh Creek, a visit to Cedar Creek makes an interesting side trip.

The best stretch of Cedar Creek is from Ott Street upstream through a pleasant, grassy park to Cedar Crest Boulevard (Route 29). The stream is not stocked here, but it holds surprising numbers of wild brown trout. Do not expect to catch a trophy here; few of the browns exceed 12 inches in length.

The fishing is difficult on Cedar Creek because the stream is clear and shallow and the wild browns are wary. Morning and evening are good times to fish. The direct sunlight of mid-day makes these trout very spooky.

Cedar Creek is stocked with hatchery trout below Lake Muhlenburg, but because of the warming effect of the lake, few trout are found here into the summer months. The best place to park your car while fishing Cedar Creek is at Cedar Creek Park, just below the Ott Street bridge.

Monocacy Creek - Northampton County
(trophy trout project, 1.9 miles)
(map: page 54)

Monocacy Creek is a limestone spring creek that offers fishing for wild brown trout on the edges of, and even in the very middle of, the city of Bethlehem. The best fishing is found in the trophy trout regulations area, which begins about 0.7 mile above the Center Street bridge and extends downstream 1.9 miles to Illicks Mill Dam. The regulations require the use of artificial lures or flies, and harvest is limited to two fish 14 inches or longer. It's possible to catch trout larger than 14 inches from the Monocacy, but such fish are unusual. No trout are stocked in this area because of the good population of wild browns.

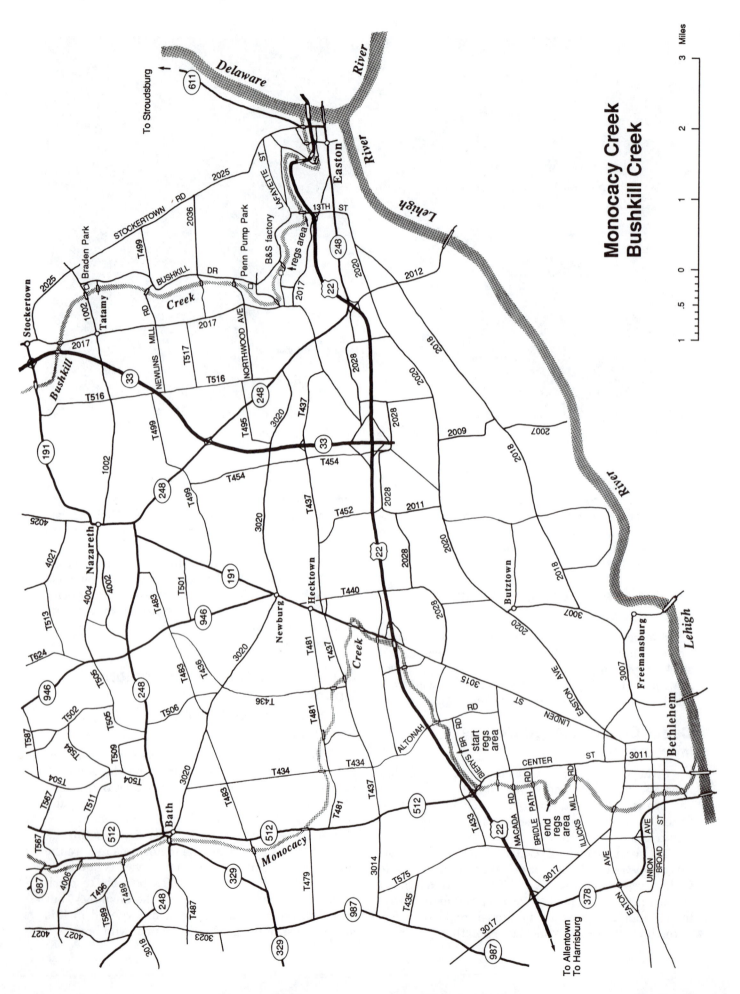

Monocacy Creek
Bushkill Creek

Monocacy Creek offers fishing for wild brown trout near Bethlehem.

In July of 1985, a truck spilled chemicals into the stream, killing many of the trout. Natural reproduction has since repopulated the stream, and fishing is good again. In the trophy trout stretch, Monocacy Creek flows through a suburban residential area, but trees flank the stream, and most of the houses are set well back from the banks.

To fish the upper part of the trophy stretch, park along the railroad tracks at the intersection of Center Street and Biery's Bridge Road. From here you can fish upstream in an attractive wooded area.

Near the middle of the trophy stretch, there is parking available on Macada Road and Bridle Path Road. Just below the bridge on Illicks Mill Road there is a large parking area, and just above the bridge the stream flows through Illicks Mill Park. From the park you can walk up along the railroad tracks that follow the west bank of the creek. The lower boundary of the trophy trout area is marked by an old mill dam.

Trout are stocked from Illicks Mill Park down through the city of Bethlehem to the mouth of Monocacy Creek on the Lehigh River, and some wild browns are also found in this lower stretch. Some anglers even report catching big browns right at the mouth on the Lehigh River, just across the river from the enormous Bethlehem Steel plant.

Trout are also stocked from above the trophy trout area upstream to the village of Bath, skipping over several posted properties. Some wild brown trout are found in this stocked stretch also, but they are not abundant. Access is made difficult along much of this stocked stretch by the many homes and businesses that line the banks of the stream. Upstream from Bath, Monocacy Creek is quite small, but it holds many wild browns there.

Fly hatches on the Monocacy are typical of Pennsylvania's limestone streams. Blue-winged Olives, Sulphurs, and Tricos are the main hatches, and several caddis hatches also appear. Terrestrial patterns such as ants and beetles are useful in the summer, and Muskrat Nymphs or more specific imitations can be used to imitate the plentiful scuds and sowbugs.

Bushkill Creek - Northampton County
(catch and release, artificials only, 1.1 miles)
(map: page 54)

There are several Bushkill Creeks in eastern Pennsylvania. This particular Bushkill Creek flows into the Delaware River at Easton. Bushkill Creek is not a very beautiful stream. Much of the lower part of the creek flows through an industrial area of Easton, and farther upstream much of the creek flows past suburban residential areas. Despite its lack of scenic grandeur, Bushkill Creek is worth including here because of its wild brown trout population and because its catch-and-release area is open to fishing year around.

Bushkill Creek originates on a ridge in the Blue Mountains and flows 24 miles before reaching the Delaware River. The upper stretches of the creek are freestone in nature, become rather shallow and warm in the summer months, and therefore hold few wild trout. Trout are stocked in this upper water, though, and a popular place to fish in the early season is in Jacobsburg State Park, which can be reached from the Belfast exit of Route 33. (This upper stretch is not shown on the map).

Limestone springs flow into Bushkill Creek near Stockertown, adding a cool, consistent flow of water. From here to the mouth, the stream holds a fair population of wild brown trout. Bushkill Drive parallels the creek, providing easy access.

The best fishing on Bushkill Creek is found in the catch-and-release area, which begins at the Binney and Smith factory and extends downstream 1.1 miles to the 13th Street bridge. Barbless hooks are required and only flies or artificial lures may be used. This stretch is in an industrial setting, but because of the special regulations and the presence of limestone springs, it holds a higher wild brown trout population than other parts of the creek. No trout are stocked here. The upper half of the catch-and-release stretch seems to hold more trout than the lower half. A dam slows the stream near the 13th Street bridge.

From the 13th Street bridge downstream to the mouth, Bushkill Creek is stocked with trout and also holds some wild brown trout. This part of the creek flows directly through the city of Easton. Another stocked section of the stream extends from the Binney and Smith factory upstream to the dam just above Penn Pump Park. The stocked stretches of Bushkill Creek are stocked by the Fish Commission before opening day and twice inseason.

Another place to try for wild browns is near the village of Tatamy. The stretch downstream from Braden Park is not stocked, but it holds fair numbers of wild browns. I hooked a heavy brown about 14 inches long at the first bridge downstream from Braden Park. Parking is available at Braden Park or along Bushkill Drive.

Bushkill Creek flows over a gravel and rock bottom, and along most of its length it is characterized by gentle riffles and pools of moderate size and depth. In the middle of Easton, the gradient increases, and there are numerous turbulent, rocky riffles.

Bushkill Creek's fly hatches include Blue-winged Olives, Sulphurs, Tan Caddis, and Tricos.

When planning a trip to Bushkill Creek, keep in mind that heavy rainfall muddies the stream quickly.

Tulpehocken Creek - Berks County
(delayed harvest, artificial lures only, 3.8 miles)
(map: page 57)

Tulpehocken Creek offers very good trout fishing right on the outskirts of Reading. A 3.8 mile section of the creek, from the first deflector below the outflow of

Tulpehocken Creek. This covered bridge marks the lower boundary of the delayed-harvest area.

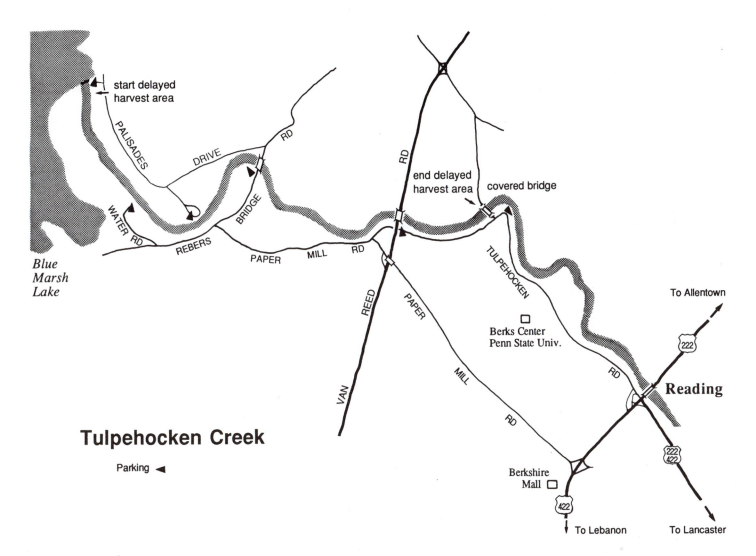

Tulpehocken Creek

Parking ◄

Blue Marsh Lake downstream to the covered bridge (the "Red Bridge") along Tulpehocken Road, is managed under delayed-harvest, artificials-only regulations. Bottom releases from the dam at Blue Marsh Lake keep the water cool all summer, and the rich limestone fertility of Tulpehocken Creek provides plenty of trout feed.

Fingerling brown and rainbow trout between 4 and 7 inches long are stocked each fall, and they grow fast in this fine habitat. Trout from 9 to 12 inches long are plentiful, 12- to 16-inchers are fairly common, and even larger fish are sometimes caught. Anglers are sometimes surprised to see many carp and suckers in Tulpehocken Creek, but they shouldn't worry. There are lots of trout, too.

The Tulpehocken is a large, wide stream with a moderate gradient. Wading the stream's gentle riffles and smooth glides is not difficult unless water levels are high. Large, picturesque sycamore trees and some thick, brushy areas line the banks.

Some good places to park along Tulpehocken Creek include the parking area just below the dam, the parking area near the bridge on Rebers Bridge Road, at the end of Water Road, under the Van Reed Road overpass, and at a parking area downstream from the covered bridge.

Tulpehocken Creek has a number of attractions that make it a popular recreation site for non-anglers as well as anglers. Covered bridge enthusiasts will enjoy the "Red Bridge," which marks the lower end of the special regulations area. This unusually long covered bridge is open to foot traffic, but closed to vehicles. Much of the land along the creek is part of a large park, and scenic trails attract walkers and bicyclists. Picnic areas and a playground for children are found along Tulpehocken Road, downstream from the special regulations area.

Because Tulpehocken Creek is one of the most productive trout streams in heavily populated southeastern Pennsylvania, fishing pressure can be intense at times. On weekends in April and May the stream is often genuinely crowded. A fair number of anglers continue to fish here through the summer and into the fall.

Sulphurs and Tricos are the main mayfly hatches on Tulpehocken Creek. Caddis hatches are also very

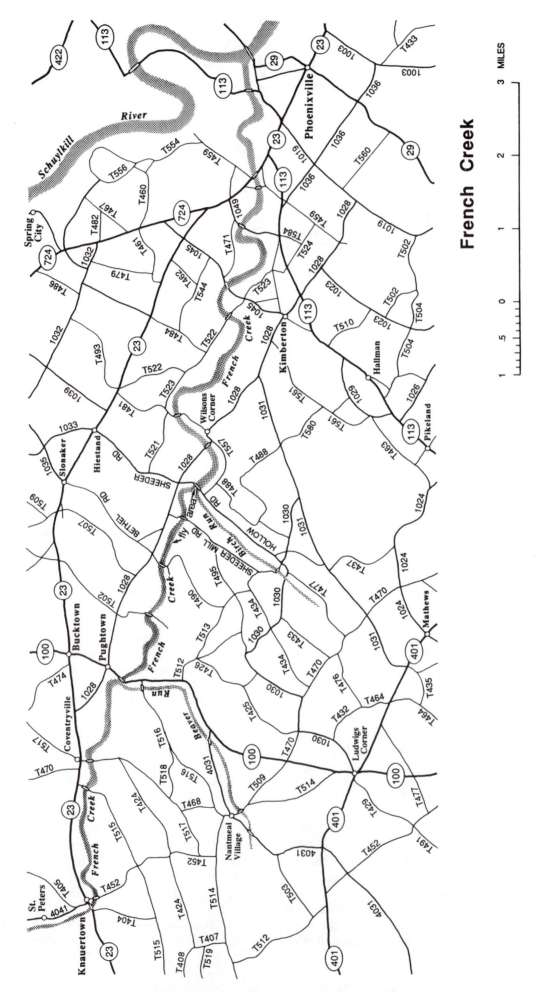

French Creek

abundant and occur from early spring into late fall.

French Creek - Chester County
(delayed harvest, fly fishing only, 0.9 miles)
(map: page 58)

French Creek is stocked over a distance of 14 miles, from the village of St. Peters downstream to Phoenixville. The fishing on French Creek is basically put-and-take, but good fishing is found at the delayed-harvest, fly-fishing-only area, which extends from an old covered bridge on Hollow Road upstream 0.9 miles to Camp Sleepy Hollow.

Because of the restricted creel limit and anglers who release most of their fish, the fly stretch holds many trout up until about late June, when the rest of French Creek has few fish remaining. In most years, water temperatures get pretty warm in July and August, though, and then fishing slows even in the fly area. In 1990, which was an unusually cool year with lots of rain, there were still many trout remaining in the fly area when I visited the stream on July 20.

Unlike most lower elevation trout streams, which tend to be heavily silted, French Creek flows

French Creek, a short distance downstream from the fly area.

fairly clean and clear over a streambed of rocks and gravel. There are few really swift-flowing sections, but many riffles connect the long pools. Large, old hardwood trees line the streambanks.

French Creek may not be one of the world's great trout streams, but it offers fishing for stocked trout in pleasant rural and suburban surroundings only a short drive from Philadelphia. Fishing pressure is very heavy early in the season. According to a Fish Commission survey, about 3,400 anglers show up for the opening day of the season.

Caddis hatches provide much of the fly fishing action on French Creek. The tan Elk Hair Caddis in sizes 14 and 16 is a good dry fly pattern here. Nymph fishers should try the Muskrat Nymph, Hare's Ear Nymph, and Green Caddis Larva patterns. When water levels drop, ants and beetles and other small terrestrial patterns work well on French Creek's broad, flat pools.

Beaver Run and Birch Run are two small tributaries to French Creek that are stocked with trout

only prior to opening day. They are best fished in the first week or two of the season.

Valley Creek - Chester County
(no kill zone, entire creek)
(map: page 60)

Wild brown trout can be found very close to Philadelphia in Valley Creek, which flows through Valley Forge National Historical Park. Valley Creek was formerly stocked with trout from Route 29 downstream 6.5 miles to the mouth, but after PCBs contamination was discovered in the stream, stocking was ended. Currently, no trout may be harvested in Valley Creek or its tributaries because of the health risks.

Since stocking ended and the no-kill restriction went into effect, the numbers of wild trout in Valley Creek increased tremendously, and the stream now holds a good population of wild brown trout. Some brown trout over 18 inches in length have been caught in recent years.

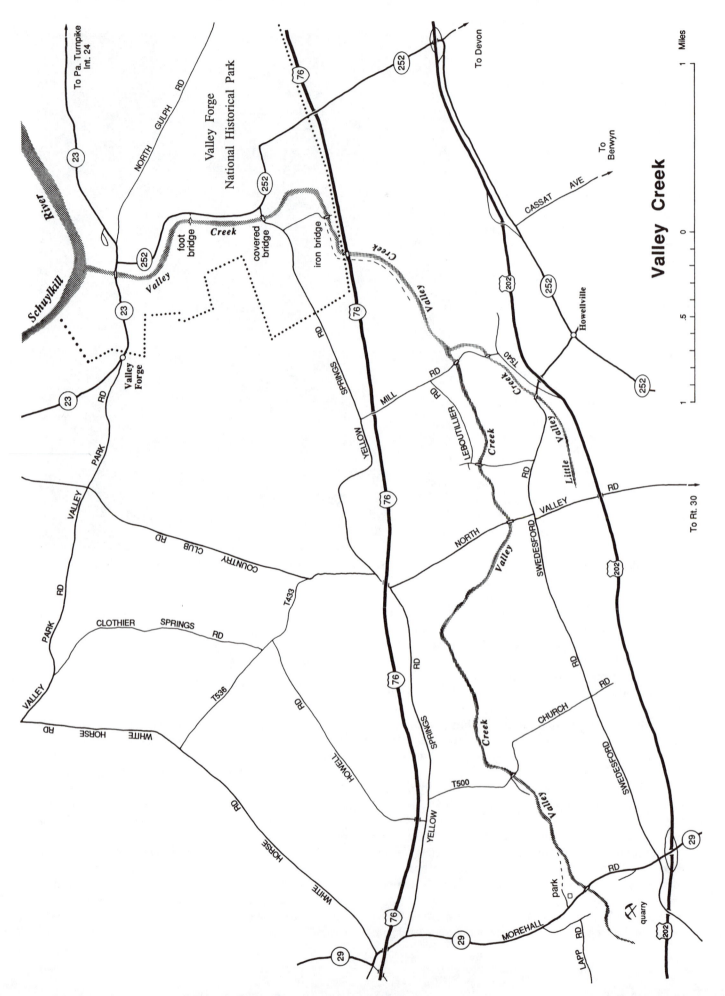

Valley Creek

It is rather surprising that Valley Creek can support wild trout. The stream flows through a suburban area near Philadelphia, it's farther south and at a lower elevation than most trout streams, and it has suffered damage from PCBs, sewage effluent, and siltation. Large housing and office developments have sprung up in the watershed. The cool limestone springs flowing in along the length of Valley Creek and the no-kill regulations make it possible for wild trout to survive despite these adverse conditions.

The lower 2 miles of Valley Creek flow through Valley Forge Historical Park, which is a beautiful expanse of rolling, grassy hills, groves of trees, and historical sites relating to the winter encampment of Washington's army during the Revolutionary War.

Route 252 (Valley Creek Road) follows the lower part of the creek as it flows through the park, and several pulloffs along the road provide easy access. A parking area is located near a covered bridge. Near the covered bridge, a gravel road leads past Maxwell's Quarters and ends at an iron bridge over the creek. From the iron bridge, a walking path continues up along the stream and under the Pennsylvania Turnpike (I-76) bridge. Above the turnpike the stream flows through a large housing development. To the great credit of the developers, they left a wide, wooded buffer strip on both sides of the stream, creating a park-like setting.

This old covered bridge crosses Valley Creek in Valley Forge National Historical Park.

All of Valley Creek upstream from the turnpike is surrounded by private property, except for a small park off Route 29, near the headwaters. Most of the stream is open to fishing, but there are a few posted stretches, and if anglers litter or otherwise create a nuisance there will certainly be more posting. A short distance below Mill Road, Little Valley Creek flows into Valley Creek, and this very small stream also holds some wild browns, especially near its mouth.

The main hatches on Valley Creek are Blue-Winged Olives, Sulphurs, and various caddis. If no flies are hatching, try fishing Muskrat Nymphs, Hare's Ear Nymphs, or Pheasant Tail Nymphs in sizes 12, 14, and 16. Freshwater scuds are abundant in Valley Creek, as they are in many limestone streams. Imitations should be tied on size 14 or 16

hooks. Dub a body with a mixture of olive, grey, and brown fur. Pick out the fur on the underside to imitate legs and trim the top and sides.

Ridley Creek - Delaware County
(delayed harvest, fly fishing only, 0.6 mile)
(map: page 62)

Ridley Creek is not a great trout stream, but it offers pleasant fishing in Ridley Creek State Park only 16 miles from center city Philadelphia. This park is a 2,600-acre oasis of rolling hills, woodlands, and grasslands in the midst of a busy suburban region. The entrance to the park is from Route 3 (West Chester Pike), about 3 miles west of Newton Square. Turn onto Providence Road or Sandy Flash Drive.

Trout stocking begins at the Colonial Pennsylvania Mansion along Sandy Flash Drive and continues

Ridley Creek

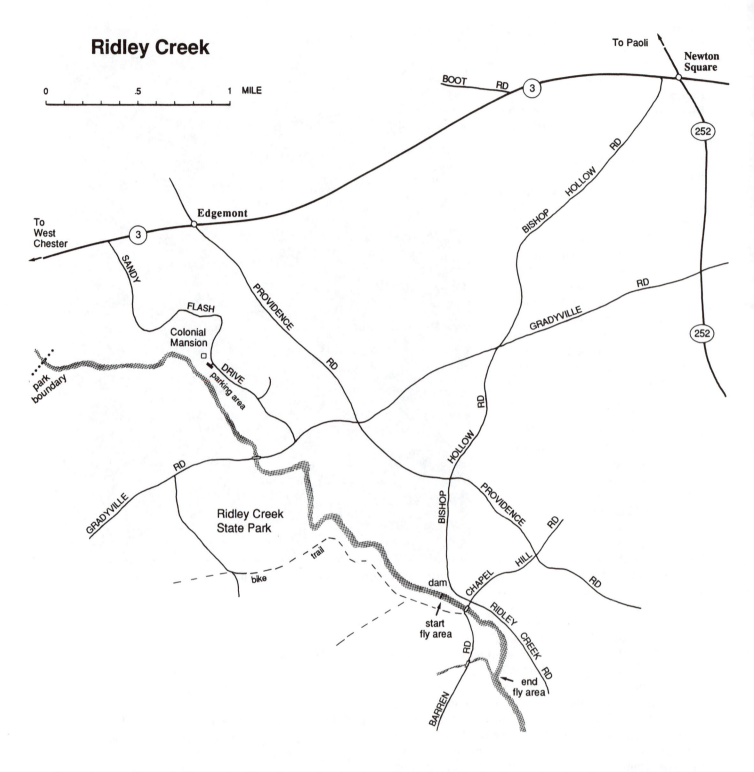

downstream through the park. The stream is about 25 feet wide and is well shaded by big sycamore trees.

A delayed-harvest, fly-fishing-only area begins at an old dam just off Bishop Hollow Road and continues downstream 0.6 mile to the mouth of Dismal Run. A large parking area is located near the old dam.

Ridley Creek has few or no wild trout, but the special regulations create good fishing until at least mid-June, and skillful and persistent anglers catch trout here even into late summer and fall. Ridley Creek is stocked prior to opening day and three times inseason, with the last stocking coming in late May.

West Branch Octoraro Creek - Lancaster County

(delayed harvest, fly fishing only, 1.9 miles)
(map: page 63)

West Branch Octoraro Creek offers perhaps the best trout fishing in Lancaster County. The stream flows through a pretty, rural area in the southern part of the county. The most consistent fishing is found in the 1.9 mile delayed-harvest, fly-fishing-only area. Driving south on Route 472 from Quarryville, you will go down a long hill, then cross a bridge over the creek. Just after the bridge, turn left onto Black Rock Road and park along the shoulder. The upper end of the fly area begins a short distance below the Route 472 bridge.

Above the fly area there are some nice pools and riffles in a pleasant woods, but this water is under general regulations, and heavy fishing pressure thins the trout out quickly after stocking. Opening day of trout season brings very heavy crowds to this stretch of West Branch Octoraro Creek. On opening day of one of the first years I fished for trout, I made a bad cast here, missed the stream completely, and hooked a fisherman on the opposite bank by his collar.

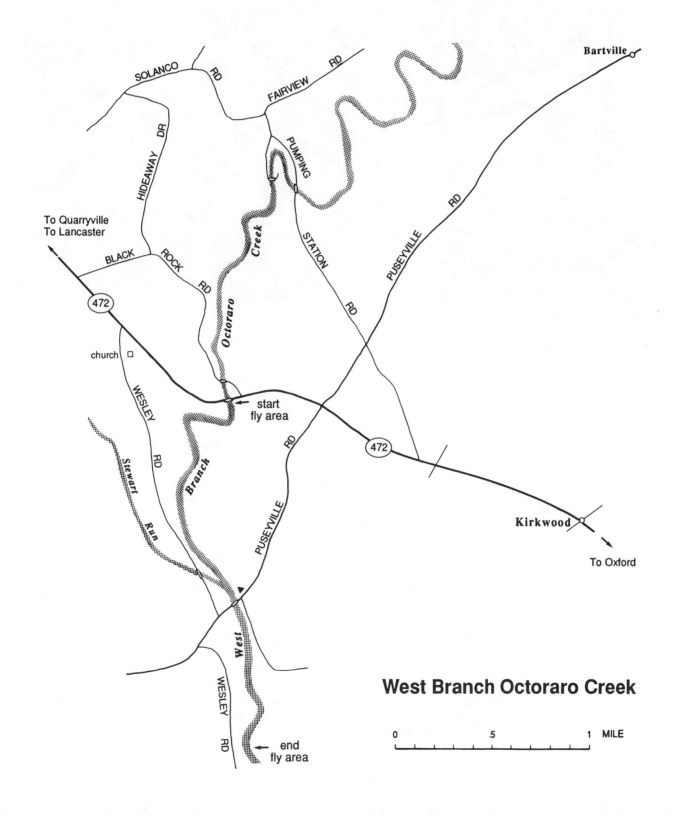

West Branch Octoraro Creek

West Branch Octoraro Creek.

To reach the lower end of the fly area, continue south on Route 472 from the Route 472 bridge for a half-mile, then turn right on Puseyville Road. In 1 mile you will cross a bridge over the creek. There is a State Game Land parking area on the right, just before the bridge. The fly area extends upstream from this bridge to near the Route 472 bridge and also downstream about another 0.7 mile.

Below the Puseyville Road bridge, the creek flows through a meadow area where there are some erosion problems and little shading. There are some deep pools in this meadow stretch, though, that hold trout well into the summer. Above the Puseyville Road bridge, the stream flows through a wooded area where there are good riffles and pools, and the streambed is mostly clean rock and gravel.

West Branch Octoraro Creek has just a very few wild and holdover trout; most of the fish are stocked. Because of the special regulations and the favorable stream habitat, many trout are found in the fly area through mid-June, and fair numbers can be found there even through the summer and into the fall.

Sadly, the rural character of West Branch Octo-raro Creek is being gradually erased by residential development near the stream. There are just a few, short posted stretches now, but as more houses are built, access problems are likely to increase.

Stewart Run, a small tributary to the West Branch, is stocked with trout before opening day only; it is best fished in the opening weeks of the season.

Muddy Creek - York County
(fly fishing only, 2 miles)
(map: page 65)

Muddy Creek, located not far from the cities of York and Lancaster, flows through a rugged, surprisingly little-developed, wooded area in southern York County. The Fish Commission stocks Muddy Creek from its origin, at the junction of the North and South Branches of Muddy Creek, downstream to the SR 2024 bridge. Stocking takes place preseason and twice inseason, with the last stocking coming in early to mid-May. The North and South Branches of Muddy Creek are also stocked trout streams.

Muddy Creek is a fairly large trout stream, which some people canoe early in the year. Swift rapids, deep pools, and large boulders are found along much

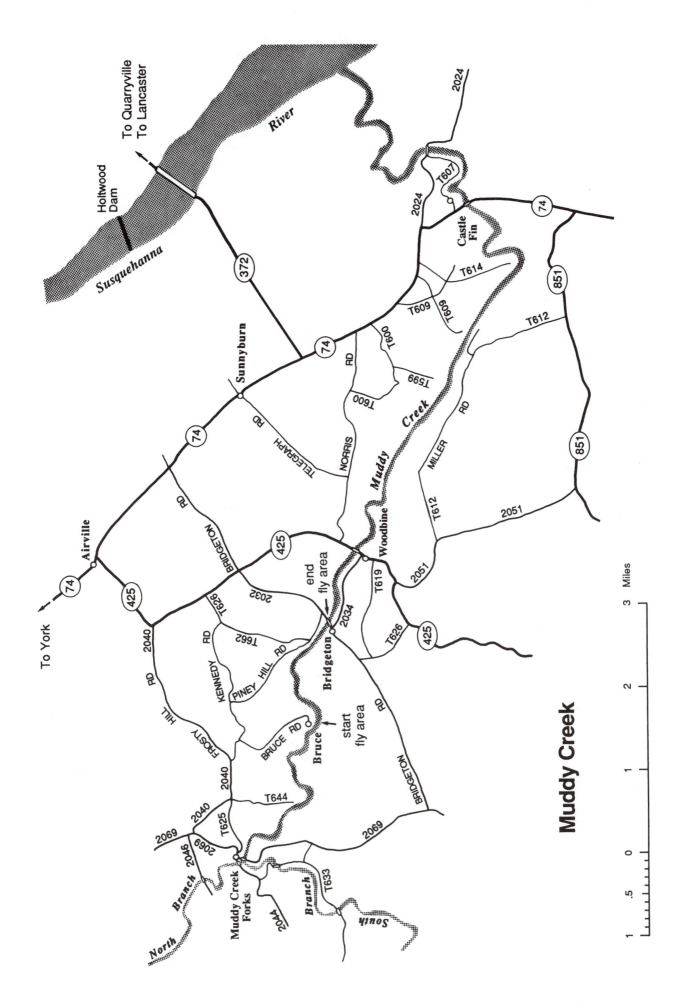

Muddy Creek

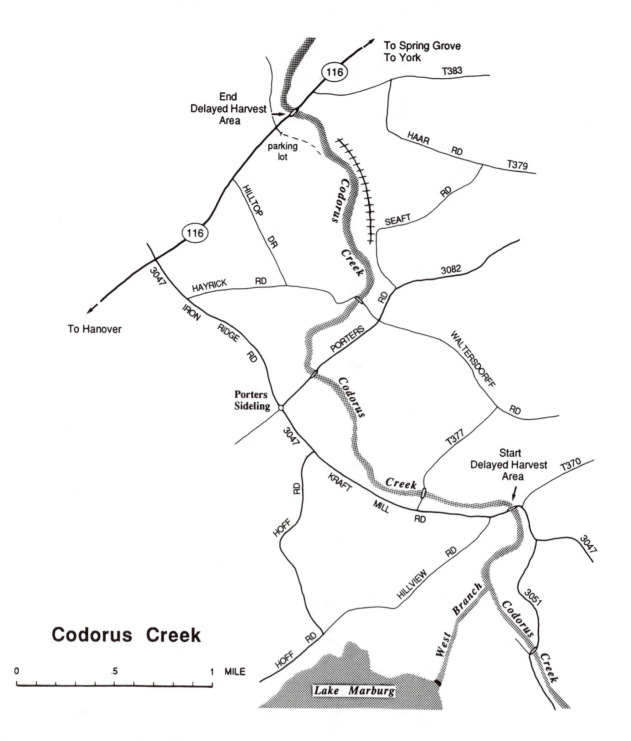

Codorus Creek

0   .5   1   MILE

of the creek, particularly from Woodbine down to the mouth, where the stream flows through a narrow gorge. In a few places, the rapids are actually too rough to canoe; I've seen wrecked canoes lying twisted among the rocks. Since warm summer temperatures and siltation prevent Muddy Creek from supporting any significant number of wild trout, few people fish for trout in Muddy Creek later than mid-June.

A fly-fishing-only area begins just above the Bridgeton Road (SR 2032) bridge at Bridgeton and extends upstream 2 miles to Bruce. The regulations keep the stocked trout from being thinned out too quickly. The stream is slower moving in the fly area

than it is in the lower stretches, but there is a good mix of riffles and deep pools.

During the summer, water temperatures rise and trout fishing slows on Muddy Creek. Fair numbers of smallmouth bass are caught in the lower reaches.

Codorus Creek - York County
(delayed harvest, artificial lures only, 3.3 miles)
(map: page 66)

The delayed-harvest, artificial-lures-only area on Codorus Creek has only been recently established, but already very good fishing is developing there. The delayed-harvest area begins at the bridge on Route 116 and extends upstream 3.3 miles to the bridge on SR 3047.

A landowner along Codorus Creek told me that Brian Berger, former Waterways Conservation Officer of York County, deserves a lot of credit for working with landowners, anglers, and all other concerned parties to get the regulations area established.

At first glance Codorus Creek doesn't look like a particularly promising trout stream. It looks like many other lowland streams: muddy banked and slow moving, with gentle riffles separating long, languid pools. But Codorus Creek has something most other lowland streams do not have: cold water. Bottom releases from Lake Marburg keep the water temperatures below 65 degrees all summer long. Trout reproduction is limited, probably by siltation, but cold water and the special regulations keep plenty of trout here through the season, and many browns hold over through the winter and take on the brighter colors of wild trout.

Codorus Creek flows through an area of woods, cornfields, and rural residences. Be particularly careful not to litter or damage any property. Before the special regulations went into effect, Codorus Creek was visited in the early season by hordes of anglers who camped overnight, trampled down banks, and left litter. These actions understandably left some landowners unhappy.

A slow-moving, wooded stretch of Codorus Creek.

Codorus Creek has good fly hatches including Hendricksons, Sulphurs, March Browns, Grey Foxes, and various caddis. This is a good stream for early season fly fishing. Hendricksons hatch in good numbers here as early as April 9, which is a week or two earlier than on most northern trout streams.

Clarks Creek - Dauphin County
(delayed harvest, fly fishing only, 1.9 miles)
(map: page 68)

Clarks Creek offers trout fishing in an attractive wooded area not far from Harrisburg. There are few wild or holdover trout in Clarks Creek, but heavy stocking provides good fishing all along the stream early in the season, and a 1.9-mile delayed-harvest, fly-fishing-only area holds trout through the summer and into the fall. Clarks Creek is stocked for opening day and three times inseason, with the last stocking coming in late May. Acid rain is probably the main reason Clarks Creek has few wild trout. Ph readings below 6 have been recorded.

Access to Clarks Creek is easy because it is followed by Route 325 for most of its length. The delayed-harvest, fly-fishing-only area begins about 2.5 miles upstream from the Route 225 bridge. Signs mark the upper and lower ends of the stretch, and parking is provided by several Game Land parking areas along Route 325.

In the fly area Clarks Creek is flat, slow moving, and clear. Tall trees line the stream, providing very good shade. Long, fine leaders and a careful presentation are required, particularly in the summer months.

Clarks Creek doesn't have very heavy fly hatches, but Hendricksons, Sulphurs, March Browns, Light

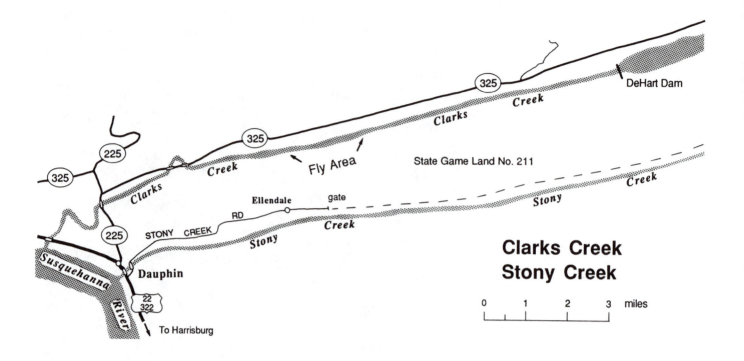

Clarks Creek
Stony Creek

0   1   2   3   miles

Cahills, and various caddis flies do appear. Terrestrial patterns such as beetles, crickets, and ants are very useful here.

Clarks Creek is semi-famous for its green inchworms, which drop from the overhanging trees limbs from late May to mid-June. Trout become very selective when feeding on these worms. Most anglers use #14 imitations constructed of either clipped green deer hair or painted cork.

Stony Creek - Dauphin County
(map: page 68)

Some streams are more notable for their attractive surroundings than for their trout fishing, and Stony Creek is one of them. Stony Creek flows into the Susquehanna River at Dauphin, just a short drive north of Harrisburg. Houses are scattered along the lower reaches, but most of the stream flows through a long, narrow, wooded valley within State Game Land No. 211.

The gravel access road that follows the creek through Game Land No. 211 is gated, and no motor vehicles are permitted. Even when the fishing is slow, this is an enjoyable place to hike and explore. The access road provides an easy walking path that is also suitable for bicycles. Some people even ride in on horseback. There are few places so remote and undeveloped, yet so close to urban areas.

The fishing on Stony Creek relies almost entirely on hatchery fish. Acid rain and drainage from old, long-abandoned coal mines make Stony Creek too acidic to support wild trout. Only a very few native brook trout are found near the headwaters. Penn State University researchers and Trout Unlimited members are experimenting with liming devices that neutralize some of the acid. Although they have had some good results, it is too early to tell whether such methods can improve Stony Creek to the point that it will support trout year around.

The Fish Commission stocks the lower 6.8 miles of Stony Creek, from the Game Land gate downstream to the mouth, preseason and three times inseason, with the last stocking coming in late May or early June. The upper part of the creek, from the Game Land gate upstream 12 miles to the upper boundary of the Cold Spring Military Reservation, is stocked inseason only. Trout are not stocked preseason in this upper stretch because early in the year the water is often too acidic to ensure the survival of the stocked trout.

Other Southeast PA Streams
(no maps)

No maps were included for the following streams and the descriptions were kept brief, but these streams are also well worth fishing.

Manada Creek - Dauphin County
A delayed-harvest, artificial-lures-only area was added to Manada Creek, starting with the 1990 trout season. This should produce consistent fishing not far from Harrisburg, Hershey, and Lebanon. Manada Creek is stocked with trout and it also has a limited population of stream-bred brown trout. Manada Creek is crossed by Route 443 about 3 miles west of the Penn National Race Course, which is near Grantville. The delayed-harvest, artificial-lures-only

area extends from Fogarty Road downstream 1.8 miles to Furnace Road (T616).

Middle Branch White Clay Creek - Chester County

Middle Branch White Clay Creek holds few or no wild trout, but a delayed-harvest, artificial-lures-only area offers consistent fishing for hatchery trout through mid-June. The stream is located in southern Chester County, near the intersection of the Pennsylvania, Maryland, and Delaware borders. The nearest town is Kemblesville. The special regulations area extends from SR 3009 (Good Hope Road) downstream 1.7 miles to the confluence with East Branch White Clay Creek. The East Branch and the main stem of White Clay Creek are also stocked with trout.

Donegal Creek - Lancaster County

Donegal Creek originates from cool limestone springs and has the potential to be a very good trout stream, but because siltation limits natural reproduction, the fishing on this farm-country stream is for stocked trout. A delayed-harvest, fly-fishing-only area begins about 200 yards below the Route 772 bridge and extends downstream 1.9 miles to near the second tributary below SR 2010. Route 772 (Mount Joy Pike) crosses the stream between Mount Joy and Marietta.

Wissahickon Creek - Philadelphia County

Wissahickon Creek flows about 4 miles through beautiful, wooded Fairmont Park near the Roxborough, Mount Airy, Andorra, and Chestnut Hill neighborhoods of Philadelphia. Several roads cross the stream, but no roads parallel it, so vehicle access is limited. A broad path that parallels the stream is popular with hikers and bicyclists.

You won't find any wild trout in Wissahickon Creek, but it's a fine place for early season angling. Trout are stocked heavily here, and although opening day finds the banks crowded with anglers, fishing pressure is just as intense on opening day on many rural streams. Wissahickon Creek gets quite warm in the summer months, but trout can sometimes be found at the mouths of feeder streams as late as July.

Bear Creek - Schuylkill County

Bear Creek is a tributary to the Schuylkill River, which it meets near the town of Auburn. A delayed-harvest, artificial-lures-only area extends from 800 yards above the T662 bridge downstream 1.9 miles to the T676 bridge. Route 895 parallels most of the length of the stream. Bear Creek is a small to medium-sized stream, about 20 to 30 feet across, which is bordered on its banks by trees, brush, and scattered houses. The fishing is mostly for hatchery trout, but there are some wild brook and brown trout in the unstocked headwaters above Summit Station.

West Valley Creek - Chester County

One of Pennsylvania's newest special regulations areas is located on West Valley Creek, a small limestone stream. The 1.2-mile delayed-harvest, artificial-lures-only section begins at Colebrook Run, upstream from SR 2020 (Boot Road), and extends downstream to a point 400 yards below a railroad tunnel. This section is located about 1 mile east of Downingtown. West Valley Creek flows through a rapidly growing suburban area, but members of local conservation organizations are making valiant efforts to preserve and upgrade the stream.

Southcentral Pennsylvania

Big Spring Creek, Cumberland County.

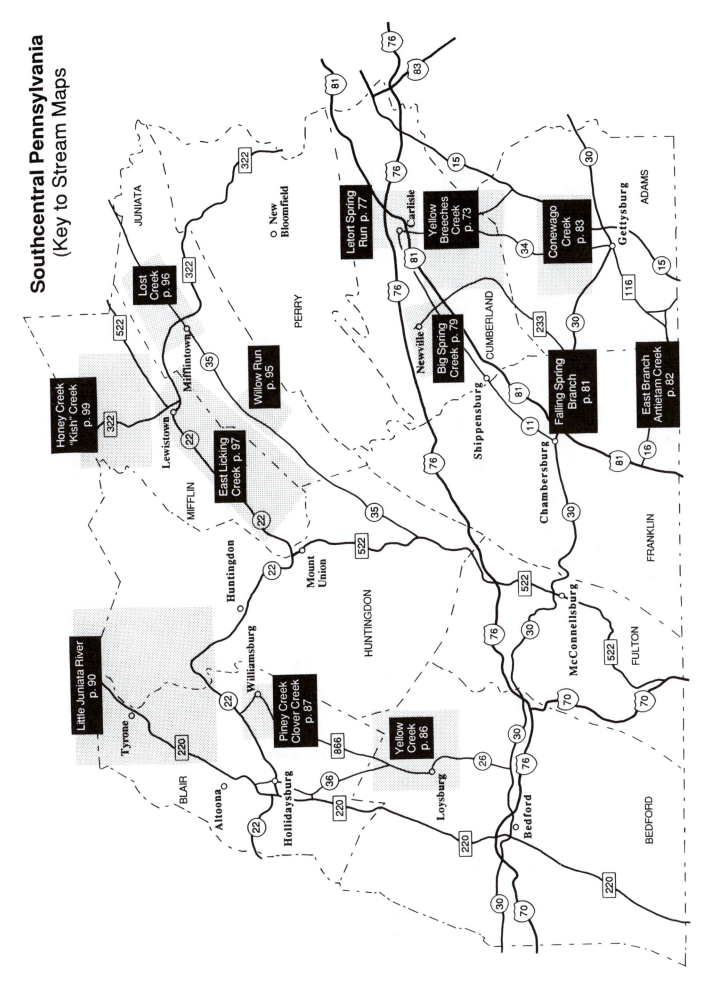

Southcentral Pennsylvania
(Key to Stream Maps)

Southcentral Pennsylvania

Yellow Breeches Creek - Cumberland County

(catch and release, artificials only, 1 mile)
(map: page 73)

The Yellow Breeches is often mentioned with the other well-known southcentral limestone streams such as the Letort, Big Spring, and Falling Spring, but it is really quite different than those streams. It is a much larger stream, approximately 60 feet wide in its middle stretch, and wider where it's backed up by numerous old mill dams. The Breeches is also a much longer stream; trout are stocked over a distance of about 30 miles, from the Route 233 bridge downstream to the mouth on the Susquehanna River. And while the Letort, Big Spring, and Falling Spring are almost entirely spring fed, the Yellow Breeches is fed by both limestone springs and by freestone tributaries such as Mountain Creek. Consequently, its flow varies more with rainfall than these other limestone creeks, and it becomes high and muddy after heavy rainfall. During the summer months, much of the Breeches becomes too warm to offer good fishing, while strong spring flows keep water temperatures cool on the Letort, Big Spring, and Falling Spring.

Farms, residential areas, and patches of woods border the Yellow Breeches. Nearly all of this land is private property, and there is some posting, but not very much. At its upper stocking point, the Route 233 bridge, the Breeches is a small, shallow stream about 12 feet wide. Large springs at the Huntsdale fish hatchery greatly increase the flow. You can park near the hatchery or at road crossings farther downstream.

Although most of Yellow Breeches Creek does not have the weedbeds that are typical of spring creeks, there are several stretches downstream from the Huntsdale hatchery that do have extensive weedbeds. From Huntsdale down to about Route 34, the stream maintains cooler water temperatures than in the lower part of the stream in the summer months. Stream surveys turned up fair numbers of trout here even in late summer, including juveniles. Some of these juvenile trout come from natural reproduction and some escape from the hatchery.

Catch-and-Release Area

A mile-long stretch of stream, from the outlet of Boiling Springs Lake downstream to the Allenberry Playhouse, is managed as a catch-and-release area. Only the use of flies or artificial lures is permitted. Fishing is open here year around and this is where most people fish in the middle to late season. Fishing remains good here in the summer and fall because the regulations prevent the harvest of fish and because cold spring water from Boiling Springs Lake moderates summer water temperatures.

The spring water flows from the lake down a short channel and then into the Yellow Breeches. This channel is also under catch-and-release regulations. The channel provides good spawning habitat, and the catch-and-release section holds a mix of stocked and wild trout. In the warmest part of the summer, trout concentrate along the north bank of the Breeches to take advantage of the cool water flowing down from the lake. The parking lot beside the outlet channel provides good access to Boiling Springs

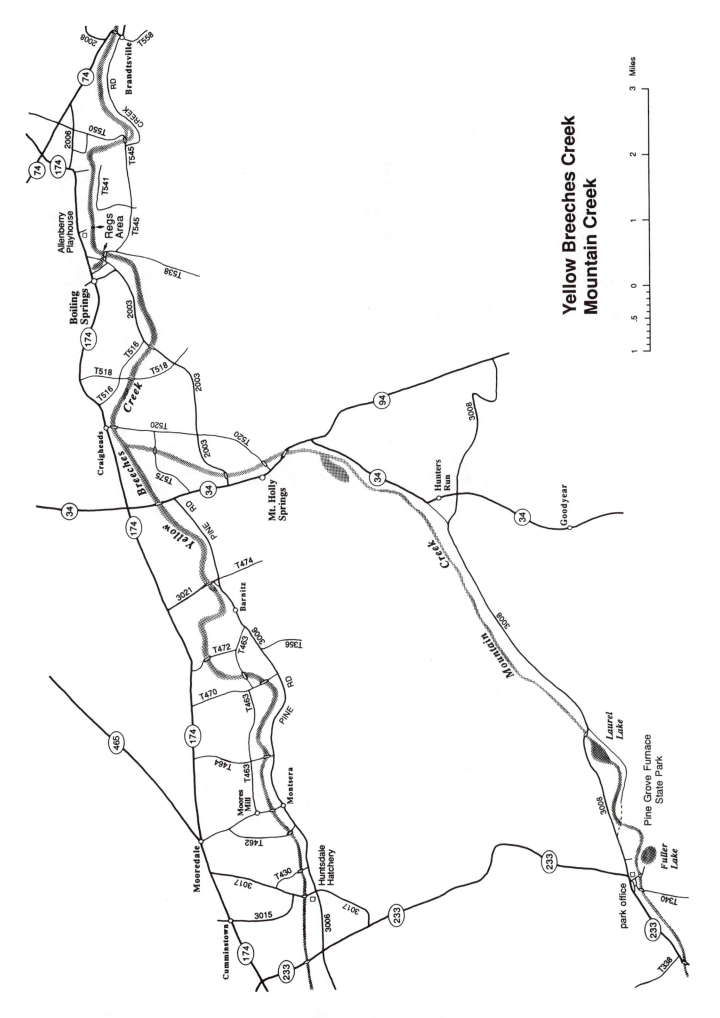

Yellow Breeches Creek
Mountain Creek

Yellow Breeches Creek at the old mill dam at Allenberry Playhouse.

Lake and to the upper part of the catch-and-release area. Boiling Springs Lake is also stocked with trout, and it has some fly hatches early in the season. The Yellow Breeches Fly Shop is located right beside the lake, along Route 174.

The lower end of the catch-and-release area can be reached by driving just east of Boiling Springs on Route 174 and turning right into the entrance of the Allenberry Playhouse and Resort. Park your car at the first parking lot on your left and walk down the road past the tennis courts to the stream. This access is generously provided by the owners of the Allenberry, and over the years this stretch has become something of a mecca among fly fishers. Here an old mill dam backs up a very long, flat pool that provides challenging dry fly fishing. Below the dam are some riffles and runs that are favored by nymph fishers. The catch-and-release stretch ends a short distance below the milldam.

The catch-and-release stretch is often rather crowded, and if you'd like more elbow room, you might try fishing some of the attractive stretches from Boiling Springs downstream to Brandtsville and on down to Williams Grove. Creek Road parallels the stream near Brandtsville, providing good access to this wooded stretch. Trout are also stocked from Williams Grove to the mouth, but this lower water warms very quickly as the season progresses.

The Fish Commission stocks trout prior to opening day and three times inseason, with the last stocking coming in mid-May. The Yellow Breeches Anglers Club, a local sportsmen's group, stocks trout from their cooperative hatchery throughout the year, and some of these are big trout over 18 inches long. Most trout you catch in the Yellow Breeches are stocked trout. There is some reproduction of trout in the upper stretches and near Boiling Springs, but most of the stream lacks good spawning habitat.

Fishing pressure on the Yellow Breeches is heavy in the early season. The catch-and-release area at Boiling Springs can be fished year around, and it is often crowded with anglers on the weekends preceding opening day. In the first several weeks of the season, the Breeches is very popular with fly fishers, lure fishers, and bait fishers alike. On one opening day early in my fishing adventures, I dead-drifted my

Hare's Ear Nymphs just like my fly fishing books said I should, but discovered that my fishing buddies were having much better luck drifting their Velveeta cheese "nymphs."

Fly Fishing

Fly fishing starts early on the Breeches if the weather permits. When there is a lot of rain early in the year, the stream runs high and muddy, but if water levels are moderate, visitors to the catch-and-release area can enjoy dry fly fishing to Blue-winged Olive hatches as early as mid-March. Other mayfly hatches on the Breeches include March Browns, Sulphurs, Tricos, and White Mayflies.

The White Mayflies have become a famous hatch on Yellow Breeches Creek. They usually emerge from mid to late August and appear at dusk in tremendous numbers. Most people fish this hatch in the catch-and-release area because there are more trout here late in the season than in other parts of the stream. The incredible numbers of flies on the water and the short time to fish before darkness falls make this hatch a frantic and sometimes frustrating affair, but many people enjoy fishing it because of the spectacular flurry of flies.

Besides the mayfly hatches, there are also many caddis and midge hatches on the Breeches. After the early season hatches taper off, terrestrial imitations such as ants and beetles often provide the most consistent dry fly fishing. Sculpin imitations, marabou streamers, and Wooly Buggers can be effective when water levels are high.

Mountain Creek - Cumberland County
(map: page 73)

Mountain Creek originates in northern Adams County and flows northeast through Cumberland County to meet Yellow Breeches Creek about 3 miles east of Boiling Springs. Because of its infertile freestone water chemistry, Mountain Creek is suffering the effects of acid rain. It does hold wild brown and brook trout in Pine Grove State Park, though, and wild brook trout can also be found far upstream into the headwaters.

The Fish Commission stocks Mountain Creek from the border of Adams and Cumberland Counties the whole way downstream to the mouth, a distance of about 16 miles. Trout are usually stocked for opening day and twice inseason, with the last stocking coming around the third week in May. In some years, though, Mountain Creek is too acidic early in the year to allow stocking prior to opening day. In these years, trout are still stocked twice inseason.

A good place to fish is at Pine Grove Furnace State Park. This is a scenic, forested area, the access is good, and the stream in this area holds both wild

and stocked trout. Also, camping is available here. Take Route 233 south from I-81 until you come to a T intersection at the State Park. Turn left on SR 3008 (Hunters Run Road) and park at the Fuller Lake parking area. Good fishing is found from here downstream 2 miles to Laurel Lake. Both Fuller Lake and Laurel Lake are also stocked with trout. Laurel Lake warms Mountain Creek, and below the lake the stream holds few trout by midseason.

To reach the upper stretches of Mountain Creek, travel south on Route 233. About 1.5 miles past the park office, Route 233 crosses the creek. About 1 mile farther south on Route 233, Woodrow Road turns to the right and crosses the creek.

Letort Spring Run - Cumberland County
(limestone springs wild trout waters, 1.5 miles)
(map: page 77)

The Letort is well known to many people from the writings of Vince Marinaro, Charlie Fox, Ed Koch, Ed Shenk, and other skilled anglers who have developed many new fly fishing techniques and fly patterns attempting to fool the creek's wary brown trout. The clear, smooth-flowing waters produced, and still produce, large wild brown trout difficult to catch with "standard" Catskill-style flies.

Patterns imitating terrestrial insects such as ants, beetles, crickets, grasshoppers, and jassids (leafhoppers) were first commonly used on the Letort and neighboring limestone spring creeks. Previously, some terrestrial patterns existed, but they were seldom used and were considered to be of minor importance compared to the aquatic insects. Innovative fly fishers of the Cumberland Valley improved upon the old terrestrial patterns and developed new ones, then demonstrated the effectiveness of these flies on the Letort and neighboring streams. Now patterns such as the Letort Hopper and Letort Cricket are used on trout streams everywhere. The ant and beetle patterns developed here have also become very popular.

Other techniques popularized on the Letort and neighboring streams include the use of marabou in streamers, the use of very long, fine leaders, and the use of tiny midge imitations. The Letort and similar streams swarm with freshwater crustaceans known as sowbugs and scuds (commonly called cress bugs), and patterns were developed for their imitation also. Marinaro's thorax-style duns, with their well-defined wing silhouettes, inspired the more recent no-hackle duns and compara-duns. Many accomplished anglers believe that the thorax-style is still the best way to tie imitations of mayfly duns for fishing over selective wild brown trout.

So much fly fishing history has taken place here, and so much fame and mystique have accumulated about the stream, that the first-time visitor may be somewhat disillusioned when he sees the Letort. Highways and residential developments have erased some (certainly not all) of the rural beauty of the area that was captured so well in Vince Marinaro's photographs. Also, the stretch of the Letort where most of this history took place, from above Bonny Brook downstream to Letort Spring Park, is only about 1.5 miles long. But as Marinaro wrote in *The Modern Dry Fly Code*: "Here many noble battles were won or lost."

The Letort originates from limestone springs in commercial watercress bogs and flows north past the Bonny Brook quarry, then through the famous meadow stretch. After passing under the Interstate 81 bridge, the stream flows through Letort Spring Park, then through Carlisle and the Carlisle Barracks. After flowing out of the Carlisle Barracks, the Letort flows past meadows, homes, and patches of trees on its way to Conodoguinet Creek.

Upper Letort

To reach the upper, classic stretch of the Letort, take Route 34 south from Carlisle. After driving under the I-81 overpass, drive on another 0.6 miles, then turn left just past a tire store onto T481 (Bonny Brook Road). This road soon leads to a bridge over the Letort. A special regulations area begins 300 yards above the Bonny Brook Road bridge and extends downstream 1.5 miles to an old railroad bridge in Letort Park. No trout may be killed in this area, and only fly fishing with barbless hooks is permitted.

The quiet, clear waters of the Letort.

Above the Bonny Brook Road bridge, the Letort is a small, narrow meadow stream with good numbers of very skittish trout. Below the bridge, the stream gathers more volume from a smaller branch, then flows past a quarry in a gravelly, riffled section that provides good spawning habitat.

Below the quarry, an old railroad grade follows the stream through the famous meadow stretch, where many large trout have been caught. Much of this meadow stretch has grown up in heavy brush and weeds in recent years, making casting and even walking along the stream banks difficult in places.

The upper Letort is not stocked with trout, and it has been known for many years for its excellent wild brown trout population. In 1981 many of the fish in this stretch were killed by a pesticide used on the watercress beds. To maintain the original wild strain of brown trout, the Fish Commission did not stock the stream, but instead allowed the surviving browns to reproduce and repopulate the stream. This has been successful, and the trout are now back in their former abundance. After the fish kill, someone stocked some rainbow trout in the Letort, and there is now a small, reproducing population of rainbow trout, most of

Letort Spring Run

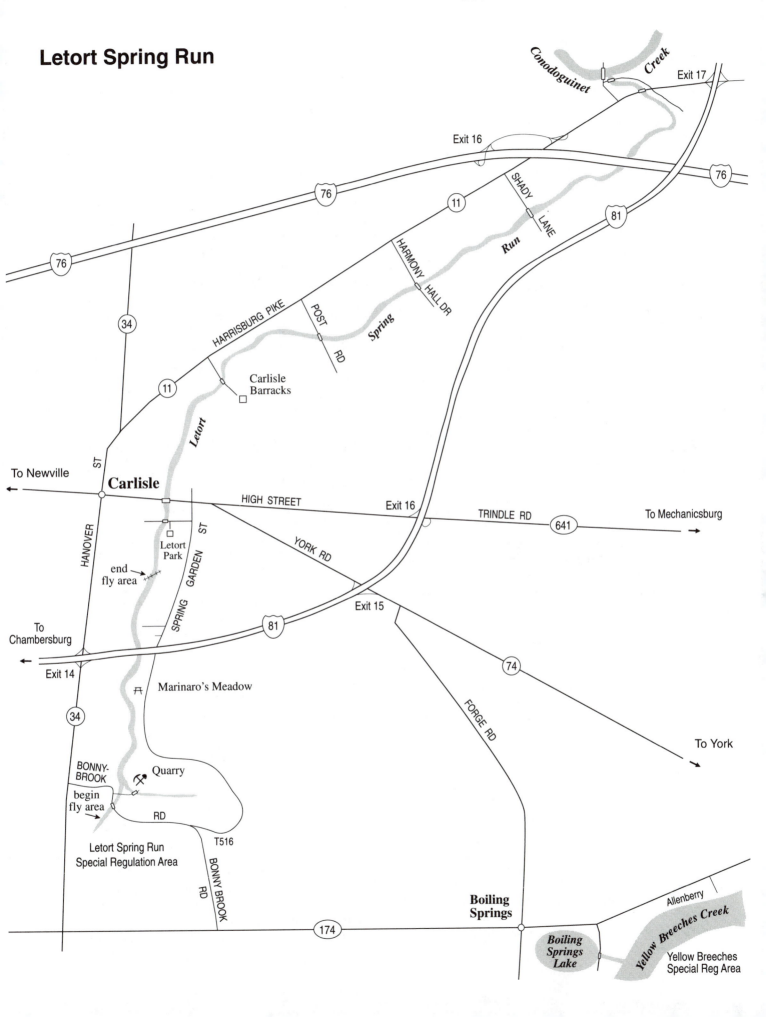

Conodoguinet Creek

Exit 17

Exit 16

76

11

SHADY LANE

Run

81

76

34

HARRISBURG PIKE

POST RD

Spring

HARMONY HALL DR

11

Letort

Carlisle Barracks

To Newville

ST

Carlisle

HIGH STREET

Exit 16

TRINDLE RD

To Mechanicsburg

641

HANOVER

Letort Park

YORK RD

end fly area

SPRING GARDEN ST

81

Exit 15

74

To Chambersburg

FORGE RD

Exit 14

Marinaro's Meadow

34

To York

BONNY-BROOK

Quarry

begin fly area

RD

T516

Letort Spring Run Special Regulation Area

BONNY BROOK RD

Boiling Springs

Allenberry

174

Boiling Springs Lake

Yellow Breeches Creek

Yellow Breeches Special Reg Area

which are found in the upper area near the Bonny Brook limestone quarry.

After the Letort flows under I-81 and past the lower boundary of the special regulations area, it flows into Letort Spring Park on the edge of Carlisle. In the park the stream still holds fair numbers of trout, but below the park it flow into the city of Carlisle and is of little interest until it emerges from the Carlisle Barracks at Post Road.

On East High Street in Carlisle, several blocks from Letort Park, you'll find fly tackle and stream information at the Cold Spring Anglers fly shop.

Lower Letort

The lower Letort, from Carlisle to the mouth, was badly polluted by sewage for many years. In 1981, Carlisle opened a new sewage treatment plant, and since then the lower Letort has been improving dramatically. The wild brown trout population has been increasing, and the Fish Commission has been stocking fingerlings. Trout are now well established in the lower Letort.

To reach the lower Letort, take Route 11 east from Carlisle, and turn right on Post Road, Harmony Hill Road, or Shady Lane. These roads all cross the Letort, but parking is limited. The stream flows past meadows and patches of woods here, and you'll find some deep holes at undercut banks and tree roots.

The lowest stretch of the Letort, from Route 76 to the mouth, is seldom fished, but this short section holds trout also. To reach this area, drive east on Route 11, pass under the Route 76 bridge, and you will soon cross a bridge over the Letort. Immediately after the bridge, turn left onto Mill Road, which follows the stream down towards its mouth on Conodoguinet Creek. Trout are sometimes caught even in the Conodoguinet, a warmwater stream, just below the influx of the Letort.

Although the Letort is one of best known streams in Pennsylvania, it is rarely crowded, and on some days you can have the stream virtually to yourself. Because the fishing is difficult, many people stop and fish a bit, more to see the stream than to really try for its wary trout, then travel on to fish for the easier trout of Yellow Breeches Creek.

Fly Hatches

The Letort usually does not have heavy fly hatches. Blue-winged Olives and Sulphurs provide some dry fly activity, and Tricos are an important summer hatch, particularly in the lower Letort downstream of Carlisle. Most dry fly fishing is done with terrestrial imitations. Cress bug imitations can be successful all year around. Some hardy anglers catch trout on cress bug imitations even during the winter months. Pennsylvania often has warm spells in midwinter when air temperatures rise into the 40's or 50's and these are good times to fish the Letort and other limestone spring creeks. Trout fishing in really wintery weather, when the air temperatures are well below freezing, is not much fun, though, because ice forms in the guides of your fishing rod.

When heavy rains cloud the Letort, streamers such as Black or Yellow Marabous, Wooly Buggers, Zonkers, and sculpin imitations work well. Anglers skilled at tying and fishing sculpin imitations catch many of the largest browns.

Most of the Letort is smooth flowing with few riffles. Because of this, the trout are easily spooked. Long leaders, light lines, and a careful approach are necessary. Some fly fishers prefer to stand a great distance back from the fish and make long casts; others prefer to sneak up close to the fish, staying low and using the cover of brush and other obstacles to hide their approach. The upper Letort has lush weedbeds that produce complicated currents. Getting a drag-free drift is a real challenge.

If your fishing on the Letort turns out to be frustrating, keep in mind that you're in good company. Many Letort regulars, who are some of the most skillful anglers to be found anywhere, consider a catch of one or two trout a successful outing on the Letort.

Big Spring Creek - Cumberland County
(limestone springs, wild trout waters, 1.1 miles)
(map: page 79)

Big Spring Creek does not hold as many wild trout as its neighboring limestone spring creeks, such as the Letort and Falling Spring Creek, or as many as some of the northern limestone streams, such as Fishing Creek and Spring Creek.

Big Spring Creek originates from large limestone springs and has a consistent flow of cool, fertile water, just as the other limestone streams do. In earlier years it was considered a very good trout stream; its reputation ranked right up with that of the Letort. In 1945, Don Martin caught a 15 1/2 pound brown trout from Big Spring, a state record at that time. Some anglers blame Big Spring's decline on the construction of a large fish hatchery at the headwaters. The hatchery has probably affected the stream's water quality, but there may also be other factors at work. In some stretches aquatic weedbeds have died back, and this may have been caused by the runoff of agricultural pesticides.

Another reason Big Spring holds less trout than some of the other limestone streams may be that only the first 1.1 miles of the stream are under special regulations. The rest of the stream is stocked with hatchery trout and has a bag limit of eight trout.

Even though Big Spring may have seen better days, it still offers some interesting and challenging fishing, and it still produces some large trout. A short stretch of the stream below the hatchery outflow is

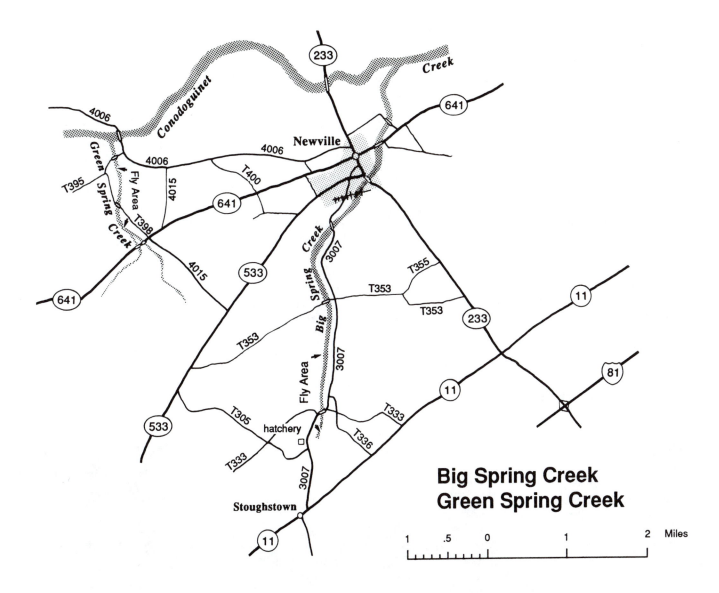

**Big Spring Creek
Green Spring Creek**

1 .5 0 1 2 Miles

managed as a wild brook trout area. In contrast with the rest of the stream, this brook trout stretch, which is often called "The Ditch," holds an incredible number of fish. The numerous cress bugs that feed on detritus carried down from the hatchery provide abundant feed for these trout. Most of the trout in "The Ditch" are brook trout, but there are also some large browns and rainbows.

Brook trout grow unusually fast here. In the small, infertile mountain streams that are their usual home, brook trout reach a length of about 6.5 inches by their third year. In Big Spring brook trout reach a length of 13 inches in the same period of time. A few of the brookies have reached lengths up to 18 inches.

Anglers accustomed to the often gullible brook trout of the mountain streams may be surprised to find how selective these Big Spring brookies are. The water here is crawling with cress bugs, and fishing their imitations is the most consistently effective technique. Terrestrial imitations and tiny midge patterns

also work well. Another fly used here is just a hook wrapped with red floss or thread, which imitates worm-like midge larvae that wash down from the hatchery.

From the source of Big Spring downstream 1.1 miles to Strohm Dam, the stream is managed under limestone-springs, wild-trout-waters regulations. Only fly fishing is permitted, and two fish per day over 15 inches may be killed. The upper part of this fly area, which is "The Ditch" described above, has aquatic weedbeds and undercut banks that provide good cover for the trout. The lower part of the fly area is wide and shallow and the weedbeds have died back. Very few trout are found in this barren stretch.

To find better fishing, follow the road downstream along the creek until you find weedbeds again. From the T353 bridge downstream to Newville, the weedbeds are in better condition. These weedbeds provide cover and shade for the trout and also cover for the insects and cress bugs which the trout eat.

Below the fly area, Big Spring is stocked with hatchery trout, and it also holds some wild and hold-over trout. These wild and holdover trout, while not numerous, sometimes grow very large. The clear, smooth water and the tricky currents among the weedbeds create challenging fishing here. Several Fish Commission parking lots along SR 3007 provide easy access to the stream.

Just upstream from Newville, the road and the creek pass under a railroad grade. Below the railroad grade, there is a large pool that has a reputation among local anglers for giving up trophy trout. The creek then flows past the houses of Newville and continues on towards its mouth on Conodoguinet Creek.

Just above the Route 641 bridge, there is a scenic old mill dam. This is a good place for taking pictures, but not such a good place for fishing. Parking spaces are limited and finding access is difficult in the lower stretches of Big Spring Creek, from Newville downstream to the mouth.

Big Spring seldom has heavy mayfly hatches, but some Blue-winged Olives, Sulphurs, and Tricos do appear. Terrestrials, cress bugs, and midges are the most popular fly patterns.

Green Spring Creek - Cumberland County
(fly fishing only, 1 mile)
(map: page 79)

This tiny limestone spring creek flows through scenic meadows and farmland east of Newville. If you are in the Newville area to fish Big Spring Creek, this stream makes a nice side trip. From Newville, take Route 641 west about 2.7 miles, then turn right on Bulls Head Road (T-398). In about a half-mile, you will come to a bridge over Green Spring Creek. This is a good place to park and fish up or downstream. The mile-long fly-fishing-only stretch is located here.

In the meadow above the bridge, the stream moves slowly through weedbeds, and the old willow trees along the banks make this a picturesque spot. Downstream from the bridge, Green Spring Creek flows through gentle riffles and small pools at under-cut banks, as it winds through more meadows on its way to Conodoguinet Creek. If you follow T398 downstream along the creek, you will come to another bridge, which provides a good access point for fishing the lower stretches.

Green Spring Creek, a small, scenic limestone stream.

Green Spring Creek has the cool, nutrient-rich water of other spring creeks, but its heavily silted streambed lacks good gravel spawning areas, so natural reproduction is limited. Trout are stocked for opening day and once inseason, usually between mid-April and early May. Fishing pressure is light, and fishing can be good here even in late summer.

Fly fishers can expect hatches of typical limestone creek mayflies, such as Blue-winged Olives, Sulphurs, and Tricos. Terrestrials and cress bug imitations work well when the flies aren't hatching. Ants, beetles, and crickets are good summer patterns.

Falling Spring Branch - Franklin County

(limestone springs wild trout waters, 2.4 miles)
(map: page 81)

Falling Spring Branch is a small limestone spring creek and one of the very few streams in Pennsylvania with a good population of wild rainbow trout. It also holds a good brown trout population, and both species grow large in this fertile stream. Trout up to 14 inches are common, and 18- to 20-inch fish are

caught occasionally. Falling Spring flows through meadows and farmland interspersed with increasing suburban development.

Publicity about Falling Spring's Trico hatch attracts many anglers to the stream. Most first-time visitors will probably be surprised to see how small this little meadow stream is. If they spend some time along its banks, though, they may also be surprised at the number and size of brown and rainbow trout this little stream holds.

To reach Falling Spring Branch, take the Chambersburg exit off I-81, go east on Route 30 several hundred yards and take the first right turn, onto SR 2029 (Falling Spring Road). This road parallels the stream up to its source. No trout are stocked above the I-81 bridge. Most of this water is protected by no-harvest, fly-fishing-only regulations. Barbless hooks are required.

Driving up from Route 30, the first good access is at the bridge on Quarry Road. Below the bridge the stream flows through a somewhat eroded meadow, but stream improvement devices built by the Falling Spring Chapter of Trout Unlimited have created some good holding water.

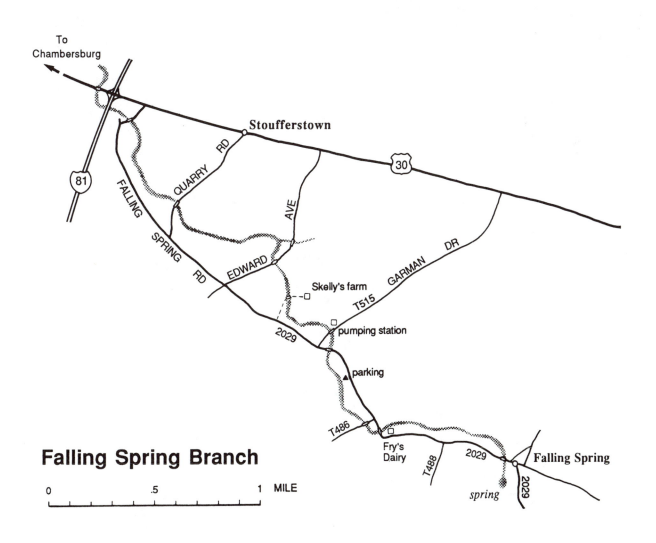

Falling Spring Branch

0   .5   1 MILE

Directly above Quarry Road, there is a large pool, where I once saw a rainbow trout about 16 or 17 inches long rising steadily. After about an hour of trying for this fish, I became convinced that wild rainbow trout can be every bit as wary and selective as wild browns. Except for this one pool, the stretch from Quarry Road up to the next bridge, on Edward Avenue, is scarcely worth fishing because the stream flows here through a severely eroded meadow, where the water is too shallow and silted to hold many fish. Parking is very limited on Edward Avenue.

From Edward Avenue upstream to Fry's Dairy is perhaps the best stretch of Falling Spring Creek. Some anglers walk down the lane at Skelly's farm to reach the stream. Other anglers park near the pumping station along Garman Drive. A little farther upstream is a small parking area along SR 2029, which is marked with a Trout Unlimited sign. There are also a few places to pull off onto the shoulder along SR 2029, but generally parking is pretty tight. In recent years, several housing developments have been built along the upper stretch of the stream.

Falling Spring has hatches typical of meadow limestone streams, including Blue-winged Olives, Sulphurs, and Tricos. The Tricos hatch daily from about July 1 into early November, and they attract fly fishers from far and wide. Falling Spring is famous for its Trico hatch, but be aware that this is difficult fishing. Falling Spring's trout have seen a lot of Trico imitations, and most of them have probably been hooked by a few. Terrestrial imitations such as ants and beetles are effective when no flies are hatching, and cress bug imitations are always worth a try.

East Branch Antietam Creek - Franklin County

(fly fishing only, 1 mile)
(map: page 82)

East Branch Antietam Creek is best known for its mile-long fly fishing area, located just east of Waynesboro. This stretch begins at Route 16 and extends downstream to the bridge on Welty Road. Parking is available at a small park adjacent to the Renfrew

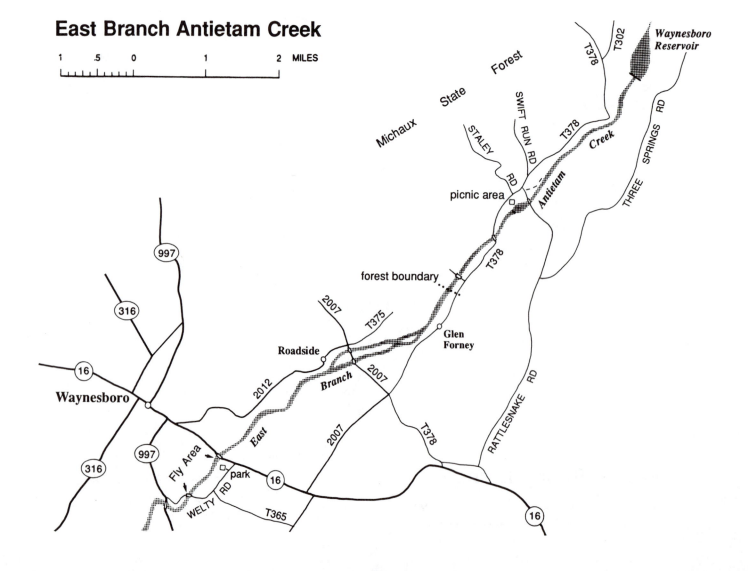

East Branch Antietam Creek

Museum. The parking area is located off Welty Road, just south of Route 16. You can also park at the lower end of the fly stretch, near the Welty Road bridge.

The upper half of the fly area is well shaded by trees, and the lower half flows through grassy cow pastures. Because of siltation, the fly area does not have a naturally reproducing trout population, but the special regulations prevent the stocked fish from being quickly removed. Water quality is good enough to allow trout to hold over from year to year, and summer stream surveys turned up a fair number of brown trout from 13 to 17 inches long and even one of 20 inches. Water temperatures get quite warm in the fly area in the summer months. The fly stretch is the lowest section of East Branch Antietam Creek that is stocked with trout.

The middle section of the creek, from the fly area upstream to near Roadside, is stocked with trout also, but some of this section is posted, and the stream suffers here from erosion and siltation. This stretch holds few trout into mid-season.

In the upper section of East Branch Antietam Creek, from Roadside upstream to the spillway of Waynesboro Dam, there is better trout habitat. Much of this stretch is in Michaux State Forest. This upper water is stocked along with the rest of the creek, and it also holds a good native brook trout population. Tall trees keep water temperatures cool here, making this a good bet for summer fishing.

To reach this upper stretch from the fly area, turn right onto Route 16 from Welty Road, travel east 1.1 miles, and turn left on SR 2007 (Old Forge Road). You will enter Michaux State Forest after driving about another 3.5 miles.

Conewago Creek - Adams County
(fly fishing only, 1.1 mile)
(map: page 83)

The fly-fishing-only area on Conewago Creek is a popular stretch for many visiting anglers. It extends from the bridge on Route 34 upstream 1.1 mile to

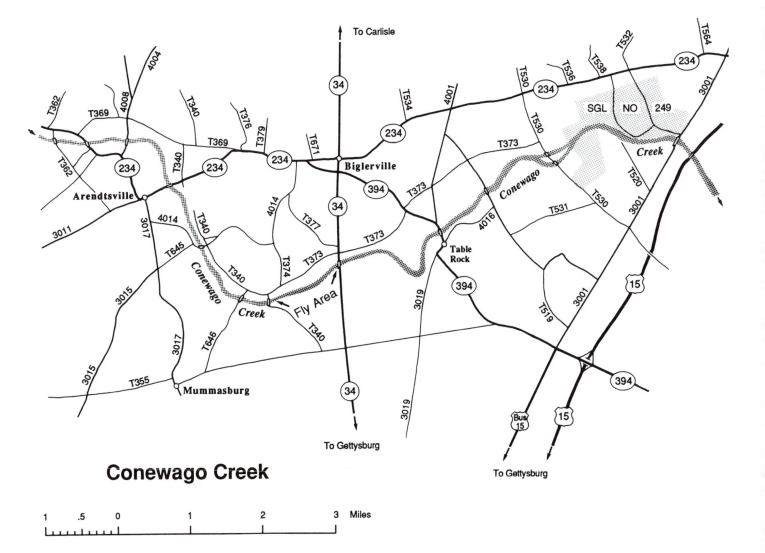

Conewago Creek

near the T340 bridge. Parking is difficult but not impossible along the narrow shoulder of Route 34. In the fly area Conewago Creek is of medium size, about 30 feet wide, and it meanders slowly through wooded bottomlands. Few wild trout are found here, but the regulations ensure good fishing for stocked trout through about mid-June, or even later in cool years. In July and August, water temperatures rise and the fishing slows. The Adams County and the Northern Virginia chapters of Trout Unlimited have been making efforts to improve stream habitat in the fly area.

Another popular fishing stretch is in State Game Land No. 249. The stream is larger here and mostly slow moving. A short distance downstream from State Game Land No. 249, the Route 15 bridge marks the lower end of the stocked water. The Fish Commission stocks Conewago Creek for opening day and also twice inseason, with the last stocking coming in early or mid-May.

The best trout habitat on Conewago Creek is in the "Narrows" stretch upstream of Arendtsville. Here the stream flows swiftly over a rocky streambed and holds good numbers of wild brown trout. Unfortunately, the stream is posted here. Rumor has it that the landowner sometimes allows politely requesting anglers to fish.

Yellow Creek - Bedford County
(delayed harvest, fly fishing only, 0.9 mile)
(map: page 86)

From its origins near Woodbury downstream to Loysburg, Yellow Creek is a limestone spring creek flowing through meadows in a wide farming valley. Wild browns are found in much of this stretch, but some of the land is posted. It is best to ask permission here before fishing. This upper stretch of Yellow Creek would probably support a very good wild trout population if erosion and siltation were controlled. Cattle grazing in meadows along the stream has broken down the banks in many places.

Currently the Fish Commission stocks 10 miles of Yellow Creek, from the mouth of Beaver Creek at Loysburg downstream to the mouth at Hopewell. Trout are stocked prior to opening day and also once inseason, in early to mid-May. The stocked portion of Yellow Creek is a medium-sized stream, about 35 feet wide at Loysburg and nearly twice that wide at the mouth, with deep holes in places. Fishing pressure is heavy early in the year.

Just below Loysburg, Yellow Creek flows through the Loysburg Gap in Tussey Mountain. Here the stream rushes over large boulders and through deep holes. This section has a reputation for producing big brown trout.

A delayed-harvest, fly-fishing-only area extends from the mouth of Maple Run (usually called Jacks Run locally) upstream 0.9 mile to Red Bank Hill. The upper end of the fly area can be reached by fishing down from the Route 36 bridge.

To reach the lower end of the fly area, turn off Route 36 onto SR 1024 at the New Frontier Restaurant, and follow this road to a bridge over Yellow Creek. Parking is limited here, but there are a few parking spots near the bridge, and if you wade upstream, you will soon be in the fly area. The fly area holds many trout year around.

Mayfly hatches on Yellow Creek include Blue-winged Olives, Blue Quills, Sulphurs, Light Cahills, Isonychia, Tricos, and White Mayflies. During the summer months, terrestrial patterns such as ants and beetles are effective. Weighted nymphs and sculpin imitations are good choices for fishing the swift water at Loysburg Gap.

From Loysburg Gap downstream to the Route 26 bridge, anglers catch a fair number of wild and hold-over brown trout year around, but from Route 26 to the mouth, the stream gets too warm in the summer to hold many trout, and few people fish in this lower stretch of the creek after mid-June.

Potter Creek - Bedford County
(map: page 86)

Although Potter Creek is the largest of Yellow Creek's tributaries, it is still quite a small stream, only about 15 feet wide. This little limestoner flows through grassy pastures and farm lands before joining Yellow Creek at the village of Waterside. The Fish Commission stocks trout preseason and once inseason, in late April or early May, from the mouth upstream 3.4 miles to the T609 bridge.

Limestone springs flow in along the length of the creek, keeping summer water temperatures cool. There is some reproduction of brown trout in Potter Creek, and browns seeking cooler water also move up from Yellow Creek in the summer months. Some good-sized browns lie beneath this little stream's undercut banks.

Three Springs Run - Bedford County
(map: page 86)

Three Springs Run is a small stream that flows through dairy cow pastures and past rural residences. Trout are stocked from the mouth on Yellow Creek upstream 2 miles to the Route 869 bridge at New Enterprise. Access is a problem on this stream because parking places are limited. Some parts of the stream flow through the landowners' backyards, so it is difficult to fish here without feeling that you are invading someone's privacy.

Three Springs Run is fed by several limestone springs and it could potentially be a good trout stream, but erosion and lack of cover are limiting the trout population.

Yellow Creek in the Narrows below Loysburg.

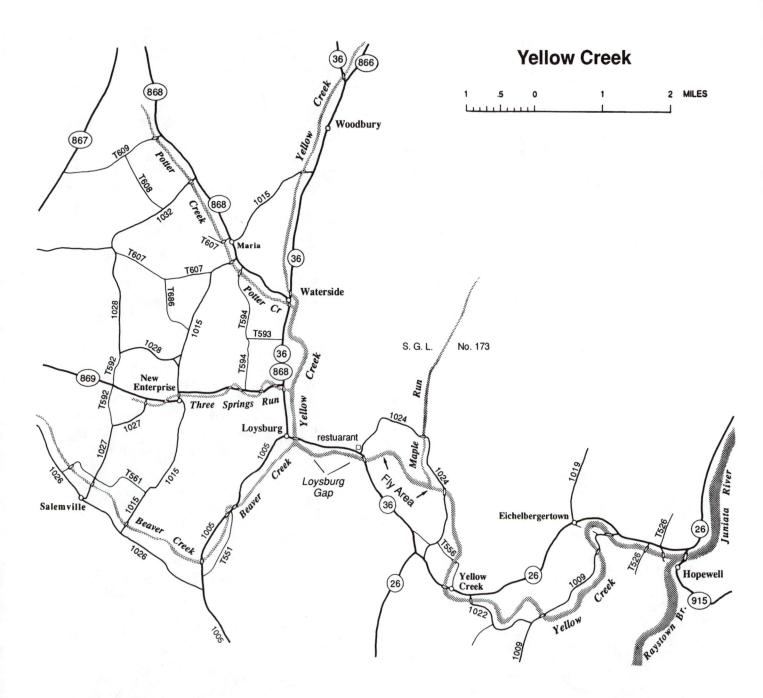

Beaver Creek - Bedford County
(map: page 86)

Beaver Creek is a small, farm-country stream that flows into Yellow Creek at Loysburg. Most of the stream flows through eroded cow pastures. Limestone springs feed Beaver Creek with a consistent flow of cool, fertile water, but because the streambed is silted, shallow, and lacking in cover, there are few wild trout and few hatchery trout remain in the stream through the summer months. The Fish Commission stocks Beaver Creek preseason and once in-season, from the mouth upstream 4.7 miles to the SR 1027 bridge near the village of Salemville.

Maple Run - Bedford County
(map: page 86)

Most of Yellow Creek's tributaries are meadow spring creeks, but Maple Run is a small freestone stream. It tumbles down from the wooded hills of State Game Land No. 173 and joins Yellow Creek at the lower boundary of Yellow Creek's fly area. The Fish Commission stocks the lower 2.3 miles of Maple Run, from its mouth upstream to the Game Land border. This stocked stretch also holds a few wild browns and brook trout. The main access is the bridge on SR 1024. Maple Run is not stocked in Game Land No. 173, but you can find some wild brook trout there.

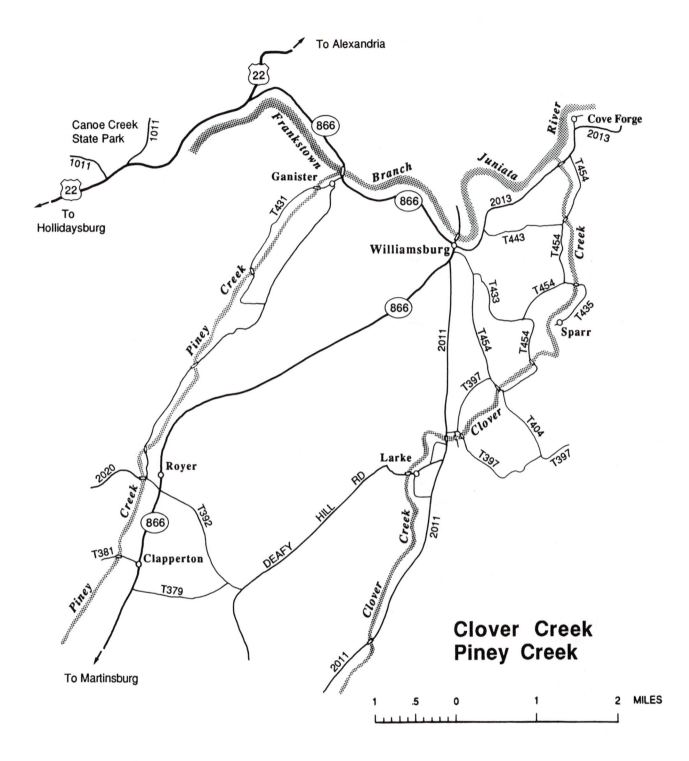

**Clover Creek
Piney Creek**

Clover Creek - Blair County
(map: page 87)

Clover Creek is less well known than many of Pennsylvania's other limestone spring creeks, perhaps because it is farther away from the cities than many of the others. Also, because it is a fairly small stream, it rarely gives up the big trophy trout that are sometimes caught on the larger spring creeks. But Clover

Creek has a very good population of brown trout. One midsummer day I watched, and even helped a little, as a Fish Commission crew surveyed Clover Creek with electro-fishing gear. The number of trout turned up in this smallish stream was surprising. I didn't see any trophy trout, but there were plenty of browns 10 to 14 inches long and a few 15 to 16 inches long.

If you have ever had the idea that fisheries work would be an easy occupation, think again. There is a lot of hard physical work involved in stream surveying. The fisheries technician who wades upstream over rocks and logs and through waist-deep pools towing the heavy, roaring, gasoline-powered generator has a particularly tough job.

Clover Creek flows through a long valley in rural Blair County. Trout stocking begins at the SR 2005 bridge below Henrietta (this upper area is not shown on the map) and continues downstream for about 7 miles to the bridge at Larke. This upper stretch of Clover Creek flows through a heavily farmed area and suffers from siltation. There are not many wild trout here, but occasionally large browns are taken from the deeper holes.

From Larke downstream 6 miles to the mouth, Clover Creek is managed as a wild brown trout stream; no trout are stocked. In this lower stretch, the water quality is improved by springs, there is more shading from stream-side trees, and the water flows more quickly. Much of this stretch is wooded and somewhat brushy, but in most places the stream is open enough to allow reasonably easy fly casting.

Some hatches to be prepared for on Clover Creek are Sulphurs, Blue-winged Olives, and Tricos. The Sulphurs are the best hatch, and they usually appear from around May 10 into early June. Terrestrial imitations are also effective. Clover Creek is rich in fish food and contains large numbers of minnows, scuds, and crayfish.

Big browns are sometimes caught below the mouth of Clover Creek in the Frankstown Branch of the Juniata. The lower 2 miles of Clover Creek are followed by T454 (Clover Creek Road). This stretch is mostly wooded, with a few homes and cottages scattered along the stream. Farther upstream, Clover Creek flows through dairy farms, and open meadows and occasional trees adjoin the creek. There is little or no posting on Clover Creek, but it is a good idea to ask permission before fishing on these farms. The open meadow stretches have good Trico hatches in the summer and fall.

Piney Creek - Blair County
(map: page 87)

Piney Creek is a small limestone spring creek with a good population of wild brown trout. It is similar in many ways to Clover Creek, which flows through the next valley to the south. In 1987 stocking was ended on Piney Creek, and the stream is now managed as wild brown trout water.

From its headwaters north of Martinsburg, Piney Creek flows north to join the Frankstown Branch of the Juniata at Ganister. From its origin downstream to Royer, Piney Creek is small, slow moving, and badly silted in places. Near Royer large springs increase the flow and improve the water quality. The Fish Commission bought land near Royer, planning to build a hatchery at these springs. The hatchery was never built, but this land now provides parking and access to the stream.

From Royer down to the mouth, Piney Creek flows along through riffles and pools, and trees along the banks keep the water well shaded. This 4.5 mile stretch has a good population of brown trout. Because the stream is fairly small, you should not expect trophies, but 14- to 15-inch trout are possible. Tree branches and brush create challenges for fly casters.

To reach Piney Creek from the Altoona/Hollidaysburg area, take Route 22 east approximately 9 miles, then turn right on Route 866. In 1.5 miles you will come to a bridge over the Frankstown Branch of the Juniata. Piney Creek flows in just upstream of this bridge. Because parking is limited on the lower part of Piney Creek, you may wish to park on the left (north) side of Route 866, just before the bridge over the Frankstown Branch. From here you can fish the lower end of Piney Creek and also try a few casts on the Frankstown Branch.

The Frankstown Branch is too warm and silted for trout along much of its length, but big brown trout are sometimes caught near the mouths of Piney Creek and Clover Creek and at other places where cold tributaries and springs enter the stream.

Secondary roads follow Piney Creek upstream from the mouth. There are several places to park along T431, near some old quarries.

Because of the influence of limestone springs, Piney Creek has cool summer temperatures (57-60 degrees in August) and a fertile water chemistry. Blacknose dace, longnose dace and sculpins are common forage-fish. Scuds and crayfish are also important trout foods. Fly hatches on Piney Creek include Blue-winged Olives, Sulphurs, Olive Caddis, Light Cahills, and Tricos. Terrestrials such as ants, crickets, and beetles are effective in the summer.

Careful wading and casting are necessary on Piney Creek because much of the stream is shallow and the wild browns are easily spooked.

Little Juniata River - Blair and Huntingdon Counties
(map: page 90)

The Little Juniata River provides an excellent example of how a waterway can rejuvenate itself with a little help. For years the Little Juniata was badly polluted, but beginning around 1970, changes in the operations of the paper mill at Tyrone and improvements in sewage treatment have greatly reduced the flow of pollutants. Since then conditions in the stream have improved dramatically. Limestone springs feed the river, and their cool, alkaline flows support a rich crop of trout food in the form of insects, minnows, and

The Little Juniata River above the village of Spruce Creek.

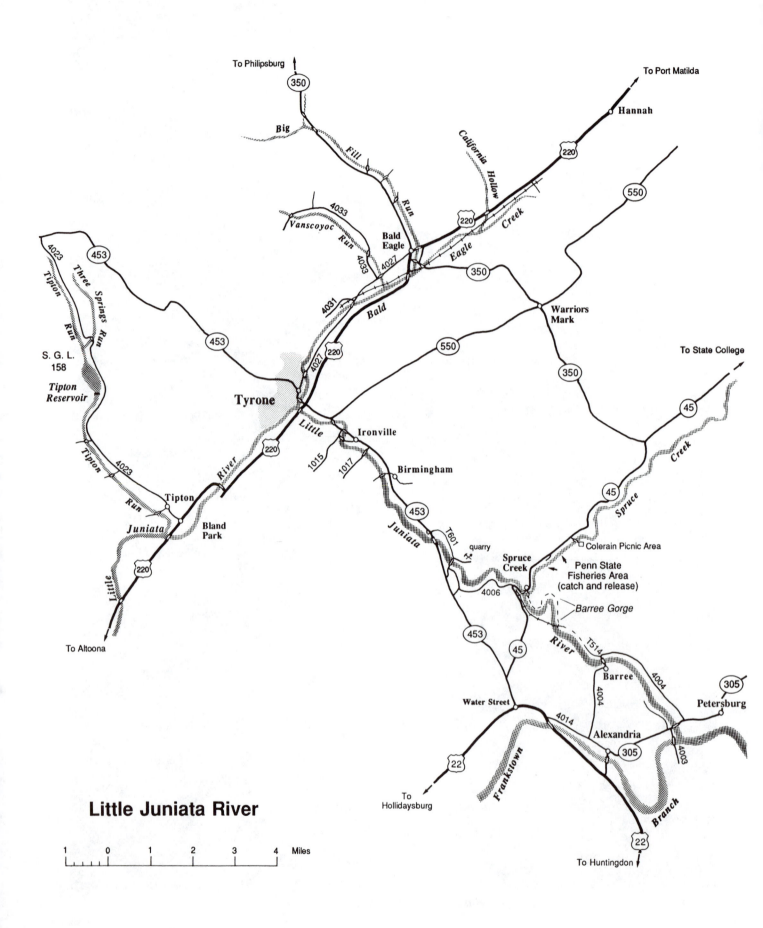

Little Juniata River

crayfish. Insect life was previously dominated by caddis flies, but now mayfly hatches are also very good and seem to be improving each year.

Trout grow fast in the Little Juniata and some real lunkers over 8 pounds have been taken. Since the cleanup, numerous fish over 18 inches have been caught each year. In 1984 a pesticide spill caused an extensive fish kill, but the river has recovered rapidly from this setback.

Trout Population

The Little Juniata is not stocked with legal-sized trout like most other trout streams. Instead the Fish Commission stocks about 100,000 brown trout fingerlings each fall. Growing up in the stream and feeding on the rich supply of natural aquatic foods, these trout soon take on the appearance and behavior of wild trout. In addition to these nearly wild trout, the Little Juniata has many truly wild trout—that is, fish resulting from natural spawning.

As fine as the fishing on the Little Juniata can be, many central-Pennsylvania anglers feel that it could be much better. The stream is fished hard and over-harvest is probably hurting the trout population. The catch in recent years has been dominated by small trout, 6 to 9 inches in length. Middle-sized trout of 10 to 14 inches in length are less abundant than you might expect in a stream with such good habitat.

Because of the success of special regulations in increasing resident trout populations in many other Pennsylvania trout streams, similar regulations have been proposed for the Little Juniata, but so far none have been approved. It's a good idea to release all or nearly all of your Little Juniata trout. Just remember that the river still receives treated sewage from the cities of Altoona and Tyrone, effluent from countless industries, and pesticides and fertilizers from farm runoff, and you will be less tempted to keep your catch for dinner.

Despite the heavy fishing pressure, the river is still far from being fished out. The Little Juniata River has some relatively inaccessible areas and some very deep pools, and just the sheer size of the stream, 80 to 90 feet wide, insures that some large fish escape capture.

The Little Juniata is an interesting stream to explore because of the variety you'll encounter along its course: from gentle riffles and shallow flats to swift, rocky rapids and deep, wide pools. A railroad parallels the stream, crossing over many scenic bridges. Be careful whenever you are near the railroad tracks; this is a very busy rail line.

Upstream of Tyrone, the Little Juniata's trout population is limited by warm summer temperatures. At Tyrone the influx of Bald Eagle Creek adds cool water and increases the size of the stream. Good trout fishing begins at Tyrone and gets even better a few miles downstream, around Ironville and Birmingham.

In this area the flow becomes swifter and numerous springs add their cool water. There are about 15 miles of good trout water from here downstream to the mouth, where the Little Juniata meets the Frankstown Branch of the Juniata.

South From Tyrone

Follow the river south from Tyrone on Route 453. There are places to park along Route 453 and some side roads leading to the river. About 1.5 miles south of Birmingham, turn right from Route 453 onto a secondary road (T601). This road turns off just before Route 453 crosses a bridge over the river. It continues downstream for about 1.2 miles before crossing a bridge over the Little Juniata near an entrance to a large quarry. You can park near this bridge, and there is good fishing upstream or down.

Driving downstream from the bridge near the quarry, you will pass by an auto wrecking yard, which lies between the road and the river. After passing the wrecking yard, turn left at the next two intersections, and you will find yourself on SR 4006, which parallels the river down to the village of Spruce Creek. This stretch has some beautiful riffles and glides and classic pools.

Spruce Creek Area

At the village of Spruce Creek, next to the Route 45 bridge over the Little Juniata, you will find Spruce Creek Outfitters, where you can find fly tackle and learn what's been hatching lately on the river.

Downstream from the Route 45 bridge, the Little Juniata River borders the Espy farm for approximately 1 mile. The owner previously provided access for anglers, but this land is now posted against trespassing. In addition to closing his land, Mr. Espy has tried to prevent anglers from wading the river, even if they come in from the opposite bank or wade downstream from the bridge. Whether he has the legal right to prohibit fishing in the stretch of river adjoining his land is an issue that has created a heated controversy. As of this writing (March 1993), a court battle seems likely. The outcome of this case may set a precedent that influences public access to rivers and streams throughout Pennsylvania.

Barree Gorge

Below Espy's farm the Little Juniata River cuts through a picturesque gorge. There are wide, unusually deep pools here, and in many places the deep water extends to the tree-lined banks, making wading and casting difficult. No roads go through this gorge, but railroad tracks follow the river after passing through a tunnel, and a good walking trail parallels the east bank along the length of the gorge. It is about 2 miles from Espy's farm downstream through the gorge to a parking area at the lower end of the gorge, above the village of Barree. This stretch of the river is within Rothrock State Forest.

To drive from Spruce Creek to the lower end of the gorge, take Route 45 south to Route 453, then drive south on Route 453 to Route 22 at Waterstreet. Turn left and follow Route 22 south about 0.7 mile, then turn left on SR 4014, which goes toward Alexandria. Drive 1.8 miles, to just past the Mead Products factory, then turn left on SR 4004, which takes you to a bridge over the Little Juniata at Barree. Turn left after the bridge and follow T514 until it ends at the parking area at the lower end of the gorge.

To fish the Little Juniata's lower water, follow SR 4004 south from Barree to Route 305. There is ample parking at the Route 305 bridge, and from here you can fish upstream in deep, slow pools or fish downstream in swift rapids to the mouth, which is about 0.3 mile below this bridge. Here the Little Juniata flows into the Frankstown Branch of the Juniata, and trout can be caught even a short distance below this junction, although water temperatures get pretty warm here in midsummer.

Fly Hatches

Hatches appearing on the Little Juniata include Blue-winged Olives, Blue Quills, Sulphurs, Olive Caddis, Grey Foxes, Green Drakes, Isonychia, Light Cahills, and White Mayflies. The Olive Caddis and the Sulphurs are very important hatches because they are on the water almost daily from early May through mid-June. In addition to the Olive Caddis, numerous other caddis hatch on the Little Juniata in a variety of sizes and colors.

The Green Drake hatches on the Little Juniata are not nearly as heavy as they are on Penns and Fishing Creeks, but they seem to be improving yearly. The best Green Drake hatches appear from Spruce Creek downstream to the mouth. The peak of the hatch usually occurs on last few days of May and the first few days of June

The White Mayfly, which is a popular hatch on the Yellow Breeches in Cumberland County, also produces good late-season fishing on the Little Juniata. These flies descend at dusk like snow, from late August through mid-September. In 1989, White Mayflies hatched through the whole month of September and even into October. This late hatching was probably caused by unusually cool weather that year.

Many of the larger trout in the Little Juniata are taken by bait fishers using crayfish, which are an abundant food source in the stream. Fly fishers should try specific crayfish imitations or Wooly Buggers, which may suggest crayfish. Sculpin imitations are also effective and account for many of the larger fish caught by fly fishers. In the summer months water temperatures rise on the Little Juniata, but good fishing can still be had at dusk, in the early morning, and at night.

There is no closed season on trout fishing on the Little Juniata from the mouth of Bald Eagle Creek at Tyrone downstream to the mouth. Many people enjoy getting a jump on the regular trout season, and the Little Juniata is a very popular fishing spot on warm weekends in late March and early April.

Spruce Creek - Huntingdon County
(catch and release, artificials only, 0.5 mile)
(map: page 90)

Spruce Creek is a productive spring-fed limestone stream that has been well publicized since former President Jimmy Carter began fishing it. Unfortunately, nearly all of Spruce Creek is posted against public fishing. The only stretch of Spruce Creek that is clearly, unequivocally open to the public is the stretch owned by Penn State University. If you inquire locally, you may find other short stretches where landowners allow fishing.

The Penn State stretch, recently named the George Harvey Experimental Fisheries Area, can be reached by traveling north on Route 45 for about 1 mile from the village of Spruce Creek. Look for the sign and a narrow drive to the right. This 0.5 mile stretch is managed under catch-and-release, artificials-only regulations. A large pool is located at the upper end of this stretch. Below this pool the creek splits into several smaller channels.

The trout population in Spruce Creek is mostly wild brown trout, but there are also many hatchery trout from private stockings. The practice of stocking hatchery trout on top of good wild trout populations is, unfortunately, quite common in Pennsylvania.

Spruce Creek is a fertile, alkaline stream with numerous fly hatches, including Blue-winged Olives, Grannoms, Olive Caddis, Sulphurs, March Browns, Green Drakes, Light Cahills, and Tricos. Spruce Creek makes a worthwhile side trip to fishing the Little Juniata, especially in midsummer when Spruce Creek's cooler water temperatures may produce more active trout.

(Little) Bald Eagle Creek - Blair County
(map: page 90)

This stream is shown on most maps as Bald Eagle Creek, but anglers often refer to it as Little Bald Eagle Creek to distinguish it from the larger and better-known Bald Eagle Creek located nearby in Centre County.

Little Bald Eagle Creek begins in Blair County near the Centre County line and flows southwest to Tyrone, where it joins the Little Juniata River. Some sections of this stream are rather shallow and appear to have been channelized, but the Little Bald Eagle has good water quality, which produces good fly hatches and fair numbers of wild brown trout in addition to hatchery trout. Fishing pressure is quite heavy early in the season, soon after stocking, but light the rest of the year. The nearby Little Juniata River, a much larger trout stream, draws more middle and late season anglers.

The Fish Commission stocks trout in 6.7 miles of the Little Bald Eagle, from the confluence with California Hollow downstream to a dam at the paper mill at Tyrone. Trout are stocked prior to opening day and twice inseason, with the last stocking coming in mid to late May. Stream surveys in mid-July showed that Little Bald Eagle Creek holds a fair population of wild brown trout from 2 to 14 inches long.

To reach the upper end of Little Bald Eagle Creek, begin at the traffic light at the village of Bald Eagle, drive north 3 miles on Route 220, then turn right onto a dirt road, which soon crosses railroad tracks. Turn right and drive down alongside the railroad tracks for a mile, and you will reach the stream. Bald Eagle Creek is small and brushy in this area. Some of this upper part of the creek flows through State Game Land No. 278. You can follow the stream down along the railroad tracks, but there is some posting from the Game Land boundary down to the Route 350 bridge, and the brush is very thick on this part of the stream.

The Route 350 bridge is a good access spot, and from here you can fish downstream past the confluence of Big Fill Run. Big Fill Run is a good wild brown trout stream, and its cool flow approximately doubles the size of Little Bald Eagle Creek.

Another good access point is the SR 4027 (old Route 220) bridge over Vanscoyoc Run. Park along the shoulder of SR 4027 and walk down along Vanscoyoc Run, which holds both stocked and wild trout. This middle section of Little Bald Eagle Creek flows through a wooded area called the Papermill Woods, and this is perhaps the best section of the creek.

Further downstream, SR 4027 crosses over the creek, and some parking is available near the bridge on the shoulder of SR 4027 and also along SR 4031, which turns off near the bridge. Above this bridge there is an open, shallow stretch, but upstream from this you will find good riffles and pools and tall trees shading the creek.

Fly hatches on Little Bald Eagle Creek include Blue Quills, Sulphurs, Green Drakes, and Isonychia. If no flies are hatching you may want to try a stonefly nymph imitation; the stream has some big Perlid stoneflies. Muskrat Nymphs are also worth a try. I had some fast fishing with these on a day in May when nothing else seemed to work.

Big Fill Run - Blair and Centre Counties
(map: page 90)

Big Fill Run is a small, tumbling freestone stream with a good wild brown trout population and good fly hatches. Unfortunately, scattered posting along the stream makes it difficult to know where you can fish and where you can't. The Fish Commission manages Big Fill Run as a wild trout stream and no longer stocks any fish.

The lower end of the creek, from the mouth on Little Bald Eagle Creek upstream to the Route 350 bridge, flows through a brushy, wooded area. Some deep holes and undercut banks are located here. On one fishing trip I saw posting signs on this stretch, but several other times it was not posted.

Upstream from the village of Bald Eagle, Big Fill is paralleled by Route 350, and several secondary roads cross the creek. Here the stream flows through a dense woods scattered with houses, and several stretches are posted.

About 3.8 miles north of the traffic light at Bald Eagle, Route 350 crosses over Big Fill Run. The stream is small in this upper water, but it holds a lot of small brown and brook trout. Downstream from the bridge, there is a wooded stretch about 1 mile long with no posting and no buildings along the creek. This area is not completely idyllic, though, because of the roar of truck traffic on Route 350.

Big Fill Run has varied fly hatches, including Blue Quills, Sulphurs, Olive Caddis, March Browns, Green Drakes, and Light Cahills.

Vanscoyoc Run - Blair County
(map: page 90)

Vanscoyoc Run is a small freestone stream with good fishing for stocked trout, wild brown trout, and native brook trout. There are few pools of even moderate size on Vanscoyoc Run; in most places you'll be fishing small pockets formed by tree roots, rocks, and undercut banks. Hardwood trees and rhododendron bushes form a dark tunnel over much of the length of the stream. These tight quarters make casting difficult, but if you can manage to flick a dry fly under the branches to likely-looking pockets, you have a good chance of catching some fish.

Vanscoyoc Run has very good numbers of mostly small wild trout. Brook trout predominate in the upper reaches and both brown and brook trout are found in the lower half of the stream.

The Fish Commission stocks trout from the mouth on Little Bald Eagle Creek upstream to the upper SR 4033 bridge. Trout are stocked preseason and once inseason, usually about a week after opening day. Fishing pressure on Vanscoyoc Run is fairly heavy in the opening weeks of season, but after the end of May, few people fish here.

The land along the stream is privately owned and most of it is open to fishing. In the lower part of the creek, there is a short posted stretch above the SR 4027 bridge. In the upper part of the creek, there is a short posted stretch just above the SR 4033 bridge. Do not litter. Littering in the past nearly resulted in the closure of a long stretch of Vanscoyoc Run.

Tipton Run - Blair County
(map: page 90)

Tipton Run begins in remote, mountainous country in State Game Land No. 58. It flows south into Tipton Reservoir, then continues south to meet the Little Juniata River at the village of Bland Park. This rocky freestone stream is no longer stocked because it has a good population of both wild brown and wild brook trout.

To reach the stream from Tyrone, take Route 220 southwest for about 4 miles to Bland Park. Turn right onto SR 4023. This road is easy to miss. On Route 220 you will pass a PPG factory and several small businesses on the right before you reach SR 4023. Look for the sign to Houtzdale.

The lower part of the creek is somewhat inaccessible because of numerous homes along the banks and a long stretch of posted property. About 2.8 miles north from Route 220, you will see Game Land No. 158 signs. From here upstream to the headwaters, Tipton Run is on public land and is open to fishing. Tipton Reservoir, however, is closed to fishing.

From the Game Land border upstream to Tipton Reservoir, there is plenty of parking along the road. The stream is larger here than most "runs," and it flows swiftly through a heavily-wooded area. There are some good riffles and small pools and enough brush and overhanging tree limbs to challenge your casting ability. In this stretch below the reservoir, the stream holds mostly brown trout.

Above the reservoir the road parallels the stream for about 0.3 mile, and you can park here and walk through the woods to the stream. Then the road takes a hairpin turn away from Tipton Run and crosses over Three Springs Run, a small tributary stream that holds native brook trout. The road then turns back toward Tipton Run and follows it upstream, but it climbs high on a hillside above the stream. It's a very steep drop down to the creek. The best way to get access to upper Tipton Run is to park along the road between the reservoir and the hairpin turn and walk up along the stream from there.

Above the influx of Three Springs Run, Tipton Run is quite small. From the reservoir upstream, there are about 2 miles of water before the run dwindles to a trickle. Above the reservoir most of the trout are brookies, but some brown trout are also found there.

Tipton Run's fly hatches include Quill Gordons, Blue Quills, Sulphurs, and Light Cahills.

Fly fishers often find themselves embroiled in minor controversies, such as whether or not it's proper to use strike indicators, whether using weighted nymphs and streamers is really sporting, whether egg patterns are in keeping with the fly fishing tradition, etc. One famous angler even objected to graphite rods because they looked "greasy." Before you spend much of your time and mental energy on such quibbles, consider this: Blair County's Waterways Conservation Officer once caught some fellows along Tipton Run *shooting* trout on their spawning beds with shotguns.

Willow Run - Juniata County
(map: page 95)

Willow Run is classified as a wild brown trout stream from its headwaters downstream 6 miles to McCullochs Mills, and trout are no longer stocked. Fishing pressure is very light on this stream for the following reasons: it is located in a lightly-populated rural area, no well-known trout streams are nearby, some sections of the stream are very brushy, and wild brown trout are often difficult to catch. The fishing is not easy on Willow Run, but some anglers will enjoy this stream's challenges.

In its upper reaches, from the headwaters downstream to State Game Land No. 215, Willow Run flows through a narrow, wooded valley, and tall hemlocks and hardwoods provide deep shade. The stream bed is mostly rock and gravel here, although silt has collected in some of the slower stretches. Undercut banks and pools formed by tree roots and downed timber provide good cover for numerous small wild brown and brook trout.

To reach this upper water, turn off Route 35 at Peru Mills onto T327 (Patterson Road). This dirt road crosses Willow Run, then follows it for another 0.6 miles. Near the intersection of T327 and T304, a rough dirt track turns off from T327 and follows the creek downstream, along the south bank.

In State Game Land No. 215, Willow Run's valley begins to widen and there are fewer tall trees. Heavy brush has grown up along the banks here, in some places completely closing over the top of the stream. Brown trout are plentiful up to 10 inches in this stretch, and some reach 14 inches.

From the State Game Land boundary downstream to the T316 bridge, Willow Run is bordered by heavy brush. The best way to fish this stretch is to wade directly upstream because the brush prevents walking along the banks. Lack of room for backcasts makes fly fishing frustrating here. I began to catch some nice brown trout in this area after putting my fly rod back in the car and switching to Mepps and Roostertails fished with spinning tackle. Several pickerel and rock bass also found these lures appealing. These warmwater fish are found along with the brown trout in the lower half of the stream.

From the T316 bridge downstream to its mouth on Tuscarora Creek, Willow Run is much less brushy and fly casting is easier. Meadows, fields, trees, and several houses border the banks here. Tributaries and

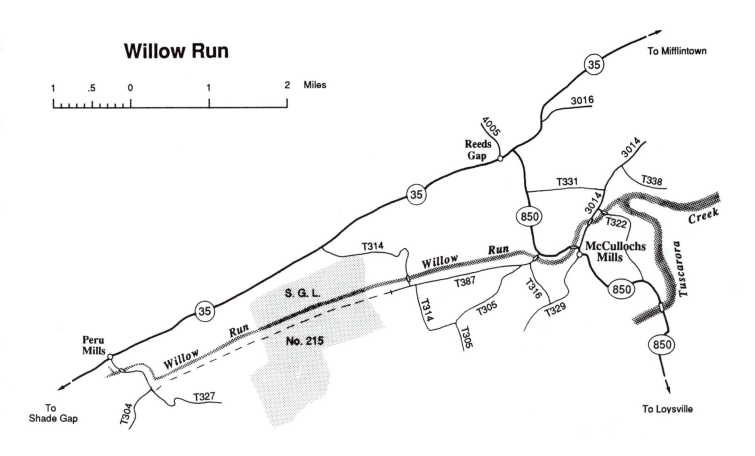

springs increase the size of Willow Run in this lower water, and deep pools hold some brown trout over 18 inches long.

Caddis of the genus *Hydropsyche*, often called Spotted Sedges or Tan Caddis, are the most common aquatic insect in Willow Run. Muskrat Nymphs in sizes 12, 14, and 16 make good imitations of their larvae and tan-bodied Elk Hair Caddis make good dry fly imitations of the adults.

Lost Creek - Juniata County
(map: page 96)

Lost Creek originates as a narrow brook in a forested, mountainous area near the Juniata/Snyder County line, and it flows south and east through a rural valley to meet the Juniata River at Cuba Mills, north of Mifflintown.

In the headwaters above Route 235, Lost Creek flows through a heavily wooded area that is posted against trespassing. Trout are stocked from Route 235 downstream to the mouth, a distance of about 13 miles. The Fish Commission stocks trout for opening day and twice inseason, with the last stocking coming around the third week in May.

From Route 235 down to about Oakland Mills, Lost Creek is mostly a woodland stream with good shade and continuous riffles and pockets. This stretch holds a good population of wild trout in addition to the stocked fish. Most of these wild trout are browns, but there are also some brookies, especially in the upper reaches near Route 235.

Below Oakland Mills, Lost Creek flows through a farming area, where the stream becomes wider and slower. From Oakland Mills to the mouth, siltation and summer warming limit the wild trout population, and trout fishing is generally poor after midseason. The lower reaches of Lost Creek hold some smallmouth bass and rock bass.

Big Run - Juniata County
(map: page 96)

Big Run is a small, freestone tributary of Lost Creek. The Fish Commission stocks 2 miles of the stream, from the mouth up to the T527 bridge. Stocking takes place preseason and once inseason, in mid to late May.

In the upper part of the stocked stretch, Big Run flows past woods and hunting camps, and farther downstream it flows through open, eroded meadows. A large retirement home is located along the stream near the intersection of T398 and SR 1002. A fair number of wild brown and brook trout can be found

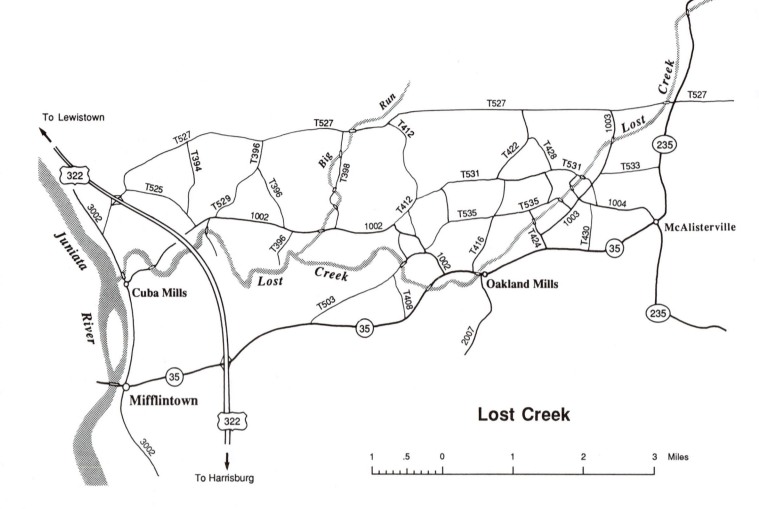

Lost Creek

in the upper part of Big Run's stocked water, but scattered posting and limited parking make this stream less than a joy to fish.

In the narrow, unstocked headwaters upstream from T527, Big Run flows through a remote, heavily wooded area. The stream is tiny here, but it holds a lot of small native brook trout.

East Licking Creek - Juniata and Mifflin Counties
(map: page 97)

East Licking Creek is stocked with hatchery trout over a distance of 20 miles, from its headwaters in Tuscarora State Forest downstream to its mouth on Tuscarora Creek, near Port Royal.

Upstream from Clearview Reservoir, East Licking Creek flows through an attractive forested area and holds a fair number of native brook trout and also a few wild browns. The best wild trout fishing is found from the Karl Guss Picnic Area upstream into the headwaters. Here a gravel forest road follows East

Licking Creek as it flows through an undeveloped area in Tuscarora State Forest. You can catch brook trout here all season long, but they are not as abundant as in many similar-looking woodland streams in Pennsylvania. Silt from the forest roads is filling in some of the pools, and this may be limiting the wild trout population, or the fault may lie with that too familiar culprit, acid rain.

Below Clearview Reservoir the stream becomes wider and deeper as it leaves the forests and enters a farming area. Because of the warming effect of the reservoir, summer water temperatures get too warm for lower Licking Creek to support many wild trout. Lower East Licking Creek is an enjoyable place to fish for stocked trout early in the season, though, because the stream flows through a scenic rural valley. Tall sycamore trees flank the stream as it courses towards its mouth on Tuscarora Creek. Unlike many streams in farming valleys, East Licking Creek is little affected by erosion, so its waters flow over a clean, rocky bed. The Fish Commission stocks East Licking Creek preseason and three times inseason.

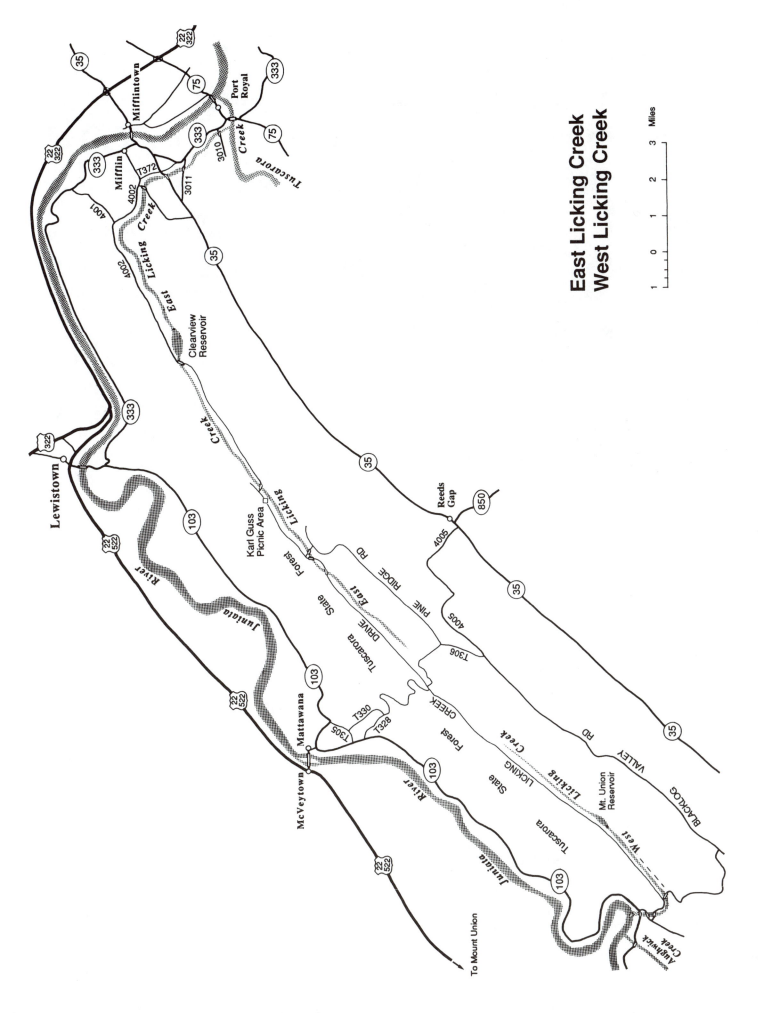

East Licking Creek
West Licking Creek

Kishacoquillas Creek in the Narrows, after a spring rain.

West Licking Creek - Mifflin and Huntingdon Counties
(map: page 97)

West Licking Creek originates in Tuscarora State Forest in Mifflin County and flows south into Huntingdon County, where it joins the Juniata River along Route 103, east of Mount Union. This small, woodland freestone stream flows most of its length through Tuscarora State Forest, but there is some private land near the mouth. A forest road follows the stream up to its headwaters.

The Fish Commission stocks West Licking Creek for opening day and twice inseason, with the last stocking coming around the first week of May. The stream is stocked from its mouth upstream 5.5 miles. The upper stocking limit is in Mifflin County, about 1.3 miles above the very small Mount Union Water Supply Reservoir.

Besides stocked trout, West Licking Creek holds good numbers of wild brown and brook trout. Expect to catch brookies 5 to 6 inches long and browns 5 to 9 inches long. Brown trout predominate in the lower part of the stream. On hot summer days when many trout streams are sluggish, this cool, tumbling stream is well worth a try.

To reach West Licking Creek from Mount Union, begin at the intersection of Route 747 and Route 522 in downtown Mount Union. Drive south on Route 522 about 1.3 miles to Allenport, then turn left onto Route 103, which parallels the Juniata River. After driving another 2.4 miles, you will cross a bridge over Aughwick Creek. Proceed another 1.1 miles and you will come to a bridge over the much smaller West Licking Creek.

Kishacoquillas Creek - Mifflin County
(map: page 99)

Kish Creek, as this stream is referred to locally, is a big, central Pennsylvania limestone stream that is not as well known as some other big limestone streams, such as Penns Creek, Fishing Creek, and Spring Creek. Many anglers undoubtedly cross over Kish Creek without a glance as they drive north on Route 322, heading towards these much better known trout streams.

Kish Creek originates southwest of Belleville, and the upper part of the stream flows through a wide, open farming valley. (This upper area is not shown on the map.) Siltation and lack of shade limit the wild trout population where the stream flows through this

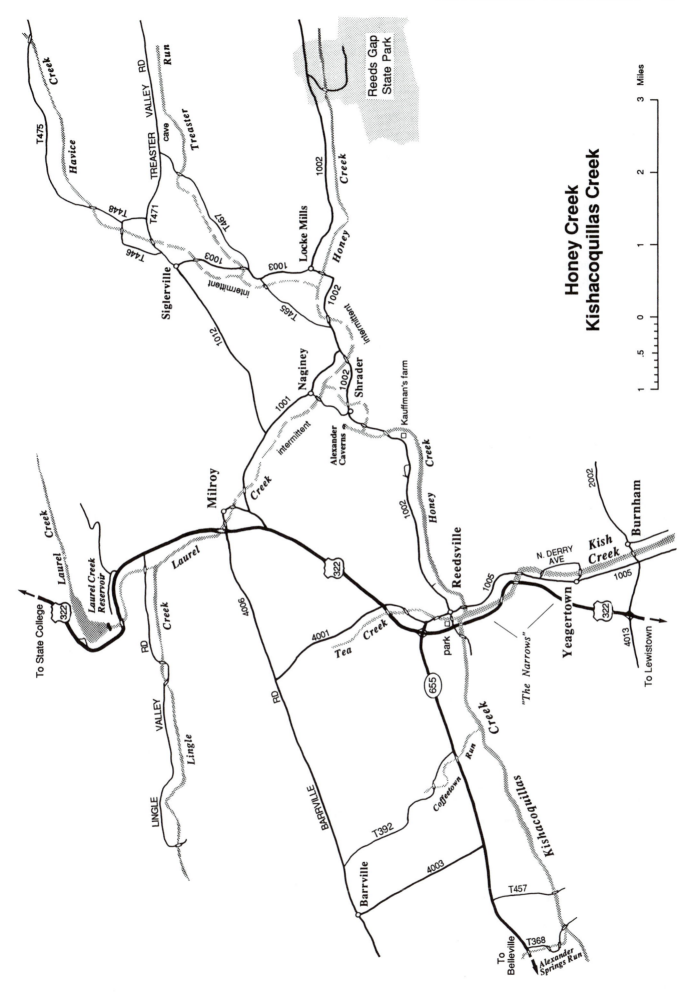

Honey Creek
Kishacoquillas Creek

farmland, and the fishing is mostly for stocked trout, although big holdover or wild browns are sometimes caught from the deeper holes. Stocking on Kish Creek begins at the bridge on T340, about 3.2 miles upstream of Belleville, and continues downstream to Burnham.

A few miles downstream of Belleville, Kish Creek leaves the farm country and flows into a wooded area, where conditions begin to improve. Alexander Springs Run and Coffeetown Run are small spring creeks that add their cool flows to Kish Creek and probably also provide some spawning habitat. A small hatchery is located on Alexander Springs Run, and some fish escape and find their way into Kish Creek.

From Alexander Springs Run downstream to Reedsville, Kish Creek flows through a wooded area with limited access. The stream is about 50 feet wide here and mostly shallow and riffled, with little cover other than that provided by small pockets and several rather shallow pools. I was fishing in this area when two young fishermen using minnows came downstream. When I asked them if they'd had any luck, one of them emptied his canvas creel onto the ground, and out spilled a 20-inch brown, a 14-inch brown, and several smaller trout. Perhaps this stretch is better trout water than it looks.

Summer stream surveys indicate that the Alexander Springs-to-Reedsville stretch holds a lot of stocked trout into the summer, but that natural reproduction is limited. Access to this stretch is available at the T368 bridge near Alexander Springs Run or at the Mifflin County Park in Reedsville. There has been some posting near the middle of this stretch. Note: the upper stretch of Kish Creek, from the headwaters downstream to Reedsville, is referred to by many people as the West Branch.

Tea Creek and Honey Creek, which are both limestone spring creeks with good wild brown trout populations, join Kish Creek at Reedsville. Mifflin County Park provides good access to all three streams. Another access point is a large parking area located along SR 1005, near the bridge over Honey Creek. The influx of cold spring water from these tributaries greatly increases the volume and water quality of Kish Creek downstream from Reedsville.

The Mann Narrows

From Reedsville downstream to Yeagertown, Kish Creek passes through a gap in Jacks Mountain called the Mann Narrows. In the Narrows the stream flows through large pools and swift, bouldered runs. This is the prime water on Kish Creek. The Narrows holds a good population of wild and holdover browns, including some big fish ranging from 14 to 21 inches. One way to reach the Narrows is to just fish downstream from Reedsville. Driving south from Reedsville on SR 1005, you can park at several places along the road,

including near the SR 1005 bridge over Kish Creek. After crossing this bridge, take the first left, onto North Derry Avenue in Yeagertown. This road leads to a bridge over the creek near a baseball field. This is a good access point for fishing the lower part of the Narrows.

There is also good fishing found downstream from North Derry Avenue, but houses and industries increase along the stream. Burnham marks the end of the stocked water. Local anglers say browns are sometimes caught as far downstream as the mouth of Kish Creek on the Juniata River at Lewistown, but that trout are scattered in the lower stretches.

Be careful when wading Kish Creek. The rocks on the bottom are coated with a layer of algae that's as slick as grease. While fishing near Yeagertown, I slipped and fell flat on my face, something I usually manage to do at least once each year.

Fly Hatches

The Green Drake hatch was once very heavy on Kish Creek. Local residents recall that the insects were sometimes so thick that driving became hazardous on the roads paralleling the stream. A few Green Drakes still appear, but only very sporadically. The main hatches now are Olive Caddis, Sulphurs, Tan Caddis, Light Cahills, and Isonychia. Kish Creek also has lots of stoneflies, particularly in the Narrows, and sculpins are also plentiful.

Kish Creek turns the color of chocolate milk after heavy rains because of all the topsoil washed in from the farms near Belleville. If Kish Creek is too muddy to fish, you might want to fish Honey Creek, which clears much more quickly after a rain.

Tea Creek - Mifflin County
(map: page 99)

Tea Creek is a tiny limestone spring creek that flows into Kishacoquillas Creek at Reedsville. No trout are stocked, but the stream holds many small wild browns. Only the lower mile of the stream, from the mouth upstream to the Route 322 bridge, is really worth fishing. Above the Route 322 bridge, Tea Creek is very small and its banks are severely eroded. A good place to park your vehicle is at Mifflin County Park, right beside the mouth of Tea Creek.

Honey Creek (lower) - Mifflin County
(map: page 99)

The upper and lower sections of Honey Creek are entirely different from one another in terms of size, appearance, water chemistry, and trout populations. First I will describe lower Honey Creek; a separate description of upper Honey Creek follows.

Lower Honey Creek emerges from the Alexander Caverns and flows southwest 3.8 miles before joining

Honey Creek holds a good population of wild brown trout.

Kishacoquillas Creek at Reedsville. After emerging from the caverns, Honey Creek is a true limestone spring creek, with a consistent supply of cool, fertile water. It flows through riffles and some deep pools along its way past farms, woods, and houses.

The appearance of the stream is different than the spring creeks of the Cumberland Valley, such as the Letort and Big Spring. Those meadow spring creeks flow slowly and smoothly and have silt bottoms and extensive weedbeds. Honey Creek has a rocky bottom and the alternating sequences of riffles and pools that are usually considered typical of freestone trout streams.

Wild Browns

Because of its fine wild brown trout population, lower Honey Creek is managed as a wild trout stream and hatchery trout are no longer stocked. Lower Honey Creek has a reputation among anglers of being a tough stream. There are times when it seems there are no fish in the creek. But with a good hatch of flies, the water comes alive with trout. Stream surveys turn up many browns from 6 to 12 inches and fair numbers from 13 to 17 inches.

To reach lower Honey Creek, take the Reedsville exit off Route 322 and drive south into Reedsville. Go straight through at the traffic light, and in about 1 block you will cross a bridge over Honey Creek. Just past the bridge there's a large parking area on the right. This is a good access site for fishing Honey Creek, Kishacoquillas Creek, and tiny Tea Creek. This lowest section of Honey Creek, from Reedsville downstream to the mouth, has a fair population of wild brown trout and also some stocked trout that move up from Kishacoquillas Creek.

To continue up along Honey Creek, drive back over the bridge and turn right at the traffic light (Reedsville has just one traffic light) onto SR 1002. This road follows the stream the whole way up to its headwaters.

About 0.5 mile up from the traffic light, there is a small park, which is a good access site. Continuing upstream, there are numerous pulloffs along both sides of SR 1002.

About 2.5 miles upstream from Reedsville, just below Kauffmans' dairy farm, there's an old bridge abutment with a large pool. Several other good pools and runs are found downstream from here. The first mile or so below Kauffmans' farm is perhaps the most productive stretch of Honey Creek.

About 0.5 mile upstream from Kauffmans' farm, SR 1002 crosses a bridge over Honey Creek. Immediately after this bridge, there is a parking pulloff on the left next to a very deep pool at another old bridge abutment.

Nearly all of the land along lower Honey Creek is privately owned. Most of the stream is open to fishing, but several landowners do not allow fishing on Sundays. Alexander Caverns and approximately the first quarter-mile of the stream below the caverns are posted against trespassing.

Fly Hatches

Some hatches to look for on Honey Creek include Blue-winged Olives, Olive Caddis, Sulphurs, Green Drakes, Light Cahills, and Tricos. The Green Drake hatch used to be very good, but it has diminished over the years. In 1988, 1989, and 1990, the Green Drakes hatched in fair numbers, so they may be making a recovery. The Sulphurs now produce the best fly fishing action on Honey Creek. They hatch most heavily from mid-May into early June.

Tributaries

Lower Honey Creek is fed by a number of small tributary streams, including upper Honey Creek. These streams all originate as infertile, mountain freestone streams. As they flow from their narrow mountain valleys into wider agricultural valleys, they begin to sink into the ground. The lower stretches of these streams have intermittent channels that flow with water early in the year, but dry up by midsummer in years with low rainfall. The water that sinks into the ground flows through limestone formations and emerges again at Alexander Caverns to create lower Honey Creek.

Four of these headwater streams that are of interest to the angler are upper Honey Creek, Treaster Run, Havice Creek, and Lingle Creek. These small streams all hold both wild and stocked trout. None of them has as good a wild trout population as lower Honey Creek, however.

Honey Creek (upper) - Mifflin County
(map: page 99)

Upper Honey Creek, also called New Lancaster Valley Run, flows mostly through privately owned land, but short stretches flow through Bald Eagle State Forest and Reeds Gap State Park. This small freestone creek holds some wild brown and brook trout, but most of its trout are from the hatchery.

The Fish Commission stocks trout for opening day and once inseason, usually around the end of May or the beginning of June. The stream is stocked over a distance of 9.5 miles, from the junction with Treaster Run near Locke Mills upstream to the SR 1002 bridge near the Mifflin/Snyder County line. (The upper part of the creek is not shown on the map.)

Around Locke Mills the stream begins to lose volume as its waters seep into the underlying limestone rock layers. At normal water levels, the stream sinks completely at a quarry near Naginey. When water levels are high, some water flows above ground in a brushy flood channel.

To reach upper Honey Creek, just continue following SR 1002 east from Reedsville. The road takes many twists and turns, but the route number stays the same. Camping sites are available at Reeds Gap State Park.

Treaster Run - Mifflin County
(map: page 99)

Treaster Run is perhaps the best of the headwater streams in the Honey Creek drainage. (Only the lower part of Treaster Run is shown on the map.) The Fish Commission stocks Treaster Run from near a cave east of Siglerville upstream 5 miles to the bridge on Treaster Valley Road, near the Bear Gap Picnic Area. Stocking takes place preseason and twice inseason, with the last stocking coming around the third week in May. Near the cave the stream begins to sink, and some of the lower parts of the creek dry up completely in midsummer.

Treaster Valley Road, a gravel forest road, follows Treaster Run along its stocked stretch through a beautiful pine forest, which is part of the Bald Eagle State Forest. There are a few cabins along the lower part of the road, but most of this area is remarkably unspoiled.

In the headwaters above the Bear Gap Picnic Area, Treaster Run is quite small and has a good population of wild brook trout. Below the picnic area, you will find wild brook and brown trout as well as stocked fish. As you go farther downstream closer to the cave, the numbers of wild trout decrease.

Havice Creek - Mifflin County
(map: page 99)

Havice Creek is a small stream that flows into Treaster Run south of Siglerville. This stream also sinks in its lower stretch. From Siglerville to its mouth, Havice Creek is a dry channel much of the year. From Siglerville, follow Havice Valley Road, which parallels the creek up into its headwaters. In these upper waters, Havice Creek is a small, freestone brook flowing through Bald Eagle State Forest, where you can find stocked trout and also some wild browns and brookies. Trout are stocked by the Fish Commission for opening day and also once or twice inseason, with the last stocking coming in early to mid-June.

Lingle Creek - Mifflin County
(map: page 99)

Lingle Creek is a small freestone stream that can be reached off Route 322 near Milroy. From Milroy, go north on Route 322 about 1 mile, then turn left onto Lingle Valley Road. This forest road parallels the creek upstream. Lingle Creek flows through a pretty wooded area in Rothrock State Forest and drains into Laurel Creek near Route 322. Lingle Creek is stocked with trout and it also holds fair numbers of small wild brown and brook trout.

The Fish Commission stocks trout for opening day and twice inseason, with the last stocking coming around the third week in May. Trout are stocked from the mouth upstream 5.5 miles to Camp Savage. Lingle Creek itself does not sink, but its receiving stream, Laurel Creek, sinks near Milroy. Laurel Creek is not stocked with trout.

Other Southcentral PA Streams
(no maps)

No maps were included for the following streams and the descriptions were kept brief, but these streams are also well worth fishing.

Standing Stone Creek - Huntingdon County

Standing Stone Creek can be reached by following Route 26 north from Huntingdon or south from State College. In its headwaters in Rothrock State Forest, Standing Stone Creek is a small, shallow, woodland stream that offers good fishing for stocked trout and wild browns and brookies. Above the Alan Seeger Natural Area, the stream is so choked with rhododendron that is nearly unfishable. The stretch just below the Alan Seeger Natural Area is still wooded, but more open and easier to fish.

From the state forest border downstream to McAlevys Fort, the stream flows through privately owned woodlands, meadows, and farms. Some of this land is posted, but some is open to fishing. The open stretches are stocked with trout, and this water also holds wild brown trout.

In July of 1987, there was an extensive fish kill caused by a liquid manure spill about a half-mile above McAlevys Fort. The stream seems to be recovering quickly, though, and I caught many small (6 to 9 inches) wild browns upstream from McAlevys Fort in June of 1990.

Below McAlevys Fort, Standing Stone Creek becomes wider and shallower. Farmland, woods, and scattered dwellings border the stream. Trout are stocked downstream as far as the first Route 26 bridge above Huntingdon. Some wild brown trout are found for several miles downstream from McAlevys Fort, but the lower stretches of the creek become warm in the summer months and hold more bass and suckers than trout in the late season. Siltation is a serious problem in Standing Stone Creek. A Green Drake hatch appears in late May and early June.

Laurel Run flows into Standing Stone Creek below McAlevys Fort. Trout are stocked from the mouth upstream to Whipple Dam State Park. Above Whipple Dam State Park, Laurel Run flows through Rothrock State Forest. No trout are stocked in this upper stretch of the creek, but you may find some wild brook trout.

Detweiler Run meets Standing Stone Creek at the Alan Seeger Natural Area in Rothrock State Forest. Tall hemlock trees shade this small stream. If you are willing to fight your way through thick growths of rhododendron, you can find some wild brook trout here. The upper stretches of Detweiler Run are a long hike from the road.

East Branch Standing Stone Creek is stocked with trout, and it holds wild brown and brook trout in its upper reaches in Rothrock State Forest. The lower half of the stream becomes too warm in the summer months for good trout fishing, and there have been some posting problems in this area.

Conococheague Creek - Franklin and Adams Counties

A good place to begin fishing Conococheague Creek is at Caledonia State Park, which is located along Route 30 about 10 miles east of Chambersburg. There is good access here, campsites are available, and this stretch is stocked heavily and often. Stocking begins a few miles upstream, at the Chambersburg Reservoir in Michaux State Forest. Trout are stocked from here downstream to Chambersburg. The fishing in Conococheague Creek is mostly for stocked trout, but some wild brook trout are found in the forested upper reaches.

Carbaugh Run is a small brook trout stream in the Conococheague drainage. It flows 5 miles through the hills of Michaux State Forest to its mouth at Caledonia State Park. Trout are stocked in the lower 1.4 miles of the stream, where it parallels Route 30. Above the stocked stretch, the stream flows through a roadless wooded area, where it holds fair numbers of wild brook trout.

Bobs Creek - Bedford County

Bobs Creek is a long freestone stream in northern Bedford County. In its forested upper stretches, where it flows through State Game Land No. 26 and Blue Knob State Park, you can find good fishing for stocked trout and for small wild brown and brook trout. A long stretch within S. G. L. No. 26 has no road access. Campsites are available at the state park. From the state park down to the mouth, Bobs Creek flows through farmlands and woods. Trout are stocked in this lower water, but the stream becomes very warm and shallow here in the summer months.

Northcentral Pennsylvania

Elk Creek, a spring-fed tributary of Penns Creek, in the Millheim Narrows.

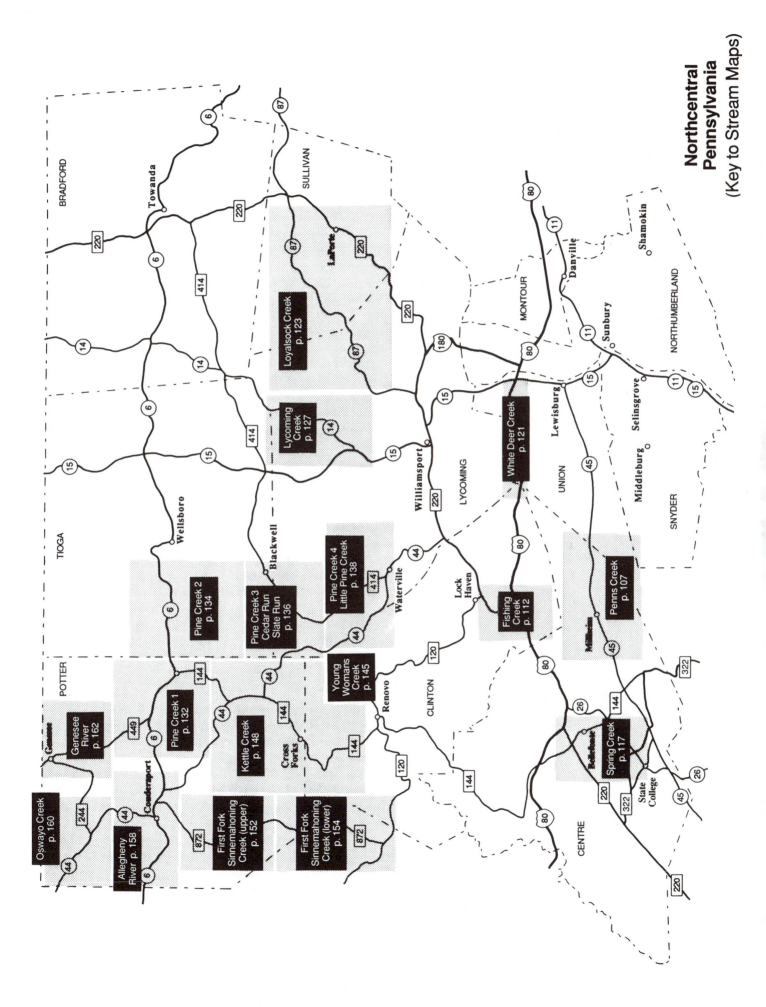

Northcentral Pennsylvania
(Key to Stream Maps)

Northcentral Pennsylvania

Penns Creek - Centre, Mifflin, and Union Counties
(catch and release, 3.9 miles)
(map: page 107)

To many anglers, Penns Creek means Green Drakes. These big, floppy mayflies appear in tremendous numbers in late May and early June and attract crowds of anglers to the stream. But Penns Creek offers much more than just Green Drakes. A great variety of mayflies and caddis hatch throughout the season, often bringing trout to the surface.

Although wild trout are not as plentiful in Penns Creek as in such streams as Spring Creek (Centre County) or Fishing Creek (Clinton County), wild browns and hatchery fish are abundant enough to provide good fishing. Trout are stocked from Spring Mills downstream about 30 miles to Glen Iron, skipping over the catch-and-release area, which is managed as a wild trout fishery. A long stretch of Penns Creek, from below Coburn downstream to below Cherry Run, flows through a mountainous, wooded area. Road access is limited in this area and deer, wild turkeys, hawks, pileated woodpeckers, and even bear are often seen.

Penns Creek has a reputation of being an unpredictable stream. There are days when the fishing is very good, particularly when there are flies hatching, and there are days when even your best efforts produce little or no success. Even the highly skilled Penns Creek veterans, who have fished the stream for years, get skunked sometimes. Despite this inconsistency, few streams have such a devoted following. It is the remarkable beauty of the stream and its surroundings, as well as the fishing, that brings people to Penns Creek again and again.

Penns Creek is a long stream, and newcomers may be puzzled about where they should begin. I recommend that you fish anywhere between Coburn and the lower end of the catch-and-release area. This is the most scenic part of the creek and it also offers the best fishing. Once you are familiar with this water, you may want to explore the upper and lower stretches of the creek.

When planning a trip to Penns Creek, keep in mind that it flows very high and muddy for several days after heavy rains. If you drive to Penns Creek and find it too muddy to fish, you may want to try Elk Creek or one of Penns Creek's other tributaries. Nearby Fishing Creek also clears more quickly than Penns Creek.

Penns Cave to Spring Mills

Penns Creek emerges from the mouth of Penns Cave, a commercially developed cavern. In this upper water, Penns Creek is a small limestone spring creek, approximately 15 to 20 feet wide. Unfortunately, nearly all of this stretch is posted against trespassing. (This stretch is not shown on the map.)

Spring Mills to Coburn

At Spring Mills a large spring flows into Penns Creek near the Route 45 bridge, and Sinking Creek flows in a short distance downstream. The additional water from these two sources approximately doubles the volume of Penns Creek, creating a medium-sized stream about 30 to 40 feet wide.

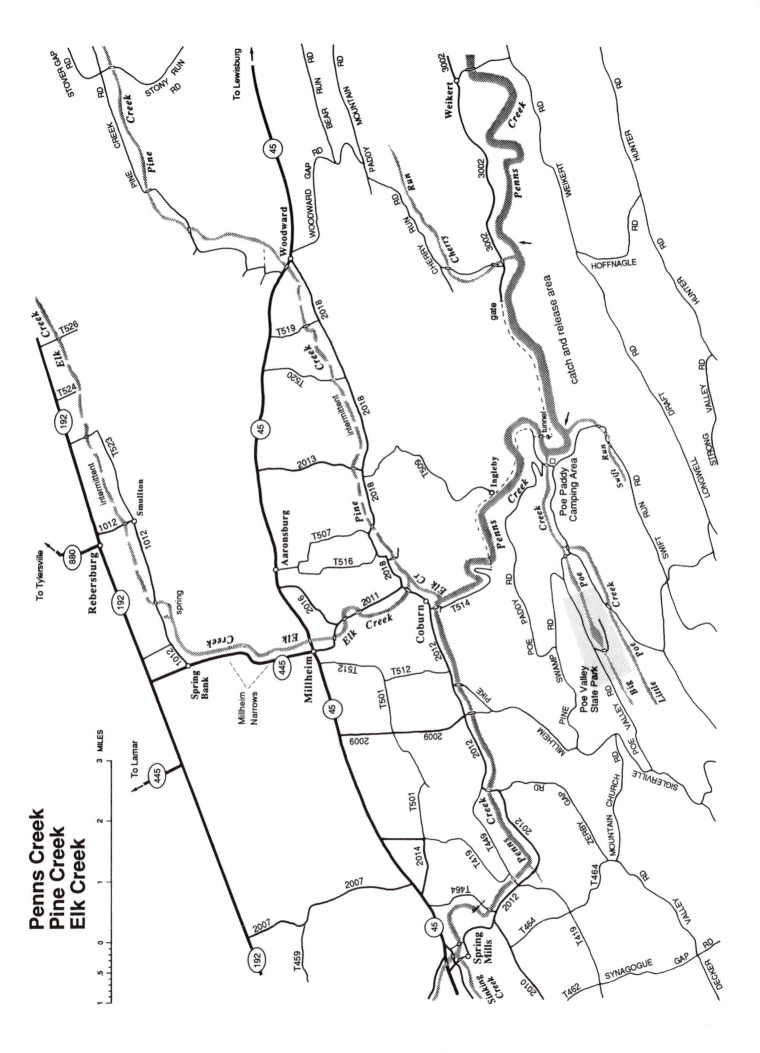

Penns Creek
Pine Creek
Elk Creek

From Spring Mills to Coburn, a distance of about 7 miles, Penns Creek flows slowly past farms, meadows, and scattered houses. Trees shade some of this stretch, but other areas are unshaded. Many anglers frequent this part of Penns Creek in the early season, but few people fish here later than Memorial Day weekend.

A fair number of wild and holdover brown trout are found in the Spring Mills-to-Coburn stretch, but water temperatures become quite warm here in midsummer and the fishing slows. Because there are several posted properties in this stretch, the Fish Commission stocks trout preseason only.

Coburn to Catch-and-Release Area

At Coburn, Elk Creek flows into Penns Creek and provides it with a healthy supply of cool spring water. This greatly improves the water quality, and the stretch below Coburn holds good numbers of wild and holdover trout. A gravel road (T514) follows the creek downstream from Coburn 1.5 miles before ending at a small parking lot. The stretch along this road has several deep pools that sometimes produce big browns. From the parking lot, you can walk across a footbridge and continue down along the creek on an old railroad grade that has been converted into a walking path. From here to Poe Paddy, Penns Creek flows through a wooded area with little development other than a group of cabins at Ingleby.

If you walk across the footbridge from the parking area and walk 100 yards or so down along the railroad grade, you may notice a hiking trail leading to the left. This trail makes a short but steep climb up to an overlook. The view of the Penns Creek valley from here is spectacular and well worth the hike.

To drive to Poe Paddy from Coburn, you must negotiate some mountain roads. The best bet is to take the Siglerville-Millheim Pike (a gravel road for most of its length, despite its name) over the mountain, then turn left on Poe Valley Road and follow it past Poe Valley State Park to Poe Paddy Camping Area. You can also take Pine Swamp Road and Poe Paddy Road, but these are narrow, rough roads.

The Poe Paddy area can also be reached from Route 322 (not shown on the map). Between Potters Mills and Milroy, Route 322 crosses over the long, steep Seven Mountains grade. On the north side (Potters Mills side) of the crest of the grade, there are signs directing you to Poe Valley State Park.

Catch-and-Release Area

At the Poe Paddy campground, a parking area next to the bridge over Big Poe Creek provides good access to this little freestone stream and to Penns Creek. You can fish from here down into the catch-and-release stretch, but there's not much of a trail along this side. To reach the north side of Penns Creek, drive through the Poe Paddy campground and follow the road to a group of cabins. Park here as best you can without blocking any cabin drives, then walk across an old railroad bridge and through a tunnel under Paddy Mountain. On the other side of the tunnel, an old railroad grade that has been converted into a walking path follows Penns Creek through the catch-and-release area.

The catch-and-release area is 3.9 miles long and extends from Swift Run downstream to below Cherry Run. All fish must be released and only flies or artificial lures with barbless hooks may be used. No trout are stocked in this stretch, but a very good population of wild brown trout is found here. Trout from 12 to 14 inches are common and 15- and 16-inchers are caught occasionally.

No roads follow the stream in this beautiful area, and no buildings line the banks, except for a Fish Commission field station. The fishing is not always easy in the catch-and-release area, but the scenic surroundings never fail to please. Penns Creek is a big stream here, over 80 feet wide, and in the spring the water is deep enough to attract canoeists. Long riffles alternate with deep pools and shallow flats.

The lower end of the catch-and-release water can be reached by taking SR 3002 east from Weikert. About 2.7 miles east of Weikert, there is a small parking area along the stream. The catch-and-release water begins a short distance upstream from here. SR 3002 continues on another 1.3 miles before ending at a gate and a parking area that provides the main access to the catch-and-release stretch.

The lower end of the catch-and-release area can also be reached by driving over a mountain on Woodward Gap Road or Bear Run Road and continuing on Cherry Run Road until it meets SR 3002. Turn right on SR 3002 and you will soon be at the main parking area. It is easy to miss Woodward Gap Road where it turns off from Route 45 near Woodward because it is narrow and poorly marked.

Lower Penns Creek

Stocking resumes below the catch-and-release area, and trout are stocked downstream as far as Glen Iron. A parking area is located beside the bridge at Weikert. The deep holes upstream of Weikert are reputed to produce hefty browns. Weikert is generally considered to be the lower limit of good trout fishing. Below Weikert summer water temperatures become very warm, and finding access is more difficult because of increased numbers of houses and camps along the stream. Fair numbers of smallmouth bass are found in the lower reaches of Penns Creek.

Hatches

Penns Creek has enough insect hatches to baffle and intrigue the most avid angler-entomologists. These hatches include Blue-winged Olives, Grannoms, Hendricksons, Olive Caddis, Sulphurs, Tan

Penns Creek. To reach the upper end of the catch-and-release area, anglers cross this old railroad bridge, then walk through a tunnel under Paddy Mountain.

Caddis, March Browns, Grey Foxes, Green Drakes, Dun Caddis, Light Cahills, Isonychia, and Tricos. When no hatches are on, try drifting stonefly nymphs through some of the faster water. The brown/yellow Perlid patterns are most popular, but dark patterns like the Montana Nymph are also effective.

The catch-and-release area has no closed season, and warm weather can produce good fly fishing as early as mid-March if spring rains haven't muddied the stream. Grannom caddis appear in great numbers on Penns Creek from about April 17 through the end of April.

Green Drakes

The Green Drakes, sometimes called Shad Flies locally, usually appear from the last few days of May through the first week in June. Many anglers journey to Penns Creek over Memorial Day weekend with hopes of fishing the Green Drake hatch. In many years, though, the Green Drake hatch is just beginning on Memorial Day weekend, and the trout are more likely to be feeding on March Browns, Grey Foxes, Isonychia, and Dun Caddis than on Green Drakes. The most reliable time to meet the Green Drake hatch on Penns Creek is during the first few

days of June. Some anglers start in the lower water near Glen Iron and follow the hatch as it progresses upstream to Coburn over a period of about ten days. Few Green Drakes appear upstream from Coburn.

On cool, overcast days, the Drakes often emerge sporadically all day long, but usually the hatching begins in earnest in early evening. As dusk turns to dark, clouds of Green Drake spinners, or Coffin Flies, hover over the stream, and just as it gets too dark to really see what you're doing, these big, white flies hit the water in a blizzard-like flurry. Sometimes this produces a good rise of fish, but often it does not. It is not unusual to see many flies, Drakes and Coffin Flies both, floating down the stream and only an occasional trout rising to meet them. Why this happens is a topic Penns Creek regulars love to argue about, but probably it is because the fish become glutted and just can't eat another fly.

Some anglers believe that most of the Green Drakes are taken underneath the water as emerging nymphs. An old method of fishing the Green Drake hatch is to twitch two or three big Light Cahill wet flies down through the riffles. More modern fly fishers use a variety of nymph and emerger patterns. I have not had much luck with subsurface patterns before or during the Green Drake hatch, but it seems to me that they should work. During several Green Drake hatches, I have had good luck just fishing the water, drifting a Green Drake dry fly through likely places. Some evenings I've caught a half-dozen fish this way, even when few trout were rising. Logic tells me that this technique shouldn't work, but sometimes it does.

After the Green Drake hatch ends, warming water often slows the fishing on Penns Creek. In early July there can be good Trico hatches at dawn and a variety of flies on the water at dusk, including small (#16-22) cream or tan caddis. Fishing in the summer is best in the early morning, at dusk, or in the middle of the night. Night fishing is not permitted in the catch-and-release stretch. Fishing hours there are from one hour before sunrise to one hour after sunset.

During the very hot, dry weather that Pennsylvania often endures in July and August, water temperatures on Penns Creek can exceed 80 degrees, and then fishing is not worthwhile at all. During the drought of 1988, the water temperature just below the catch-and-release area reached 86 degrees. How the trout can even survive such temperatures is somewhat of a mystery. With the cooler temperatures of fall, good fishing returns.

Elk Creek - Centre County
(map: page 107)

Elk Creek flows into Penns Creek at Coburn, giving that famous stream a much needed boost of cool, limestone spring water. Elk Creek is not stocked with hatchery trout, but it offers good fishing for wild brown and brook trout.

The headwaters of Elk Creek originate in Bald Eagle State Forest, about 1.5 miles upstream of Stover Gap Road. (The headwaters are not shown on the map.) Here Elk Creek is a narrow, shallow freestone stream with many small native brook trout. There are a few cabins near the stream in this forested area but little other development. The best way to reach this area is to fish upstream from the bridge on Stover Gap Road. A posted stretch lies just downstream of this bridge.

Below Stover Gap Road, Elk Creek flows another 5 or 6 miles before it begins to sink into the ground near T526 (Fox Gap Road). In this stretch Elk Creek wanders through a rural patchwork of meadows, fields, and woods. A fair number of wild browns and brookies are found here, but it in many places the water is shallow, slow, and suffering from siltation. It is a good idea to ask permission of landowners before fishing in this area because they aren't accustomed to seeing many anglers since stocking ended.

Downstream from T526, Elk Creek is intermittent until a large limestone spring below the SR 1012 bridge near Spring Bank brings it back to full volume. This spring supplies a strong flow of water that keeps Elk Creek running cool all summer long. From the spring down to near the intersection of Route 445 and SR 1012, you'll find lots of small browns and brookies, in about equal numbers.

Between Spring Bank and Millheim, Elk Creek flows through a gap in Brush Mountain called the Millheim Narrows. Here the gradient increases and the stream flows swiftly over rocks and boulders and through several large holes. This stretch holds many wild browns up to 12 inches, and 14-inchers are not uncommon. Brook trout are also found in the Narrows, and indeed the whole way to the mouth, but they are outnumbered by the browns.

From Millheim downstream to the mouth of Pine Creek, Elk Creek flows through pastures interspersed with houses. This part of the creek holds good numbers of wild browns and a few brookies, but access is more difficult than in the Narrows because of houses near the stream.

Pine Creek adds a lot of water to Elk Creek, and below this junction the stream approximately doubles in width. From the confluence of Pine Creek downstream to the mouth on Penns Creek is a short stretch of water, but the long, slow pools here have produced some big brown trout.

Elk Creek's fly hatches include Blue-winged Olives, Sulphurs, and Green Drakes. The Sulphurs are the most productive hatch. The Green Drake hatch is good on the lower part of the creek, from Pine Creek down to the mouth on Penns Creek, but very spotty farther upstream. Between hatches Elk Creek can be a difficult stream, but drifting Muskrat nymphs, Hare's Ear nymphs, or Pheasant Tail nymphs will often produce some trout.

Pine Creek - Centre County
(map: page 107)

Pennsylvania has many Pine Creeks. The one we are discussing here flows into Elk Creek at Coburn a short distance before Elk Creek flows into Penns Creek. This particular Pine Creek is not well known outside of its local area.

From its mouth on Elk Creek upstream 1.5 miles to the SR 2018 bridge, Pine Creek is a typical limestone spring creek, with slow pools and a consistent flow of cool, fertile water. This part of the stream is not stocked, but it holds a fair population of wild brown trout. The best place to park is near the junction with Elk Creek. Not many people fish this stretch of Pine Creek. The trout don't seem to be as plentiful as in Elk Creek or Penns Creek, and they are difficult to catch in this slow, smooth water.

From the SR 2018 bridge upstream to the village of Woodward, much of Pine Creek is intermittent.

Sinks in the underlying limestone formations take the majority of the stream flow underground here. Most of the land along this stretch is posted.

The Fish Commission stocks Pine Creek preseason only from Route 45 at Woodward upstream 5.5 miles to the bridge on Stony Run Road. Scattered posting in this area makes finding access tricky. Pine Creek is a shallow freestone stream here, with a fair population of wild brown and brook trout.

In the unstocked headwaters above Stony Run Road, Pine Creek flows through a wooded area in Bald Eagle State Forest, where it holds plenty of small native brook trout.

Poe Creek - Centre County
(map: page 107)

Poe Creek is a small freestone stream that flows into Penns Creek at the Poe Paddy Camping area. The Fish Commission stocks 3 miles of the stream, from the outlet of Poe Lake downstream to the mouth. Trout are stocked preseason and twice inseason, with the last stocking coming in late May. Poe Lake itself is heavily stocked and heavily fished.

From the outlet of Poe Lake downstream to the confluence of Little Poe Creek, few wild trout are found because of the warming effect of Poe Lake. The cool water flowing in from Little Poe Creek rejuvenates the stream somewhat, and fair numbers of wild browns are found in the lower half of the creek. Little Poe Creek is not stocked. It may hold some wild trout, but it is a very small stream.

Fishing Creek - Clinton County
(trophy trout project, artificials only, 5 miles)
(map: page 112)

Clinton County's Fishing Creek is one of Pennsylvania's finest trout streams. The creek has excellent numbers of wild brown and brook trout and a great variety of fly hatches. Limestone springs and tributary streams flow in along the length of the creek, keeping water temperatures cool and maintaining summer flows.

Fishing Creek is quite different in appearance than the limestone spring creeks of southcentral Pennsylvania, such as the Letort, Big Spring, and Falling Springs. These streams flow slowly through grassy meadows and in many areas have silt bottoms and extensive weedbeds. Fishing Creek looks more like a freestone stream; it flows over a rocky bed and has alternating riffles and pools. In some places Fishing Creek flows through farms and residential areas, but most of the creek is well lined with trees.

An unusual aspect of Fishing Creek is that several sections of the creek are intermittent; that is, they dry up in the summer. In these places the water flows underground into limestone aquifers. Farther downstream, springs bring the water back to the surface. These intermittent stretches are beneficial to the stream because the water flowing underground is cooled and cleansed of silt, and the springs rejuvenate the stream.

Most of Fishing Creek relies on wild trout reproduction to maintain its trout fishery. The only stocked water is the 3-mile stretch from the mouth of Cedar Run downstream to the Route 150 bridge below Mill Hall. Here the Fish Commission stocks trout preseason and twice inseason, with the last stocking coming in late May. Fishing pressure is heavy on this stocked stretch early in the season.

The Narrows

The most popular destination for visiting anglers, and the best place to begin exploring Fishing Creek, is the 5-mile stretch under trophy trout regulations. This stretch begins at the SR 2004 bridge below the Lamar fish hatchery, and extends upstream to a bridge on the Tylersville fish hatchery grounds. This special regulations stretch is commonly called the Narrows because here the creek flows through a narrow valley with steep, wooded slopes rising up from the stream banks. The stream moves quickly here and swift runs alternate with deep pools.

The Narrows stretch is easily accessible. SR 2002 follows the stream and there are numerous parking pulloffs. In the Narrows, Fishing Creek holds an excellent population of wild brown and brook trout. Since the institution of special regulations, trout numbers have approximately doubled. Wild brook trout commonly reach 9 to 10 inches and occasionally 12 inches. Brown trout are plentiful up to 14 inches and 15- and 16-inchers are caught fairly frequently.

Fishing pressure is heavy at times in the Narrows. The Green Drake hatch attracts the largest crowds. At most other times you can find room to fish without great difficulty. Much of the upper part of the Narrows has "No Sunday Fishing" signs. Please respect the landowners wishes; they are very generous to allow access to this great trout water.

Downstream From the Narrows

After you are familiar with the Narrows stretch, you may want to explore some of the rest of the creek. Except for the Narrows and the stocked water around Mill Hall, Fishing Creek is lightly fished and most of the creek holds good numbers of wild trout.

The stretch extending from the bridge at Clintondale downstream to the next bridge, on SR 2004, offers good fishing. There is a short posted section in the middle of the stretch. Brook trout are still common a mile or so below Clintondale, but farther downstream the trout population is dominated by brown trout. Parking is found at the Clintondale bridge.

At the bend in the creek below the SR 2004 bridge, there is a sink and here Fishing Creek flows

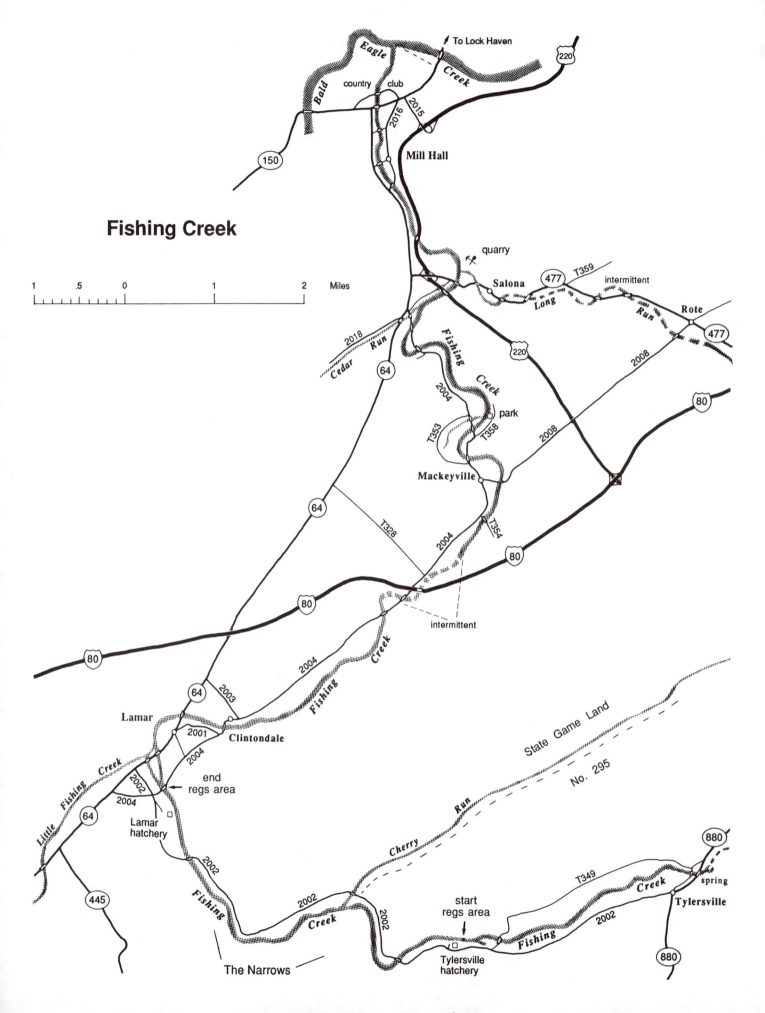

Fishing Creek

underground in dry weather. About halfway between the I-80 bridge and T354 (Rag Valley Road), there is a small spring that keeps some water flowing below it year around, but Fishing Creek doesn't reach full strength again until larger springs add their flow near Mackeyville.

Good fishing for wild browns and the occasional wild brook trout is found from Mackeyville downstream to Mill Hall. A good access point is the small park on T358 (Belle Spring Road). Most bridges also provide access.

A nice pool is located at the mouth of Cedar Run. Cedar Run is a fair-sized limestone spring creek, but much of it is posted, and it suffers terribly from siltation. No trout are stocked and wild brown trout are present but not abundant.

Parking is available at the Route 477 bridge near Salona, and there's a nice stretch of pools and deep runs from here downstream to the Route 220 overpass. I fished this stretch one evening in early June, and trout after trout hit a #10 Hares Ear Nymph. All of them were wild browns. I've fished this stretch several other times without catching a single fish. Trout fishing on Fishing Creek is unpredictable, as it is on most streams. Just downstream from the Route 220 overpass, a gravel lane turns off from Route 64 and parallels the stream, providing easy access.

In Mill Hall a portion of the stream has been channelized, and fishing pressure is very heavy early in the year, but even here some trout can be found year around.

From below Mill Hall to its mouth on Bald Eagle Creek, Fishing Creek does not seem to hold a great many trout, but local anglers consider this lower water a good stretch for trophy browns. Downstream of the Route 150 bridge, there are several deep, slow pools; then the creek flows through a country club's golf course, where fishing is prohibited. Below the golf course, Fishing Creek flows through a wooded stretch and then into Bald Eagle Creek. Bald Eagle Creek is essentially a warmwater stream here, inhabited by bass, carp, and muskies, but some anglers claim that big browns are caught in Bald Eagle Creek right at the mouth of Fishing Creek and even downstream as far as the Route 150 bridge.

I've done some fishing in lower Fishing Creek, near its mouth, and I managed to catch a big carp on a #14 Elk Hair Caddis, but the big browns eluded me. To reach the mouth of Fishing Creek, you can walk up along the banks of Bald Eagle Creek from the Route 150 bridge, or you can park a little way west of the bridge and walk in along a power line.

Upstream From the Narrows

Upstream from the Narrows, above the Tylersville hatchery, Fishing Creek is considerably smaller than below the hatchery. The springs that feed the hatchery also add a lot of water to the creek. From the Tylersville hatchery upstream to a spring above the Route 880 bridge near Tylersville, Fishing Creek is shallow and slow. This stretch carries water most of the time, but during very dry periods the flow dwindles, leaving a series of unconnected pools. Fair numbers of mostly small brown and brook trout are found here.

The stretches above Tylersville are not shown on the map. From Tylersville upstream to near Eastville, Fishing Creek flows through a broad farming valley. In this valley the stream sinks in some sections and flows above ground in others. Even the sections that flow year around are slow moving and do not seem to be flowing at full volume, probably because much of the water is carried underground in limestone aquifers. Some wild brown and brook trout can be found in this part of the stream, but they are not nearly as plentiful as in the Narrows. It is best to get permission from landowners before venturing onto private farms in this area.

From near Eastville upstream to the headwaters, Fishing Creek is a small, freestone brook trout stream that flows through a remote wooded area. Some anglers reach this upper stretch from the rest area on Interstate 80.

Hatches

Fishing Creek has a great assortment of fly hatches, including Blue-winged Olives, Blue Quills, Grannoms, Hendricksons, Olive Caddis, Sulphurs, March Browns, Grey Foxes, Green Drakes, Light Cahills, Isonychia, and Tricos. The Green Drake hatch is very heavy in the Narrows and attracts many fly fishers. The fishing can be very good during the Green Drake hatch, but as on Penns Creek, there are many times when the flies swarm in the air and on the water and few fish rise to meet them.

Nymph fishing is often the best way to catch trout on Fishing Creek. Try weighted Hare's Ear Nymphs in sizes 10 to 16. Sculpin imitations and stonefly nymphs are also effective and sometimes tempt the larger fish. The Grannom caddis hatch is very heavy on Fishing Creek and occurs at the same time as on Penns Creek, from about April 17 through the end of April. Blue Quills are also a reliable early season hatch on Fishing Creek.

Cherry Run - Clinton County
(map: page 112)

Cherry Run is an unstocked freestone stream that flows into the Narrows stretch of Fishing Creek. If you like brushy, wilderness brook trout streams, you will like Cherry Run. This stream holds a good brook trout population, and brown trout are occasionally caught in the lower part of the creek. Cherry Run carries a surprisingly large volume of water—much more than most typical little freestone brook trout streams. Excellent shading from surrounding trees and brush keeps Cherry Run's water temperature cool all summer long.

A parking area is located on the west side of the SR 2002 bridge. East of the bridge, you'll find a gated access road that follows Cherry Run upstream for several miles. Much of the stream is heavily brushed in with rhododendron, so you'll have to work for your fish. There is some private land near the mouth of Cherry Run, but most of the stream flows through State Game Land No. 295. The Western Pennsylvania Conservancy deserves a great deal of credit for their substantial role in preserving this 12,670-acre tract of forested wilderness.

Fishing Creek in the Narrows.

Little Fishing Creek - Centre and Clinton Counties

(map: page 112)

Little Fishing Creek is stocked with trout from its mouth on Fishing Creek at Lamar upstream to near Hublersburg. (Only the lower part of the creek is shown on the Fishing Creek map.) Route 64 parallels this stocked stretch. The Fish Commission stocks trout preseason and once inseason.

Although the stocked stretch of Little Fishing is fed by limestone springs, few wild trout are found here. Unfortunately, the stream has been damaged by siltation, eroded banks, and the channelization of some stretches.

From Hublersburg upstream to a sinkhole near Hecla Park (Mingoville), the streambed is completely dry much of the year. Upstream from Hecla Park (Mingoville), Little Fishing Creek is a freestone stream with good fishing for small native brook trout. This upper stretch is in Bald Eagle State Forest.

Long Run - Clinton County

(map: page 112)

Long Run is a small stream that flows into lower Fishing Creek near Salona. The Fish Commission stocks about 5 miles of water, from Rote upstream to near an old CCC bridge, where Long Run is formed by the junction of Pepper Run and Washburn Run. (Most of the stocked water on Long Run is not shown on the map, but finding access is easy because the entire stream is paralleled by Route 477.)

Trout are stocked prior to opening day and twice inseason, with the last stocking coming in late May. The stocked stretch of Long Run rushes through a narrow, steep-sided ravine. Long Run holds a good population of wild brown and brook trout. Pepper Run and Washburn Run also hold native brook trout.

Near Rote, Long Run begins to sink, and the channel is intermittent from here downstream to Salona. Limestone springs revive the stream a short distance above its mouth on Fishing Creek.

Spring Creek - Centre County

(no kill zone, from SR 3010 bridge at Oak Hall to mouth)

(Fisherman's Paradise – no harvest, fly fishing only, 1 mile)

(map: page 117)

Spring Creek is a large limestone spring creek with an interesting if not always cheery history. Theodore Gordon fished Spring Creek in the early days of trout fishing in this country, and in his time the stream was noted for its brook trout fishery. The introduced brown trout later replaced the brook trout, and Spring Creek gained a national reputation for its big browns and great fly hatches. The excellent fishing attracted such well-known fishermen as Ray Bergman, John Alden Knight, Charles Wetzel, and Edward Hewitt.

The stretch known as Fisherman's Paradise was particularly famous. This was one of the first experiments in the use of special regulations. Only fly fishing with barbless hooks was permitted. In the early days two large trout could be taken daily, and later complete catch-and-release fishing was instituted.

Fisherman's Paradise was heavily stocked with large trout, and great crowds of anglers lined the banks. George Harvey, fly fishing innovator and author of *Techniques of Trout Fishing and Fly Tying*, introduced many people to fly tying and fly fishing at Fisherman's Paradise before going on to instruct thousands more at Penn State University.

In the mid-1950's Spring Creek became severely polluted by sewage effluent, and even though stocking continued much of the stream was plagued with excessive weed growth and low oxygen levels in the summer months. Siltation from farming, road building, and construction, and pollution from gasoline spills and Kepone and Mirex releases added to the damage. Wild trout populations were low along most of the length of the stream.

In 1981 all stocking was discontinued and a no-kill policy was enacted because of the health dangers of eating fish contaminated with Kepone and Mirex. Since then the trout population has increased tremendously, and presently fishing for wild brown trout is excellent. Many water quality problems remain, but there have been some improvements made in sewage treatment. All fish must still be released from Oak Hall downstream to the mouth because of the persistence of Kepone and Mirex.

According to stream studies conducted in 1988 and 1989, brown trout populations along nearly the entire length of Spring Creek exceed the 36 pounds per acre standard that the Fish Commission uses to define Class A wild brown trout waters. Some stream sections had over 200 pounds of trout per acre, which is very good indeed.

Particularly satisfying is the large average size of the Spring Creek fish. Trout from 12 to 14 inches are very common and 15- to 16-inch fish are caught frequently. If you spend much time along the banks of Spring Creek, you will hear some amazing stories about really big fish, and at least some of these stories are true. I have heard many stories about 25- to 27-inch fish, and although I've never caught one of these monsters, I did see a fisherman catch (and measure) a heavy 25-inch brown. Several anglers have told me of a brown trout that measured over 30 inches. Many of these really large trout seem to be caught near the hatchery at Fisherman's Paradise or the hatchery at Benner Springs, so some of these whoppers may be brood fish that found their way from the hatcheries into the stream.

Headwaters

Stream conditions vary greatly along the length of Spring Creek. From the headwaters above Boalsburg downstream to the junction with Cedar Run, Spring Creek is a small stream about 10 to 15 feet wide. (This stretch is not shown on map.) Fair numbers of wild brown trout are found in this stretch, but in some places the stream goes dry in midsummer. From the junction with Cedar Run downstream to the bridge above Nadigs Quarry at Oak Hall, Spring Creek is posted against trespassing.

Nadigs Quarry to Route 26

From the bridge above Nadigs Quarry down through Lemont to the Route 26 bridge, Spring Creek is of moderate size, about 18 to 25 feet wide, and it holds a very good brown trout population. Most of this stretch is open to fishing, but there is a short posted property near the middle of this stretch.

Near the quarry Spring Creek is narrow and brushy, and the trout are very skittish. Spring Creek holds plenty of trout through Lemont, but many houses line the stream in this area. About 1 mile east of the Rt. 26 bridge, opposite the Nittany Mall, you will find Flyfisher's Paradise, a good source for fly fishing gear and information about Spring Creek.

Route 26 to Benner Springs

The section of Spring Creek from Route 26 downstream to the Benner Springs hatchery has the most serious water quality problems and the lowest trout population. Consequently, this water is fished the least, and some Spring Creek regulars like to fish here to escape fishing pressure on other parts of the creek. The section below the UAJA sewage plant has experienced several fish kills.

Benner Springs to Fisherman's Paradise

Spring Creek is rejuvenated by springs near the Benner Springs hatchery, and good fishing can be found along the hatchery property. More rainbow trout are found here than in other parts of the creek, probably as a result of trout escaping from the hatchery. The road leading to Benner Springs is gated. The gate is open between 6:30 A.M. and 9 P.M. from April 15 to September 30, and between 6:30 A.M. and 6 P.M. from October 1 to April 14.

From Benner Springs down to Fisherman's Paradise, Spring Creek flows through a wooded area owned by the Rockview State Penitentiary. A dirt road provides good walking access, but motorized vehicles are prohibited. The trout population here is moderate by Spring Creek standards. You will find more trout here than in the Route 26 to Benner Springs stretch, but not as many as in some other parts of the creek. This stretch is not fished very hard and it is the least developed, most "woodsy" part of Spring Creek.

Fisherman's Paradise

Fisherman's Paradise doesn't draw the huge crowds it once did, but it is still the first stop for most anglers new to the stream, and there are few days during the year when someone doesn't cast a line here. The regulations in this 1-mile stretch allow only fly fishing with barbless hooks, and all fish must be released. Trout are no longer stocked, but the Paradise holds both wild trout and hatchery escapees.

The great attraction of the Paradise is its ease of access. The Paradise is owned by the Fish Commission, and you can drive in, park your car at one of the parking areas, and stroll the grassy banks with fly rod in hand. Much of the Paradise is open enough to allow easy casting, and wading is prohibited, so fishing boots aren't necessary. The flat, slow-moving stretches behind the numerous dams and deflectors are good places to try your fine-and-far-off dry fly skills on sophisticated trout.

Midges often bring trout to the surface here, and ant imitations work very well in the summer months. When the trout aren't rising, a small Pheasant Tail Nymph or cress bug imitation can be used to sightfish for nymphing trout.

Aside from the fishing, the Paradise is also a pleasant place to picnic, visit the Bellefonte Hatchery, or just go for a walk. I recommend that you not spend all of your time at the Paradise, though. Too many anglers fish only this stretch and miss out on the rewarding fishing found on other parts of the creek.

Fisherman's Paradise to Route 550

Springs near Fisherman's Paradise and other springs farther downstream increase the volume and improve the water quality of Spring Creek, and the stretch from the Paradise downstream to Route 550 has an excellent trout population.

Just downstream from Fisherman's Paradise, Spring Creek flows through the popular cabin stretch, where there are many wild trout and also quite a few hatchery escapees.

About 1 mile of the stream, from Route 550 upstream to the sharp bend in the creek, had been posted for several years, but it was purchased by the Pennsylvania Fish Commision in December 1992, assuring public access to this enjoyable stretch of Spring Creek.

Route 550 to Bellefonte

From the Route 550 bridge downstream to Bellefonte, Spring Creek flows past houses, businesses, and brushy patches of trees. The trout population in this section does not seem to be as high as in the Fisherman's Paradise to Route 550 stretch, but it is still quite good.

Spring Creek
Bald Eagle Creek

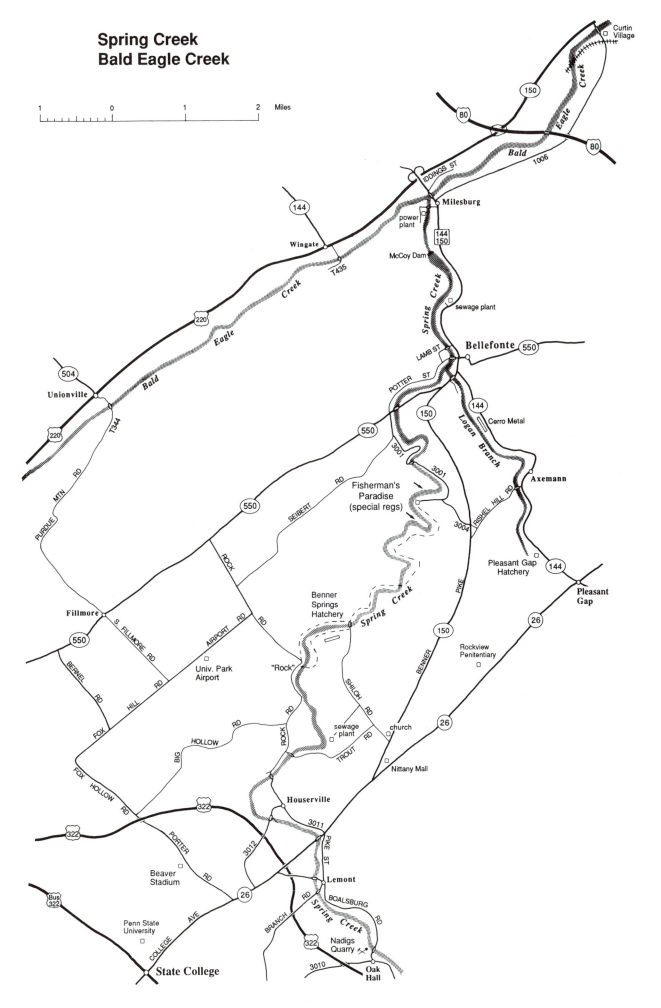

Just below the mouth of Logan Branch, there is a long, flat pool that offers challenging dry fly fishing. Upstream from here, the stream flows past Centre Oil and Gas and the SMS Sutton factory. Just upstream from the factory is a wooded stretch about a quarter-mile in length that is owned by Bellefonte Borough. A large pulloff along Potter Street provides access to this stretch.

In Bellefonte, an exhibition area where no trout fishing is allowed extends from the railroad bridge just above Talleyrand Park downstream to the Lamb Street bridge. Here large trout stocked by local businesses and flocks of ducks compete for pellets and bread thrown by picnickers.

Bellefonte to Mouth

Spring Creek is big water from Bellefonte downstream to the mouth at Milesburg. Much of Spring Creek can be waded with hip boots, but waders are recommended for this lower stretch. Logan Branch and the Big Spring in Bellefonte add a lot of cold spring water to the creek. This additional water also keeps water temperatures cool in the lower reaches.

The Bellefonte-to-Milesburg stretch held few trout when the Fish Commission surveyed the stream in 1980, but the fishing is very good now and stream surveys in 1988 and 1989 showed that the trout population has increased tremendously.

Good access is provided by a gravel lane that turns off Route 144, just above the Bellefonte sewage plant. Another good place to park is above an old power plant in Milesburg. From the small dam beside the power plant upstream to the larger McCoy Dam, you will find a few short, swift riffles and many long, flat pools that come alive with trout during a Sulphur or Trico hatch. Behind McCoy dam there is a long, shallow, silted stretch that seems to hold few trout. A large, heavily fished junction pool is located at the confluence of Spring Creek and Bald Eagle Creek.

Hatches

Spring Creek does not have many of the classic mayfly hatches. You are not likely to see any Quill Gordons, Hendricksons, March Browns, Grey Foxes, or Green Drakes here. Spring Creek once had a good Green Drake hatch, but pollution has eliminated it. Spring Creek does have good hatches of Blue-winged Olives, Sulphurs, Olive Caddis, Tan Caddis, Light Cahills, and Tricos.

Good midge fishing can be found throughout the year, even during warm spells in February and early March. I've had good luck with the Griffith's Gnat pattern on midge-sipping trout. The original Griffith's Gnat calls for a body of peacock herl, palmered with grizzly hackle. Substituting grey, black, or green dubbing for the peacock herl also produces effective midge imitations. Terrestrial patterns, particularly ants, are effective in the summer and fall.

The Sulphur hatch is the big fly fishing event on Spring Creek. Most fly hatch references list the Sulphur hatch as beginning in mid-May and lasting into mid-June, but I have seen good hatches as early as April 29 and very heavy hatches as early as May 3. These early Sulphurs are larger than the later Sulphurs (a #14 imitation is best), and they hatch most heavily between 3 and 5 in the afternoon. Some anglers call these early mayflies Pale Evening Duns rather than Sulphurs.

The Sulphurs that begin hatching in mid-May are smaller (#16), and the action is usually heaviest right at dusk. Some of the Sulphurs that hatch in June are even smaller, and are best imitated with #18 flies. Sulphurs appear most heavily in May and June, but they also appear sporadically all summer and even into early September. The term Sulphur is used loosely on Spring Creek to describe several different yellow-bodied mayfly species. If you carry Sulphur imitations in sizes 14, 16, and 18, it's not necessary to know the exact genus and species.

The problem is in deciding what Sulphur patterns to use. The trout can be very choosy during the Sulphur hatch, and this has led to a great profusion of different patterns, including standard hackled flies, cut-wing thorax patterns, no-hackles, parachutes patterns, and compara duns, all of which are capable of fooling some of the trout some of the time, but none of which seems to be consistently effective. The problem may be that the trout are more often taking emerging nymphs right at the surface than the fully emerged duns.

A simple emerger can be tied with a pale yellow dubbed body and a short wing of light grey-blue muskrat fur. One afternoon in early spring, I stood in one spot and caught a dozen trout and raised many more with this fly and was foolish enough to think that this solved the Sulphur problem. The next day I used the same fly and caught not a single fish, while the trout rose all around me. This sort of experience keeps trout fishing interesting.

Nymph fishing can be very effective before and during Sulphur hatches. I often fish two or three nymphs at a time, and one evening before the Sulphur hatch began, I hooked a 9-inch and a 14-inch fish on the same cast. I had always thought this was something that happened only in the overheated imaginations of fishing writers.

The Trico hatch provides good fishing on Spring Creek, and it doesn't attract a great many anglers. The Tricos begin hatching around July 1 and hatch daily through the summer and into late October. The hatch usually occurs between 7:00 and 10:00 in the morning and begins early in warm weather and late in cool weather. The Tricos do not hatch heavily on all of Spring Creek. The Benner Springs area, for example, has few Tricos, but there are good hatches

Spring Creek. Casting a long line for rising trout at Fisherman's Paradise.

from Fisherman's Paradise to the mouth. Trout rise most readily for these tiny mayflies in the slow, flat sections of the stream.

When the trout aren't rising, nymph fishing with Muskrat Nymphs, Green Caddis Larvae, Hare's Ear Nymphs, Pheasant Tail Nymphs, and imitations of sowbugs and scuds often produces good results. Sowbugs are very abundant in the middle stretches of Spring Creek, and scuds are plentiful in the upper and lower stretches. Muskrat Nymphs, weighted and roughly dubbed, with no unnecessary embellishments such as wings, tails, or hackle, are the most popular nymphs on Spring Creek.

Although the fishing is now excellent on Spring Creek, the stream's water quality and wild trout fishery are threatened by continuing population growth and all of its problems: increased runoff from roads and parking lots, siltation from construction, depletion of springs by pumping from wellfields, and increased volume of sewage effluent. Hopefully, proper conservation measures will be taken to preserve Spring Creek, but if you're the pessimistic sort, enjoy the fishing now while it's still available.

Logan Branch - Centre County
(map: page 117)

Logan Branch is a limestone spring creek that begins near the Pleasant Gap fish hatchery and flows north to meet Spring Creek at Bellefonte. At first glance the stream looks very small, but even though it is narrow, it has deep holes and carries a large volume of water. Route 144 closely parallels Logan Branch, and there are numerous small parking pulloffs along the road used by anglers. Logan Branch clears more quickly than Spring Creek after heavy rains, so it provides a good alternative when Spring Creek is high and muddy.

The Fish Commission stocks trout preseason and twice inseason, with the last stocking coming in late May. Fishing pressure is very heavy soon after stocking, and there are a few skilled anglers who catch trout here in all seasons of the year, including the middle of the winter.

Logan Branch has a good population of wild brown trout, and it is especially noted for producing big trout, from 18 inches up to 24 inches. The stream

Logan Branch. This tributary to Spring Creek holds some large browns, but they are difficult to catch.

is difficult to fish, though, and most fly fishers will enjoy fishing on nearby Spring Creek more than on Logan Branch.

If you want to catch one of Logan Branch's big browns, you should be prepared to put in a lot of hours fishing and getting to know the stream. There is very little dry fly water here; most of the stream consists of swift riffles and short, deep pools. Brush and trees line the banks, so about the only way to approach this water is to wade and fish directly up-stream, and the wild browns are easily spooked.

Another reason many anglers prefer to fish Spring Creek is that Logan Branch is not a very pretty stream—numerous homes and businesses are located along its banks. About one-half mile of the stream flows through the Cerro Metal factory, which is a large brass foundry.

The main fly hatches are Blue-winged Olives and Sulphurs, but Logan Branch trout take most of their food underwater. Weighted Muskrat Nymphs and sculpin imitations are the most popular fly patterns. My best luck on Logan Branch has been with a weighted marabou muddler, mottled olive-brown in color, tied with a fur head instead of a deer hair head to allow it to sink quickly.

Bald Eagle Creek - Centre County
(map: page 117)

Trout are stocked in 27 miles of Bald Eagle Creek, from the village of Hannah, near the headwa-ters, downstream to the backwaters of Sayers Dam at Bald Eagle State Park. (Only part of the stream is shown on the map.) The Fish Commission stocks trout prior to opening day and once inseason, in mid-May. The Hanna-to-Port Matilda section is stocked preseason only.

The upper part of Bald Eagle Creek, from Han-nah downstream to the junction with Spring Creek at Milesburg, is a low-gradient, marginal stream that gets very warm and low in midsummer and holds few wild trout. Only a few places near springs or below tributaries hold trout all year. This stretch is very popular in the early season, though, and opening day finds the banks crowded with anglers. In midsummer you are more likely to catch smallmouth bass than trout in the upper part of Bald Eagle Creek.

At Milesburg, Spring Creek flows in and com-pletely changes the character of Bald Eagle Creek. When water levels are high early in the year, Spring Creek and Bald Eagle are about equal in size where they meet. In midsummer, when the upper Bald Eagle slows to a trickle, perhaps 80% of the water flowing downstream from the junction is contributed by Spring Creek. The lower stretch of Spring Creek maintains a strong flow of cool water even in the hottest, driest summers, and this cool water greatly improves conditions in lower Bald Eagle Creek.

The 3-mile stretch from Milesburg downstream to the bridge at Curtin Village flows cool all summer long, and trout can be found here year around, although only a few dedicated anglers fish here after the early season. This stretch does not contain nearly as many trout as Spring Creek, but it is known locally for producing large browns. The big pools and long riffles here provide excellent holding habitat for trout, but the trout population is probably limited by lack of spawning habitat and by fishing pressure.

At Milesburg you can park at the municipal building near the Route 150 bridge. To start a little farther downstream, cross the Route 150 bridge, drive down Iddings Street past a factory, and park along the stream bank. The bridge at Curtin Village provides good access to the lower end of this stretch.

Very few people fish the Curtin Village-to-Sayers Dam stretch after the early season, but this water may also hold some big browns. Even in this lower stretch, water temperatures never get too warm for trout. Water temperatures here rarely exceed 70 degrees, even on scorchingly hot days in late July. By comparison, Penns Creek, which holds a good population of trout year around, often has summer water temperatures exceeding 80 degrees.

The upper part of Bald Eagle Creek, upstream from Milesburg, has decent fly hatches, including Hendricksons, Grey Foxes, and a variety of caddis. A good hatch of Hendricksons appeared on opening day (April 14) in 1990, but very few trout rose for them.

The trout had been stocked just the day before and were probably not yet accustomed to feeding on aquatic insects.

The lower water, below Milesburg, has hatches similar to those on Spring Creek, such as Sulphurs, Olive Caddis, and Tricos. Fly hatches are generally not as heavy as on Spring Creek, though, and perhaps the best way to tempt the big browns is with big flies such as Zonkers, Wooly Buggers, or sculpin imitations. Night fishing also produces some large browns. I once hooked a very large fish on a sculpin imitation in lower Bald Eagle Creek, but it promptly broke off my 5x leader tippet, which I had foolishly neglected to change after fishing a caddis hatch. A skeptical fishing buddy told me that maybe this big fish was a carp and maybe it was. Maybe.

White Deer Creek - Union and Centre Counties
(delayed harvest, fly fishing only, 3.1 miles)
(map: page 121)

On the lower 3 or 4 miles of White Deer Creek, you will find houses along the banks, but the rest of the stream flows through a heavily wooded area, much of which is state forest land. White Deer Creek is a tea-colored freestone stream with a fair number of wild brown and brook trout in addition to stocked fish. The Fish Commission stocks trout preseason and three times inseason, with the last stocking coming in early June.

A 3.1-mile delayed-harvest, fly-fishing-only area begins at the bridge on Cooper Mill Road and extends upstream to the Union/Centre County line. The stream is fairly small here, with gentle riffles and quiet pools. Downed trees provide much of the cover in the stream, and overhanging branches and tag

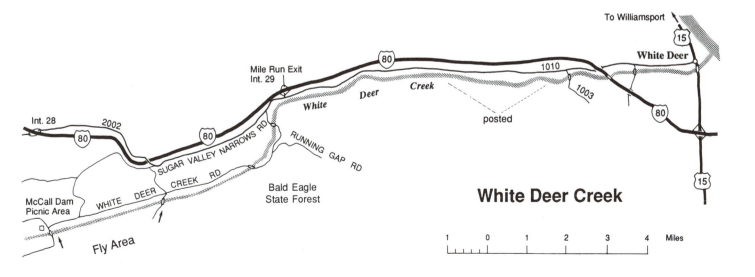

White Deer Creek

White Deer Creek in the fly area.

alders make casting a challenge. White Deer Creek's fly area receives less fishing pressure than many other fly areas in the state.

Above the fly area, White Deer Creek is small and shallow. The Fish Commission stocks this stretch preseason only, from the upper boundary of the fly area upstream 5.5 miles into the headwaters.

Downstream from the fly area, much of the creek is closely paralleled by Route 80, but this area is heavily wooded and the sights and sounds of the highway are largely blocked. About 2.5 miles of the stream has been posted against trespassing by a water supply company.

The lower end of the creek, from the Route 80 bridge downstream to the mouth, has many houses along the banks, and about 2 miles of streambed were channelized after the Hurricane Agnes flood in 1972.

White Deer Creek is a good stream for dry fly fishers because it has some good hatches, including the Green Drake, and even when there are no hatches you can often catch trout by prospecting with a general pattern such as an Adams, Grey Fox Variant, or Elk Hair Caddis. Beetle and cricket patterns work well, also.

Loyalsock Creek - Sullivan and Lycoming Counties
(fly fishing only, 1.4 miles)
(map: page 123)

The Loyalsock is a large stream. In many parts of the country it would be considered a river. Chest waders are helpful here, and caution must be exercised when wading. Fishing on the Loyalsock is mostly for stocked trout, although occasionally large holdover browns are caught, and sometimes wild trout are caught near the mouths of tributary streams. Most trout fishing is done between opening

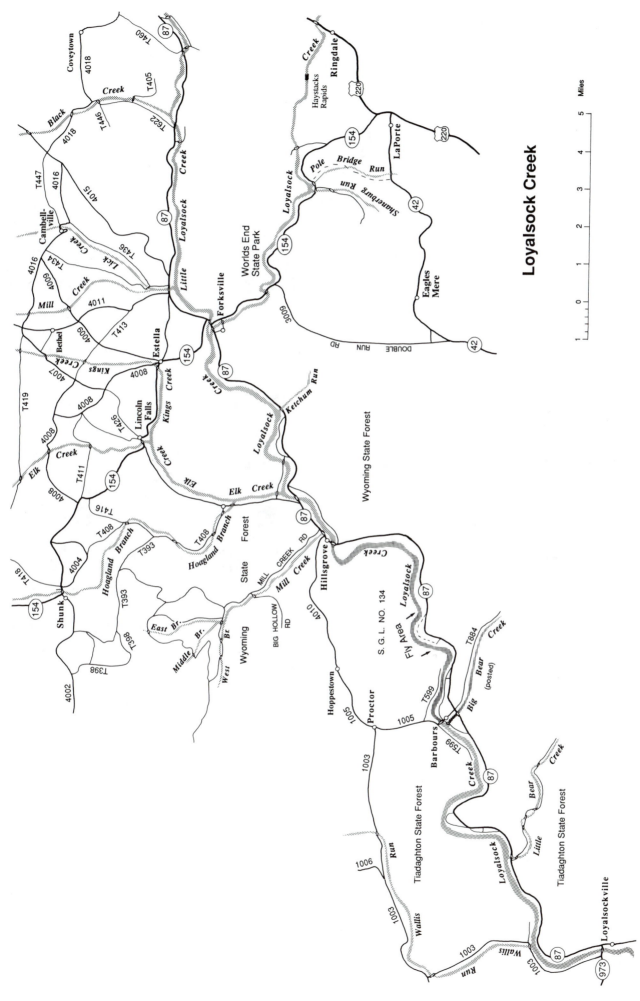

Loyalsock Creek

day and mid-June because later in the summer water temperatures rise. The lower sections of Loyalsock Creek offer fair smallmouth bass fishing.

The Fish Commission stocks trout preseason and twice inseason, with the last stocking coming in mid-May. Spring rains sometimes make water levels very high early in the year, but when water levels are more moderate the Loyalsock is an enjoyable stream to fish on the opening weekend of the season. Because it is such a large stream, and because many stretches are away from immediate road access, you can easily find places to fish without being crowded.

The month of May is the best time to fly fish the Loyalsock. When the season opens, the water is often too high for good fly fishing, and during the summer months, warm water temperatures limit the fishing. During the month of May, the fly hatches are at their peak and water flows are usually moderate. In midsummer you are more likely to find trout in one of the Loyalsock's many tributaries than in the Loyalsock itself.

Loyalsock Creek begins above the village of Lopez, near the Sullivan/Wyoming County line, and flows more than 50 miles before meeting the West Branch of the Susquehanna River near Williamsport. The upper part of the creek is affected by mine drainage and is considered too acidic to stock with trout. Some anglers have reported catching trout in the Ringdale-to-Polebridge Run stretch, particularly near the mouths of tributaries, but they are not abundant here. This remote, beautiful stretch of stream has numerous rapids, and white water boating is popular here and on the rest of Loyalsock Creek in the spring.

Stocking begins at Polebridge Run, which flows into Loyalsock Creek about 3 miles upstream from Worlds End State Park. Trout are stocked downstream as far as Loyalsockville.

From Polebridge Run down through Worlds End State Park to the junction with Little Loyalsock Creek, the Loyalsock flows through a rugged, scenic gorge. In this stretch you will find swift rapids and attractive pools. The entire stretch is paralleled by

Loyalsock Creek above Worlds End State Park.   (Tim Palmer photo)

Route 154. Camping is available at Worlds End State Park, and there are also some fine hiking trails.

At Forksville, Little Loyalsock Creek flows in and increases the size of the Loyalsock. Below Forksville, the valley widens and the stream becomes less swift. You will find pools the length and width of football fields in this area.

From the Lycoming County line downstream 1.4 miles to Sandy Bottom, the Loyalsock is managed under fly-fishing-only regulations. A gravel road turns off Route 87 and leads to a parking area near the lower end of the fly area. The road turns off at a sign reading, "Tiadaghton State Forest, Nature Trail, Sandy Bottom."

From the fly area down to the lower stocking limit, the Route 973 bridge at Loyalsockville, there is some nice trout water, but access becomes more difficult because of the increased number of homes and camps along the stream. There are places where you can get to the stream—you just have to plan a little and check out your access points.

Much of the fly fishing action on Loyalsock Creek is provided by caddis hatches, which can be heavy. Mayfly hatches include Hendricksons, March Browns, Grey Foxes, Isonychia, and Light Cahills.

Wallis Run - Lycoming County
(map: page 123)

Wallis Run flows into Loyalsock Creek a few miles north of Loyalsockville. The Fish Commission stocks trout preseason only. Some places are posted along this stream, but the lower stretches are open and offer good fishing for stocked trout and wild browns.

Little Bear Creek - Lycoming County
(map: page 123)

Little Bear Creek flows into Loyalsock Creek 5.2 miles north of Loyalsockville. A state forest road (Huntersville Road) turns off from Route 87 and follows the stream to its headwaters. Most of Little Bear Creek flows through a forested valley in Tiadaghton State Forest, where its riffles and pockets are well shaded by surrounding hemlock trees. Numerous habitat improvement structures have been built along the stream. Trout are stocked from the mouth upstream 4 miles to Red Run. Little Bear Creek also holds a fair population of both wild brown and brook trout.

Mill Creek - Sullivan County
(map: page 123)

There are several Mill Creeks in the Loyalsock drainage. This particular Mill Creek flows into Loyalsock Creek at the village of Hillsgrove. The stream originates in Wyoming State Forest and flows about 4 miles through a forested area before meeting the Loyalsock.

Mill Creek is stocked from its mouth upstream 2.8 miles to the bridge on Big Hollow Road. About half this stretch is privately owned and about half is in state forest lands. The stream flows here through a deep, narrow, heavily forested valley. Mill Creek Road parallels the stream high on the hillside above it. There are several steep trails that lead down to the stream. The Fish Commission stocks trout preseason and once again inseason, in late April. In addition to these stocked fish, Mill Creek holds a fair population of wild brown and brook trout.

Mill Creek is not stocked above Big Hollow Road, but the upper part of the creek flows through Wyoming State Forest and holds fair numbers of wild brown and brook trout. Mill Creek is formed by the West, East, and Middle Branches of Mill Creek, all of which are tiny, woodland streams that are worth a try for native brook trout.

Elk Creek - Sullivan County
(map: page 123)

Elk Creek flows into Loyalsock Creek above Hillsgrove. Trout are stocked from the mouth upstream 4.5 miles to the Route 154 bridge at Lincoln Falls. Above Lincoln Falls the stream is posted by a private club. The Fish Commission stocks trout preseason and also twice inseason. In addition to stocked trout, Elk Creek has a fair population of wild brown trout and also a few native brookies.

Most of the stream flows through woods, but there are some open areas near the mouth. This lower water is wide and shallow and has little cover for trout, so it doesn't provide as good fishing as the upper part of the creek.

Hoagland Branch - Sullivan County
(map: page 123)

This small tributary to Elk Creek flows through a forested area and offers good fishing for both stocked trout and wild trout. Good fishing can be found here even in the summer and fall. Hoagland Branch is stocked from its mouth upstream 7.5 miles to the Route 154 bridge at Shunk. The Fish Commission stocks trout preseason and twice inseason, with the last stocking coming in late May. Hoagland Branch ranges from 12 to 25 feet in width, and its pockets and small pools hold good numbers of wild brown and brook trout all along the length of the stream.

Much of the lower part of the stream flows through Wyoming State Forest. The upper part of the creek flows through privately owned woodlands.

Kings Creek - Sullivan County
(map: page 123)

Kings Creek is a small stream that meets Elk Creek at Lincoln Falls. The Fish Commission stocks trout prior to opening day but makes no inseason stockings. The many houses along the banks of this stream and several scattered posted stretches create access difficulties.

Ketchum Run - Sullivan County
(map: page 123)

Ketchum Run is a small, unstocked wilderness stream that flows into Loyalsock Creek about 3 miles south of Forksville. There is some private property near the mouth, but the rest of the stream flows through Tiadaghton State Forest. Ketchum Run holds good numbers of wild brook trout.

Little Loyalsock Creek - Sullivan County
(map: page 123)

The Little Loyalsock is the largest tributary to Loyalsock Creek, which it meets at Forksville. Trout are stocked in this medium-sized stream from its mouth upstream 10 miles to near the village of Dushore. (The upper reaches are not shown on the map.) Route 87 follows the stream along this stretch. The land along the stream is all privately owned and scattered posting makes finding access difficult in some places. The Fish Commission stocks trout preseason and once inseason.

Little Loyalsock Creek is basically a put-and-take stream with few wild or holdover trout, and the fishing is generally poor in the summer and fall. It has some attractive pools in its middle and lower stretches, though, and for the opening of the trout season this stream can sometimes be a better choice than the main branch of the Loyalsock. Early in the year, the main branch of the Loyalsock often runs too high to wade or fish easily, but the Little Loyalsock is smaller and easier to wade, and it often has good hatches in the early season.

Lick Creek - Sullivan County
(map: page 123)

Lick Creek is a small freestone stream that flows into the lower stretch of Little Loyalsock Creek. Trout are stocked preseason only, from the mouth upstream 4 miles, to just below the Bradford County line. Besides stocked fish, Lick Creek holds good numbers of wild brown trout, and good fishing can be found here even in midsummer. The stream flows through privately owned woodlands, and there are some houses and camps along its banks.

Black Creek - Sullivan County
(map: page 123)

Numerous no-trespassing signs along the banks will discourage many anglers from fishing this tributary to Little Loyalsock Creek. The Fish Commission stocks trout preseason only, from the mouth upstream 3 miles to the SR 4018 bridge. Black Creek holds a fair population of wild brown trout.

Shanerburg Run - Sullivan County
(map: page 123)

Shanerburg Run flows through a dark tunnel of evergreens before meeting Loyalsock Creek about 3

miles east of Worlds End State Park. No trout are stocked in this rocky little stream, but it holds a good population of wild brook trout. The stream is only about 3.7 miles long, and all of it flows through state forest lands except for a short section of private, posted land in the headwaters. A gravel forest road (Shanerburg Road) follows the creek upstream for 1.5 miles. To fish above that point, you must hike in.

Pole Bridge Run - Sullivan County
(map: page 123)

Pole Bridge Run is a small, woodland stream that flows into Loyalsock Creek about 3 miles east of Worlds End State Park. Route 154 crosses near the mouth, and Route 42 crosses about 2.5 miles upstream. Between the roads, the only access is a rough, ankle-busting trail that follows the creek. The Fish Commission stocks trout from the mouth upstream to Route 42. Pole Bridge Run also holds many native brook trout. The lower part of the creek flows through Wyoming State Forest.

Lycoming Creek - Lycoming and Tioga County
(map: page 127)

Lycoming Creek and its tributaries drain much of central Lycoming County. It is not nearly so large a stream as Loyalsock Creek to the east or Pine Creek to the west, but it is a medium-sized stream. The stream originates near the juncture of Lycoming, Tioga, and Bradford Counties, and it flows south about 30 miles before meeting the West Branch of the Susquehanna River at Williamsport.

Lycoming Creek has a limited number of wild and holdover trout because much of the stream is wide and shallow, and because water temperatures rise quickly as the season progresses. From opening day through about the second week in June, though, Lycoming Creek offers decent fishing for stocked trout and fairly good fly hatches. Fish can also be found later in the season in certain places, such as in the upper part of the creek and below the mouths of tributary streams. The Fish Commission stocks trout before opening day and also once inseason, usually in late May or early June.

Route 15 parallels Lycoming Creek north from Williamsport. The Fish Commission stocks trout from Cogan Station, which is about 5 miles north of Williamsport, upstream to the confluence of Roaring Branch. Around Cogan Station there are lots of houses, so you may want to start fishing farther upstream. (This lower water is not shown on the map.)

About 2.5 miles north of Cogan Station, the creek and Route 15 take a sharp bend to the right. Here a road turns off Route 15 to a small collection of cabins

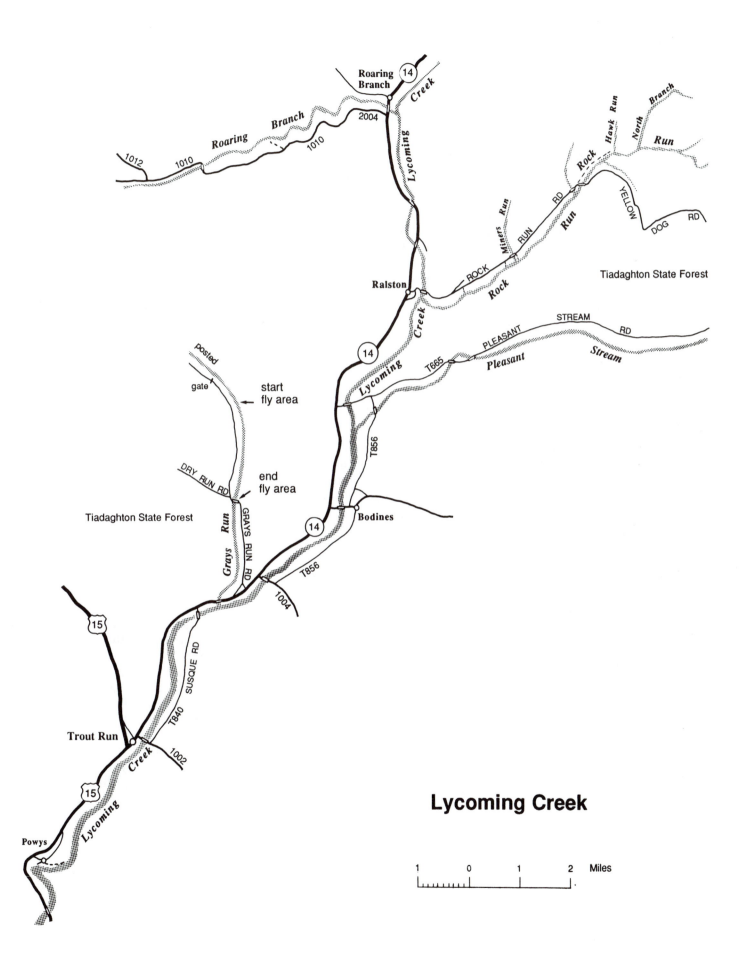

Lycoming Creek

known as Powys. A good place to park here is next to a baseball field. Upstream from the baseball field, there is an attractive, well-shaded stretch of stream.

Continuing north on Route 15, you will soon come to the village of Trout Run. Take Route 14 north from here. About one-half mile north of Trout Run, turn to the right onto a secondary road (SR 1002) and cross the creek. Then take the first left, onto T840 (Susque Road). You can park here along Susque Road, and there are some runs and pools near the bridge and a large pool is located several hundred yards upstream.

One evening I talked to some fishermen who were fishing this big pool with bass plugs in hopes of catching a trophy trout. They said big trout are caught each year in Lycoming Creek, and that many of them are "salters," which are large stocked trout.

Continue up along the creek on Susque Road, and in about 1 mile, at a bend in the road, there is a huge pool. This is a popular fishing spot and also a popular swimming hole in warm weather.

Farther up on Susque Road, you will cross a bridge over Lycoming Creek just before meeting up with Route 14 again. There is parking available at this bridge and good water up or downstream.

Continuing north on Route 14, about 0.3 miles past Susque Road you will cross a small, easy-to-miss bridge over Grays Run. Park to the right just before the bridge. Where Grays Run meets Lycoming Creek, there is a long, flat pool. Because of the cooler water flowing in from Grays Run, trout can be found here late into the season. This is a scenic, forested part of Lycoming Creek, and more deep pools are located upstream from here. This section of Lycoming Creek gets fished rather hard. Grays Run offers good fishing for both wild and stocked trout.

One mile north of Grays Run, there is a fair-sized pool and adequate parking at the SR 1004 bridge. Continuing north on Route 14, there are several pulloffs along the road that provide access to the stream. Some stretches of the stream are wooded here, and there are also some houses and campgrounds near the stream.

At the village of Ralston, turn right and follow a gravel road across the railroad tracks to a bridge on Lycoming Creek. There is good fishing above and below this bridge. Walk a short distance downstream, and you will come to the mouth of Rock Run. This tributary stays cold all summer, and trout can be found below its junction with Lycoming Creek even in midsummer. A little farther downstream, there are some deep glides near an old bridge.

Upstream from Ralston, Lycoming Creek is a small stream, but in this area the water temperature stays cool enough to hold stocked trout into late summer and there are even some wild brown and brook trout. Numerous pulloffs along Route 14 make finding access to the stream easy.

About 3.5 miles above Ralston, Roaring Branch flows into Lycoming Creek. Just above the confluence with Roaring Branch, Lycoming Creek often has a dry streambed in midsummer.

Lycoming Creek's mayfly hatches include Hendricksons, March Browns, Grey Foxes, Green Drakes (sporadic), Brown Drakes (sporadic), and Light Cahills. The water is often low and clear, so careful casting is needed.

Grays Run - Lycoming County
(fly fishing only, 2.2 miles)
(map: page 127)

Grays Run is perhaps the best of the tributaries to Lycoming Creek. This small stream flows through a heavily wooded area and offers good fishing for both stocked trout and wild browns. Some of the stream flows through private property, but much of it flows through Tiadaghton State Forest.

Traveling north on Route 14, you will cross Grays Run about 3 miles north of the intersection with Route 15. The bridge is small and easy to miss. Just before the bridge, there is a pulloff on the right. From here you can fish the short distance down to the mouth on Lycoming Creek. Above the bridge the stream is brushy and narrow, with deep pockets that hold good numbers of wild brown trout. A little farther upstream there are some houses, and a short stretch of the stream is posted.

Just north of the Route 14 bridge, turn left off Route 14 onto Lower Grays Run Road. If you miss this road, take the next left onto Upper Grays Run Road. The roads soon meet and form Grays Run Road, which follows the creek upstream. After passing a stretch of houses along the lower mile of the stream, you will enter the Tiadaghton State Forest. Here you'll find many places to pull off along the road and walk through the woods to the creek.

About 2.2 miles up from the mouth, Grays Run Road crosses over the creek. From this bridge downstream to the mouth, Grays Run is managed as a wild trout stream and no trout are stocked. This lower part of the creek holds many wild brown trout.

From the bridge upstream 2.2 miles, Grays Run is managed under fly-fishing-only regulations. Above the fly area, the stream is owned by the Grays Run Club and is closed to public fishing. The fly area is stocked once each season, prior to opening day. In addition to the stocked trout, the fly area also holds some wild brown and brook trout.

Pleasant Stream - Lycoming County
(map: page 127)

Pleasant Stream is a small tributary to Lycoming Creek that offers pleasant fishing for stocked trout, wild brown trout, and wild brook trout. The Fish

Rock Run, a scenic tributary to Lycoming Creek.

Commission stocks trout from the mouth upstream 9.5 miles to the confluence of North Pleasant Stream (which is upstream of the area shown on the map).

Despite its length, Pleasant Stream never gets very big, and even near the mouth it is little more than a brook. The stream has a moderate gradient and flows over a streambed of clean gravel and rocks. Surrounding trees provide good shade in most places. Pleasant Stream Road parallels the entire length of the creek.

The lower half of Pleasant Stream flows through private land, and cabins and houses are found along the creek. There is some scattered posting here, and there aren't many places to park.

The upper half of the creek flows through a beautiful wooded area of Tiadaghton State Forest, and this is where you will find the most enjoyable fishing. A gravel forest road and a few cabins along the road are the only developments in this upper stretch. There are few large pools, but numerous pockets and small pools provide adequate cover. An old CCC camp near the junction of North Pleasant Stream is a popular camping site.

Pleasant Stream has a good population of small wild browns and brookies, and it holds many fish through the summer and fall. The water gets very low and clear, though, so you must approach the stream carefully to avoid spooking the fish.

Rock Run - Lycoming County
(map: page 127)

This tributary to Lycoming Creek is notable for its unusual and spectacular scenery. Most of the stream flows through a steep-sided, narrow ravine. There are waterfalls and swirling potholes, and in several places the flow of the water has carved chute-like channels through solid bedrock. The water is very clear, and it is often possible to see the trout lying on the bottom of deep pools. Most of Rock Run flows through Tiadaghton State Forest.

To reach Rock Run, turn off Route 14 onto a side street at the war memorial in the village of Ralston. This street passes a bank and a store, crosses some railroad tracks, passes a trucking company, then arrives at a bridge over Lycoming Creek. You can park near this bridge and walk down along Lycoming Creek a short distance to the mouth of Rock Run. You can fish upstream on Rock Run from here, but the lower stretch of the creek is shallower, less scenic, and seems to hold fewer trout than the middle and upper stretches.

To fish farther upstream, drive up along Rock Run Road. The road follows the creek, but in many places there are sheer cliffs dropping down to the creek bottom, so you must choose your spots to hike down carefully. There are several pulloffs along Rock Road and obvious paths that lead down to the stream.

Near the mouth of Miners Run, Rock Run flows through unusually deep, narrow channels carved out of solid rock. About one-half mile downstream from Miners Run, Rock Run plunges over a waterfall into a deep pool.

About 1.8 miles above Miners Run, the road crosses a bridge over Rock Run. This is another good access spot. The stream is somewhat smaller here, but there are still some large holes in this area. After crossing the bridge, the road becomes Yellow Dog Road and winds its way up a mountain away from the creek. Just before the bridge, a rough jeep road turns off the main road and follows Rock Run upstream about 0.7 mile to Hawk Run, which is the uppermost stocking point. Above Hawk Run, Rock Run and its North Branch flow through a remote, roadless area of Tiadaghton State Forest. If you are willing to walk in, you can find some native brookies here, but they aren't really plentiful.

Rock Run is stocked over a distance of about 5 miles, from Hawk Run down to the mouth. The Fish Commission stocks trout preseason and three times inseason, with the last stocking coming in late May. In addition to stocked trout, Rock Run holds fair numbers of wild brown and brook trout. Rock Run stays cold and offers decent fishing through the summer. On hot days the deep pools are great places to go for a refreshing swim.

Roaring Branch - Lycoming and Tioga Counties
(map: page 127)

Roaring Branch, also called Roaring Brook, is a small stream that flows into upper Lycoming Creek at the village of Roaring Branch. Most of the stocked stretch of the stream flows through a narrow, steep, wooded ravine, which makes it a scenic and interesting place to fish, but which also makes access tricky.

One place to get access is near the mouth, at the Route 14 bridge. To fish farther upstream, drive up the first road south of the bridge, which is numbered SR 2004 at the lower end and SR 1010 once it crosses into Tioga County. This road parallels the creek upstream, but it is a rugged hike from the road to the creek bottom. There are some places where you can scramble down the banks, and there are also several lanes leading down to the creek. There are a lot of no-trespassing signs along the road, so it is best to walk in only where you see signs reading, "Fishing permitted, walk in only."

About 4.5 miles up from Route 14, SR 1010 crosses Roaring Branch. This is a good place to park and fish downstream. This is also the upper stocking point. Trout are stocked from here to the mouth.

From the SR 1010 bridge up into the headwaters, Roaring Branch flows through meadows and woods. Wild brook and brown trout are found in this upper stretch, but most of the land along the stream is posted against trespassing.

The Fish Commission stocks Roaring Branch for opening day and once again inseason, usually in late May. The stocked stretch of Roaring Branch holds fair numbers of wild brown and brook trout. In midsummer the stream becomes low and very clear, but it always flows cool. When water levels are low, most of the fish drop into the deeper pools. Roaring Branch is a small stream, but it has some surprisingly deep pools scattered along its length.

Pine Creek - Potter, Tioga and Lycoming Counties
(maps: pages 132, 134, 136, 138)

Pine Creek is one of Pennsylvania's longest and most celebrated trout streams. In its headwaters near Brookland in Potter County, Pine Creek is a mere trickle of a trout stream, but as it flows through some 75 miles of Potter, Tioga, and Lycoming Counties, it gathers the waters of numerous tributaries, many of which are themselves fine trout streams. In its lower stretches, the creek grows almost to river size, 200 feet wide in places.

Along its length Pine Creek and its many tributaries offer good fishing for wild and stocked trout, great fly hatches and some of the state's finest mountain scenery. The Pine Creek Gorge, or Pennsylvania Grand Canyon, with its steep, forested slopes and limited access, is a particularly wild and beautiful place to fish.

Pine Creek can be divided into four sections according to changes in the trout population:

1) From the headwaters near Brookland downstream to the confluence of Genesee Forks at West Pike, Pine Creek is not stocked and it offers good fishing for wild brown and brook trout.

2) From West Pike downstream to Galeton, Pine Creek receives hatchery trout and also holds a good population of wild brown trout.

3) From Galeton downstream to Waterville, the fishing is mostly for stocked trout, but some wild and holdover trout are caught, particularly near the mouths of tributaries. This section includes most of the length of Pine Creek's trout water.

4) From Waterville downstream to the mouth on the West Branch Susquehanna River, no trout are

Pine Creek at West Pike. Even the little ones are fun to catch.

stocked. Some hatchery trout drift down into this lower water, but you are likely to catch more small-mouth bass than trout here.

Headwaters to West Pike

In its headwaters Pine Creek is a narrow, tumbling brook that's well shaded by surrounding trees. Above Brookland, you can park along Route 449 and scramble down the bank to the stream, which is only 6 to 8 feet wide here. Just below Brookland, there is posting along 1 mile of the stream.

Downstream from Brookland, a good place to park is at the Route 449 bridge over Buckseller Run. Here Pine Creek flows through a wooded area scattered with hunting camps. Although the stream is still small at this point, there are lots of pockets and small pools at downed logs and tree roots. Brown and brook trout inhabit the creek in about equal numbers here. Buckseller Run is very small, but it also holds native brook trout.

From near the mouth of Ninemile Run downstream about 1.3 miles to the mouth of Cabin Run, Pine Creek is posted by the Brookland Club.

By the time Pine Creek reaches the Route 6 bridge between Walton and West Pike, it has grown from a brook into a medium-sized stream about 30 feet wide. There is parking available at the Route 6 bridge and good fishing is found upstream and down. Both brown and brook trout are found in this area early in the year, but in the summer you are likely to

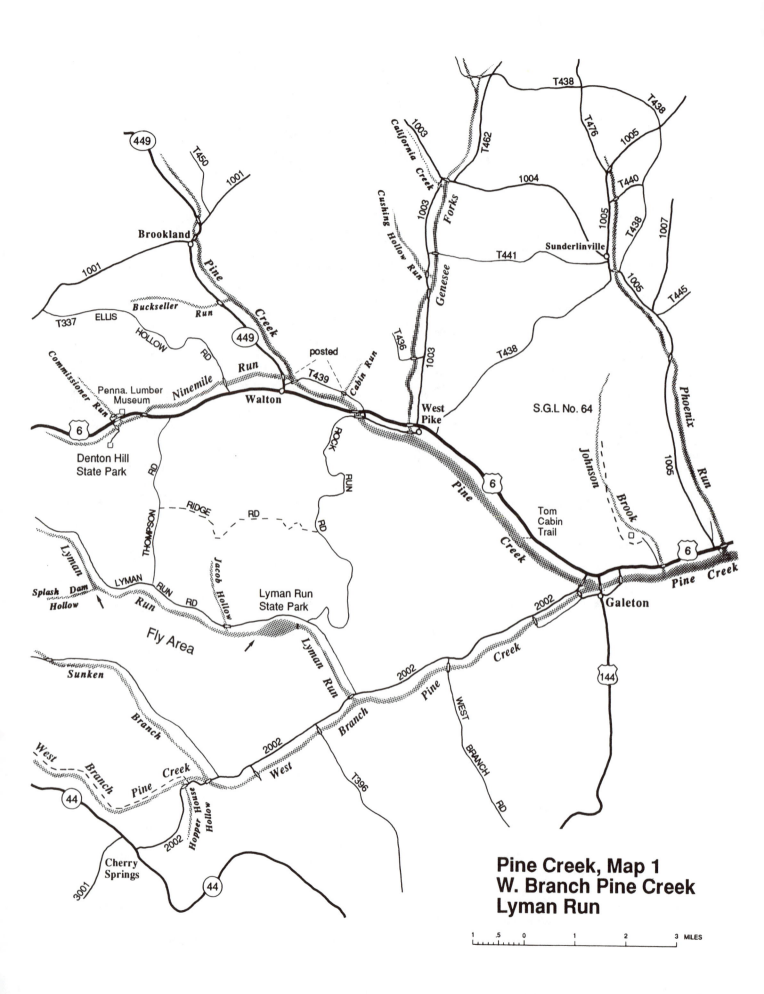

**Pine Creek, Map 1
W. Branch Pine Creek
Lyman Run**

1 .5 0   1   2   3 MILES

Pine Creek. The canyon in winter.   (Tim Palmer photo)

catch mostly brown trout. Apparently the brookies move upstream or into tributaries when the water begins to warm.

From the Route 6 bridge downstream to West Pike, Pine Creek is mostly shallow and riffly, but you can find trout in this pocket water.

West Pike to Galeton

At West Pike, Genesee Forks flows in and increases the volume of Pine Creek by perhaps one-third. Just below the junction pool, you will find fly fishing gear and fly tying materials at Jack's Tackle.

The Fish Commission begins stocking Pine Creek at the confluence of Genesee Forks, and from there downstream to Galeton you can find both wild browns and stocked fish. This stretch is paralleled by Route 6, and the stream flows here through woods and open, grassy fields scattered with houses and camps. These dwellings make access a little tricky in some spots, but there are several places where you can park along Route 6 and walk through the woods or fields without passing too close to any buildings.

Much of the West Pike-to-Galeton section is shallow, and the scarcity of large pools may displease some anglers, but this stretch holds quite a few wild brown trout. I enjoyed some fine dry fly fishing here during a Green Drake hatch.

About 1.5 miles upstream from Galeton, there is a big pulloff along Route 6 and a rough dirt road called Tom Cabin Trail leading down to the creek. Here Pine Creek flows through a wooded area, and there are several long riffles and pools.

Galeton to Ansonia

At Galeton, the largest town in this rural area, West Branch Pine Creek meets Pine Creek, and a low dam backs up a section of both creeks. The wide, open stretch behind the dam and the increasing size of Pine Creek create warm summer temperatures that are marginal for trout.

From Galeton downstream through the rest of Pine Creek's trout water, fishing is good for stocked trout through about mid-June. In warmer years fishing can get tough after the first week of June, and in

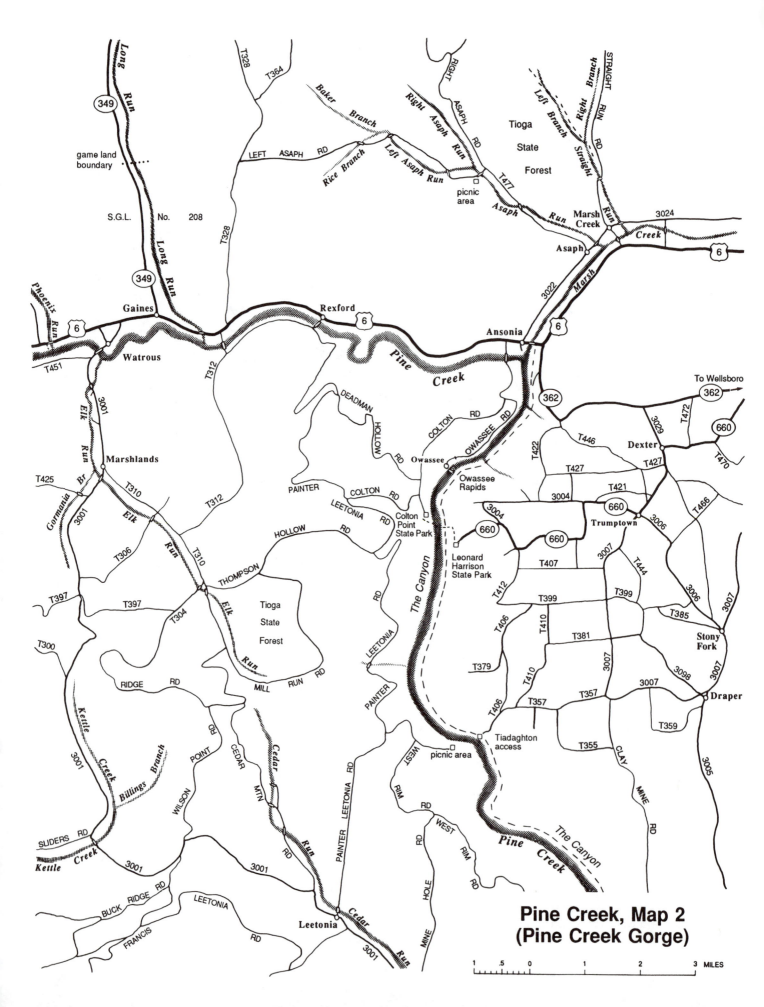

**Pine Creek, Map 2
(Pine Creek Gorge)**

cooler years fishing can remain good through the end of June. As the water temperature rises, many trout gather near the tributary mouths and many also move up into the tributaries.

Few people fish for trout in the lower stretches of Pine Creek after mid-June, but a few anglers fish at night near springs and tributaries and sometimes they catch large browns.

From Galeton to Ansonia, Pine Creek is paralleled by Route 6, but trees and stream banks isolate the stream from highway noise. Access can be gained at most bridge crossings, or by parking along Route 6 and walking down tributaries such as Johnson Brook, Phoenix Run, and Long Run. A Fish Commission access site at Ansonia is popular with canoeists and rafters. Pine Creek is a large stream, approximately 150 feet wide, by the time it reaches Ansonia.

The Canyon

At Ansonia, Pine Creek turns abruptly to the south and enters the Pine Creek Gorge, which is often called the Pennsylvania Grand Canyon by tourism officials. Anglers call it simply "The Canyon." From Ansonia downstream approximately 16 miles to Blackwell, Pine Creek is not crossed by any bridges, and access is limited by rugged mountains that rise up 800 feet on both sides of the creek. The big water, beautiful surroundings, and excellent fly hatches make the canyon a unique place to fish.

Many canoeists and rafters float from Ansonia down through the canyon to Blackwell during April and May, particularly on the weekends. By early June the water is often too low for boating. The upper part of the canyon has swift rapids alternating with long, deep pools. The largest and most dangerous rapids are Owassee Rapids. Several people have lost their lives there.

Camping is available on the west rim of the canyon at Colton Point State Park and on the east rim of the canyon at Leonard Harrison State Park. The Turkey Path, a narrow, steep trail, leads down to Pine Creek from both state parks. Usually the campsites are less crowded at Colton Point State Park than at Leonard Harrison State Park.

To fish the upper part of the canyon, drive south from Ansonia on Colton Road and turn left onto the unmarked dirt Owassee Road. This road leads downhill to the creek, then follows along the bank, providing good access. After about 2 miles, a large parking lot appears on the right. Do not drive past this point. If you continue you will find that the road winds up a hill and ends at a gate. You will be forced to turn around in a narrow spot on the edge of a cliff. Past the gate, the road leads to a group of private cabins located near Owassee Rapids. The cliffs along this side of the creek make it difficult to walk downstream towards Owassee Rapids or the pools farther downstream. In low water periods, you can wade across

Pine Creek in several places and walk down along the old railroad grade, now a walking path, that follows the eastern bank.

Another way to get to the old railroad grade is to turn from Route 6 onto Route 362 at Ansonia, drive south 0.8 mile, then turn right onto a dirt road, which continues another 0.2 mile before ending at a parking area by the railroad grade. The railroad tracks have been removed, and the grade is now state forest property. The grade is presently rather rough for bicycles, but it may soon be improved. Motor vehicles are prohibited on the grade.

About halfway through the canyon, there is an access site at Tiadaghton. The road leading down to this site is steep, and it gets muddy and rutted in wet weather. If you get your car stuck here, you won't be the first person. Around Tiadaghton, and generally in the lower part of the canyon, Pine Creek flows more evenly, without the large pools or rapids found in the upper part of the canyon.

Lower Pine Creek

Below Blackwell, Pine Creek is closely followed by Route 414 and finding access is easy. There are cabins, campgrounds, and houses along the lower Pine Creek valley, but it is still a scenic and mostly rural, forested area.

At Blackwell, Babb Creek dumps mine acid into Pine Creek, and fly hatches drop off dramatically downstream from there. Good caddis hatches still occur in lower Pine Creek, and some mayfly hatches still appear, but not in the tremendous numbers found in Pine Creek upstream from Blackwell.

Two terrific trout streams, Slate Run and Cedar Run (see pages 141 and 142), and several smaller tributaries flow into lower Pine Creek, and these offer alternatives to Pine Creek, particularly when Pine Creek is either too warm or too high to fish. Slate Run Tackle Shop, located along Route 414 opposite the mouth of Slate Run, is a good source of tackle and stream information.

Hatches

Hatches on Pine Creek include Blue Quills, Hendricksons, Olive Caddis, Grey Foxes, Green Drakes, Brown Drakes, and Isonychia. These are only the major hatches. Nearly every aquatic insect known to eastern trout fishermen appears to some extent on Pine Creek and its tributaries, so bring along all your fly boxes.

One of the heaviest fly hatches I have ever seen on any stream was a hatch of Hendricksons on Pine Creek. The fishing was very good for awhile, but at the peak of the hatch, the flies were so thick on the water that anglers began leaving the stream. Even though many trout continued to rise, the chance of a trout selecting your artificial fly from the floating mass of duns was slim.

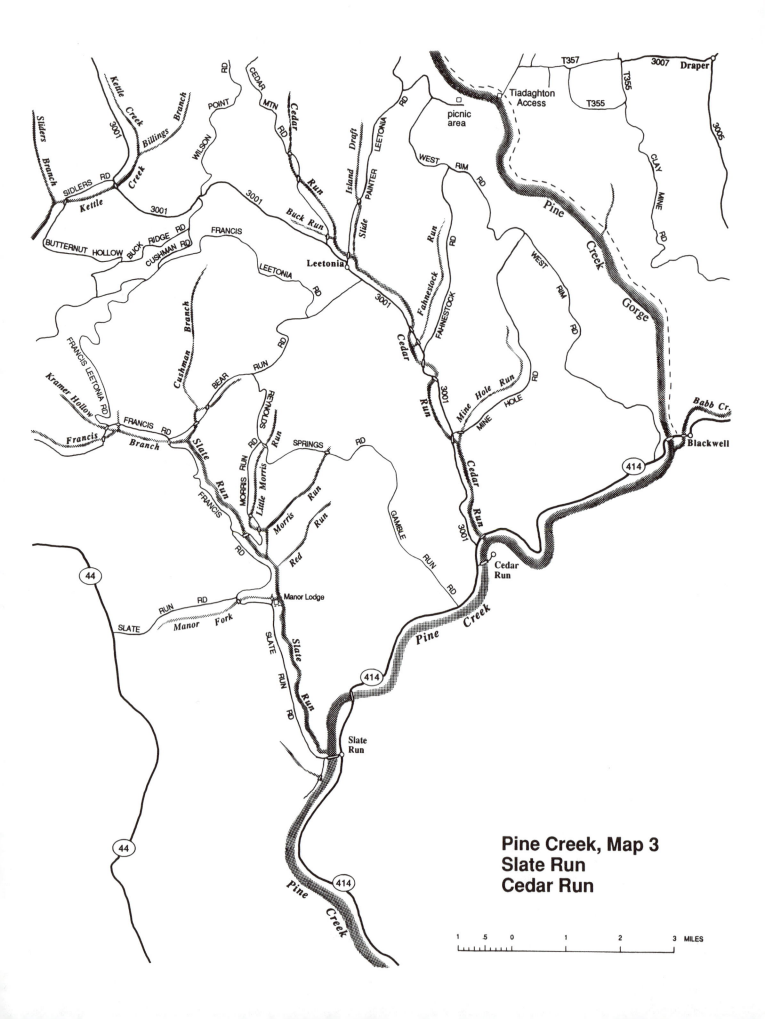

Pine Creek, Map 3
Slate Run
Cedar Run

1 .5 0   1   2   3 MILES

The Hendrickson hatch occurs from Blackwell upstream at least as far as West Pike, and probably well up into the headwaters. In warm years with low-to-moderate water levels, heavy hatches of Hendricksons can occur as early as opening day in mid-April, and in cooler years the hatch can begin as late as May 1.

The Green Drake hatch is not as heavy on Pine Creek as on some limestone streams, such as Penns Creek or Clinton County's Fishing Creek, but the trout rise readily to these big insects on Pine Creek, and they often do not on the limestoners. Good Green Drake hatches are found from the canyon upstream at least as far as the Route 6 above West Pike and also in many of Pine Creek's tributary streams.

Appearing around the same time as the Green Drakes, or slightly later, are the Brown Drakes. The peak of this hatch usually lasts only three or four days, but if you hit it right you will enjoy very heavy spinner falls at dusk. The canyon is the favored place to fish the Brown Drake hatch.

Nine Mile Run - Potter County
(map: page 132)

Nine Mile Run originates in the Susquehannock State Forest west of Denton Hill State Park, and flows east 6 miles to meet upper Pine Creek at the village of Walton. Route 6 closely parallels the stream for its entire length, providing easy access. A short stretch of the stream near the mouth at Walton is posted against trespassing.

Nine Mile Run flows over rocks and gravel, and it is well shaded at most places by trees and shrubs. Mature hardwood trees line the lower part of the stream, and some of the middle and upper stretches are bordered by thick brush.

Because of its good population of wild trout, Nine Mile Run is no longer stocked with hatchery fish. Summer stream surveys turned up good numbers of brown trout from 6 to 10 inches long and a few fish around 12 to 14 inches. Brook trout are also present, even in the lower stretches of the creek.

Above the confluence with Commissioner Run at Denton Hill State Park, Nine Mile Run is very small, but it holds many wild brook trout. Commissioner Run also holds wild brook trout.

Nine Mile Run is a challenging stream to fish. Low hanging branches make casting tricky, and when the water level drops, the stream becomes very clear, making the wild browns even more wary than usual. The Green Drake hatch, which usually occurs around the first week in June, causes the browns to lose some of their caution.

Fishing pressure is fairly light on Nine Mile Run. You may see some other anglers here in the spring, but in the summer and fall, you are likely to have the stream entirely to yourself.

Genesee Forks - Potter County
(map: page 132)

Genesee Forks is a tributary to upper Pine Creek, which it meets at the village of West Pike, about 5 miles west of Galeton. Don't confuse this stream with the Genesee River, which also flows through Potter County, but in a completely different drainage.

Genesee Forks originates at the junction of Lehman Hollow and Baldwin Hollow and flows south 7.6 miles past woods, small farms and overgrown meadows. Trout are no longer stocked because of the good wild trout population found along the length of the stream. Most of the trout are browns, but brook trout are mixed in with the browns in the upper part of the creek, from around Cushing Hollow Run up into the headwaters. Most of the browns you catch in Genesee Forks are likely to be 5 to 10 inches long, but the stream also produces some brown trout over 12 inches long.

While exploring the Genesee Forks, you may encounter some access problems. All of the stream is on private property and quite a few homes are found along its banks. In the upper reaches, from SR 1004 up to the headwaters, most of the stream is posted. There are also a few short posted areas along the middle and lower stretches.

Perhaps the best way to fish Genesee Forks is to park along Route 6 and fish upstream. There are several deep pools in the lower part of the creek. Other access points include the T436 bridge and the T441 (Stiles Road) bridge. The fishing pressure is very light on Genesee Forks. Good hatches of Green Drakes appear in late May and early June.

West Branch Pine Creek - Potter County
(map: page 132)

West Branch Pine Creek has not been as widely publicized and is not fished as hard as some other Potter County streams, but it offers good fishing for both wild and stocked trout. This medium-sized stream adds considerably to the flow of Pine Creek when the two streams meet at Galeton. The Fish Commission stocks the West Branch from the mouth upstream 10.5 miles to the last point of road access, at a small tributary named Hopper House Hollow. Trout are stocked for opening day and once inseason, usually in early to mid-May. The stocked portion of the stream is easily accessible from SR 2002, which follows the stream up from Galeton.

From Lyman Run downstream to Galeton, the West Branch flows through woods and brushy fields, and many hunting camps and homes are near the stream. A large sawmill is located about 1 mile above Galeton. Some wild trout are found in this lower

Pine Creek, Map 4
Little Pine Creek

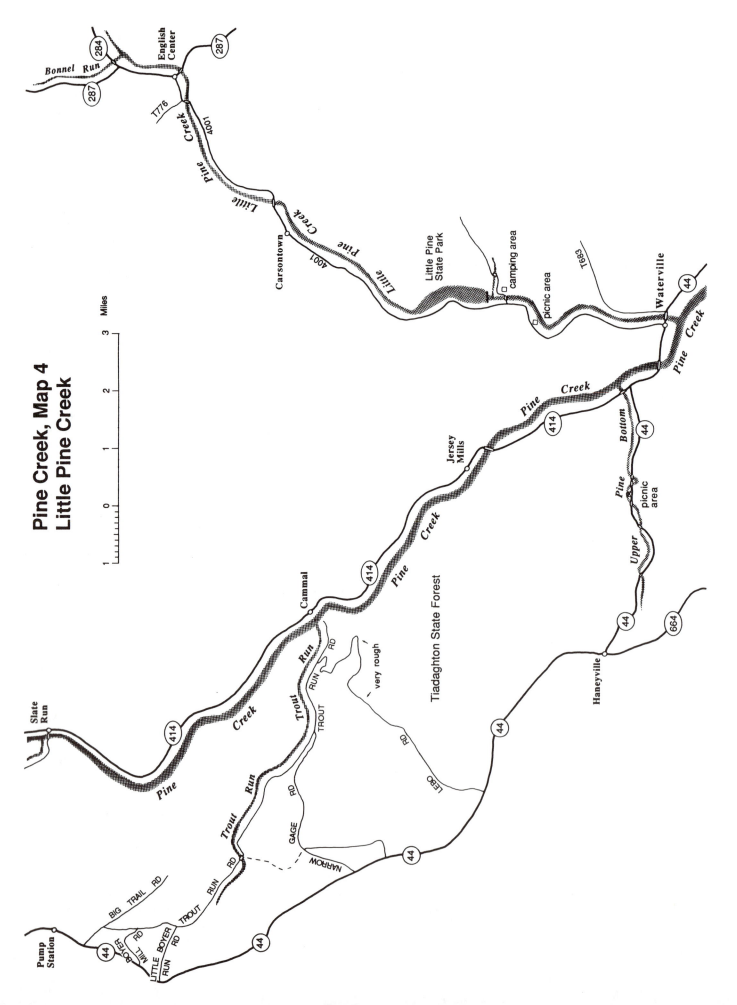

stretch, but water temperatures get pretty warm here in the summer months, especially in the lower 2 or 3 miles of the stream.

Above the confluence of Lyman Run, the West Branch is a smaller stream, and it courses through a narrow, wooded valley. There are also some hunting camps in this area, but not as many as in the lower stretch. From Lyman Run up to Hopper House Hollow, the stream is well shaded and holds a good population of wild brown trout and also some brookies. This upper part of the West Branch's stocked water consists mostly of riffles, pockets, and occasional small pools, but there are several surprisingly deep pools, one of which has a rope swing for swimmers.

At Hopper House Hollow, the West Branch and the road go their separate ways, and from here a trail follows up along the stream into the headwaters. Above the road the West Branch flows for nearly 6 miles through a remote roadless area in the Susquehannock State Forest. This is a great place to hike along the stream and fish for native brook trout. The stream is small here, but there are some decent-sized pools and beaver ponds.

The West Branch has some good fly hatches including Hendricksons, Sulphurs, Grey Foxes, and Green Drakes. The Green Drake hatch can be very good here; it usually occurs from the very end of May through the first week in June. A small (#16) Letort Cricket works well in the summer and fall.

Lyman Run - Potter County
(fly fishing only, 4 miles)
(map: page 132)

Upstream from Lyman Lake, Lyman Run is a real beauty of a small freestone stream. Protected by special regulations and well shaded by surrounding trees, this little stream has a very good population of wild brown and brook trout.

From the lake upstream about 4 miles to Splash Dam Hollow, the creek is managed under fly-fishing-only regulations and no trout are stocked. In the lower water near the lake, there are good numbers of brown trout, but the farther upstream you go, the more common the brook trout become.

A Potter County fisherman who fishes Lyman Run often told me that he sometimes catches nice browns here, but that often the brook trout grab his fly before the browns have a chance. Above Splash Dam Hollow, there are another 1.5 miles of brook trout water in the narrow headwaters.

Despite the small size of the creek, 10-inch brown trout are fairly common and 12-inchers are caught occasionally. Native brook trout are abundant up to 6 or 7 inches, and 9-inch brookies are not unusual.

Lyman Run flows clear most of the time, and careful casting is required to avoid spooking the fish.

Lyman Run above the lake is a particularly good place to fish in midsummer, when many larger streams have warmed and fly hatches have tapered off. Try terrestrials such as deer-hair beetles and crickets or light-colored dry flies such as the Light Cahill or Grey Fox Variant.

Lyman Run State Park, on the shores of Lyman Lake, offers camping, swimming, and picnicking. Lyman Lake is well stocked with trout and it offers good fishing into early June.

The lower part of Lyman Run begins at the spillway on Lyman Lake and continues another 2.3 miles before meeting the West Branch of Pine Creek. The best way to reach this stretch is to park your car near the spillway and fish downstream from there. Trout are stocked in this lower section of Lyman Run for opening day and twice inseason, with the last stocking coming in mid-May. This lower part of Lyman Run is warmed by Lyman Lake; water temperatures in the summer can reach the 70's. There are not nearly as many wild trout here as above the lake, but there are fair numbers of wild browns in addition to the stocked fish.

Lyman Run has a good Green Drake hatch, as do many of the other tributaries to Pine Creek.

Johnson Brook - Potter County
(map: page 132)

Johnson Brook is a very small stream, only about 7 to 8 feet wide, and the access to it is sort of tricky, but if you like little brook trout streams, you may want to try this one. Johnson Brook flows under Route 6 and into Pine Creek about 1.3 miles west of Galeton. You can fish upstream from the Route 6 bridge, and the stream does hold trout there, but there are some houses along the banks in this area.

To get to the upper, wilder part of the stream, drive 0.8 mile up the road that parallels the stream, which will bring you to a sign reading "Stop, Private Road." Straight ahead you will see a house and barn. Park near the sign and walk around this homestead on side trails that lead to the left and the right. The trail to the left (west) is easier going. Be sure to close all gates behind you. Above this property Johnson Brook flows 3.5 miles through the remote, forested hills of State Game Land No. 64. Here you will find lots of native brook trout, few of which exceed 6 inches in length.

Phoenix Run - Potter and Tioga Counties
(map: page 132)

Phoenix Run flows into Pine Creek about 2.5 miles east of Galeton. This stream is no longer stocked because it has a very good wild brown and brook trout population. The best fishing is found from the mouth upstream 4.5 miles to the first SR 1005 bridge. Much of this stretch lies within State Game Land No. 64. Most of the lower part of the creek is well shaded by tall trees, and the stream flows quickly over a rock and gravel bed.

There is some parking available near the Route 6 bridge. On the west side of the bridge, a dirt track leads down to the junction of Phoenix Run and Pine Creek.

SR 1005 follows Phoenix Run from Route 6 upstream to the headwaters. Just above Route 6, a dirt road turns off from SR 1005 and leads to a group of cabins along the stream. Upstream from the cabins, Phoenix Run flows through State Game Land No. 64, where small pools and pockets at undercut banks and downed trees hold lots of wild brown and brook trout. Most of these fish are 10 inches or less in length, but a few exceed 12 inches.

Farther upstream, near the SR 1005 bridge, the stream is less shaded and grass and brush are found along the stream banks. The upper boundary of Game Land No. 64 is about 0.3 mile upstream of the first SR 1005 bridge.

If you continue north on SR 1005 towards the village of Sunderlinville, you will find Phoenix Run flowing through farms and meadows. More houses appear along the streambanks here, and much of this upper water is posted against trespassing. Trout numbers are much lower here than downstream in State Game Land No. 64.

Phoenix Run has good hatches of Green Drakes in late May and early June.

Elk Run - Tioga County
(map: page 134)

Elk Run is a good news, bad news stream. The good news is that Elk Run has a good population of wild brown and brook trout. The bad news is that scattered posting and numerous houses along the stream make access difficult. Elk Run originates in Tioga State Forest and flows north 7 miles to join Pine Creek near Watrous.

The best fishing with the least posting is found from the village of Marshlands upstream into the headwaters. If you want to avoid private property problems altogether, do your fishing in the headwaters above Thompson Hollow Road, where Elk Run flows through tall timber in Tioga State Forest. The stream is very small here, only about 8 to 9 feet wide, but native brook trout are plentiful.

Downstream from the state forest land, Elk Run flows past small farms, houses, woodlots, and brushy meadows. Elk Run is included in the Fish Commission's wild trout program and receives no stockings of hatchery trout.

Long Run - Tioga County
(map: page 134)

Long Run is a small stream that flows through State Game Land No. 208 before meeting Pine Creek near the village of Gaines. The Fish Commission stocks trout from the mouth upstream 4.5 miles. Trout are stocked preseason and three times inseason with the last stocking coming in early May.

Long Run is a gently flowing stream with some shallow, barren areas, but pockets along tree roots and undercut banks hold trout all year around. Most of the larger pools are found in the lower mile of the creek. Long Run has a fair population of wild brown and brook trout.

Access to Long Run is easy. You can park along Route 6 near the mouth or at various places along Route 349, which parallels most of the stream. Above the stocked stretch, Long Run is quite small, but there are wild brown and brook trout in the headwaters and fishing pressure there is light.

Asaph Run - Tioga County
(map: page 134)

Asaph Run flows into Marsh Creek at the village of Asaph, which is located about 2 miles northeast of Ansonia. (Marsh Creek is stocked with trout, but it has pollution and posting problems and it gets warm in the summer months.) T477 follows Asaph Run up from the village of Asaph.

Asaph Run is stocked with trout from its mouth upstream 3 miles to its origin at the junction of Left and Right Asaph Runs. The Fish Commission stocks trout for opening day and twice inseason, usually the first and second week after opening day. Asaph Run also holds a good population of wild brown and brook trout, most of which are fairly small, but some of the browns reach 10 to 12 inches.

The lower part of Asaph Run, approximately the first mile upstream from the mouth, flows through private land, which is currently open to fishing. Above this stretch the stream flows through Tioga State Forest, where it is well shaded and tumbles over rocks and boulders. The Youth Conservation Corps has installed some stream improvement devices in this area, but most of the stream remains quite shallow. There is a picnic area at the upper end of Asaph Run, where its branches meet.

Left Asaph Run - Tioga County
(map: page 134)

Left Asaph Run flows 2 miles through Tioga State Forest, and it offers fishing for both stocked and wild trout. This shallow, rocky, swift-flowing brook is well shaded by trees and shrubs. The Fish Commission stocks trout before opening day and twice inseason, usually in the first and second weeks after opening day. Left Asaph Run also has a good native brook trout population, with many fish between 3 and 6 inches and a few larger fish.

Left Asaph Run is paralleled along its length by a forestry road appropriately named Left Asaph Road. In its headwaters, Left Asaph Run is formed by the junction of Baker Branch and Rice Branch, which are very small brook trout streams.

Right Asaph Run - Tioga County
(map: page 134)

Right Asaph Run flows 1.7 miles through Tioga State Forest and it offers good fishing for native brook trout. No trout are stocked. Stream surveys show that Right Asaph Run holds many brook trout between 3 and 6 inches long and also some larger ones. Right Asaph Road follows the stream for most of its length. The headwaters of Right Asaph Run arise in the Black Swamp Natural Area of the Tioga State Forest.

Straight Run - Tioga County
(map: page 134)

Straight Run is a small, unstocked brook trout stream that flows into Marsh Creek about 2.5 miles northeast of Ansonia. The stream is 1.8 miles long from its mouth upstream to its origin at the junction of Left and Right Straight Runs.

Straight Run has very good numbers of small brook trout. The lower part of Straight Run flows through private land, but most of the stream flows through Tioga State Forest. Straight Run Road, a forest road, parallels the creek.

Left Straight Run is a small, unstocked stream that flows 2.5 miles through a remote area in Tioga State Forest. Although the stream is narrow and shallow, it holds many brook trout.

Right Straight Run also flows through Tioga State Forest. It holds some brook trout, but fewer than Straight Run or Left Straight Run.

Cedar Run - Tioga and Lycoming Counties
(trophy trout project, artificials only, 7.2 miles)
(map: page 136)

Cedar Run is a beautiful mountain freestone stream that flows some 11 miles through State Forest lands before joining Pine Creek at the village of Cedar Run. The beauty of the stream's tumbling riffles and long ledge pools and its excellent wild trout population make fishing Cedar Run a rare experience.

The entire length of the stream is managed as a wild trout stream, so there is no stocking. From the mouth upstream 7.2 miles to Buck Run, Cedar Run is under Trophy Trout regulations, which requires the use of flies or artificial lures. The limit is two trout per day, with a minimum size of 14 inches. In this section the trout population is dominated by brown trout, although brook trout are also present and become more common the farther upstream you go. Several of Cedar Run's small tributaries also hold wild brook trout.

Stream surveys show that Cedar Run holds excellent numbers of brown trout between 5 and 10 inches and pretty good numbers between 11 and 14 inches. A few fish between 15 and 18 inches were also found.

In the headwaters above Buck Run, Cedar Run has a mixed brown and brook trout population, with the brook trout taking over in the extreme headwaters. Above Buck Run, Cedar Run is quite small, little more than a trickle in midsummer. Most of the large ledge-rock pools are found in lower Cedar Run, from the mouth upstream to the first bridge on SR 3001. Above this you'll find mostly riffles and pocket water, and some small pools, but trout are plentiful in these areas also.

Although Cedar Run has an excellent trout population, it is not always an easy stream to fish. Its waters are crystal clear and its wild browns are wary. In the early part of the year, when water levels are up, trout can be found in the riffles and runs, and nymph and wet fly fishing are most effective. From late April into early June, when the fly hatches are at their best, fishing can be excellent to rising trout.

In midsummer, after water levels drop, fish move out of the shallow water and into the deeper pools. Fishing these long, flat pools demands a careful approach and long, fine leaders. Even with the best of efforts, fishing on bright summer days can be slow. During the summer, fishing is generally best in the early morning or late evening. Some Cedar Run regulars prefer to fish at night during the summer months.

Some anglers have complained that fishing is not as good now on Cedar Run as when the stream was stocked. Probably the catch rate has decreased a bit. This is not due to a lack of trout, but it is simply because wild brown trout are much more difficult to catch than stocked fish. According to Fish Commission stream surveys, the number of trout from 9 to 14 inches long has increased by 65% since the special regulations have gone into effect. The trout are there. The challenge to the angler is to figure out how to catch them.

Cedar Run can be perplexing. On a bright summer day, you may peer into the depths of a perfectly clear pool with your polarized fishing glasses and count the stones on the bottom without seeing many trout, but the trout are there somewhere, probably hiding under the rock ledges.

A friend and I fished the lower stretch of Cedar Run one July night and only caught two or three

A small tributary tumbles into Cedar Run.

trout between us, but before we left, we pointed our flashlights into the pool where we had been fishing, and the pool was as thick with trout as a hatchery pond. Many of these fish had probably migrated up from Pine Creek to find cooler water.

Cedar Run has good fly hatches, including Blue-winged Olives, Blue Quills, Quill Gordons, Hendricksons, March Browns, Grey Foxes, Green Drakes, and Isonychia. After water levels drop in the summer, try ant and beetle imitations.

Slate Run - Lycoming and Tioga Counties

(fly fishing only, 6.5 miles)
(map: page 136)

Few streams in Pennsylvania have a combination of mountain scenery and wild trout comparable to Slate Run's. From its origin at the junction of Cushman Branch and Francis Branch, Slate Run flows 7 miles through a narrow, forested valley before meeting Pine Creek at the village of Slate Run. Rock ledges form surprisingly deep pools and even a small waterfall.

Slate Run is managed as a wild brown trout stream and is no longer stocked. Fly-fishing-only regulations are in force over the entire length of the stream. Stream surveys indicate that Slate Run has an excellent wild brown trout population. A few brook trout are found also, particularly in the upper reaches. Large trout are not common here, but surveys turned up a few browns between 18 and 20 inches, surprisingly big fish for a mountain freestone stream. Even though no trout are stocked in Slate Run, some hatchery trout move up into it from Pine Creek. I once saw a palomino trout in Slate Run almost 2 miles upstream from the mouth.

Slate Run is paralleled by roads along its entire length, but in most places a hike is required to reach the stream because the roads are high on the hillsides above the stream. To get to Slate Run, follow Route 41 and Route 414 up along Pine Creek from Waterville until you reach the bridge over Pine Creek at the village of Slate Run. Near this bridge, along Route 414, you will find the Slate Run Tackle Shop, a good source for fly fishing tackle and information about Slate Run, Cedar Run, and Pine Creek. Turn left across the bridge and park near the Hotel Manor. This is the easiest access to the lower part of Slate Run. From here you can fish the short distance down to the mouth on Pine Creek—or even better—fish upstream on Slate Run, and you will soon find yourself fishing some really attractive pools and riffles.

To reach the upper water, drive up Slate Run Road. This road follows Slate Run, but travels high on the hillside above it. There are several trails that lead from the road down to the creek. A parking area is located next to Manor Lodge at the junction of Slate Run and Manor Fork. If you fish upstream from here, you will soon come to the very scenic Manor Falls Pool, where a small waterfall plunges into Slate Run's deepest hole.

After Slate Run Road crosses over Manor Fork, turn right onto Francis Road, which follows Slate Run the rest of the way up to its origin. Morris Run Road, an unimproved dirt road, turns off from Francis Road and crosses Slate Run, providing access near the middle of the creek. Francis Road also provides access to Slate Run's headwater tributaries, Francis Branch and Cushman Branch, which are small streams with good fishing for wild brown and brook trout.

Slate Run has good fishing all season long. In the spring there are excellent fly hatches. Because of Slate Run's cool water temperatures, fly hatches occur later than on larger, warmer streams such as Pine Creek and Kettle Creek. For example, Hendricksons usually emerge about a week later on Slate Run than on Pine Creek.

In the summer months, Slate Run gets low and very clear, and fishing on bright days can be tough. Long leaders and careful presentations are required to avoid spooking the trout. At this time of year, fishing at dawn and dusk with small ant and beetle patterns is effective.

Autumn also provides fine fishing. Trout become more active as temperatures drop and as spawning season nears. Some anglers even fish Slate Run during warm spells in December and January.

Rattlesnakes are often seen along the banks of Slate Run. The only person I've ever met who actually was bitten by a rattler in Pennsylvania was bitten while fishing here.

Fly hatches on Slate Run include Blue-winged Olives, Blue Quills, Hendricksons, Sulphurs, March Browns, Grey Foxes, Green Drakes, Light Cahills, Isonychia, and Tricos. Terrestrial imitations are very good in summer and fall.

Slate Run's small tributaries, such as Manor Fork, Morris Run, and Red Run, hold wild brook trout and also some wild browns. The lower end of Red Run flows through a very scenic mini-gorge.

Francis Branch - Tioga and Potter Counties

(fly fishing only, 2 miles)
(map: page 136)

Francis Branch originates in Potter County and flows into Tioga County, where it joins the Cushman Branch to form Slate Run. Most of this small mountain stream flows through Tioga State Forest. No trout are stocked here, but wild brown and brook trout are found in good numbers.

Francis Branch is about 5.5 miles long, including the narrow upper reaches. The lower 2 miles, from the mouth upstream to Kramer Hollow, are managed under fly fishing only regulations. Brown trout are common in the fly area, and stream surveys turn up many browns between 8 and 10 inches long and even a few 12-inchers. Farther upstream, you'll find mostly brook trout.

Most anglers fish Francis Branch as a side trip from Slate Run. Francis Branch receives much less fishing pressure than Slate Run, probably because of its small size and the thick brush that lines much of the length of the creek.

Cushman Branch - Tioga County
(map: page 136)

Cushman Branch is a small stream that flows through remote, mountainous country in Tioga State Forest before joining Francis Branch to form the headwaters of Slate Run. No trout are stocked here, but the stream holds a good mixed population of wild browns and brookies. Most of the browns run 4 to 8 inches long and a few exceed 10 inches. Brook trout between 4 and 6 inches are very numerous, but few exceed 8 inches.

Bear Run Road follows along the lower half-mile of Cushman Branch. Above this point the stream can be reached only by walking.

Trout Run - Lycoming County
(map: page 138)

Trout Run flows through Tiadaghton State Forest and meets Pine Creek opposite the village of Cammal. There is no bridge across Pine Creek at Cammal, but when water levels are low you can wade across Pine Creek to the mouth of Trout Run. The mouth of Trout Run on Pine Creek's Wagon Wheel Pool is a popular fishing spot.

Several rugged forest roads lead in to Trout Run from Route 44. Lebo Road is extremely rough and dangerous and should be avoided. Some people refer to it as "Scary Road." Narrow Gage Road is narrow and steep, but in dry weather it is usually passable by ordinary automobiles. Trout Run Road follows the length of Trout Run. It gets muddy and rutted in some places in wet weather.

Most of Trout Run consists of fast-flowing, shallow riffles and pocket water. A few larger, deeper ledge-rock pools are found in the lower part of the creek, from Narrow Gage Road downstream to the mouth. The stream is well shaded by trees all along its length. In the summer months Trout Run becomes very low and clear.

The Fish Commission stocks Trout Run from the mouth upstream 5 miles. Trout are stocked preseason and twice inseason, with the last stocking coming in late May. Trout Run holds a fair population of wild brown and brook trout.

Upper Pine Bottom - Lycoming County
(map: page 138)

Upper Pine Bottom is a small, tumbling stream that meets Pine Creek near the junction of Routes 44 and 414, north of Waterville. The Fish Commission stocks trout from the mouth upstream 3.5 miles. Trout are stocked prior to opening day and twice inseason, with the last stocking coming in late May or early June.

Upper Pine Bottom is very small. It slows to a trickle in midsummer, but it holds a surprising number of wild browns and brook trout. The lower end of the creek flows through a steep, narrow ravine that's well shaded by tall pines. In this stretch the streambed is jumbled with rocks and downed timber.

Farther upstream, Upper Pine Bottom is closely followed by Route 44. Getting access to the stream is easier in this upper stretch, but there is less cover for trout. A small picnic area along Route 44 provides a pleasant place to have lunch and enjoy a cool drink from an old cast-iron hand pump.

Little Pine Creek - Lycoming County
(map: page 138)

Little Pine Creek is a major tributary to Pine Creek, which it meets at Waterville. The stream originates at the junction of Blockhouse Creek and Black Creek (not shown on the map), and it flows about 14 miles past woods, open grassy areas, and scattered houses and hunting camps.

The first 2.5 miles, from the origin downstream to Bonnel Run, are posted by the Texas Blockhouse Club. The Fish Commission stocks trout from Bonnel Run downstream to the mouth. Most of this water is open to public fishing, but there are a few posted properties between English Center and Carsontown.

Little Pine Lake, a 94-acre impoundment at Little Pine State Park, also receives stocked trout. A long stretch of the stream above the lake, and a shorter stretch below the lake, lie within the boundaries of the state park. Parking is available at the camping and picnic areas downstream from the lake and at several places along SR 4001 upstream from the lake.

Little Pine Creek has good fly hatches from mid-April through the end of May, and the stream is wide enough for easy fly casting. In early to mid-June, though, fishing slows because of rising water temperatures. Much of the stream is wide and shallow, and long stretches are unshaded or only partially shaded. Summer water temperatures sometimes reach 80 degrees in the lower part of the creek, downstream from the lake.

Some wild browns are found upstream from the lake, but most of Little Pine's fish come from the hatchery. Trout are stocked before opening day and three times inseason. The last stocking is in late May.

Young Womans Creek - Clinton County
(fly fishing only, 5.5 miles)
(map: page 145)

Young Womans Creek is a scenic freestone stream that flows about 10 miles through a forested valley before meeting the West Branch of the Susquehanna at the village of North Bend.

A fly fishing stretch begins 0.7 mile above the junction with Left Branch Young Womans Creek and extends upstream 5.5 miles to Beechwood Trail. Much of the fly stretch lies within Sproul State Forest, but approximately 2 miles of the fly stretch is in private land that is also open to fishing. Despite the houses and cabins found here and there along the stream, the valley is still mostly wooded.

The fly area is not stocked with trout and it holds very good numbers of wild brown and brook trout. Browns are common up to about 11 inches, and occasionally larger ones are caught. Brook trout are plentiful up to 7 or 8 inches.

When there's a good hatch of flies on this stream, the fishing can be fast and furious. Young Womans Creek has few really large pools, but the pockets and small pools are productive. In midsummer the water gets very low and clear, but water temperatures remain cool.

Above and below the fly area there are two stretches that receive hatchery trout. The Fish Commission stocks these areas preseason only.

The upper stocked section begins at Beechwood Trail and extends upstream 2 miles to the origin of Young Womans Creek, at the confluence of County Line Branch and Baldwin Branch. This stretch is entirely within Sproul State Forest.

The lower stocked stretch begins at the lower end of the fly area and extends downstream about 3 miles to the mouth. This stretch is all privately owned and open to fishing. Both the lower and upper stocked areas hold many wild trout. Despite Young Womans Creek's distance from any large cities, the fishing pressure in these stocked areas is intense on the opening weekend of the trout season.

Because Young Womans Creek is well shaded, water temperatures remain cool in the summer the whole way to the mouth, and plenty of trout can be found year around, even in the lower stretches where the stream flows past the houses of Gleasontown and North Bend.

Young Womans Creek's fly hatches include Bluewinged Olives, Blue Quills, Hendricksons, Olive Caddis, Sulphurs, Green Drakes, and Isonychia.

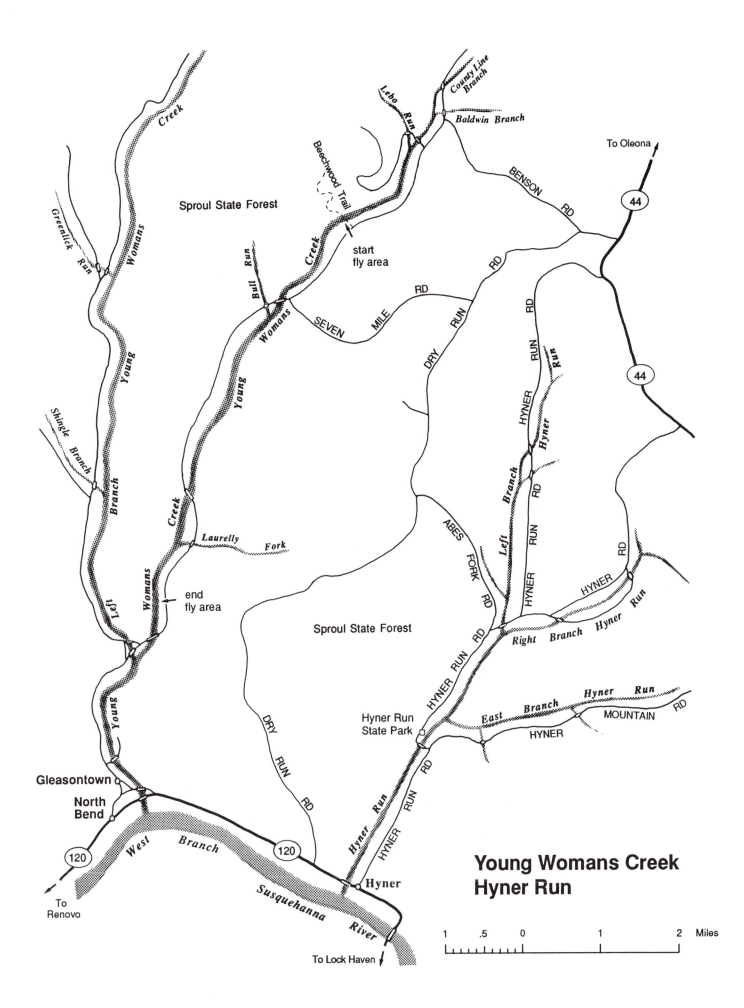

**Young Womans Creek
Hyner Run**

Left Branch Young Womans Creek - Clinton County
(map: page 145)

Left Branch Young Womans Creek is somewhat smaller and shallower than the main branch. Virtually all of the stream lies within state forest lands, and tall trees provide good shade along most of its length. A narrow, dirt forest road follows the Left Branch from its mouth to its origin.

Like the main branch, the Left Branch has few large pools, but fishing the pocket water is productive. Some stream improvement devices have been built to provide deeper holding water. Wild brown and brook trout are found in good numbers along the length of the Left Branch, but they are not as plentiful as in the main branch of Young Womans Creek, and their average size is smaller.

The Fish Commission stocks trout from the mouth upstream 8.5 miles to a forest road bridge. (The upper reaches are not shown on the map.) Trout are stocked preseason and three times inseason, with the last stocking coming in late May.

Few people fish the Left Branch after the stocked trout have been thinned out, but fishing can be good in the summer and fall for wild trout. Fewer cabins have been built along the Left Branch than along the main branch, so the Left Branch retains more of a deep woods quality. The road along the Left Branch is also more primitive. In some places it is steep and narrow and lacking in parking pulloffs.

Hyner Run - Clinton County
(map: page 145)

After Hyner Run is formed by the junction of its Left and Right Branches, it flows 4.5 miles through a wooded area before joining the West Branch of the Susquehanna River. The lower half of the creek flows through privately owned land, and the upper half flows through Hyner Run State Park and Sproul State Forest.

The Fish Commission stocks Hyner Run preseason and twice inseason, with the last stocking coming in early to mid-May. Hyner Run holds a fair number of wild brown and brook trout, but not as many as nearby Young Womans Creek, which is a much larger stream.

Most of Hyner Run is shallow, with the exception of two very large pools located just downstream of the Route 120 bridge. Houses are located along the stream for about the first mile above the Route 120 bridge, but above this the stream is forested. Hyner Run Road follows the stream through Hyner Run State Park and on up to the headwaters. A camping area, swimming pool, and picnic area are located in Hyner Run State Park.

East Branch Hyner Run is a very small, unstocked tributary to Hyner Run. It nearly disappears into the rocks in dry summers, but it holds many 4- to 5-inch native brook trout. You can fish upstream from the mouth in Hyner Run State Park or stop along Hyner Mountain Road and walk down the bank to the creek.

Right Branch Hyner Run - Clinton County
(map: page 145)

Right Branch Hyner Run is a small, rocky headwater stream that is shallow and generally lacking in cover, but you can find stocked trout and native brookies in the pockets and scattered small pools.

The Fish Commission stocks the lower 2 miles of the stream preseason and twice inseason, with the last stocking coming in early to mid-May. The Right Branch flows amid tall trees in Sproul State Forest.

Left Branch Hyner Run - Clinton County
(map: page 145)

Left Branch Hyner Run is a small, rather shallow stream that flows through Sproul State Forest. The Fish Commission stocks the lower 1.8 miles preseason and twice inseason, with the last stocking coming in early to mid-May. The Left Branch holds good numbers of small wild brook trout.

Kettle Creek - Tioga, Potter, and Clinton Counties
(Catch and release, artificials only, 1.7 miles)
(map: page 148)

Kettle Creek is one of the best known of Pennsylvania's north-country streams. Along with its numerous tributaries, Kettle Creek has provided good trout fishing for many years. In earlier days, when the area was first being opened up for logging, Kettle Creek and its tributaries swarmed with native brook trout. Brook trout from 12 to 14 inches in length were not unusual, and some fish over 18 inches were taken. Brook trout were found not just in the upper reaches of Kettle Creek, but also far downstream near the mouth. The heyday of the Kettle Creek brook trout fishery ended around 1920.

Logging, road building, and forest fires stripped the watershed of its trees, and the resulting erosion widened Kettle Creek's channel. Native brook trout are now found mostly in the headwaters and small tributary streams. The wider, warmer creek became better suited to the introduced brown trout that now make up most of Kettle Creek's wild trout population.

The trees have grown back since the early logging days, and most of Kettle Creek's drainage area is now

Kettle Creek. Fishing the evening rise at the lower end of the catch-and-release area.

forested, mountainous country, scattered with small settlements and hunting camps. This area is popular not only with anglers, but also with hunters, who pursue deer, bear, and turkey in these woods.

Upper Stretches

From its origin downstream to the influx of Billings Branch, Kettle Creek is a very small, unstocked brook trout stream. Billings Branch is a similarly small brook trout stream.

Stocking on Kettle Creek begins at the confluence of Billings Branch and continues downstream about 32 miles. From Billings Branch downstream to Germania Branch, a distance of about 4 miles, Kettle Creek holds a fair population of wild brown and brook trout in addition to the stocked fish. Brook trout are more plentiful than browns in the upper part of this stretch.

A dirt road (T433) crosses Kettle Creek about 0.7 mile below the mouth of Germania Branch. From this bridge downstream about 3 miles to the Route 44 bridge, Kettle Creek flows through a beautiful wooded area. This roadless stretch of stream holds fair numbers of wild browns and also some native brook trout.

Below the Route 44 bridge, Kettle Creek's valley widens, and open, grassy fields as well as trees line the stream banks. Signs of civilization become more frequent, too. Cabins and houses appear along the stream and paved roads, Routes 44 and 144, follow

Kettle Creek downstream. From the Route 44 bridge downstream about 6 miles to the catch-and-release area, Kettle Creek supports a fair wild brown trout population in addition to the stocked fish.

At the village of Oleona, Little Kettle Creek flows into Kettle Creek and approximately doubles its size. A few miles south of Oleona, at Ole Bull State Park, there is a children's fishing area and campsites are available.

Catch-and-Release Area

The catch-and-release area on Kettle Creek extends from just below the Route 144 bridge upstream 1.7 miles. The regulations allow only the use of artificial lures or flies, and barbless hooks are required.

The catch-and-release regulations maintain a good supply of trout here year around, so this is a good place to fish in the middle and late season, when the trout have been thinned out elsewhere on Kettle Creek. This is also the most popular stretch of Kettle Creek and it gets crowded at times.

Lower Stretches

Trout are stocked downstream to Kettle Creek Lake (Alvin Bush Dam) and also another 3 miles below the lake to a low dam known as the recreation dam. Kettle Creek Lake is also stocked with trout. Campsites are available at Kettle Creek State Park.

Below the catch-and-release area, Kettle Creek begins to take on the characteristics of a marginal

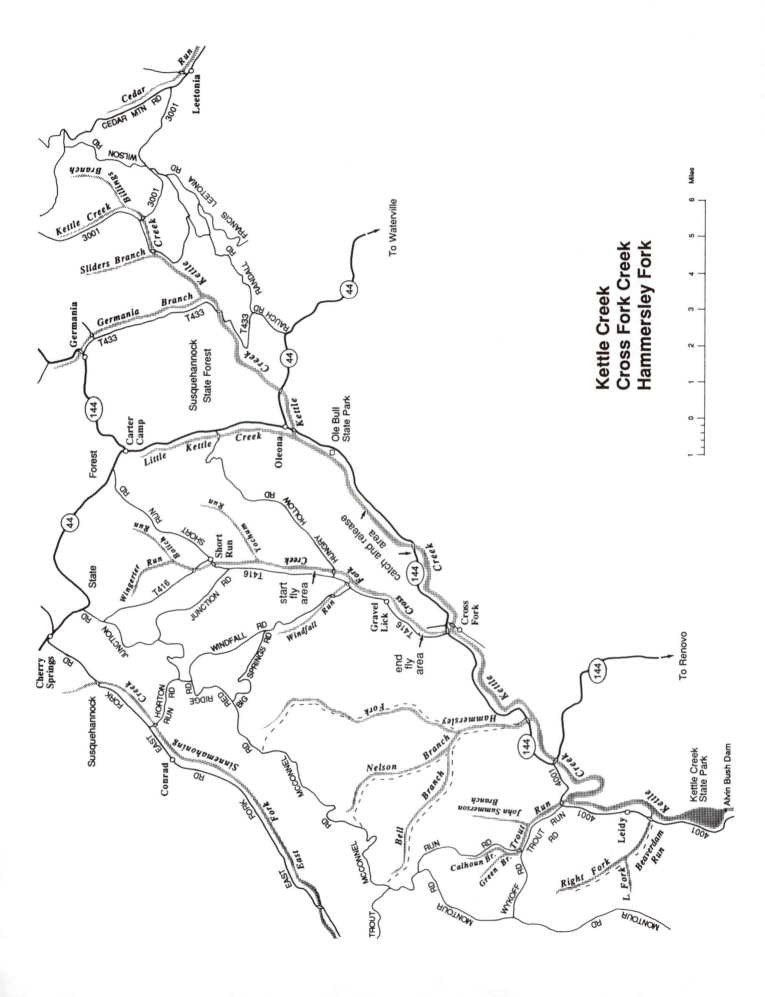

Kettle Creek
Cross Fork Creek
Hammersley Fork

trout stream, with warm summer temperatures and few wild trout. Fishing for stocked trout is good in the early season, though, and fly hatches can be excellent. Because Kettle Creek clears and drops quickly after rains, it is a good choice when other streams are too high and muddy to fish.

As the water temperatures rise in early June, trout migrate to the mouths of tributaries such as Cross Fork Creek, Hammersley Fork, and Trout Run. As the water warms even more, many of the fish move up into these feeder streams.

By late June trout become scarce in Kettle Creek anywhere below the village of Cross Fork. Then it is time to fish the catch-and-release area, the headwaters of Kettle Creek, or one of the tributary streams.

Fly Hatches

Kettle Creek has good fly hatches, which include Blue-winged Olives, Blue Quills, Quill Gordons, Hendricksons, Olive Caddis, Sulphurs, March Browns, Grey Foxes, Green Drakes, Brown Drakes, Isonychia, and Tricos.

Warm spring weather can produce Hendrickson hatches as early as opening day, but usually they begin hatching about a week later. Kettle Creek has a good Green Drake hatch that usually appears in the first week of June.

In the summer and fall, Kettle Creek becomes very low and clear, and then it's fun to try fooling the trout in the long, flat pool at the Route 144 bridge at the lower end of the catch-and-release area. These trout become very wary as the season progresses, and they'll often drift downstream peering at your fly before deciding not to take it. If you think that stocked trout in a freestone stream can't be selective, these fish may convince you otherwise. Small ant, beetle, or midge imitations seem to work best.

The Kettle Creek valley is served by two tackle shops: the Cross Fork Tackle Shop in the village of Cross Fork and the Kettle Creek Tackle Shop, which is located south of Cross Fork, along Route 144.

Starting at the headwaters and moving downstream, Kettle Creek's major tributaries are Billings Branch, Germania Branch, Little Kettle Creek, Cross Fork Creek, Hammersley Fork, Trout Run, and Beaverdam Run. All of these streams hold trout.

Billings Branch - Tioga County
(map: page 148)

Billings Branch, a small, unstocked brook trout stream, flows 2 miles through a remote area in Tioga State Forest before joining upper Kettle Creek. The forest road that follows upper Kettle Creek provides access to the mouth of Billings Branch, and anglers must walk up from there. In midsummer this stream nearly dries up, but small, native brook trout are plentiful in the pockets and pools.

Germania Branch - Potter County
(map: page 148)

Germania Branch originates north of the village of Germania in Potter County and flows 6 miles to its mouth on upper Kettle Creek. The upstream reaches flow through fields and woods, and there are many houses along the creek near Germania. The lower part of the stream, downstream from Germania, flows through Susquehannock State Forest. T433 parallels the creek south from Route 44 at Germania, providing easy access.

Trout are stocked for opening day and twice inseason in the lower 2.2 miles of the stream, where it flows through the state forest land. Trees provide good shade and cover along this attractive stretch. Germania Branch holds a fair number of wild brown and brook trout.

Little Kettle Creek - Potter County
(map: page 148)

Little Kettle Creek flows into Kettle Creek at the village of Oleona, near the intersection of Routes 44 and 144. Route 44/144 follows it upstream from Oleona, providing easy access. Trout are stocked from the mouth at Oleona upstream 4.3 miles. Above this stretch, some areas of the stream are posted. Most of the lower, stocked section of the stream flows through Susquehannock State Forest.

Little Kettle Creek is an attractive woodland stream with rocky riffles and many pockets and small pools. Good cover is provided by roots and downed trees. Tall trees form a canopy over the stream, keeping it in deep shade.

The Fish Commission stocks trout for opening day and three times inseason. Little Kettle holds some wild brown and brook trout, but despite its good cover and shade it does not hold as many wild trout as some other Kettle Creek tributaries, such as Cross Fork Creek and Hammersley Fork.

Cross Fork Creek - Potter County
(fly fishing only, 5.4 miles)
(map: page 148)

This tributary to Kettle Creek is managed as a wild trout stream and trout are no longer stocked. Like many streams that have been designated wild trout streams, Cross Fork Creek's trout population has increased since stocking was ended and fishing pressure has decreased. Cross Fork Creek holds both wild brown and brook trout. Brook trout predominate in the headwaters, a mixed brown-brook trout population is found in the middle stretches, and brown trout are most common in the lower part of the stream. Brown trout are plentiful up to 12 inches, and occasionally 14- to 16-inch fish are caught.

Cross Fork Creek is a pleasant freestone stream of moderate gradient, with alternating riffles and pools. It flows through a wooded area scattered with hunting camps. There are few really large pools and much of the stream is fairly shallow, but the many small pools and pockets shelter trout. A canopy of trees provides good shade in most places, keeping water temperatures cool throughout the summer months. Cross Fork Creek is a sentimental favorite of mine because it was here, when I just learning fly fishing, that I first hooked a good-sized wild trout: a heavy, brightly-colored 14-inch brown.

Most of Cross Fork Creek is under fly-fishing-only regulations. The fly area begins at an abandoned bridge located a little less than a mile above the mouth and continues upstream for 5.4 miles to Rhulo Hollow, which is located above the bridge on Hungry Hollow Road. Above the fly area, there is also good fishing for wild brown and brook trout.

Cross Fork Creek flows into Kettle Creek a short distance below the village of Cross Fork. Just east of the Route 144 bridge, a road turns off Route 144 and follows Cross Fork Creek upstream to the abandoned bridge that marks the lower end of the fly area. This is a good place to park to fish the lower water.

West of the Route 144 bridge, a gravel road (T416) turns off from Route 144 and follows upstream along Cross Fork Creek to the headwaters. Most of Cross Fork Creek flows through the Susquehannock State Forest, but there are houses on private properties at several places along the creek. Because of these private properties and because T416 in most places is located on the hillside well above the creek, you'll need to do a little exploring to find the good access points.

Cross Fork Creek has good fly hatches, which include Blue-winged Olives, Blue Quills, Quill Gordons, Hendricksons, March Browns, Grey Foxes, Sulphurs, Green Drakes, Brown Drakes, Light Cahills, Isonychia, and Tricos.

Hammersley Fork - Potter County
(map: page 148)

Hammersley Fork originates in a remote, mountainous area of the Susquehannock State Forest in Potter County and flows south approximately 9 miles to its mouth on Kettle Creek. This near-wilderness stream is accessible only from a road near the mouth or by hiking into the headwaters. Hammersley Fork is one of the larger tributaries to Kettle Creek; it's approximately the same size as Cross Fork Creek.

Hammersley Fork was known historically as a great brook trout stream. Fish Commission surveys in the summers of 1981 and 1982, however, indicated that brown trout were replacing the brook trout in the lower half of the stream.

All stocking was ended in 1983, and Hammersley Fork is now managed as a wild trout stream. In recent years anglers report catching mostly brook trout, even in the lower stretches of the creek, so the trout population may be swinging back towards the brook trout. Most of the brookies are less than 7 inches long, but fair numbers reach 8 to 9 inches.

Fishing pressure on Hammersley Fork is light compared to most trout streams. I fished the stream on a weekend in early May and saw no one else along the stream. The same day I saw at least a dozen anglers fishing in one pool at the bridge on Kettle Creek's catch-and-release area.

Hammersley Fork is far from being an untouched fishery, though. Many hikers camp and fish along the stream and some anglers illegally drive vehicles up along the creek. Hammersley Fork veterans recall that years ago the fishing pressure was very light and the brook trout often reached 10 to 12 inches.

Route 144 crosses Hammersley Fork near its mouth about 4 miles west of the village of Cross Fork. A dirt road follows the creek's east side for 0.7 mile before coming to a ford.

The road continues from the ford up along the west side of the creek for about 1 mile, passing several cabins, but it is extremely rough and there are signs at the ford prohibiting further vehicle travel. The best bet is to park near the ford and walk upstream from there. At the last cabin there are more signs prohibiting vehicles and above this point you enter the real backcountry of the Hammersley Fork drainage.

About 1 mile upstream from the last cabin, Nelson Branch flows into the Hammersley Fork. The two streams are about equal in size where they meet. Both Nelson Branch and its tributary, Bell Branch, hold native brook trout. The headwaters of Hammersley Fork can be reached by hiking in on trails that lead south from McConnel Road.

Trout Run - Clinton County
(map: page 148)

This tributary to Kettle Creek is quite small, less than half the size of Hammersley Fork or Cross Fork Creek, but it offers good fishing for stocked trout and native brook trout. A large parking area located at the SR 4001 bridge provides access to the lower stretch of Trout Run and also to Kettle Creek. From here Trout Run Road, a dirt forest road, follows up along the stream to its headwaters. Trout Run flows through Susquehannock State Forest, where surrounding trees provide deep shade.

The Fish Commission stocks trout once each season, prior to opening day, from the mouth upstream to where Trout Run is formed by the confluence of Calhoun Branch and Green Branch. Besides the stocked fish, Trout Run holds a good population of native brook trout.

About 2 miles upstream from the mouth, Trout Run is joined by the John Summerson Branch, a very small, unstocked stream with a good population of brook trout. No roads follow this little "trickle trib," but a trail follows it up from Trout Run Road. Water levels get extremely low here in the summer months.

Calhoun Branch and Green Branch, which join to form the headwaters of Trout Run, are very small, unstocked streams that hold native brook trout.

Beaverdam Run - Clinton County
(map: page 148)

Beaverdam Run flows 1.7 miles through a forested valley and meets Kettle Creek a short distance above Kettle Creek State Park. Most of the stream flows through Sproul State Forest, but there is some privately owned land near the mouth. A dirt road follows along the west bank. The road is in good condition along the lower half of the stream, but farther upstream it becomes narrow and rough.

The Fish Commission stocks Beaverdam Run with brook trout preseason and twice inseason, with the last stocking coming in early or mid-May. Wild trout are not plentiful, but the stream does hold some native brook trout. The Left Fork and Right Fork of Beaverdam Run also hold some native brook trout.

First Fork Sinnemahoning Creek - Potter and Cameron Counties
(map: page 152 and 154)

The First Fork of the Sinnemahoning is a long, wide, mostly shallow freestone stream, which, along with its tributaries, drains much of southwestern Potter County. It is formed by the junction of Prouty Run, which is a good trout stream, and Borie Branch, which is not. The Fish Commission stocks the First Fork heavily from its origin downstream nearly 30 miles to its mouth on Sinnemahoning Creek in Cameron County.

In the first several miles of the First Fork, from its origin downstream to the concrete bridge on SR 3003 above Costello, there is a good population of wild brown trout and many trout can be found throughout the season. This stretch is mostly wooded, but scattered hunting camps and homes are found near the stream. There are a few, short posted stretches that make finding access a little tricky. The easiest way to get access to this stretch is to park at the concrete SR 3003 bridge and walk upstream from there. A broad path follows along the south side of the stream.

From the SR 3003 bridge downstream to Costello, the First Fork flows through a broad valley of farms, meadows, and hunting camps. This stretch holds some wild and holdover brown trout, but they're not as plentiful as in the upper reaches. Because much of this stretch is unshaded, summer water temperatures become warm here. The pool at the mouth of South Woods Branch often offers good fishing.

Another nice piece of water is in a meadow about a half-mile upstream of the bridge at Costello. Here the stream narrows and carves out deep holes, and good cover is provided by undercut banks and tree roots. These holes hold trout even in the summer, when much of the rest of the stream gets too shallow to provide good cover. Parking is available at the bridge at Costello.

At Costello, Freeman Run flows in and increases the volume and width of the First Fork. The stretch from Costello to Wharton offers good fly fishing from opening day through about the first week in June, mostly for stocked trout. This stretch has a mix of riffles and long, flat, open pools. Heavy fly hatches produce good dry fly fishing. By the time the Green Drake hatches are over, the trout have been thinned out, and many of the remaining fish have begun to migrate to find cooler water. By mid-June trout will be found mostly at the inlets of cool tributary streams or in deep holes. Few wild trout are found in this stretch or anywhere downstream from here.

At Wharton the First Fork is joined by East Fork Sinnemahoning Creek, which is smaller than the First Fork and a fine trout stream. Below Wharton the First Fork is a put-and-take stream, with few trout remaining into the summer. Fair numbers of smallmouth bass are found in this lower water.

The George B. Stevenson Reservoir is stocked with trout preseason and three times inseason. Campsites are available near the reservoir at Sinnemahoning State Park. An interesting place to fish is just below the George B. Stevenson dam. There is a picnic area here, and just opposite the parking lot there are some nice rapids, runs, and pools. The water also gets quite warm here in the summer, but the deep runs and pools below the dam hold trout later into the season than the rest of the lower creek. In early July I saw a large fish swimming around in the concrete tailrace immediately below the dam. At first I thought this big, dark fish was a carp, but after looking more carefully, I saw that it was a heavy brown trout over 20 inches long. No, I didn't catch it.

The First Fork has heavy fly hatches, including Blue-winged Olives, Blue Quills, Quill Gordons, Hendricksons, Sulphurs, Tan Caddis, March Browns, Grey Foxes, Green Drakes, Brown Drakes, Light Cahills, Isonychia, and Tricos.

Although most of the First Fork gets too warm and low to offer good fishing in the summer months, many of its tributaries do fish well through the summer and into the fall. Some of the better ones are Prouty Run, East Fork Sinnemahoning Creek, Bailey Run, Lushbaugh Run, and Lick Island Run.

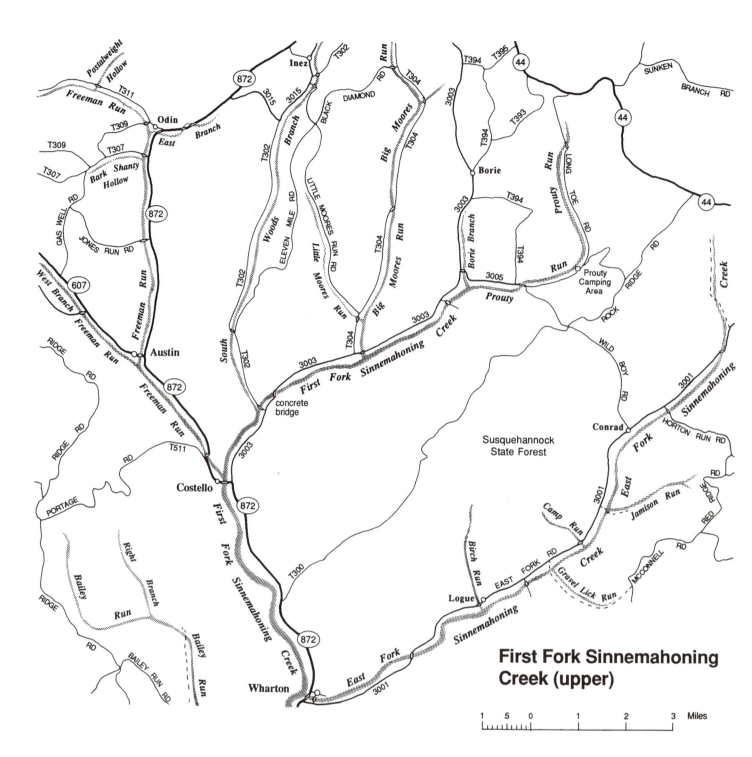

First Fork Sinnemahoning Creek (upper)

Prouty Run - Potter County
(map: page 152)

Prouty Run, or Prouty Branch as it is often called, is a small stream that flows into the upper end of First Fork Sinnemahoning Creek. The lower section of the stream holds an excellent population of wild brown trout, and native brook trout are found in the headwaters.

Prouty Run joins Borie Branch to form the First Fork near the intersection of SR 3003 and SR 3005.

From here upstream about 2.7 miles to the camping area at Prouty Place State Park, Prouty Run holds mostly brown trout and also a few brookies. Above the camping area, Prouty Run flows through a narrow valley shaded by tall evergreen trees. In this area you will find mostly brook trout. Continuing upstream, Prouty Run soon becomes very small and in dry summers these headwaters slow to a trickle.

Upstream from Prouty Place State Park, the creek flows through an undeveloped wooded area and finding access is not a problem. From the State Park downstream to the mouth, however, the stream is all privately owned, and there are many houses along the banks. SR 3005 parallels this stretch, but there are few parking spaces. As of this writing, there is little posted property along Prouty Run, except for a short stretch owned by Prouty Trout Farm, a fee fishing operation.

Big Moores Run - Potter County
(map: page 152)

Big Moores Run flows into First Fork Sinnemahoning Creek north of Costello. T304 follows the stream from near the mouth up into the headwaters. Much of the property on the lower and upper sections of the creek is posted against trespassing, but in the middle part of the creek there is a wooded stretch where you will find pleasant fishing for hatchery fish and wild brown and brook trout. This stretch starts about a half mile below the bridge on Black Diamond Road and extends downstream 4 miles. Most of this stretch is in Tiadaghton State Forest. In this area Big Moores Run is 12 to 15 feet wide and well shaded by trees and shrubs.

Most of the land along the upper reaches of Big Moores Run, upstream from the bridge on Black Diamond Road, is posted, but if you can get permission to fish from landowners, you will find good numbers of wild brook trout.

(Note: Little Moores Run is not stocked and it often goes nearly dry in the summer.)

South Woods Branch - Potter County
(map: page 152)

South Woods Branch meets First Fork Sinnemahoning Creek about 1.7 miles north of Costello. From the mouth upstream about 1.5 miles to the first bridge on T302, the creek flows through open meadows, but upstream from this bridge the creek flows through a well-forested area. Much of this forest land is within Susquehannock State Forest and most of the stream is open to fishing, but there are several short posted stretches.

South Woods Branch is stocked with hatchery trout preseason and three times inseason with the last stocking coming in mid-May. In addition to the stocked trout, the stream also holds good numbers of small wild brown and brook trout.

Freeman Run - Potter County
(map: page 152)

Freeman Run is a tributary to First Fork Sinnemahoning Creek, which it meets at Costello. From the headwaters downstream to the confluence of Bark Shanty Hollow near Odin, no trout are stocked and most of the land along the creek is posted against trespassing. If you can persuade a landowner to allow you to fish, you will find good numbers of native brook trout here. On some maps, this upper part of Freeman Run is labelled Odin Run.

Trout are stocked from the confluence of Bark Shanty Hollow downstream 7.5 miles to the mouth. Route 872 closely parallels the stream, providing good access. The upper part of the stocked stretch, from Bark Shanty Hollow downstream to Austin, is mostly wooded, but there are some scattered houses. The bridge on Jones Run Road is a good place to park and fish upstream or down.

About 1 mile above the small town of Austin, you will see the crumbling remains of an old concrete dam that collapsed years ago, drowning many people. From Austin downstream to the mouth, Freeman Run is still partially wooded, but more houses appear along the banks.

The Fish Commission stocks trout for opening day and once inseason, usually in late April or early May. Wild trout are not abundant in the stocked stretch of Freeman Run, but wild browns and brookies are sometimes caught. Fishing is best early in the year, before the stocked fish have been thinned out.

West Branch Freeman Run is a very small woodland brook that flows into Freeman Run at Austin. Because of the West Branch's small size and its wild trout population, no trout are stocked. This little tributary holds a good population of wild brook trout, mostly 4 to 6 inches long. Route 607 parallels the entire length of the stream. Many houses line the lower mile of the West Branch, but farther upstream the banks are mostly tree-lined and access is easier.

East Fork Sinnemahoning Creek - Potter County
(map: page 152)

East Fork Sinnemahoning Creek begins as a remote brook trout stream near Cherry Springs and flows southeast 14 miles before joining First Fork Sinnemahoning Creek at Wharton. Along its way the East Fork offers native brook trout in the upper reaches, hatchery trout mixed with wild brown and brook trout in the middle reaches, and mostly stocked trout at the lower end.

The East Fork is smaller than the First Fork—perhaps half its size. It is a gently flowing stream, and its trout lie in small pools and pockets. Because it is well shaded along most of its length and fed by numerous small, cold tributaries, the East Branch remains fairly cool in the summer months.

Except for about 2 miles of the headwaters, the entire stream is paralleled by SR 3001, which can be reached from Route 872 at Wharton. Above Conrad the East Fork lies mostly within the Susquehannock State Forest. From Conrad downstream to the mouth

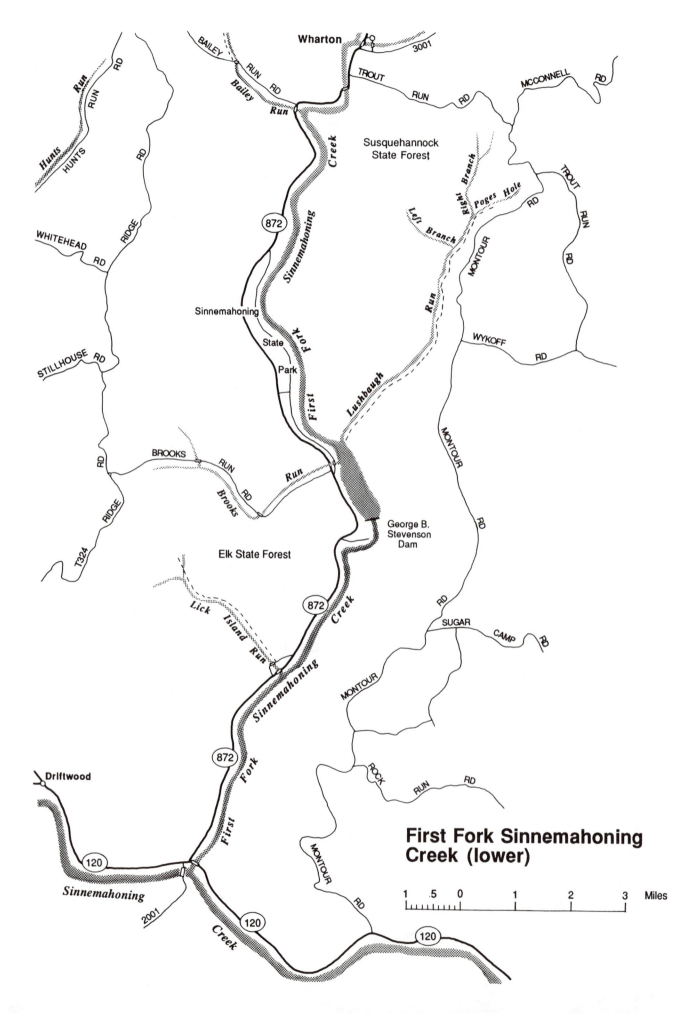

**First Fork Sinnemahoning
Creek (lower)**

East Fork Sinnemahoning Creek between Wharton and Logue.

at Wharton, there are homes and camps as well as trees along the stream.

The East Fork is stocked with hatchery trout from the mouth at Wharton upstream to the upper SR 3001 bridge, skipping over the stretch between Conrad and Camp Run. This 2.9-mile stretch is not stocked because of its good wild brown trout population and because scattered posting limits access.

In the lower 3 miles of the East Branch, from the mouth at Wharton upstream to the first SR 3001 bridge, the fishing is mostly for stocked trout. This stretch is mostly unshaded and water temperatures climb here in the summer months.

From the lower SR 3001 bridge upstream to Conrad, there are good numbers of wild browns, and wild brookies are mixed in with the browns in the upper part of this stretch.

From Conrad upstream, you will find a mixed population of brown and brook trout, with the brook trout taking over in the upper reaches. About 2.5 miles above Conrad, SR 3001 crosses a bridge over the East Branch. Near the bridge there are several cabins that make access difficult, but about a half-mile farther up along SR 3001 you'll find a hiking trail that continues up along the stream. From here to the headwaters, you can fish for native brook trout in wilderness solitude.

The East Fork Sinnemahoning's waters run clear, and careful wading and casting are required to avoid spooking the trout. Many of the trout are found where cover is provided by undercut banks, tree roots, or downed logs. In the summer, try casting terrestrials such as Letort Crickets or beetle patterns to these spots. The East Fork's tiny tributaries, such as Birch Run, Gravel Lick Run, and Jamison Run, are worth a try for native brook trout.

Fly hatches on the East Fork include Blue-winged Olives, Blue Quills, Quill Gordons, Hendricksons, Sulphurs, March Browns, Grey Foxes, Green Drakes, Brown Drakes, Light Cahills, Isonychia, and Tricos.

Bailey Run - Potter County
(map: pages 152 and 154)

Bailey Run flows into First Fork Sinnemahoning Creek about 2 miles south of Wharton. Parking is available near the mouth at the Route 872 bridge. Bailey Run Road follows the stream up from the mouth for 1.5 miles; then it crosses a bridge over Bailey Run and turns away from the stream. From this bridge downstream 1.5 miles to the mouth, Bailey Run is stocked with trout and it also holds a good population of wild brown and brook trout. Most of this lower stretch is in woods and grassland, but there are a few dwellings along the stream.

From the bridge upstream to the headwaters, a distance of about 6.5 miles, Bailey Run is not stocked, but it offers good fishing for wild brown and brook trout to those who are willing to do some walking. There are many cabins near the bridge, but once you walk upstream about a half-mile you enter the Susquehannock State Forest, which provides a wilderness setting up into the headwaters.

Lushbaugh Run - Cameron and Potter County

(map: page 154)

Lushbaugh Run is a small brook trout stream that flows through a roadless area of Susquehannock State Forest. The stream flows into the upper end of the George B. Stevenson Reservoir on First Fork Sinnemahoning Creek. You can reach the mouth of Lushbaugh Run by wading the First Fork above the reservoir, then walking south along the shore of the reservoir. The upper stretches of Lushbaugh Run can

be reached by walking in over mountainous terrain from Montour Road.

Lushbaugh Run is about 4.3 miles long from its mouth upstream to where it splits into Left and Right Lushbaugh Runs. The stream is densely shaded by trees and it holds a good population of small brook trout. The Left and Right Branches also hold brook trout and also flow through remote, wooded areas.

Geological survey maps aren't really necessary for exploring most Pennsylvania streams, but if you decide to hike into the headwaters of Lushbaugh Run and explore the branches, you may find these maps useful. The lower part of Lushbaugh Run is on the First Fork quadrangle map, and the upper part is on the Hammersley Fork quadrangle map.

Brooks Run - Cameron County

(map: page 154)

Brooks Run is a fast-falling little stream that flows into the George B. Stevenson Reservoir at Sinnemahoning State Park. Most of the stream lies within Elk State Forest, and a paralleling forest road provides easy access.

As it courses through a narrow, deeply shaded ravine, Brooks Run tumbles over short drops into

Lushbaugh Run.

small plunge pools and pockets. The Fish Commission stocks Brooks Run preseason and three times inseason, with the last stocking coming in late May or early June. Several wired refuge areas are closed to fishing from opening day until June 15.

Lick Island Run - Cameron County
(map: page 154)

Lick Island Run is a small, unstocked brook trout stream that flows into First Fork Sinnemahoning Creek about 3 miles south of George B. Stevenson Dam. The stream is about 4 miles long and it flows most of its length through a scenic, wooded area in Elk State Forest.

A secondary road turns west from Route 872 and crosses a bridge over Lick Island Run. There are several cabins and houses near this bridge, so finding a parking place is difficult. A short distance north of the bridge, a narrow, rough dirt road turns off and follows the stream up into the state forest lands. This road is easy to miss because it is so narrow that you may mistake it for a cabin drive. Lick Island Run holds a good population of native brook trout.

Allegheny River - Potter County
(map: page 158)

The Allegheny River, which carries tug and barge traffic near its mouth at Pittsburgh, begins life as a trout stream in Potter County.

In the headwaters above Seven Bridges, the Allegheny is a very small stream that holds native brook trout. Unfortunately, much of the land along the stream is posted in this upper area.

From Seven Bridges down to Colesburg, the Allegheny is still quite small but it holds good numbers of wild brown and brook trout. In the upper part of this stretch, the Allegheny flows through grassy meadows and farther downstream, near Colesburg, it wanders through brushy, tangled swamps.

Stocking begins at Colesburg, and from here down to Coudersport, a distance of about 9 miles, the Allegheny offers good fishing for both stocked and wild trout. The wild trout here are mostly browns, but there are also some brookies. The brown trout population in this stretch is quite good. Stream surveys taken here in late summer turned up many browns up to 12 inches, fair numbers to 14 inches, and a few larger fish up to 18 inches.

Through the town of Coudersport, the Allegheny is contained within a concrete flood control channel, and fishing is not permitted. This channel is wide, shallow, and mostly unshaded, and it warms the water in the summer months. Mill Creek, which is an unstocked stream with a good wild brown trout population and some difficult access problems, meets the Allegheny in Coudersport.

Trout are heavily stocked in the 10-mile stretch between Coudersport and Roulette, and this is pretty good trout water early in the year. Most trout caught in this area are stocked, but some wild trout are also present as a result of spawning in tributary streams such as Dingman Run and Reed Run. (Reed Run is posted against trespassing.)

The Coudersport-to-Roulette stretch has long been known for producing large brown trout. This stretch does get warm in the summer, though, and as temperatures increase, trout move to areas of cooler water, such as deep pools, spring holes, and mouths of tributaries. Anglers who know the stream well can find these trout and sometimes catch big trout while night fishing. Summer fishing is generally much better above Coudersport, though, where there is a good wild trout population and cooler water temperatures.

The Allegheny is also stocked below Roulette, as far downstream as Port Allegheny in Mckean County, but this lower water is really warmwater habitat and holds few trout after the stocked fish are caught in the spring. This stretch offers good fishing for smallmouth bass and muskies.

The Fish Commission stocks the Allegheny for opening day and once inseason, usually between mid-May and the first week of June.

Mill Creek - Potter County
(map: page 158)

Mill Creek is an unstocked stream that flows into the Allegheny River in Coudersport. It holds a good population of wild brown trout throughout most of the stream, and wild brook trout are found in the headwaters. Mill Creek is well shaded and fed by springs, and it maintains cool water temperatures even in midsummer.

Access is a problem on Mill Creek because the lower reaches flow right through Coudersport, and even the upper stretch of the creek has homes and businesses along the banks. If you have come to Potter County looking for a wilderness trout stream, this is not the place.

Parking is available at a pulloff near the Route 44 bridge at Sweden Valley. Above this bridge the stream splits into two small branches: the upper stretch of Mill Creek, which is paralleled by Route 44, and Trout Run, which is paralleled upstream by Route 6. Both branches are very small and hold mostly native brook trout. Mill Creek can be fished upstream from the Route 44 bridge for about a half-mile, but then you will encounter posted property.

Downstream from the Route 44 bridge, Mill Creek flows through a wooded area scattered with houses. The stream is slow moving here and has some deep holes. Heavy brush makes casting and even walking a challenge. From this area downstream, brown trout predominate.

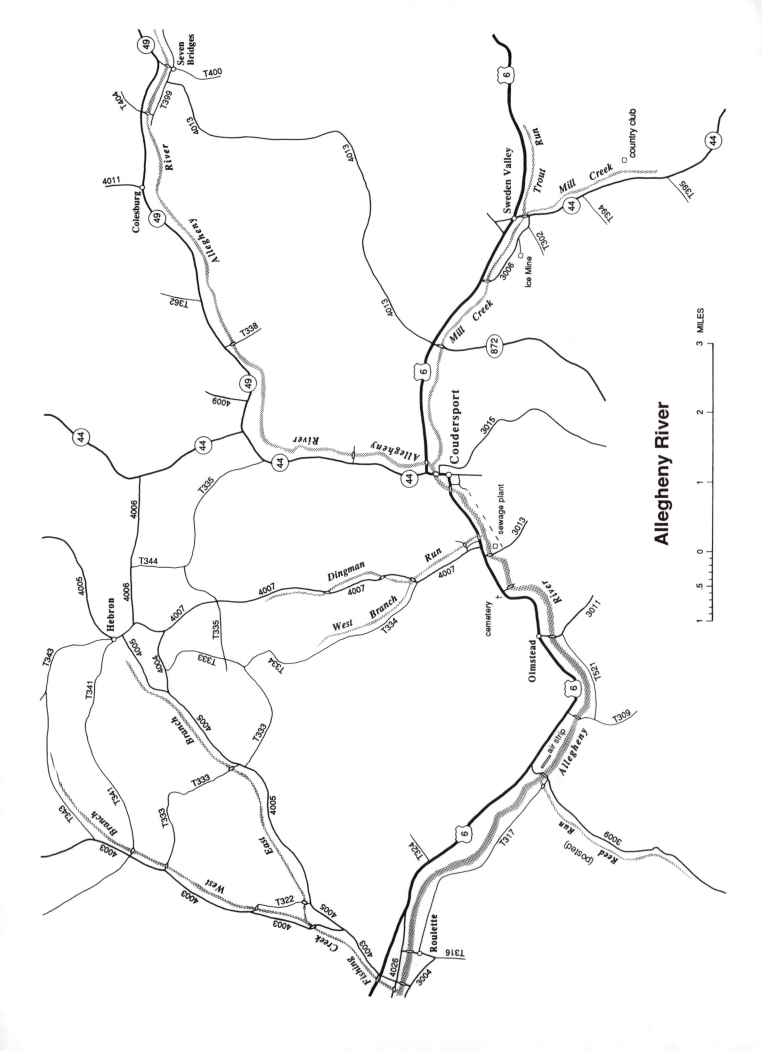

Allegheny River

Another access point to Mill Creek is the Route 872 bridge. Here the stream is surrounded by low trees and thick brush. Houses and businesses are found near the stream in this area also.

Dingman Run - Potter County
(map: page 158)

Dingman Run is a small freestone stream that flows through a brushy, wooded area before meeting the Allegheny River about 1 mile west of Coudersport. The stream was previously stocked over a distance of 3 miles, but stream surveys show that Dingman Run has a fine population of wild brown trout and also some brook trout, so the stream is now managed as a wild trout stream and fish are no longer stocked. The stream holds many trout from 4 to 10 inches long, and an occasional brown reaches 14 inches.

A road follows Dingman Run from Route 6, near the mouth, upstream to the headwaters. About 1 mile up from Route 6, the road forks. The road to the right follows Dingman Run, the road to the left follows its small tributary, West Branch Dingman Run.

West Branch Dingman Run is a very small, densely shaded stream, with a good native brook trout population. The stream becomes too small to fish about 1 mile above its mouth.

There is little parking near the Route 6 bridge and there are houses along the stream in this area. Probably the best way to fish Dingman Run is to park at the first bridge above Route 6 and fish up towards the junction of Dingman Run and the West Branch. On a recent visit, much of the West Branch and the upper reaches of Dingman Run were posted.

Fishing Creek - Potter County
(map: page 158)

Potter County's Fishing Creek is a stocked trout stream that joins the Allegheny River near Roulette. It originates at the junction of its East and West Branches and flows 2 miles through a valley of farms and scattered houses. The Fish Commission stocks trout preseason and once inseason, usually two or three weeks after opening day. Fishing is best in the early season, because Fishing Creek warms in midsummer and holds few wild trout.

East Branch Fishing Creek - Potter County
(map: page 158)

East Branch Fishing Creek is a small, shallow stream that is stocked with trout, but which holds few wild trout because of siltation problems. The Fish Commission stocks trout preseason and once inseason, usually a week or two after opening day.

West Branch Fishing Creek - Potter County
(map: page 158)

West Branch Fishing Creek provides better trout habitat than either the main branch of Fishing Creek or the East Branch. The West Branch is stocked from its mouth upstream 3 miles to Fisk Hollow, which flows in just below the T341 bridge. The Fish Commission stocks trout preseason and once inseason, usually two or three weeks after opening day.

In addition to the stocked trout, West Branch Fishing Creek also holds a fair population of wild brown trout. Alternating riffles and pools provide good holding water, and much of the stream is shaded by surrounding trees.

Oswayo Creek - Potter County
(map: page 160)

Oswayo Creek is not as widely known as some other Potter County trout streams, such as Pine Creek, Kettle Creek, or First Fork Sinnemahoning Creek, but it offers very good fishing for wild brown trout. For many years Oswayo Creek has produced big brown trout for the small group of anglers who fish the stream seriously. Many of the bigger fish have been caught at night.

Above the Fish Commission hatchery located near the village of Oswayo, Oswayo Creek is very small and most of the land along the creek is posted. Near the hatchery, springs and tributaries increase the flow of the stream and keep it running cool all through the summer.

From the hatchery downstream 6 miles to the mouth of Clara Creek, no trout are stocked in Oswayo Creek because of the plentiful wild brown trout found here. In the upper part of this stretch, near Oswayo, the stream flows through brushy meadows and past occasional houses. Some access points include the hatchery parking lot, the bridge on Calhune Road, and the T354 bridge. There is a short posted stretch directly below the T354 bridge.

Farther downstream, you can find parking along the shoulder near the Route 244 bridge. The stream is narrow here, but it carries a surprising volume of water even in dry summers. Upstream from the Route 244 bridge, the banks are lined with heavy brush, and the creek has carved out short, deep holes and undercut banks.

Still farther downstream, you can park near the T351 bridge and enjoy good fishing upstream or down. From the T351 bridge downstream past Clara Creek, and almost as far as the mouth of Elevenmile Creek, Oswayo Creek flows through a heavily wooded area, and here you will find deep pools and tangles of downed trees, which make wading difficult in spots,

Oswayo Creek

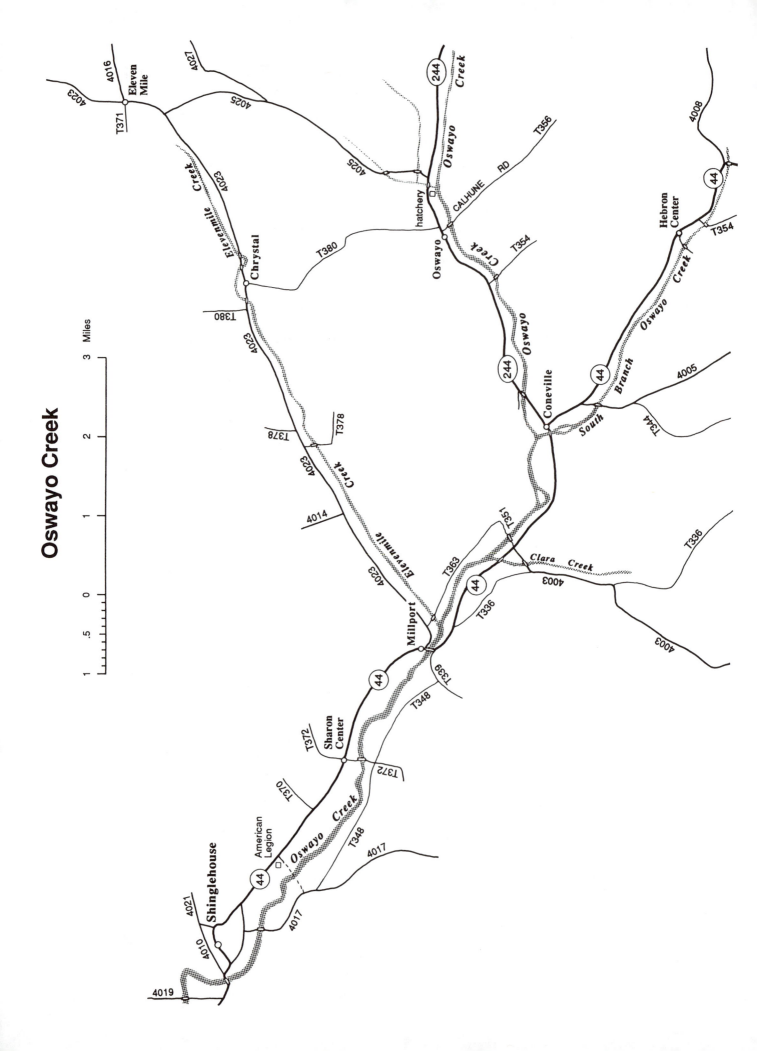

but provide excellent cover for trout. Some anglers park alongside Route 44 near the bridge over Clara Creek and walk from there to Oswayo Creek.

Oswayo Creek's stocked water begins at the mouth of Clara Creek and continues downstream 3.7 miles to the T372 bridge near Sharon Center. The Fish Commission stocks trout prior to opening day and once inseason, in late April or early May. The stocked stretch holds a good population of wild and holdover brown trout, but there are not as many wild trout here as in the unstocked water farther upstream. Near the mouth of Elevenmile Creek, there is a stretch of open meadows along the stream, but in most places the banks of Oswayo Creek are wooded.

From Sharon Center downstream to Shinglehouse, there are some very deep pools. In this lower water, Oswayo Creek gets rather warm in the summer months, and smallmouth bass and muskies inhabit this stretch. Hatchery trout that have drifted down from upstream stockings are caught here in the early season, though, and big browns are sometimes caught as far downstream as Shinglehouse and occasionally even below Shinglehouse.

Oswayo Creek has good fly hatches, including Sulphurs, Grey Foxes, Green Drakes, and Isonychia.

South Branch Oswayo Creek - Potter County
(map: page 160)

You can find good fishing for both wild and stocked trout on South Branch Oswayo Creek, a small, brushy tributary to Oswayo Creek. Most of the stream flows through old meadows growing up in brush and low, scrubby trees. The upper part of the creek is more heavily wooded.

The Fish Commission stocks trout from the T354 bridge above Hebron Center downstream to the mouth. Stocking takes place prior to opening day and once inseason, usually in late April or early May. South Branch Oswayo Creek holds a good population of wild browns up to 12 inches in length and lesser numbers of wild brook trout.

Elevenmile Creek - Potter County
(map: page 160)

This small tributary to Oswayo Creek offers fishing for both wild brown trout and stocked trout. It originates near the village of Eleven Mile in northwest Potter County and flows 7.5 miles before it reaches its confluence with Oswayo Creek at the village of Millport. The stream flows past woodlots, open meadows, brushy areas, and rural residences.

Elevenmile Creek is closely paralleled by SR 4023 from its mouth to its headwaters. Turn onto this road from Route 44 at Millport. Unfortunately, parking spaces along this road are scarce. The land along the creek is all privately owned, but most of it is open to fishing. A short stretch near the middle of the stream is posted against trespassing.

From the mouth at Millport upstream 4 miles, Elevenmile Creek is stocked with hatchery trout and it also holds a good wild brown trout population. The Fish Commission stocks trout prior to opening day and once inseason, usually in early or mid-May. Stream surveys in midsummer found good numbers of trout from 2 to 10 inches and fair numbers up to 14 inches. Most of the fish remaining late in the season were wild trout, but a few fish left over from stocking were also found.

Above the stocked stretch, Elevenmile Creek is managed as a wild trout stream and receives no hatchery trout. The stream is very small in this upper stretch and slows to a trickle in dry years. Water quality is good, though, and this section holds a good brown trout population. Stream surveys found many trout from 2 to 10 inches and a few up to 15 inches.

Genesee River - Potter County
(map: page 162)

The Genesee River originates near Ulysses in Potter County and flows north about 9 miles before crossing into New York state. In Pennsylvania, the Genesee is a small stream coursing through a valley of farms, meadows, and patches of woods. It is a gently flowing stream with few fast riffles or deep pools. The Genesee is joined by the Middle Branch of the Genesee at Hickox and by the West Branch of the Genesee at the town of Genesee. Nearly all of the land along the Genesee and its branches is privately owned, so gaining access is not so easy as on streams surrounded by state forest and game lands.

In the headwaters the Genesee is joined by Ludington Run, a small stream that is no longer stocked because of posting. The Fish Commission stocks the Genesee from the confluence of Ludington Run downstream 5.4 miles to the New York line. Trout are stocked before opening day and once inseason. The upper part of the Genesee River holds some wild brown and brook trout, but they aren't abundant.

Fly hatches on the Genesee are seldom heavy, but Blue Quills appear in late April and Light Cahills emerge in early summer.

Middle Branch Genesee River - Potter County
(map: page 162)

The Middle Branch Genesee River begins near the village of Gold and flows north to join the Genesee River at Hickox. Some anglers call this stream the Gold Branch. The Middle Branch flows through a rural valley of farms, woodlands, and scattered cabins and homes.

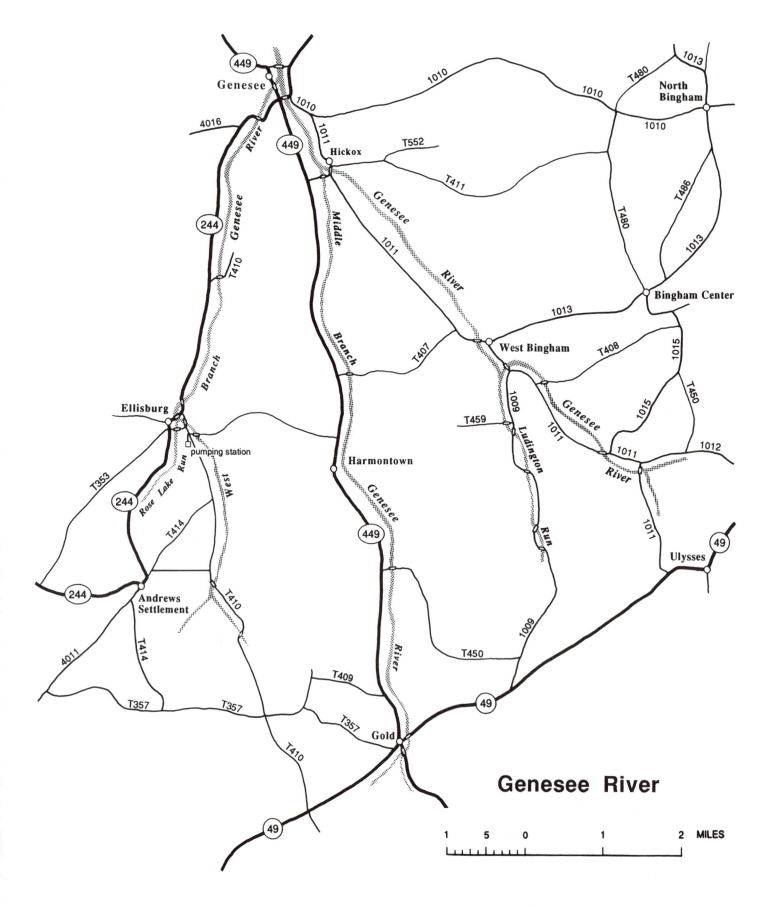

Genesee River

In the headwaters near Gold, the Middle Branch Genesee River has good fishing for native brook trout, but several posted stretches make access difficult. A sportsmen's club stocks trout in this area.

The Fish Commission begins stocking 1 mile downstream from Gold and stocks trout from this point to the mouth. Stocking takes place prior to opening day and once inseason. The stocked stretch of the Middle Branch also holds fair numbers of native brook trout and a few wild brown trout.

West Branch Genesee River - Potter County
(map: page 162)

The West Branch Genesee River originates near Andrews Settlement and flows north 7 miles to join the main branch of the Genesee River at the town of Genesee. The West Branch is a small, moderate-gradient stream that drains a watershed of woods, farms, and hunting camps.

From Ellisburg upstream into the headwaters, the West Branch is not stocked, but this stretch holds a dense population of small brook trout. From Ellisburg downstream 4.6 miles to the mouth, the West Branch is stocked with hatchery trout and this stretch also holds a good brook trout population and a few wild browns. The Fish Commission stocks trout preseason and once inseason.

Other Northcentral PA Streams
(no maps)

No maps were included for the following streams and the descriptions were kept brief, but these streams are also well worth fishing.

Middle Creek - Snyder County

Middle Creek is stocked from the village of Middle Creek downstream to the town of Middleburg. This farm-country stream is limestone influenced and it has good insect hatches, but its water gets very warm in the summer months. The water temperature reached 90 degrees at the Route 522 bridge during the drought of 1988. The fishing is mostly put-and-take, but large browns are occasionally caught where springs and tributaries flow in.

Swift Run is perhaps the best of Middle Creek's tributaries. This small freestone stream is stocked and it holds a good population of wild brook trout in its upper stretches, where it flows through Bald Eagle State Forest.

South Branch Middle Creek, North Branch Middle Creek, and Kern Run are other stocked tributaries to Middle Creek.

Buffalo Creek - Union County

Buffalo Creek is stocked with trout from T366 (Aikey Road), which crosses the stream west of the village of Pleasant Grove, downstream about 12 miles to Cowan. The fishing here is mostly put-and-take.

North Branch Buffalo Creek is stocked with trout from its mouth on Buffalo Creek near Mifflinburg upstream about 7 miles to the Mifflinburg Reservoir. Most of this stretch is forested, but some farms and homes appear along the lower end of the creek. A few wild brown and brook trout are found in this stocked stretch of the stream, and many stocked trout carry over into early summer.

Above the reservoir, another 7 miles of North Branch Buffalo Creek flow through Bald Eagle State Forest. No trout are stocked in this remote upper stretch, but fishing is good for wild brook trout.

Panther Run is a small, unstocked tributary to North Branch Buffalo Creek that also holds wild brook trout.

Rapid Run is heavily stocked from Halfway Lake (which is also stocked) at Raymond B. Winter State Park downstream 11 miles to its mouth on Buffalo Creek, which it meets near Cowan. The entire stream is easily accessible from Route 192. Most of the stream is wooded, and much of the upper part of the stream flows through Bald Eagle State Forest. Some wild brown and brook trout are caught in Rapid Run, and many hatchery trout remain into early summer.

Other stocked tributaries to Buffalo Creek include Spruce Run and Little Buffalo Creek.

Philipsburg Area - Centre County

Flowing through Philipsburg and forming the border between Centre and Clearfield Counties is Moshannon Creek, sometimes called the "Red Mo" because of its mine-drainage-tainted waters. Even though Moshannon Creek is badly polluted, many of its tributaries in northern Centre County offer good trout fishing. These streams flow through rugged, mountainous country, much of which is within Moshannon State Forest.

Cold Stream Run, located just south of Philipsburg, holds hatchery trout and wild browns and brookies. Fishing pressure is heavy early in the year.

Black Bear Creek is crossed by Route 504 a few miles east of Philipsburg. This small, scenic stream is stocked, and it also holds many wild brook trout.

A few miles farther east, Route 504 crosses over Sixmile Run. This clear, beautiful stream is stocked and it also holds scattered wild brook and brown trout. Dirt forest roads follow the entire stream.

A few miles farther east, Route 504 crosses over a lake in Black Moshannon State Park. Black Moshannon Creek is stocked from the spillway of this lake downstream 14 miles to T325, which crosses the stream just south of the village of Moshannon. A dirt road follows downstream along the creek for about 2 miles, and below this there is a long, roadless stretch. Forests surround most of the stream, but strip-mined areas border the lower reaches below Route 80.

Black Moshannon Creek gets warm in the summer months and its waters are rather acidic, so it doesn't hold many wild trout, but big browns are sometimes caught below the mouths of tributaries.

Benner Run flows into Black Moshannon Creek about 3.5 miles downstream from the state park. This small, unstocked wilderness stream has good fishing for wild brook and brown trout.

Rock Run meets Moshannon Creek farther downstream, where Moshannon Creek is paralleled by Route 80. Rock Run flows through a remote mountainous area and it holds a good population of wild brook trout.

Route 144 Brook Trout Streams - Centre and Clinton Counties

Between Snowshoe and Renovo, Route 144 crosses a high, forested plateau. To either side of the road, small brook trout streams have cut deep, narrow ravines as they descend towards either Beech Creek or the West Branch of the Susquehanna. Most of this area is in Sproul State Forest. Dirt forest roads provide some access, but reaching most of these streams requires a long, steep hike.

As you are driving north from Snow Shoe towards Renovo on Route 144, the streams to the left (west) side of the road include Spruce Run, Bougher Run, Fields Run, Yost Run, Burns Run, and Fish Dam Run. These streams all flow into the West Branch of the Susquehanna. None of them are stocked.

On the right (east) side of Route 144, you will find Sandy Run (unstocked), Wolf Run (stocked), Panther Run (unstocked), Eddy Lick Run (stocked), and Big Run and its branches (unstocked). These streams all drain southeast to Beech Creek, which is polluted.

The wild brook trout in these streams are usually small, and their numbers vary from stream to stream, but the adventurous angler will enjoy exploring this remote area. The Sproul State Forest map is almost a necessity for finding these streams, and topographic maps provide even greater detail. This mountainous region is prime rattlesnake habitat.

Schrader Creek - Bradford County

Schrader Creek flows through a forested corner of southwest Bradford County, and much of the stream lies within the boundaries of State Game Lands No. 12 and 36. Trout are stocked from the Sullivan County line, near the headwaters, downstream 15.6 miles to Coal Run, which dumps mine acid into the creek about 3 miles below Laquin.

Most of Schrader Run flows through a remote wooded area accessible only by walking in along a gated game land road. There is a gate at the lower end of this stretch near Laquin and another at the upper end near the Sullivan County line. In addition to stocked trout, Schrader Creek holds some wild brook trout, but their numbers may be limited by acid rain. Some wild brook trout are also found in beaver ponds near the headwaters. Water temperatures in Schrader Creek remain cool through the summer months, and trout can be caught on terrestrial patterns through the summer and into the fall.

Little Schrader Creek flows into Schrader Creek a few miles above Laquin. This small stream is stocked and it also holds some wild brook trout. It nearly dries up in the summer months. Like Schrader Creek, this is a good stream to fish if you enjoy remote walk-in areas.

Millstone Creek meets Schrader Creek at Weston. Trout are stocked in the lower stretch of this stream, and wild brook trout are found in the headwaters above Deep Hollow Run.

White Deer Hole Creek - Lycoming and Union Counties

Don't confuse this stream with White Deer Creek, which is located several miles farther south in Union County. White Deer Hole Creek offers good fishing for wild brook trout and also some wild browns in its upper 4 or 5 miles of water, where it flows through Bald Eagle State Forest.

After it leaves the state forest, White Deer Hole Creek flows past the village of Elimsport and through an open farming valley on its way to its mouth near Allenwood. Trout are stocked in this lower water, but water temperatures get pretty warm in the summer months. Large brown trout are occasionally caught where cool limestone springs flow into the stream.

Muncy Creek - Lycoming and Sullivan Counties

Muncy Creek is a long freestone stream that is similar in many ways to Lycoming and Loyalsock Creeks but not as well known as those streams. Trout are stocked from the village of Nordmont in Sullivan County downstream to the mouth on the West Branch Susquehanna River at Muncy. The land along the stream is occupied by farms, woodlots, and rural villages. Although all of this land is in private ownership, there is little posting.

Most of the fishing is for stocked trout, but some wild brown and brook trout are found in the middle and upper reaches. In midsummer, water flows become low and fairly warm, and the remaining trout are usually found in the deeper pools and near springs and the mouths of tributaries. Many of the larger pools, including several that are 6 to 8 foot deep, are found in the middle stretch of the creek, near Glen Mawr and Picture Rocks.

Muncy Creek has good fly hatches, including Quill Gordons, Green Caddis, Sulphurs, Tan Caddis, March Browns, Grey Foxes, and Slate Drakes.

Northwest Pennsylvania

Venango County's Pithole Creek.

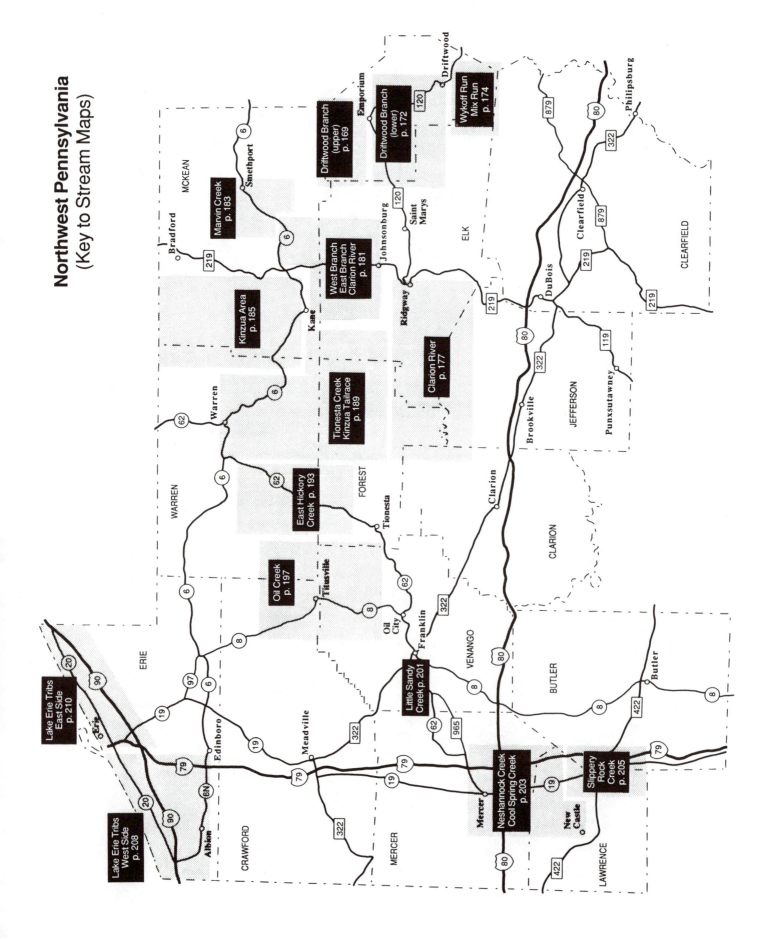

Northwest Pennsylvania
(Key to Stream Maps)

Northwest Pennsylvania

Driftwood Branch Sinnemahoning Creek - Cameron County

(delayed harvest, fly fishing only, 1 mile)
(maps: pages 169 and 172)

The Driftwood Branch is stocked with trout over a distance of 30 miles, from its junction with Elk Fork downstream to its mouth on the Bennet Branch of the Sinnemahoning. Along its way it grows from a small brook into a nearly river-sized stream.

In the unstocked headwaters above the junction with Elk Fork, the Driftwood Branch flows through a heavily forested area. A gravel road, SR 4004, follows the stream to its origin. The stream is small in this upper stretch, averaging about 15 feet in width. There is a good wild trout population here, a mixture of brown and brook trout in the lower end near Elk Fork, and mostly brookies farther upstream.

Fishing is good in this upper part of the Driftwood Branch even in midsummer because the stream is well shaded and water temperatures remain cool. The water does get low and clear, though, and the fish are easily spooked. There are some very small tributaries to this upper stretch of the Driftwood Branch that also hold native brook trout.

Below the junction with Elk Fork, the Driftwood Branch flows out of the deep woods, and from here down to Emporium, it winds past brushy meadows, woodlots, and scattered houses. The creek widens here and is less well shaded; water temperatures get pretty warm in midsummer. The upper part of this stretch, from Elk Fork down to about Bobby Run, holds fair numbers of wild brown trout, but there are only scattered wild trout in the Driftwood Branch below this. Some big browns are caught each year, though, all along the length of the Driftwood Branch.

A nice pool is located where Clear Creek meets the Driftwood Branch, and parking is available here along SR 4004. A gigantic ledge pool is located about a five-minute walk upstream from the junction with Clear Creek. A fisherman who lives near the stream told me that he once caught a 28-inch brown trout from this pool.

A 1-mile delayed-harvest, fly-fishing-only stretch is located along Route 46, north of Emporium. Parking near the bottom of the stretch is available at the county fairgrounds. At the top of the stretch, you can park near the Shippen Township building.

The fishing in the fly stretch is mostly for stocked trout, but the regulations keep good numbers of trout here, providing consistent fishing for most of the year. The water temperatures can get pretty warm here in July and August, though, and then fishing slows. The fly stretch is open to fishing year around, and it is a good place to try when warm weather in late March or early April brings on a case of trout fever. Fly fishing tackle can be purchased at Craig Hudson's Fisherman's Attic, which is located along the right (east) side of Route 46 about 1 mile north of the fly stretch.

From Emporium downstream to the mouth, the Driftwood Branch is a large stream where you can catch smallmouth bass as well as stocked trout. Route 120 parallels this lower water, but in many places it is a long, steep hike down to the creek. Railroad tracks also follow the stream here, but there is little other development in this rugged, forested area. The

Driftwood Branch Sinnemahoning Creek near the village of Cameron.   (Thad Bukowski photo)

trout fishing in this lower water is mostly put-and-take, and few people fish here later than mid-June, but anglers who know the stream well sometimes catch big browns in the summer, usually from deep pools or near the mouths of tributaries.

Elk Fork - Cameron County
(map: page 169)

Elk Fork is a small stream that flows through a forested area before joining the Driftwood Branch of the Sinnemahoning. Getting access to this stream is very difficult. It is posted against trespassing at the only bridge crossing, the SR 4004 bridge near the mouth. Where SR 4004 crosses the Driftwood Branch, a dirt road leads north past a few houses, then follows Elk Fork up into the mountains. This road is very rough and in wet weather it is nearly impassable. The Fish Commission discontinued stocking of Elk Fork because of the posting in the lower stretch, but the upper stretches may be worth exploring because Elk Fork holds good numbers of wild brown trout and brook trout.

Bobby Run - Cameron County
(map: page 169)

Bobby Run is an unstocked tributary to the Driftwood Branch that holds fair numbers of native brook trout. A dirt road turns off from SR 4004 at a lumber mill and follows the creek upstream. Most of Bobby Run is owned by a lumber company and is closed to public fishing, but one section of the stream flows through Elk State Forest.

Cooks Run - Cameron County
(map: page 169)

This unstocked tributary to the Driftwood Branch of Sinnemahoning Creek offers good fishing for wild brown and brook trout to anglers who are willing to do some walking. SR 4004 crosses Cooks Run near its mouth, and a gravel road goes upstream 100 yards or so to a cemetery, but above this there is no road access. The stream drains a mountainous, wooded tract owned by a paper company.

Clear Creek - Cameron County
(map: page 169)

Clear Creek is a small tributary to the Driftwood Branch of Sinnemahoning Creek. The lower 4 miles of the stream are paralleled by SR 4003. The stream averages about 20 feet in width and flows through meadows, brush, and patches of woods. Houses and hunting camps along the roadside create some access problems. About a half-mile of the stream is posted. The Fish Commission stocks Clear Creek with hatchery trout prior to opening day, but makes no inseason stockings.

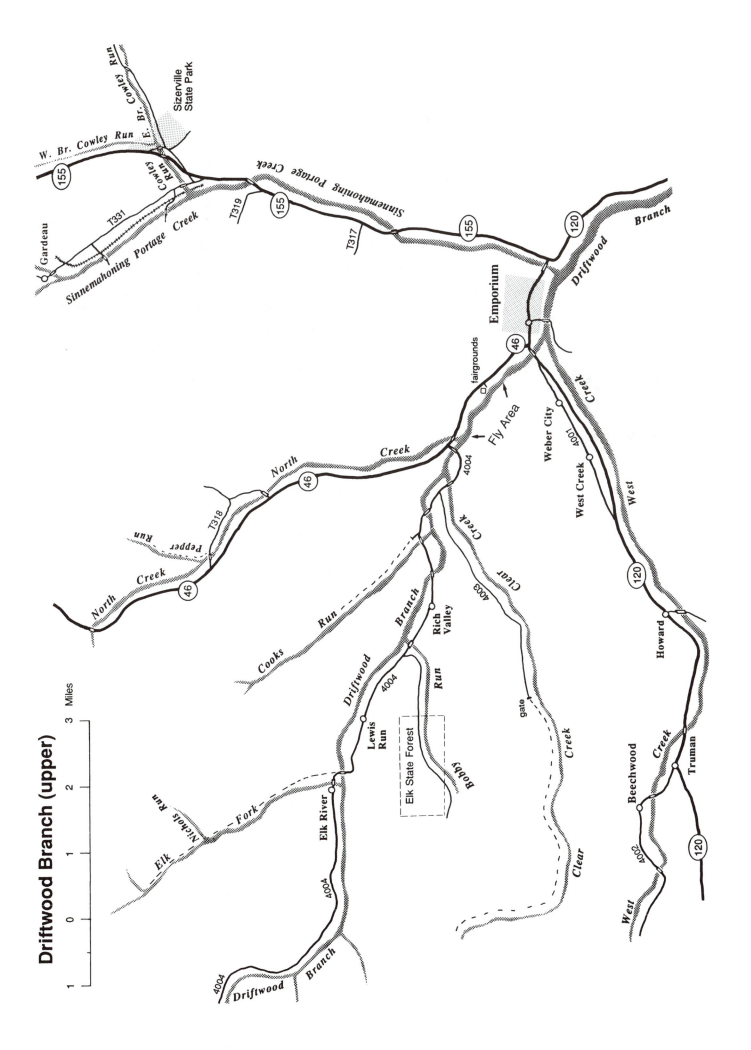

Driftwood Branch (upper)

A misty morning on Sinnemahoning Portage Creek.

At the end of SR 4003, there is a gate and a parking area on the left. Walk-in fishing above this gate is permitted, and in its headwaters, Clear Creek flows through an undeveloped wooded area. The stream is pretty small in this upper stretch, but it holds fair numbers of wild brown and brook trout and offers uncrowded fishing in a near-wilderness setting.

North Creek - Cameron County
(map: page 169)

North Creek's headwaters are in a dense stand of hemlocks in Elk State Forest. Most of the stream flows through privately owned land, however. Some of this land is wooded, and some of it is in meadows and brush. Homes and cabins have been built in some places near the stream. North Creek is about 20 feet wide and flows at a moderate pace. It has few large pools; most of the stream consists of shallow riffles and pocket water.

The Fish Commission stocks trout preseason and once inseason, from the mouth of North Creek on the Driftwood Branch upstream a little less than 6 miles. North Creek holds some wild brown trout, but siltation may be limiting trout reproduction.

West Creek - Cameron County
(map: page 169)

West Creek is a tributary of the Driftwood Branch of Sinnemahoning Creek and meets that stream at Emporium. The Fish Commission stocks trout preseason and once inseason, from the mouth upstream to Truman. All of this stretch is paralleled by Route 120. Because of water quality problems caused by acid mine drainage in the headwaters, West Creek has few wild trout.

Sinnemahoning Portage Creek - Cameron County
(map: page 169)

Sinnemahoning Portage Creek, or just plain Portage Creek as it is known locally, is a tributary to the Driftwood Branch of Sinnemahoning Creek, which it meets at Emporium. Portage Creek is stocked with trout for 6.5 miles, from its mouth upstream to Cowley Run. The Fish Commission stocks trout preseason and once inseason, usually in late April or early May. The stocked stretch of the creek is paralleled by Route 155, and there are numerous houses and businesses along the road. The stream is mostly wide, shallow, and unshaded here, and few wild trout are found in this stretch.

A large pool is located at the confluence of Cowley Run. Above the confluence with Cowley Run, Portage Creek is not stocked, but it holds a good population of wild brown trout. T331 (Gardeau Road) parallels the creek up to Gardeau. Railroad tracks also follow the stream. The first half-mile of the stream above Cowley Run is straight and shallow and looks as if it has been channelized. Farther upstream there are some short, deep pools surrounded by thick, shrubby willows. Upstream from these pools are several huge pools. The largest pool even has a diving board. One evening, at dusk, I cast a Letort hopper out into the middle of one of these big pools, and it was quickly grabbed by a 14-inch wild brown trout. A good way to get to this area is to park along T331, close to where it crosses over the railroad tracks. The big pools are downstream from here a little way.

Parker Run meets Portage Creek at Gardeau, and above this point Portage Creek is small, but wild browns and brookies can be found here if you are willing to fight your way through heavy brush. Parker Run may hold some trout, but a local fisherman told me that it receives some acid mine drainage.

Cowley Run - Cameron County
(map: page 169)

Cowley Run originates at the junction of its East and West Branches in Sizerville State Park and flows downstream 1 mile to its mouth on Portage Creek. No trout are stocked in Cowley Run, but it holds a good population of wild brown trout, and stocked trout move in from the East and West Branches and from Portage Creek. A good place to park your car is near the bridge on T331 (Gardeau Road). There is a large pool at the railroad bridge downstream from T331 and another large pool where Cowley Run meets Portage Creek.

East Branch Cowley Run - Cameron and Potter Counties
(map: page 169)

This small stream originates in the Susquehannock State Forest in Potter County and flows approximately 5 miles before meeting West Branch Cowley Run at Sizerville State Park. The Fish Commission stocks trout preseason only, from the mouth upstream 3.2 miles to a power line crossing. The East Branch also holds a good population of wild brown and brook trout. Brown trout are more numerous in the lower stretch near the park, and brookies are more common farther upstream. Much of the creek flows through open, grassy areas, where it's enjoyable to walk along the banks and cast a fly to pockets created by tree

roots and undercut banks. I caught a 7-inch brook trout here that was one of the most brilliantly colored fish I've ever seen. To get to East Branch Cowley Run, drive into Sizerville State Park and follow the road past the park office and the swimming pool. The road soon turns to gravel and follows the stream to its headwaters.

West Branch Cowley Run - Cameron and Potter Counties
(map: page 169)

The lower end of West Branch Cowley Run flows past the camping area of Sizerville State Park. This is a good spot to camp close to good fishing. Upstream from the park, the stream is paralleled by Route 155. The Fish Commission stocks trout from the mouth upstream about 2.5 miles, to Slabtown Road. West Branch Cowley Run offers fishing not only for stocked trout, but also for small wild brown trout, which are abundant here. The upper reaches of West Branch Cowley Run flow through brushy beaver swamps.

Hunts Run - Cameron County
(map: page 172)

Hunts Run is an unstocked tributary to the Driftwood Branch of Sinnemahoning Creek. This small woodland stream offers good fishing for wild brown trout from its mouth upstream to McNuff Branch. Above McNuff Branch, Hunts Run is much smaller and brook trout become more common. Stream surveys indicate that most of Hunts Run's browns are between 4 and 8 inches long and that few exceed 12 inches in length. Some local anglers report, though, that big browns over 18 inches long are sometimes caught in Hunts Run.

Most of Hunts Run lies within Elk State Forest, but there is some private land along the creek. There are quite a few houses and camps near the mouth of the stream at the village of Cameron, and there are scattered camps and summer homes farther upstream. Hunts Run Road, a gravel forest road, parallels the stream. In some places, the road lies close to the creek, but in other spots it climbs on the hillside far above the creek.

A scenic trail follows up along McNuff Branch, a small tributary to Hunts Run. Some wild trout can be found in this stream also, but in most places the water is very shallow. Hiking along McNuff Branch one autumn morning, I spotted a bobcat and watched it for about five minutes as it dragged a groundhog along the stream bank.

Hicks Run - Elk County
(map: page 172)

Hicks Run is formed by the confluence of the East and West Branches of Hicks Run, and it flows 2 miles

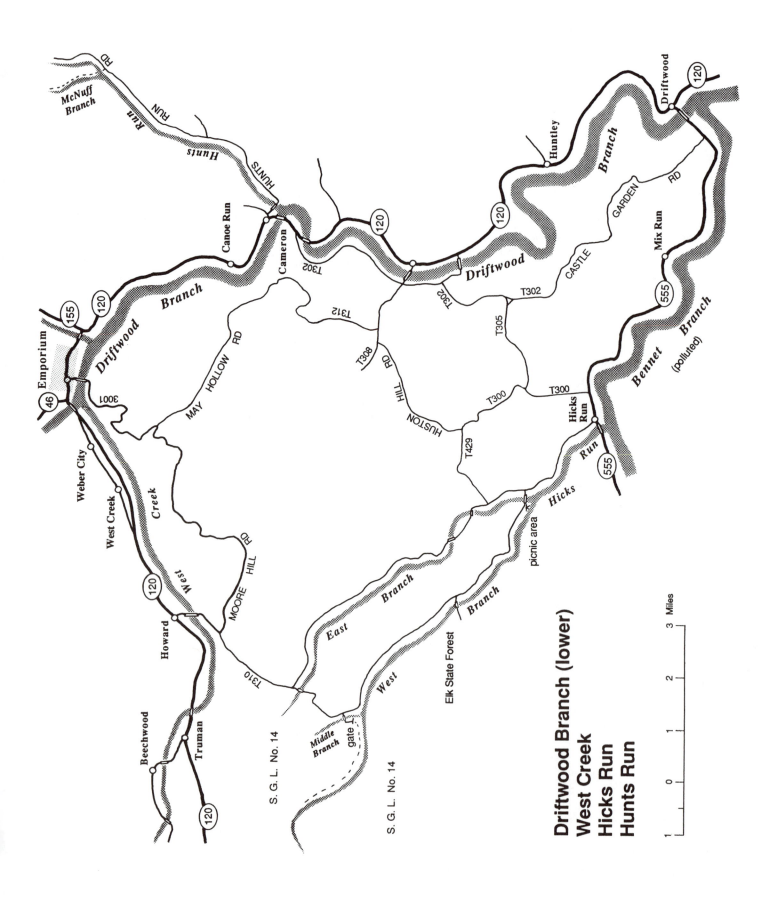

Driftwood Branch (lower)
West Creek
Hicks Run
Hunts Run

through a wooded valley. The upper mile lies within Elk State Forest, and the lower mile flows past many cabins. Good access can be found at the Route 555 bridge near the mouth and at a state forest picnic area at the confluence of the branches. A gravel road, Hicks Run Road, follows along the stream, but cabins along the road limit access in some places. The stream is wide and shallow near the mouth, but it is narrower and faster up near the picnic area.

The Fish Commission stocks Hicks Run preseason and three times inseason. Hicks Run doesn't hold a great many trout into the summer and fall, but the diligent angler can find a few trout in some of the deeper holes.

West Branch Hicks Run - Elk and Cameron Counties
(map: page 172)

West Branch Hicks Run flows through a heavily wooded area in State Game Land No. 14 and Elk State Forest. The watershed is mostly undeveloped except for a few hunting camps and a forest road that follows the lower part of the stream.

The Fish Commission stocks trout preseason and three times inseason along 6 miles of the West Branch, from the mouth up to the confluence of tiny Middle Branch Hicks Run. This stretch has some wired refuge areas, and stream improvement devices have been built. The fishing is mostly for stocked trout in this part of the creek, but there are also some wild browns and brookies.

There is good fishing for wild brook trout in the unstocked headwaters in State Game Land No. 14. Park at a gate near the confluence of Middle Branch Hicks Run and walk up along the access road that follows the West Branch to its origin. Pennsylvania's elk herd roams this area, and if you are lucky you may see one of these majestic creatures.

East Branch Hicks Run - Elk County
(map: page 172)

East Branch Hicks Run flows through an undeveloped wooded area in Elk State Forest and State Game Land No. 14. A gravel road follows the stream, providing easy access. The Fish Commission stocks the East Branch preseason and three times inseason from the T310 bridge downstream 7 miles to the mouth. Above the T310 bridge, the stream is very small and walled in by heavy brush. Below the T310 bridge, there are marshy areas and beaver ponds for about 2.5 miles. These beaver ponds are sheltered by thick brush, but if you fight your way through the tangle of roots and branches, you will find good fishing for native brook trout.

Below this marshy area, the stream flows more swiftly through riffles, small pockets and washtub-sized pools. Jack dams, deflectors, and other stream improvement devices have been built here.

East Branch Hicks Run has a good population of native brook trout in the headwaters and a good mixed brown and brook trout population farther downstream.

Mix Run - Cameron and Elk Counties
(map: page 174)

Mix Run is a narrow, rocky stream that flows through Elk State Forest before meeting the Bennet Branch of Sinnemahoning Creek. There are a few cabins along the lower end of the creek, but most of the watershed is unspoiled forest land. A dirt forest road (Red Run Road) parallels the lower 4 miles of the stream, making access easy, but because this area is far from any large or even medium-sized towns, fishing pressure is relatively light. In the summer and fall, you are likely to have the stream to yourself.

The Fish Commission stocks Mix Run preseason and three times inseason, from the mouth upstream 4 miles to the confluence of Red Run. The stream also holds some wild brown and brook trout, not in tremendous numbers, but enough to make fishing worthwhile even in the summer and fall, after most of the stocked fish are gone. The water becomes low and perfectly clear in midsummer, and then the trout are usually found in the deeper pools and pockets. Terrestrial patterns, such as beetles, small crickets, and ants work well in the summer.

Above Red Run, Mix Run flows through a remote area, and the adventurous angler can hike along the stream and find some native browns and brookies.

Red Run is stocked by a sportsmen's cooperative hatchery, but not by the Fish Commission. Red Run is rather acidic and holds few wild trout.

Wykoff Run - Cameron County
(map: page 174)

Wykoff Run begins as a small brook trout stream and flows 9 miles through a wooded area before meeting Sinnemahoning Creek. Most of the stream is narrow, riffly, and rocky, with few large pools. The lower part of the creek is wider and slower moving. Access is made easy by SR 2001 (Wykoff Road), which follows the entire stream. Elk State Forest surrounds the stream along most of its length, but there are private holdings and houses along the lower 2.5 miles.

The Fish Commission stocks Wykoff Run preseason and twice inseason, from the mouth upstream 6.5 miles to Big Spring Draft. Both Big Spring Draft and the unstocked headwaters of Wykoff Run hold native brook trout. The stocked section of Wykoff Run has a good population of both wild brown and brook trout. Many of the browns reach 10 to 12 inches, respectable fish for a stream of this size.

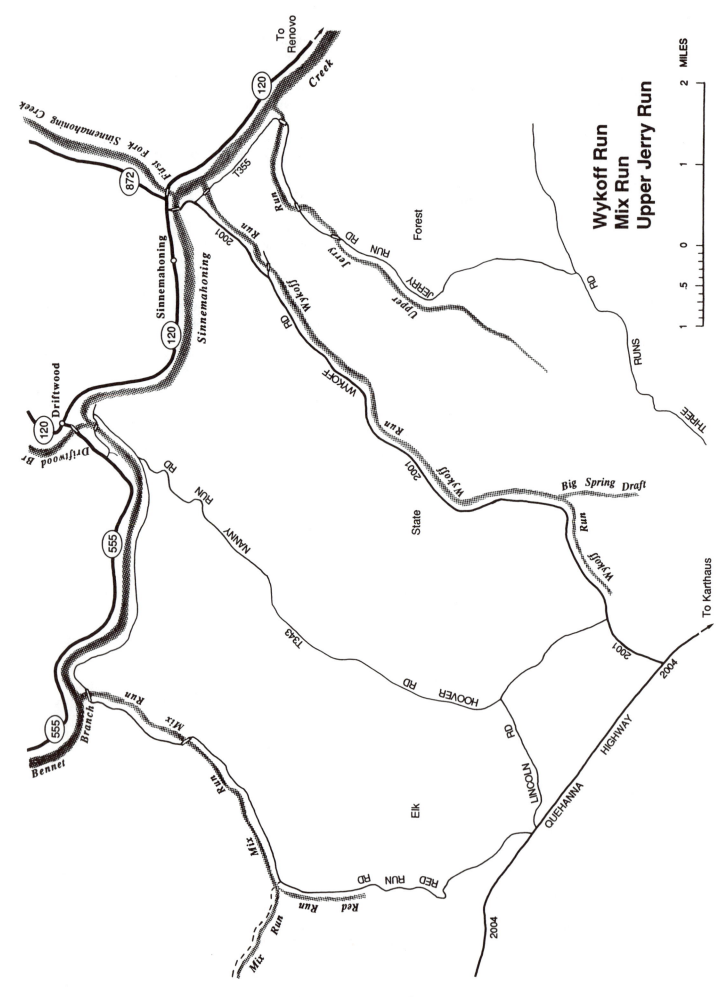

Wykoff Run
Mix Run
Upper Jerry Run

Upper Jerry Run in Elk State Forest.

Upper Jerry Run - Cameron County
(map: page 174)

Upper Jerry Run is a very pretty little stream that tumbles down through a narrow, deep-shaded hollow in Elk State Forest. Although this stream carries only a small volume of water, it has a lot of good holding places for trout because it continually bounces from one pocket or pool to another.

The Fish Commission stocks hatchery trout in the 3.8 miles of the stream paralleled by the forest road, Jerry Run Road. Trout are stocked preseason and twice inseason, with the last stocking coming in late May or early June.

The unstocked headwaters and the upper part of the stocked stretch hold many wild brook trout up to 6 inches long and a few larger ones. The lower part of the creek holds wild brown and brook trout.

Most of Upper Jerry Run's drainage is undeveloped, except for a group of cabins near the mouth and the forest road that follows the stream. This road is in good condition in its lower stretch, but up near the junction with Three Runs Road it is potholed and strewn with large rocks.

Clarion River - Elk, Jefferson, Forest, and Clarion Counties
(map: page 177)

For many years the Clarion River was severely polluted and held few fish. Some water quality problems still persist, but reductions in mine drainage, improvements at the paper mill in Johnsonburg, and pollution reductions by several smaller industries have resulted in cleaner water. The Clarion River is much larger than most trout streams, and it gets pretty warm in the summer, but cold water releases from a dam on the East Branch Clarion River keep temperatures cool enough for trout survival.

Since 1980 the Fish Commission has been stocking the Clarion with 50,000 to 100,000 fingerlings annually, in the 42-mile stretch from Ridgway downstream to the Route 36 bridge at Cooksburg State Park. In recent years many large brown trout, 18 to 20 inches and even larger, have been caught.

The Clarion may not be everyone's ideal trout stream. The water is still turbid, approximately the color of coffee with cream, and a sulphurous paper mill odor is noticeable, particularly in the upper part of the river. Dry fly purists should go elsewhere because hatches of insects that bring trout to the surface are rare. Also, the Clarion is a big river, and the trout are not evenly distributed. Some stretches are slow moving and muddy bottomed, with few riffles or rapids, and these areas hold few trout.

The Clarion does have some real attractions, though. The primary attraction is the chance of catching a trophy brown trout. Smallmouth bass also offer good fishing in the Clarion, especially in the lower stretches downstream from Hallton.

Much of the land along the Clarion is public land under the management of the Pennsylvania Game Commission, Kittanning State Forest, Clear Creek State Park, and Cook Forest State Park. Developed campsites are located at Clear Creek State Park and at Cook Forest State Park. There are some private holdings and houses along the river, but generally finding access is not a problem.

The Clarion flows through a scenic, forested area, and camping and canoeing are popular here. The river has some moderate riffs and rapids, but little heavy white water. A canoe can take anglers to places on the river that are seldom fished by anglers on foot. Canoe traffic can be heavy on weekends, particularly on the lower river near Cooksburg.

Spinning lures are very popular on the Clarion River, especially black Rooster Tails and gold-colored Mepps. Bait fishermen do well with the old standbys: night crawlers and minnows. The few fly fishers who fish the Clarion favor big nymphs and streamers.

Concentrate on fishing areas of the river that look like trout water: rocky riffs, deep runs, and pools with fast water flowing into them. The mouths of tributaries are also hot spots. Avoid the slow, muddy, weedy stretches, which hold more carp than trout.

The fishing on the Clarion is best from opening day through early June and again in the fall. The first week of the trout season is often produces very good fishing if water levels aren't too high. Fishing slows in the summer because water temperatures rise, sometimes reaching 80 degrees.

Note: the Johnsonburg-to-Ridgway stretch of the Clarion River is not shown on the map. No trout are stocked there because of questionable water quality. Local anglers report that trout are sometimes caught in this stretch, though.

Access Points

The best stretch of the Clarion for trout fishing is from Ridgway downstream to Hallton, but trout are found as far downriver as Cooksburg and even below. The following are some good fishing and access sites on the Clarion, starting at Ridgway and moving downstream:

(1) A lot of trout are caught right in Ridgway. You can park near the Route 219 bridge in the middle of town. Next to the bridge you'll find Loves' Canoes, where you can rent canoes and buy fishing tackle. Ask to see their photos of Pennsylvania elk.

(2) There are some good riffs just downstream from the mouth of Little Toby Creek.

(3) At Portland Mills, turn off Route 949 opposite a white church and follow a bumpy, dirt track to a canoe launching site on the riverbank. There are rapids and deep pools here, and Bear Creek flows in on the opposite shore.

(4) The bridge at Arroyo is a good access point for canoeists, and there are swift runs and deep holes here that provide good fishing.

(5) The stretch near the mouth of Spring Creek at Hallton is productive. A canoe access site is located a few miles east of Hallton along SR 3002.

(6) The mouth of Callen Run, located near a large pumping station along Route 949, is worth a try.

(7) There are stretches of fast water and deep holes located upstream of the bridge at Belltown. Belltown Canoe Rental is located downstream from the bridge.

(8) There are deep holes downstream from the mouth of Millstone Creek.

(9) The mouths of Clear Creek and Maple Creek are worth a try.

(10) The mouth of Cathers Run, at Gravel Lick, is a good spot and this is probably the last good stretch for trout. Downriver from here you will find bass and other warmwater fish, but few trout.

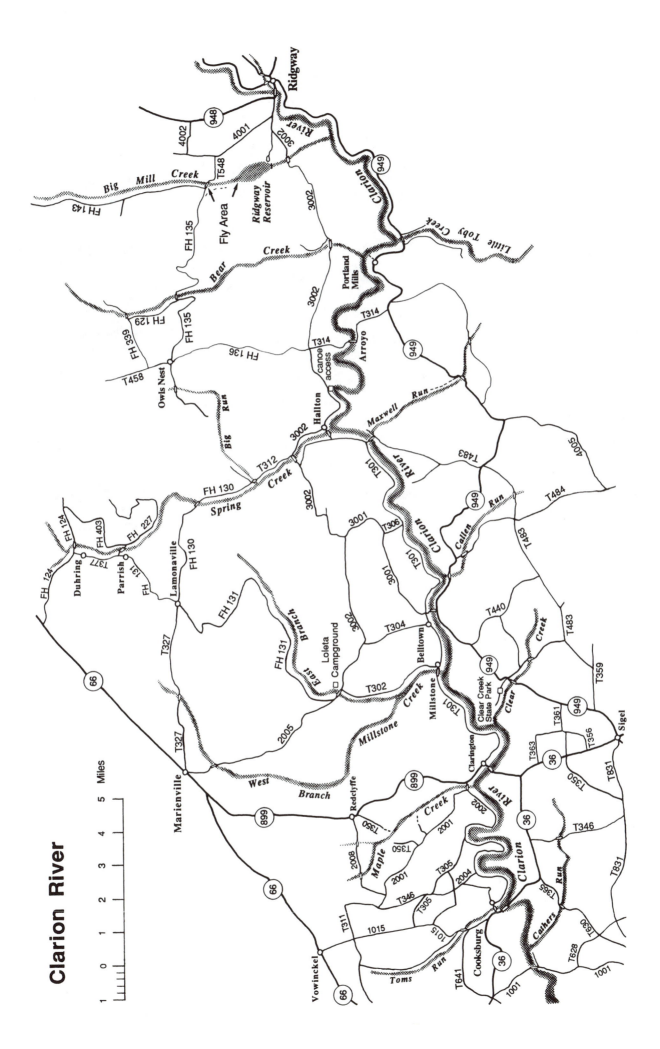

Clarion River

A quiet stretch of the Clarion River near Hallton.

Addresses and Phone Numbers (Clarion River)

Clear Creek State Park, R.D.1, Box 82, Sigel, PA 15860. Tel: (814) 752-2368. Camping and cabins are available. Cabins require reservations.

Cook Forest State Park, P.O. Box 120, Cooksburg, PA 16217. Tel: (814) 744-8407. Camping and cabins are available. Cabins require reservations.

Loves' Canoes, Route 219 bridge, downtown Ridgway. Tel: (814) 776-6285

Belltown Canoe Rental, Route 949 at Belltown bridge. Tel: (814) 752-2561

Clarion River Tributaries
(map: page 177)

The following stocked trout streams (Big Mill Creek through Cathers Run) are tributaries that flow into the Clarion River between Ridgway and Cooksburg. Most of these streams flow through forested areas with little development other than some logging and oil and gas exploration. These streams all have essentially put-and-take fisheries, with few wild trout. The geology of the region produces infertile streams with low alkalinity. This makes them very susceptible to damage from acid precipitation. Stocked trout can be caught from opening day to early June, but few trout remain into the summer. These streams get very low and clear in midsummer. Big brown trout from the Clarion River are sometimes caught in the lower stretches of these streams.

Big Mill Creek - Elk County
(fly fishing only, 1 mile)
(map: page 177)

Big Mill Creek's fly-fishing-only stretch extends from the T548 (Bingham Road) bridge downstream 1 mile to the backwaters of Ridgway Reservoir. The stream also has some wired refuge areas, which are closed to fishing during the regular season, but open after June 15. The Fish Commission stocks trout pre-season and three times inseason, with the last stocking coming in late May. Few trout were found in this creek in midsummer surveys.

Little Toby Creek - Elk County
(map: page 177)

For many years Little Toby Creek was badly polluted by acid mine drainage, but the water quality has improved, and the Fish Commission recently added this stream to their stocking list. The lower miles of the stream flow through the remote forests of State Game Land No. 44.

Bear Creek - Elk County
(map: page 177)

Bear Creek flows through a heavily wooded area of the Allegheny National Forest where there is only limited road access. The Fish Commission stocks trout preseason and once inseason, usually in late April. Big browns from the Clarion River are sometimes caught in the lower reaches of Bear Creek.

Spring Creek - Elk and Forest Counties
(map: page 177)

Spring Creek is one of the largest tributaries to the Clarion. It flows for most of its length through the Allegheny National Forest. Trout are stocked from the mouth at Hallton upstream to the village of Duhring. The Fish Commission stocks trout preseason and once again inseason, usually around mid-May.

Big Run - Elk and Forest Counties
(map: page 177)

This small tributary of Spring Creek is stocked preseason only with brook trout. Few fish were found in Big Run during summer stream surveys.

Maxwell Run - Jefferson County
(map: page 177)

Maxwell Run flows most of its length through State Game Land No. 44. The Fish Commission stocks this brushy little stream with hatchery brook trout before opening day and once inseason, usually in mid-May.

Callen Run - Jefferson County
(map: page 177)

Callen Run is a small stream that flows through Kittanning State Forest and meets the Clarion River near a pumping station along Route 949. The Fish Commission stocks trout preseason and once inseason, usually around two weeks after opening day.

Millstone Creek - Elk County
(map: page 177)

Millstone Creek flows through the Allegheny National Forest. Trout are stocked from its mouth at Millstone upstream approximately 2 miles to its origin at the junction of its East and West Branches. The Fish Commission stocks trout preseason and three times inseason, with the last stocking coming around late May.

East Branch Millstone Creek - Elk County
(map: page 177)

The East Branch flows through the Allegheny National Forest, and it is stocked from its junction with the West Branch upstream 4 miles. The Fish Commission stocks trout preseason and three times inseason, with the last stocking coming around late May. The Allegheny National Forest's Loleta Campground is located along the East Branch.

West Branch Millstone Creek - Forest County
(map: page 177)

The West Branch is stocked only in its upper stretches, at the T327 bridge east of Marienville and at the SR 2005 bridge south of Marienville. The Fish Commission stocks trout preseason and once inseason, around mid-May. The remote, roadless stretch that extends from SR 2005 downstream to the junction with East Branch Millstone Creek is not stocked. This desolate area may be interesting for hikers to explore, but do not expect to find many trout.

Clear Creek - Jefferson County
(map: page 177)

The lower stretch of Clear Creek flows through Clear Creek State Park, and it is easily accessible to campers and visitors there. Corbett Road, a forest road, follows the creek upstream from Route 949. The Fish Commission stocks trout preseason and three times inseason, with the last stocking usually coming in late May.

Maple Creek - Forest County
(map: page 177)

Maple Creek flows through a heavily wooded area in the Allegheny National Forest. Because of its limited accessibility, Maple Creek is not fished hard. The Fish Commission stocks trout preseason and once inseason, in mid-May, from SR 2008 (Bear Run Road) down to the mouth. The stream is posted against trespassing for a short distance above the bridge near the mouth. T350 (Coon Road) and an unnamed dirt road a little farther south both provide access to the middle stretch of Maple Creek.

Toms Run - Forest County
(map: page 177)

Toms Run flows through Cook Forest State Park and meets the Clarion River near the park office at Cooksburg. Tourists and campers flock to this area and frequent stockings attract many anglers, so don't expect to fish in wilderness solitude.

The Fish Commission stocks Toms Run preseason and five times inseason, with the last stocking coming in mid-May.

Cathers Run - Clarion and Jefferson Counties
(map: page 177)

Cathers Run drains a heavily forested watershed, most of which lies within State Game Land No. 283. The Fish Commission stocks trout preseason and once inseason, usually in late April. Large brown trout sometimes move into the lower end of the creek from the Clarion River.

West Branch Clarion River - Mckean and Elk Counties
(delayed harvest, fly fishing only, 0.5 mile)
(map: page 181)

The West Branch of the Clarion River is stocked with trout from the Route 219 bridge above Halsey downstream approximately 14 miles to its junction with the East Branch Clarion River at Johnsonburg. The West Branch in its upper reaches is a small, fairly shallow stream that flows through an undeveloped wooded area. Much of this area appears to have burned over and then grown back in thick brush and scrubby trees. Fair numbers of wild browns and a few native brook trout are found in these upper reaches. Some of the tiny tributaries to the upper West Branch also hold native brook trout.

As you continue downstream, scattered houses begin to appear along the stream as you approach the village of Wilcox. At Wilcox the volume of the stream is increased by the addition of Wilson Run, and below Wilcox the stream widens, slows, and deepens as it wends its way towards Johnsonburg.

Three miles below Wilcox you'll find a delayed-harvest, fly-fishing-only area, which begins near the intersection of Route 219 and SR 4003 and extends upstream one-half mile. Wading is prohibited and fishing is allowed only from the east bank. Most of the trout in the fly area are stocked, but the regulations keep good numbers of fish here at least through June 15. After June 15, when it becomes legal to harvest fish here, some anglers seem determined to fish the stretch out, but fair numbers of trout can be found here throughout the summer, particularly in the deeper pools in the upper half of the fly area.

The creek moves slowly through the fly stretch and becomes low and clear in the summer months. A local fisherman, who fishes the fly area often, has good luck through the summer using McMurray Ants. Hatches are usually not heavy on the West Branch, but some Hendricksons, March Browns, Grey Foxes, Green Drakes, and Light Cahills appear.

The Fish Commission stocks the West Branch preseason and once inseason, usually around mid-May. Fishing pressure is heavy soon after stocking, but light the rest of the year. After the stocked fish have been thinned out, the best places to fish are the fly area and the headwaters near Halsey. The lower water, from Wilcox downstream to the mouth, holds only a few wild trout, but big brown trout are occasionally caught in this area, some of which exceed 20 inches in length.

Wilson Run - Elk and Mckean Counties
(map: page 181)

This small tributary to the West Branch Clarion River is easily accessible from Route 321 between Kane and Wilcox. The stream is lined with trees and brush, which help maintain cool water temperatures through the summer. It looks like it should be a good trout stream, but it holds only a limited number of wild trout—brookies in the headwaters and browns in the lower water.

The Fish Commission stocks trout preseason and once inseason, usually in late May, from the mouth upstream 5 miles to the Elk/Mckean County line. Wilson Run is heavily fished early in the season, but few people fish it the rest of the year.

Hoffman Run - Elk County
(map: page 181)

Hoffman Run is a very small tributary to Wilson Run, which is a tributary to the West Branch Clarion River. Trout are stocked from the mouth upstream 2 miles to a small lake at Allegheny National Forest's Twin Lakes Campground. A fair number of small wild brown and brook trout are found in this stretch.

The Fish Commission stocks trout preseason and twice inseason, with the last stocking coming in late May or early June. Upstream from the lake, Hoffman Run is little more than a trickle, but some wild brook and brown trout also inhabit this headwater stretch.

East Branch Clarion River - Elk County
(map: page 181)

Because it is fed by bottom releases from the dam at East Branch Lake, the East Branch Clarion River flows cold and full all summer long. During the summer months its water temperatures are in the 50's or low 60's when most sizeable freestone streams have water temperatures in the 70's or even 80's. This strong flow of cold water should provide an excellent trout habitat, but the fishery has been limited because of acidity from mine drainage on some of the tributaries of East Branch Lake. During the 1960's pollution abatement programs helped to reduce the

West Branch Clarion River
East Branch Clarion River

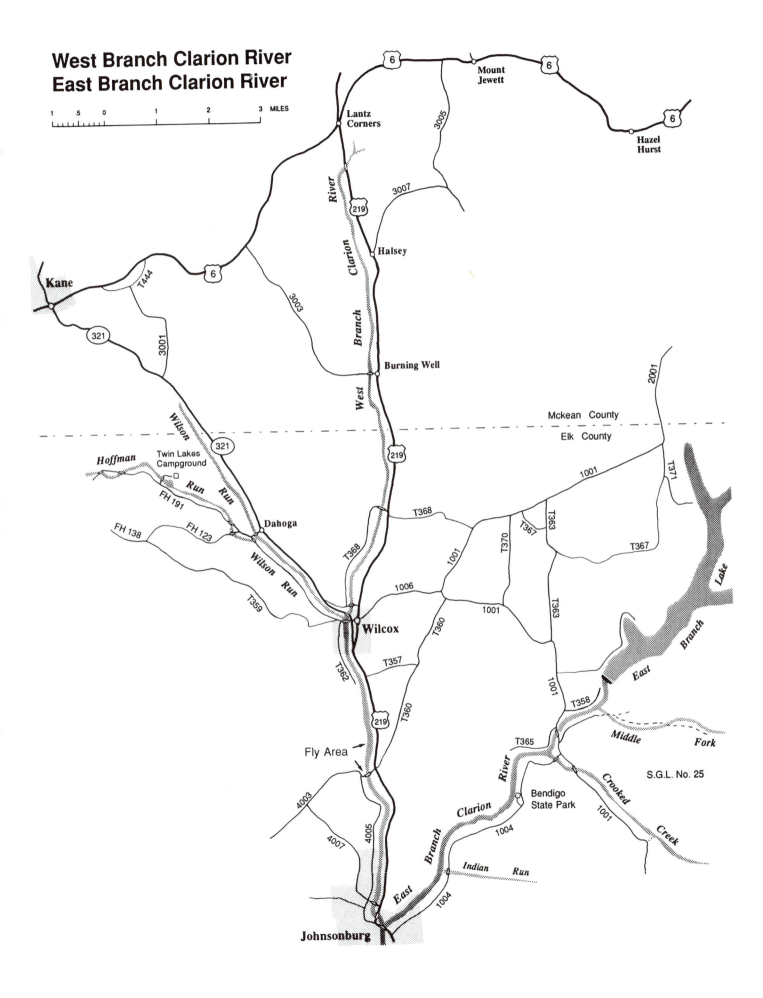

acid mine drainage, making it possible for the East Branch to be stocked with trout.

The Fish Commission now stocks trout preseason and three times inseason, with the last stocking coming in late May or early June. In addition to the adult "catchable" trout, fingerlings are also stocked. Trout are stocked from the dam downstream to the mouth of Indian Run, which is polluted by mine drainage.

Stocked trout can be caught all through the summer, and the East Branch also holds some wild brown and brook trout, but not in great numbers. Fly fishers will find caddis hatches and some sporadic mayfly hatches. If the cleanup of mine drainage in the headwaters continues to improve water quality, the East Branch may develop into an excellent trout fishery.

The upper stretch of the East Branch, from the dam down to SR 1001, is paralleled on both sides by dirt roads. The road on the east side is in good condition and several pulloffs provide easy access to this beautiful stretch of water. On the west side, T358 is a very rough and some marshes lie between the roadside and the streambank.

Two tributaries to East Branch Lake, Straight Creek and South Fork Straight Creek (not shown on map), offer good fishing for stocked trout and wild brown and brook trout in Elk State Forest.

Middle Fork - Elk County
(map: page 181)

This very small tributary to the East Branch Clarion River flows entirely within State Game Land No. 25. The stream is only 6 to 12 feet wide, and it is well shaded and protected by trees and brush. A Game Land access road follows the creek, but it is gated, so you must walk up from the parking area located near the mouth. The Fish Commission stocks trout preseason and once inseason in the lower 2.5 miles of Middle Fork. Middle Fork also holds good numbers of native brook trout and a few wild browns.

Crooked Creek - Elk County
(map: page 181)

Crooked Creek is a small stream that flows into the East Branch Clarion River about 1.5 miles upstream from Bendigo State Park. Most of the stream lies within heavily forested State Game Land No. 25, but there is some private property near the mouth. Trout are stocked from the SR 1004 bridge upstream 3 miles. SR 1001 closely follows the lower reaches of Crooked Creek, but a fair hike through the woods is required to reach the middle and upper reaches. At the point where SR 1001 bends sharply away from the creek, there is a parking pulloff and a gated access road that leads to the stream.

The Fish Commission stocks Crooked Creek with trout preseason and three times inseason, with the last stocking coming in early to mid-May. Crooked Creek holds some wild brook trout in its stocked stretch, but they aren't very plentiful. You may find more brookies in the unstocked headwaters.

Marvin Creek - Mckean County
(delayed harvest, fly fishing only, 1.1 mile)
(map: page 183)

Marvin Creek is a tributary to Potato Creek, in the Allegheny River drainage. The major attraction of Marvin Creek is the delayed-harvest, fly-fishing-only section, which can be found along Route 6, about 2 miles west of Smethport. A large sign marks the lower boundary of the fly area, and a power line crosses the upper boundary. The regulations reduce the harvest of trout, and plenty of fish can be found here throughout the season. Parking is limited to the narrow shoulder along Route 6. The shoulder is widest near the downstream border of the fly area.

Trout are stocked along 10 miles of Marvin Creek, from Smethport upstream to Hazel Hurst. Fair numbers of wild trout are found in the upper water near Hazel Hurst, but most of the rest of the stream holds few wild trout. The Fish Commission stocks trout preseason and three times inseason, with the last stocking coming around the third week in May.

Marvin Creek drains a broad valley of meadows, trees, brush, and farmland. The valley is lightly populated, but houses have been built near the stream in some places.

Allegheny Reservoir (Kinzua Dam) and Tributary Streams - Warren and Mckean Counties
(map: page 185)

The Allegheny Reservoir is a huge 12,000-acre lake created by the impoundment of the Allegheny River behind Kinzua Dam. The reservoir is very popular with boaters and anglers, and several boat launch sites and campgrounds are scattered along its shores. The reservoir is primarily a warmwater fishery, with good fishing for panfish, bass, walleyes, pike, and muskies, but it also produces some gigantic brown and rainbow trout.

There is also good trout fishing in the reservoir's tributaries: South Branch Kinzua Creek, Kinzua Creek, Chappel Fork, Sugar Run, North Branch Sugar Run, and Willow Creek. These streams flow, for the most part, through scenic, well-forested areas in the Allegheny National Forest, and they offer fishing for both stocked and wild trout. Typically, these streams harbor native brook trout in their headwaters and wild browns and rainbows in their lower stretches. Wild rainbow trout are very unusual in Pennsylvania. They are found in these tributary

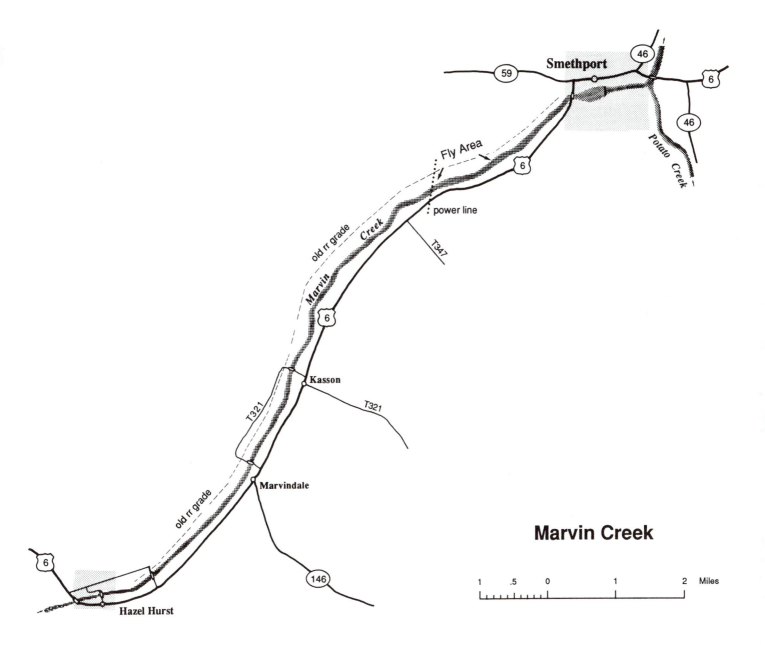

Marvin Creek

streams as a result of spawning by rainbows that move up from the reservoir.

Fly hatches on the tributaries to the Allegheny Reservoir include sporadic hatches of Quill Gordons, Blue Quills, and Hendricksons in the early season and better hatches of March Browns, Grey Foxes, and Light Cahills from mid-May through June. Caddis hatches also appear, and terrestrial patterns are effective in the summer months.

Large trout from the lake are sometimes caught at the mouths and in the lower stretches of these tributary streams, particularly during the spawning season of late October and early November. To get an idea of the size of some of the trout caught in the reservoir and in the lower parts of the tributaries, take a look at the fish photos at "Paul's," a store located on Route 321, about 1 mile south of the bridge over

Kinzua Creek. They have photos of numerous trout between 4 and 8 pounds and some bigger ones. The mounted musky on the wall looks like the freshwater equivalent of "Jaws."

An excellent map of the Allegheny National Forest, which includes the entire Kinzua Dam area and information on boat launches and camping, is available at the cost of $2.00 from the Allegheny National Forest, Supervisor's Office, 222 Liberty Street, P.O. Box 847, Warren, PA 16365.

South Branch Kinzua Creek - Mckean County
(map: page 185)

South Branch Kinzua Creek is perhaps the best trout stream in the Kinzua area. Tall trees provide excellent shade, keeping the stream cool in the summer months. The clean, clear water supports a good population of wild brown trout. Native brook trout are found in the upper part of the South Branch and also in its tiny tributaries. There are even some stream-bred rainbow trout in the South Branch as a result of spawning by rainbow trout that move up from the Allegheny Reservoir. In midsummer the stream becomes low, clear, and shallow, but it still holds a lot of trout. I had good fishing here in late July.

South Branch Kinzua Creek is stocked from its mouth upstream to the influx of Hubert Run. This section of the creek is paralleled by Route 321, and in most places a short hike through the trees is required to reach the stream. The Fish Commission stocks trout preseason and twice inseason, with the last stocking coming in mid-May.

To reach the unstocked headwaters, start at the intersection of Route 6 and Route 321 in Kane, drive east 3 miles on Route 6 to just past an old drive-in theater, then turn left onto T311, a gravel road that soon becomes Forest Highway 186. This road first crosses Glad Run, then South Branch Kinzua Creek.

Kinzua Creek - Mckean County
(delayed harvest, artificial lures, 2.3 miles)
(map: page 185)

Kinzua Creek is the largest of the Allegheny Reservoir tributaries. In years past this stream suffered from water quality problems caused by oil and gas operations, and no trout were stocked. Improvements have been made, and the Fish Commission now stocks trout preseason and three times inseason, with the last stocking coming around the second or third week in May.

Besides stocked trout, some sections of Kinzua Creek hold fair numbers of wild brown trout, but it is not as good a wild trout stream as the other tributaries to the Allegheny Reservoir.

A delayed-harvest, artificial-lures-only area has been approved for Kinzua Creek, starting in 1991. These regulations should help maintain good numbers of trout throughout the year. This stretch starts at the Route 219 bridge at Tallyho and extends downstream 2.3 miles to Camp Run. The stream has some nice riffles and pools here, and the banks are well forested. Access is made easy by Forest Highway 321.

Trophy browns are caught each year near the Route 321 bridge, often called the Red Bridge, which crosses the upper arm of the reservoir a short distance below the confluence of Kinzua Creek and South Branch Kinzua Creek.

Most of Kinzua Creek flows through Allegheny National Forest, and forest roads provide good access. Several of Kinzua Creek's small tributaries are worth a try for wild brown and brook trout.

Chappel Fork - Mckean County
(map: page 185)

Chappel Fork is a small, pleasant stream that flows 7 miles through the Allegheny National Forest before flowing into the Allegheny Reservoir. The Fish Commission stocks trout preseason and twice inseason, with the last stocking coming in mid to late May. Route 321 parallels the lower 2 miles of Chappel Fork. In most places this stretch of the creek is not visible from the road, and a short walk through the woods is required. The headwaters can be reached from a road that turns off from Forest Highway 455, but much of the upper part of the stream can be reached only by walking.

In addition to the stocked trout, wild brown and brook trout are found in Chappel Fork, particularly in the upper part of the creek, from the Route 321 bridge up into the headwaters. This upper stretch is the best place to fish through the summer and fall.

In the lower end of the creek, from the Route 321 bridge down to the reservoir, the water flows more slowly, and a section of the stream flows along a power line cut, where there are few trees to provide shade. Chappel Fork has some very small tributaries that hold native brook trout.

Sugar Run - Mckean County
(map: page 185)

Sugar Run is a scenic stream that flows most of its length through the Allegheny National Forest before meeting the Allegheny Reservoir. Route 321 follows the stream, making access easy. Good fishing can be found here for both wild and stocked trout.

The Fish Commission stocks trout in Sugar Run preseason and twice inseason, with the last stocking coming in mid to late May. Wild browns and rainbows are plentiful in the lower stretches of Sugar Run, and brook trout are found in the upper half of the stream. Sugar Run is a good choice for summer fishing because tall trees all along the length of the stream keep water temperatures cool.

There are several wired refuge areas on Sugar Run. These short stretches are closed to fishing during the early part of the trout season, but they are open after June 15. A boat launch is located on the Allegheny Reservoir near the mouth of Sugar Run.

North Branch Sugar Run - Mckean County
(map: page 185)

North Branch Sugar Run is smaller than Sugar Run, and its upper reaches become a mere trickle in the summer months. This attractive stream flows through a rugged, heavily forested area in the Allegheny National Forest. There is no vehicle access

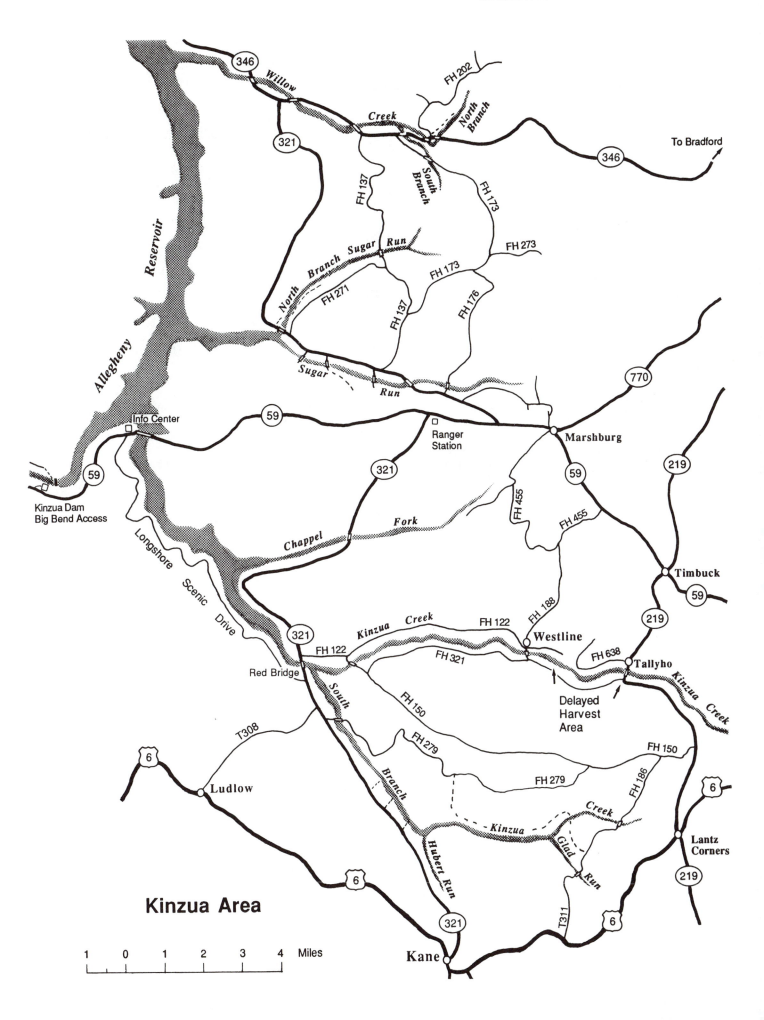

346

Willow

321

Creek

FH 202

North Branch

346

To Bradford

FH 137

South Branch

FH 173

Reservoir

North Branch Sugar Run

FH 273

FH 271

FH 173

Allegheny

North Branch

FH 137

FH 176

Sugar

Run

770

59

Info Center

Ranger Station

Marshburg

59

Kinzua Dam
Big Bend Access

59

321

Chappel

Fork

FH 455

FH 455

219

Longshore

Scenic

Drive

Timbuck

FH 188

59

321

Kinzua   Creek

FH 122

Westline

219

FH 122

FH 321

FH 638

Tallyho

Red Bridge

Kinzua Creek

Delayed
Harvest
Area

South

FH 150

FH 150

T308

FH 279

FH 186

6

6

Ludlow

Branch

FH 279

Kinzua   Creek

Glad

6

Lantz
Corners

Hubert Run

Run

T311

219

6

Kinzua Area

321

Kane

1   0   1   2   3   4   Miles

Chappel Fork has a mix of woods and grassy areas along its banks.

other than at the Route 321 bridge, near the mouth, and at the Forest Highway 137 bridge, near the headwaters. Forest Highway 271 parallels the stream, but it is a long hike from the road down to the stream bottom. A good way to explore this stream is to walk along the gated dirt road that follows the creek up from Route 321.

North Branch Sugar Run is stocked with trout preseason and three times inseason, with the last stocking coming in mid-May. The stream also holds a good population of wild brown and brook trout.

Part of the enjoyment of exploring trout country comes from chance encounters with wildlife. As I was driving towards the upper bridge on the North Branch, I was stopped by a ruffed grouse and a half-dozen, fuzzy grouse chicks in the middle of the forest road. They didn't seem in any hurry to move, so I stopped the car and walked toward them, to see how close I could approach. As I got closer, the grouse chicks scampered into the woods. The hen grouse followed them, then turned and charged out of the woods directly at me, with wings outstretched and neck ruff expanded. Grouse are often said to be elusive and shy of humans, but apparently they can be aggressive when protecting their young.

Willow Creek - Mckean County
(map: page 185)

Willow Creek is more "civilized" than the other Kinzua area streams. It flows through privately owned land as well as through Allegheny National Forest land, and there are houses scattered here and there along its length. There is little or no posting, though, and the stream offers fishing for both stocked and wild trout. Route 346 parallels Willow Creek, providing easy access and parking.

The Fish Commission stocks trout preseason and twice inseason, with the last stocking coming around mid-May. Most of Willow Creek's wild trout are browns, but some wild rainbows are also found, and brookies inhabit the headwaters. The Allegheny National Forest's Willow Bay Campground is located at the mouth of Willow Creek.

Kinzua Tailrace and Allegheny River - Warren County
(maps: pages 185 and 189)

The tailrace below Kinzua Dam is a popular fishing spot that produces many large trout, both browns and rainbows. The Fish Commission stocks fingerling

Sugar Run is well shaded by surrounding trees.

trout in this stretch each year, and they grow rapidly in this big water.

From below the spillway downstream 0.75 mile, fishing is open all year, and the daily limit is three trout. At Big Bend Access Area, off Route 59, you will find a parking lot, restrooms, and a boat ramp. The water is deep and slow here, and you will often see anglers sitting on lawn chairs along the water's edge, fishing bait with bobbers.

From the Big Bend Access Area downstream to Warren, there are several pulloffs along Route 59 where anglers park their cars and scramble down steep banks to the river. A particularly popular spot is the long stretch of riffles that run along Dixon Island, which is located about a mile below the dam. This stretch can be easily waded when water levels are moderate to low and often produces good fly fishing.

Caddis hatches are very heavy here and provide most of the fly fishing action. A Tan Elk Hair Caddis in size 14 is a good dry fly caddis pattern. Be sure to also bring some subsurface caddis patterns, such as grouse hackle wet flies or Antron Caddis Pupa patterns. When no flies are on the water, stripping large streamers such as Wooly Buggers, Zonkers, Marabou Muddlers, and Matukas can produce savage strikes.

To reach the north shore of the tailrace, take Route 6 across the river towards Warren and turn right onto Hemlock Road. Near the end of the road, you will come to a gate. Park on the right and walk down the trail that leads past the fence of a fish hatchery to the tailrace. The flow is much swifter here than on the Big Bend Access side of the river.

Downstream from the tailrace, there are several pulloffs along Hemlock Road and steep trails that lead to the river. From here you can fish along Dixon Island and several smaller islands.

Fly fishing begins to get good in the spring after the water flows have decreased to moderate levels. Fly fishing is best after water releases from the dam are reduced to 1,200 cubic feet per second or less. May and June are usually the peak months for fly fishing here.

When water temperatures exceed 70 degrees, as they often do from mid-June through early September, trout fishing is best late in the evening, very early in the morning, or at night. Because the water from the dam is drawn from the top of the reservoir rather than the bottom, summer water temperatures are much warmer than in such icy-cold tailwaters as the Youghiogheny. You can find out about water flow

Kinzua Tailrace looking downstream from the dam. Big Bend Access Area is on the left and a fish hatchery is on the right.

and water temperatures by calling (814) 726-0164, the Kinzua Dam fishing information number.

Some of the largest trout are caught by anglers who use bait, spinners, or spoons when water flows are high and cold, such as in the early spring and in fall and early winter. The Kinzua tailrace holds not only trout, but also bass, walleye, and muskies.

Downstream from the tailrace area, the Allegheny River becomes so large that many stretches ares difficult to fish without a boat. Boaters catch many trout in the Allegheny River by drifting from the Big Bend Access down to Warren. Boaters can take their boats out at Warren, at the Fish Commission access site at Starbrick, or at the Buckaloons Campground, which is an Allegheny National Forest facility located near the mouth of Brokenstraw Creek.

Trout are also found far downstream from Warren and are sometimes caught even as far downstream as Oil City, but the Allegheny is a big river here and the trout are scattered. As water temperatures warm in the river in early summer, trout can sometimes be found at the mouths of cooler tributary streams, such as Thompson Run, East Hickory Creek, West Hickory Creek, and others. Fly fishers sometimes catch large browns on dry flies during the evening rise at these creek mouths. These tributaries are shown on the East Hickory Creek map on page 193.

Tionesta Creek - Warren and Forest Counties
(map: page 189)

The main branch of Tionesta Creek is formed by the confluence of the West and South Branches of Tionesta Creek near Barnes. The Fish Commission stocks 23 miles of the stream, from the confluence of the branches downstream to Kelletville. Tionesta Creek is stocked preseason and three times inseason, with the last stocking coming around the third week in May. Most of the fishing is for stocked trout, but some big holdover browns are caught each year.

The Tionesta is a large stream, over 150 feet wide in its lower water, and it is popular with canoeists in the spring. It has a moderate gradient; gentle riffles separate long, flat pools. As with many large trout streams, Tionesta Creek is best fished in the spring because water temperatures rise quickly in early summer. In early to mid-June, as the water warms,

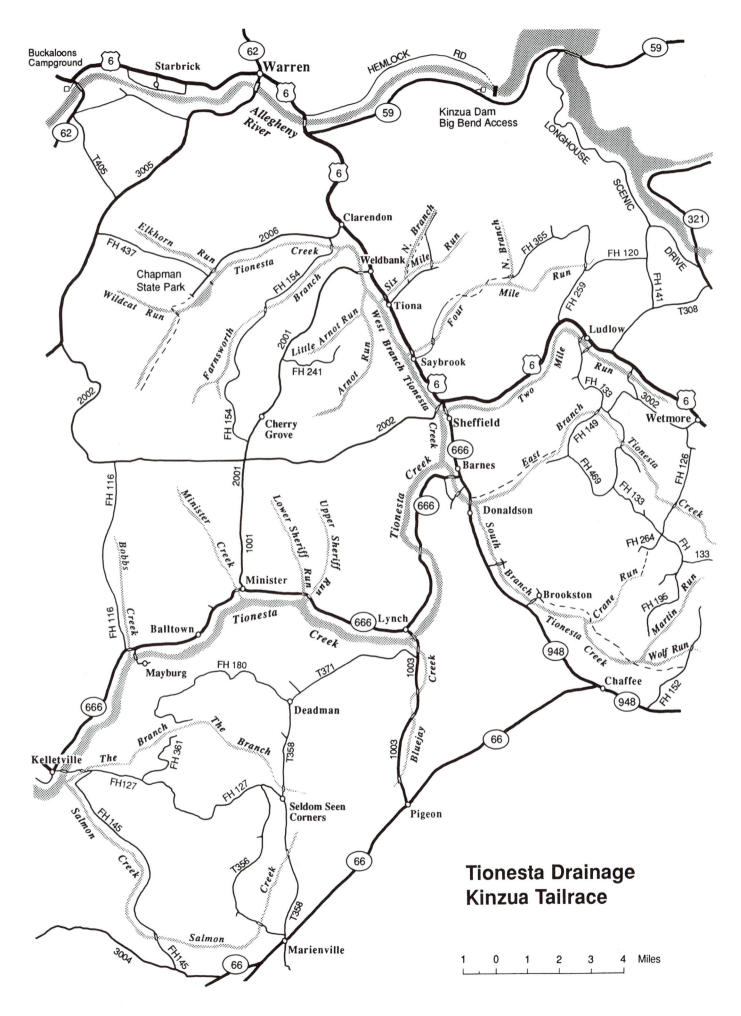

**Tionesta Drainage
Kinzua Tailrace**

trout often concentrate at the mouths of colder tributaries. Fishing in July and August is very slow.

Most of Tionesta Creek is easily accessible from Route 666; there are many places to pull off and park along the road. The upper stretch of Tionesta Creek, from the junction of the South and West Branches downstream to the Route 666 bridge, is not so easily accessible. Route 666 parallels the stream here also, but the stream is separated from the road by steep, wooded slopes.

The Tionesta has only scattered hatches of such early-season mayflies as Blue Quills and Quill Gordons, but it has better hatches of March Browns, Grey Foxes, and Light Cahills in late May and early June. Good caddis hatches occur throughout the season. The best fly fishing is found from the origin of Tionesta Creek downstream to Mayburg.

Bobbs Creek, Minister Creek, Upper Sheriff Run and Lower Sheriff Run are all small tributaries to Tionesta Creek. These streams are not stocked, but they hold low to fair numbers of wild brown and brook trout. Minister Creek is the largest and best of these streams. Allegheny National Forest's Minister Creek Campground has six tent camping sites connected by foot trails along Minister Creek. For further information on camping here, call the Sheffield Ranger District at (814) 968-3232.

Most of Tionesta Creek flows through the Allegheny National Forest, and a superb map, which includes the Tionesta drainage, the Kinzua area, and many other streams in Forest and Warren Counties, is available from the Supervisor's Office, Allegheny National Forest, 222 Liberty Street, P.O. Box 847, Warren, PA 16365. The cost is $2.00.

Salmon Creek - Forest County
(map: page 189)

Salmon Creek is a beautiful, back-country stream that flows through a remote part of the Allegheny National Forest before meeting Tionesta Creek near Kelletville. Its width varies from 20 to 40 feet and it has abundant riffles, pockets, and pools that provide good holding areas. The only thing it lacks is a good trout population. Because of the naturally low fertility of the water and the damaging effects of acid rain, few wild trout inhabit this stream. The fishery is almost entirely dependent on hatchery trout.

The Fish Commission stocks Salmon Creek preseason and four times inseason, with the last stocking coming in late May. Despite the name, do not expect to catch any salmon here.

The Branch - Forest County
(map: page 189)

Like its larger neighbor Salmon Creek, The Branch flows through a wild, inaccessible part of the Allegheny National Forest before meeting Tionesta Creek at Kelletville. Trees and rhododendron bushes keep it in deep shade. The Branch has only a few wild brookies; naturally low fertility, acid rain, and water quality problems from oil drilling limit the wild trout population.

The Fish Commission stocks trout preseason and once inseason, usually in late May or early June, from the mouth upstream to T358.

Bluejay Creek - Forest County
(map: page 189)

There are a lot of cabins crowded along the banks of the lower stretches of Bluejay Creek, but farther upstream, where Bluejay Creek flows through the Allegheny National Forest, the surroundings are more attractive. Bluejay Creek is stocked from the uppermost bridge on SR 1003 (Bluejay Creek Road) down to its mouth on Tionesta Creek at Lynch.

The Fish Commission stocks trout preseason and three times inseason, with the last stocking coming in late May. This stream has been damaged by acid rain and holds very few wild trout. Despite its low wild trout population, Bluejay Creek is a popular place to pursue hatchery fish in the early season.

South Branch Tionesta Creek - Warren, Forest, and Elk Counties
(map: page 189)

South Branch Tionesta Creek is stocked with trout from its mouth near Barnes upstream 5.5 miles to Brookston. Stocking takes place preseason and once inseason. The lower part of the creek, from the junction with the East Branch downstream to the mouth at Barnes, is a medium-sized stream with some deep holes. The South Branch flows slowly here and has a sandy streambed. In the summer months, this stretch gets too warm for good trout fishing. Most of this lower stretch of the creek flows through woodlands, but there are also numerous dwellings along the banks. A good place to park your car is next to the Route 666 bridge.

Above the junction with East Branch Tionesta Creek, the South Branch is a smaller stream that flows through a wooded area with few houses near the stream other than at the village of Brookston. Access is provided by Route 948 and several forest roads that cross the creek.

Above Brookston, South Branch Tionesta Creek is not stocked, but it holds a fair population of wild browns. This upper part of the creek flows through a remote part of the Allegheny National Forest.

Crane Run, Martin Run, and Wolf Run are small tributaries to the South Branch that hold good numbers of wild brown and brook trout. A tar pit that was once a dump site for a chemical company is located on the upper reaches of Wolf Run. Fish Commission personnel have noticed a reduction in aquatic insects in the stream near this dump.

East Branch Tionesta Creek - Warren and Mckean Counties
(map: page 189)

East Branch Tionesta Creek flows through the Allegheny National Forest, and it is more of a backwoods stream than the other branches of the Tionesta. The mouth can be reached from Route 666 near the village of Donaldson, but this is the only place on the stream that is accessible from a paved road. Forest roads provide access at several points in the middle and upper reaches and there are some long stretches that can be reached only on foot.

The Fish Commission stocks the East Branch from its mouth upstream to Forest Highway 126. Because of its limited access, the East Branch is not stocked as heavily as the other branches of the Tionesta, and it is stocked only once inseason. The limited access means less fishing pressure, though, and stocked trout can be found well into the summer.

The water quality of the East Branch has been affected by oil and gas exploration, but there is some reproduction of brown trout, and some wild brook trout are found in the upper stretches. The middle part of the creek offers some of the best fishing. This stretch can be reached from Ludlow via Forest Highways 133 and 149. From Route 6 at Ludlow, follow the Forest Service signs directing you toward the Tionesta Scenic Area. This is a beautiful, secluded area to enjoy camping and fishing.

West Branch Tionesta Creek - Warren County
(map: page 189)

West Branch Tionesta Creek is stocked from Sheffield upstream to the lake at Chapman State Park. The stream is paralleled by Route 6 in its lower stretch and SR 2006 (Chapman Dam Road) farther upstream. Because of siltation and summer warming, the fishing is mostly for hatchery trout, but some wild and holdover trout are found near the mouths of tributary streams. Trout are stocked preseason and four times inseason, with the last stocking coming around the third week in May. Trout fishing becomes very slow after mid-June.

Camping is available at Chapman State Park, and the lake here is also stocked with trout. Wildcat Run and Elkhorn Run are small, unstocked tributaries that hold native brook trout. Wildcat Run is the better of the two streams.

Arnot Run and Little Arnot Run are also unstocked tributaries to the West Branch. Both streams provide good fishing for wild brown and brook trout.

Farnsworth Branch - Warren County
(map: page 189)

Farnsworth Branch is a small, brushy stream that flows into West Branch Tionesta Creek near Clarendon. Some houses are found near the stream in the lower reaches, but most of Farnsworth Branch flows through the Allegheny National Forest. Forest Highway 154 parallels the entire stream.

The Fish Commission stocks trout from the mouth upstream 7 miles, to near a cooperative fish hatchery. Trout are stocked preseason and three times inseason, with the last stocking coming in late May. Although the fishing is mostly for hatchery trout in Farnsworth Branch, the stream does hold some wild brook trout.

Six Mile Run and North Branch Six Mile Run - Warren County
(map: page 189)

Six Mile Run is stocked with trout from its mouth on West Branch Tionesta Creek upstream 1.5 miles to the confluence with North Branch Six Mile Run. The North Branch is also stocked with trout, from its mouth upstream 3 miles. A paved road follows Six Mile Run up from Tiona, but numerous houses along the road make finding access tricky.

The North Branch flows through a densely wooded area, where only rough jeep trails provide access to the stream. The Fish Commission stocks both streams preseason and once inseason, usually around mid-May. These streams are small, but they both have good populations of wild brown trout. Native brook trout can be found in the North Branch.

Four Mile Run - Warren County
(map: page 189)

Four Mile Run flows into West Branch Tionesta Creek near Saybrook. The Fish Commission stocks trout from the mouth upstream about 4 miles to North Branch Four Mile Run. Trout are stocked preseason and once inseason.

A good road follows the stream from Saybrook up to the first bridge. There are quite a few houses along the road here. Above the first bridge, the houses end and the road quickly deteriorates into a muddy, potholed track.

The upper water on Four Mile Run can be reached via Forest Highways 259 and 365, which turn off from Route 6. FH 365 crosses a bridge over North Branch Four Mile Run, and the North Branch and Four Mile Run meet a short distance below this bridge. Four Mile Run is not stocked above this junction, but it has a good population of wild browns and brook trout. The North Branch isn't stocked either, but it holds many small native brook trout. If you like backwoods, small-stream fishing, you will enjoy the upper part of Four Mile Run and its North Branch.

Two Mile Run - Warren and Mckean Counties
(map: page 189)

Two Mile Run is little known except to anglers who live near the stream, but it is a very enjoyable stream to fish. Access is made easy by Route 6, which parallels the stream, and trees buffer the stream from road noise. The houses of Sheffield line the stream for about 1 mile up from the mouth, but most of the rest of the stream flows through woodlands. About half the length of Two Mile Run lies within the Allegheny National Forest.

The Fish Commission stocks Two Mile Run preseason and once inseason over a 10-mile stretch, from Sheffield up to Wetmore. The stream also holds a good wild brown trout population. Native brookies are found along with the browns from Ludlow upstream into the headwaters. Some of Two Mile Run's little tributaries offer good fishing for native brook trout.

East Hickory Creek - Forest and Warren Counties
(delayed harvest, artificial lures only, 1.7 miles)
(map: page 193)

East Hickory Creek is a medium-sized trout stream that meets the Allegheny River near the village of East Hickory. A delayed-harvest, artificial-lures-only stretch and back-country fishing in the headwaters are the main attractions here. Trout are stocked from the mouth upstream to the confluence of Middle Hickory Creek. The Fish Commission stocks trout preseason and four times inseason, with the last stocking coming in mid-May.

The lowest stretch of the creek, from the Route 62 bridge downstream to the mouth, is slow moving and has some deep pools. Most of the stocked trout are gone from this stretch by midsummer, but some large brown trout are occasionally caught here in the summer months. Apparently, these fish move up from the Allegheny River in search of cooler water.

From Route 62 up to the mouth of Beaver Creek, there are numerous houses and a large lumber mill near the stream. Just past the lumber mill, turn left onto T328, a gravel road that follows East Hickory Creek upstream. Forests surround the creek from here to the headwaters, with little development other than some hunting camps and oil and gas operations.

From Otter Creek up to Queen Creek, a distance of 1.7 miles, East Hickory Creek is managed under delayed-harvest, artificials-only regulations. These regulations maintain a high density of trout in this stretch. Access is easy here. You can park just about

anywhere along T328. Many anglers camp along the stream in the delayed-harvest area.

From the bridge at Queen upstream about 2 miles to the bridge on Forest Highway 119, East Hickory Creek flows through a wooded area with no road access. An Allegheny State Forest camping area is located just above the FH 119 bridge.

From FH 119 up to the headwaters, East Hickory Creek is accessible only by walking in. The stream is small here and mostly slow moving. Above the junction with Middle Hickory Creek, no trout are stocked, but both Middle Hickory Creek and the upper reaches of East Hickory Creek have fair populations of wild brook and brown trout.

As recently as 1963, East Hickory Creek had a good wild trout population along most of its length, but now there are only limited numbers of wild trout, except for in the headwaters above Forest Highway 119. The reasons for this decline are not clear.

Fishing tackle can be purchased at the Forest County Sports Center in Tionesta, about 7 miles south of East Hickory Creek via Route 62.

Queen Creek - Forest and Warren Counties
(map: page 193)

Queen Creek flows into East Hickory Creek at the upper end of that stream's delayed harvest area. A dirt road follows up along the lower end of Queen Creek and leads to a natural gas pumping station. A small parking area is located near the stream bank, a short distance downstream from the pumping station. From here you can walk along a gated access road that follows Queen Creek upstream.

Queen Creek is about 8 miles long, but because access is limited in the upper part of the creek, only the lower 2 miles of water are stocked. The Fish Commission stocks trout preseason and once inseason, usually in mid to late May.

A short distance downstream from the pumping station, there are several deep, swirling holes with good cover provided by undercut banks, roots, and downed trees. I caught several brown trout and had several other strikes here in mid-summer, during the severe drought of 1988.

Upstream from the pumping station, Queen Creek is well shaded by surrounding trees and flows through medium-sized pools connected by gentle riffles. Queen Creek holds some wild brown and brook trout, and many local anglers consider it to be one of the better streams in the area, but others say that the wild trout fishing has dropped off in recent years. Acid rain may be to blame.

The upper stretches of Queen Creek flow through a beautiful, remote area, which is well worth exploring even if you don't catch many fish. FH 551, a very

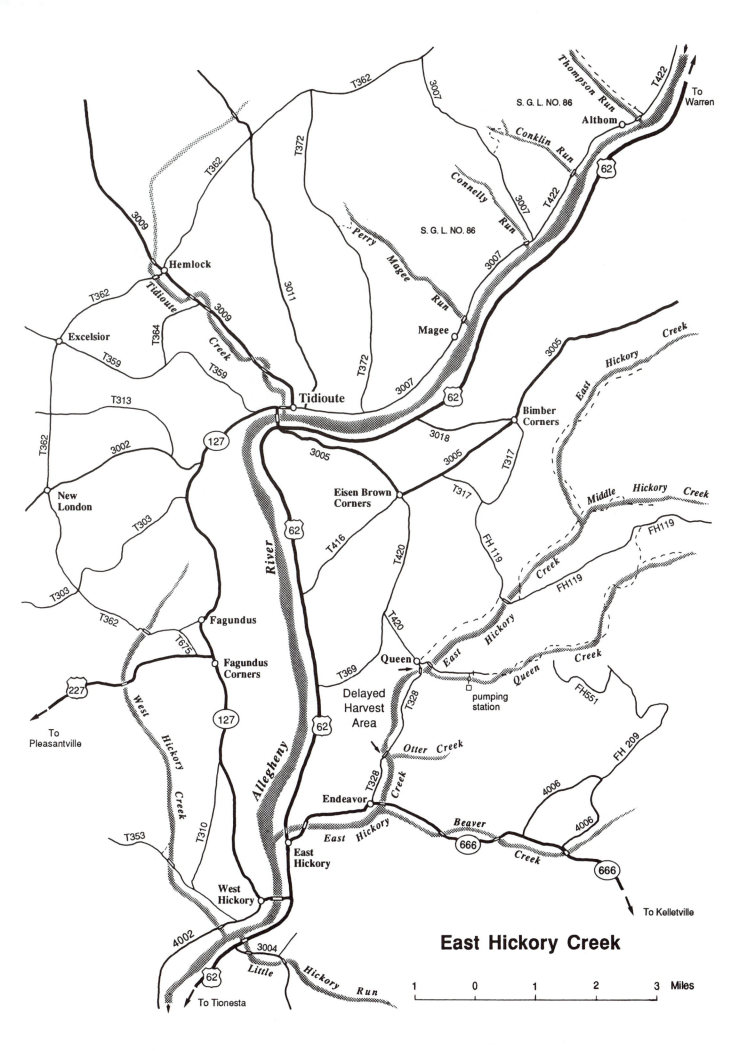

East Hickory Creek

1 0 1 2 3 Miles

East Hickory Creek in the delayed-harvest area.

rough forest road, provides some access to this upper stretch of Queen Creek.

Otter Creek - Forest County
(map: page 193)

Otter Creek is a small, unstocked forest stream that flows into East Hickory Creek at the lower end of that stream's delayed-harvest area. The lower part of Otter Creek is well shaded by trees but it is rather shallow and seems to hold few fish. Some anglers have reported catching wild brook trout in the upper stretches, though.

Beaver Run - Forest County
(map: page 193)

This small tributary to East Hickory Creek is stocked from its mouth upstream 6.8 miles to its headwaters. Route 666 follows most of the stream, but the headwaters are less accessible. The entire stream flows through forest land. The Fish Commission stocks trout preseason and once inseason. A few native brook trout are found in Beaver Run, but most of the trout come from the hatchery truck.

Thompson Run - Warren County
(map: page 193)

This pleasant little stream flows through the forested hills of State Game Land No. 86 before meeting the Allegheny River at Althom. There is a parking area near the mouth, and from here you can walk up along a gated dirt access road. This road parallels the creek, but in many places the hike down the bank to the stream is steep.

The Fish Commission stocks Thompson Run from its mouth upstream 2 miles. Trout are stocked preseason and three times inseason, with the last stocking coming around mid-May. Thompson Run has a fair population of wild brown trout in its lower waters, and native brookies can be found farther upstream.

Connelly Run and Conklin Run - Warren County
(map: page 193)

These tiny streams flow through State Game Land No. 86 and into the Allegheny River. They are not stocked, but if you enjoy exploring small streams, you *might* find some native brookies here.

Perry Magee Run - Warren County
(map: page 193)

Perry Magee Run flows most of its length through the rolling, wooded hills of State Game Land No. 86. SR 3007 crosses the creek just above its mouth on the Allegheny River. The upper end of the stocked stretch can be reached only by walking. A Game Land parking area is located along T372, about 3 miles north of the intersection with SR 3007. From here you can walk along a gated access road that winds down to the stream.

Most of Perry Magee Run's trout come from the hatchery, but the stream does hold a few wild brown and brook trout. The Fish Commission stocks trout before opening day and once inseason, usually around mid-May.

Tidioute Creek - Warren County
(map: page 193)

Tidioute Creek is stocked with trout for approximately 6 miles, from its mouth on the Allegheny River upstream to SR 3011. From the town of Tidioute up to Hemlock, the creek is followed closely by SR 3009, and finding access is tricky in spots because of the many houses along the road.

Upstream from Hemlock, Tidioute Creek flows through undeveloped forest lands. There are few wild trout in Tidioute Creek, even in the upper reaches. These upper reaches look ideal for brook trout, but for some reason there are few wild trout to be found.

West Hickory Creek - Forest County
(map: page 193)

West Hickory Creek flows through a hilly, heavily forested area and offers good fishing for both stocked and wild trout. The Fish Commission stocks 5.7 miles of the stream, from the mouth upstream to the T362 bridge. Trout are stocked preseason and once inseason, usually in late April or early May.

The bridge on SR 4002 near the mouth is a good access point. There are several deep, quiet pools between this bridge and the mouth, and sometimes large browns move into this lower stretch from the Allegheny River. Above the bridge is a faster-flowing stretch of riffles and pockets.

Near the T353 bridge, there are many cabins, but if you drive up past the cabins, you can park along the road on the right and follow a trail through the woods to the creek. Upstream from here, you will find a heavily-wooded stretch that is not fished very hard. The stream is narrow here and hemmed in by trees and brush. Most of this water is fast flowing and fairly shallow, but pockets and small pools at tree roots and downed logs provide good cover, and a few of the larger holes are waist deep.

West Hickory Creek has a fair wild brown trout population in the stocked portion of the stream and fair numbers of native brook trout in the headwaters above T362. Some of the creek's tiny tributaries are worth trying for native brook trout.

Little Hickory Run - Forest County
(map: page 193)

Little Hickory Run is a small brook with rocky, shallow riffles and some good pocket water. A few houses are found near the mouth, but most of the creek flows through a wooded area in the Allegheny National Forest.

To reach this small stream, take Route 62 north from Tionesta. Travel 5 miles up along the Allegheny River, and you will reach the bridge over Little Hickory Run. Just before the bridge, turn right onto SR 3004 (Little Hickory Road), which provides access to the lower part of the creek.

The Fish Commission stocks trout preseason and once inseason, around mid-May. Little Hickory Run holds fair numbers of wild trout. Brown trout predominate in the lower stretches, and brook trout can be found in the headwaters.

Oil Creek - Crawford and Venango Counties
(delayed harvest, artificial lures only, 1.6 miles)
(map: page 197)

Oil Creek may not sound like a proper name for a trout stream, but don't let the name fool you. In the early years of Pennsylvania's oil boom, the stream often flowed black from oil spills, but today Oil Creek is one of the most popular trout streams in the northwest region of the state. Oil Creek also has several tributaries that offer trout fishing, such as East Branch Oil Creek, Thompson Creek, McLaughlin Run, Shirley Run, Pine Creek, Caldwell Creek, and West Branch Caldwell Creek.

Oil Creek is stocked over a distance of 27 miles, from the confluence of Mosey Run near Lincolnville downstream to Rouseville. (The upper stretches are not shown on the map.) The Fish Commission stocks trout preseason and once inseason, with the last stocking usually coming in early or mid-May. Most of the fishing is for stocked trout, but Oil Creek is known for producing large brown trout, and some wild trout can be found at the mouths of tributaries.

Oil Creek State Park

The best place to fish Oil Creek is on the 13.5-mile stretch of stream that flows through Oil Creek State Park. This stretch is heavily stocked, and the stream flows here through pleasant, wooded hills. Road access is limited, and there are few buildings in this area, except for some historical sites from the oil boom days. Oil Creek is a big stream in Oil Creek State Park, roughly 100 to 150 feet wide, and it is popular with canoeists from March to June.

Access to the upper end of the park is found at the Drake Well Museum, off Route 8 just south of Titusville. You can park at the museum or at a parking lot on the opposite side of the creek that is also used by canoeists and bicyclists. A bike trail extends from this parking lot down along the stream to Petroleum Center, another major access site. Some of the best trout water on Oil Creek is found between the Drake Well Museum and the bridge on T635 (Miller Farm Road). Good riffles and deep pools are found here, and several springs and small tributaries flow in along this stretch. T635 is a dirt and gravel road that can get muddy after heavy rains. T621, which leads to the west side of the creek farther downstream, is an even rougher road.

Petroleum Center is the main access site in the lower end of the park. Restrooms and an information center are located here. Good park maps are available at the information center. From the information center, you can walk or ride bike up along the bike trail. Note that camping is not permitted in the park.

Delayed-Harvest Area

Oil Creek's delayed-harvest, artificials-lures-only area begins at the Petroleum Center bridge and extends downstream 1.6 miles to a railroad bridge. This special regulations area has become quite popular. When weather permits, many anglers get an early start on the season in February and March. The water usually becomes low and warm during the summer months, but many trout remain through the summer and into the fall. Fishing is open year around in this stretch, and the Oil Creek Chapter of Trout Unlimited makes supplemental stockings very early in the year and again in the fall.

Oil Creek Outfitters, located near the upstream boundary of the delayed-harvest area, is a good source for fishing tackle, additional stream information, and bicycle rentals.

The State Park stretch offers the best fishing, but Oil Creek is also worth fishing upstream from Titusville. You can get access at most bridge crossings. There are good riffles and pools at the Route 408 bridge at Hydetown, and big browns are sometimes caught in this stretch. At Tryonville the water is deep and slow moving. Above Centerville, where East Branch Oil Creek flows in, Oil Creek is small, slow moving, and marshy in spots.

Oil Creek has good fishing and fly hatches from the early season up to about mid-June, but its waters become low and warm after that. More bass than trout are caught in Oil Creek during July and August.

Oil Creek. A fisherman fights a trout in Oil Creek State Park.   (Thad Bukowski photo)

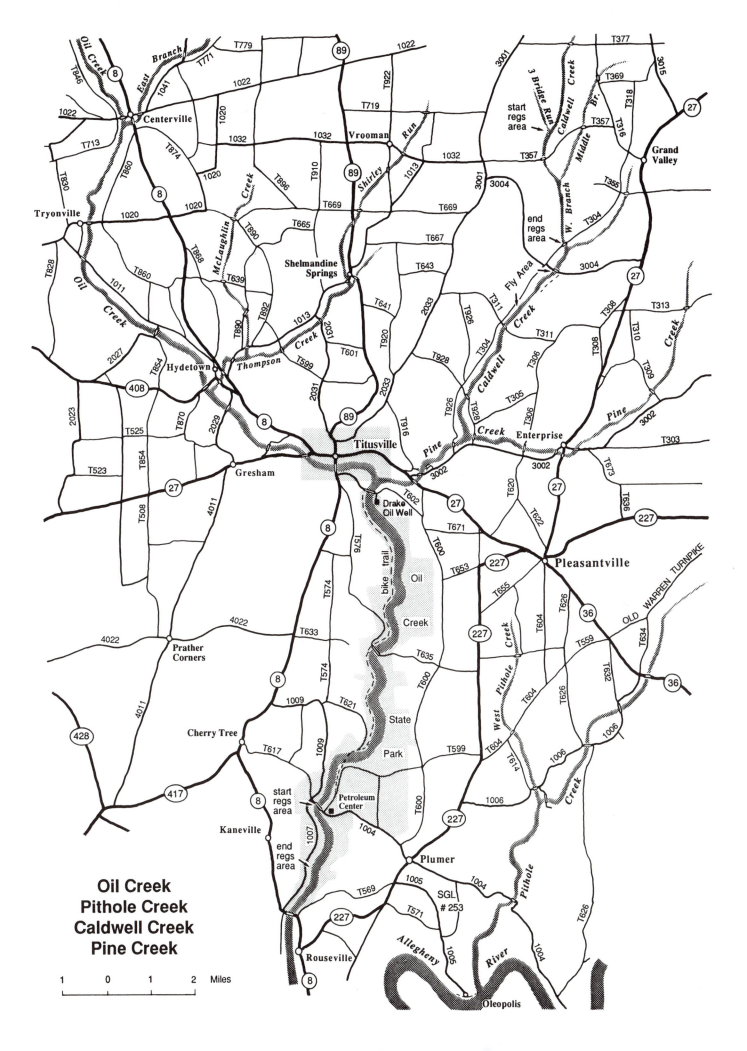

Oil Creek
Pithole Creek
Caldwell Creek
Pine Creek

Fly hatches on Oil Creek include Sulphurs, March Browns, Grey Foxes, Light Cahills, and a variety of caddis. Crayfish are an important food source here, so you might try imitative crayfish patterns or a suggestive pattern such as the Wooly Bugger.

East Branch Oil Creek - Crawford County
(map: page 197)

East Branch Oil Creek flows through a countryside of woods and farms before meeting Oil Creek at the village of Centerville. It is stocked from its mouth upstream to Spartansburg, a distance of about 10 miles. The Fish Commission stocks trout preseason and also once inseason, around mid-May. This slow-moving creek has an essentially put-and-take fishery, with few wild or holdover trout. Fishing pressure is heavy in the opening weeks of the season.

Thompson Creek - Crawford County
(map: page 197)

Thompson Creek, often called Thompson Run locally, flows into Oil Creek at the village of Hydetown, just below the Route 408 bridge. This small stream is stocked from its mouth upstream about 3 miles to the SR 2031 bridge. The Fish Commission stocks trout preseason and once inseason, usually around the second week in May. Thompson Creek has excellent water quality and holds fair numbers of wild brown trout.

Parking is limited along the lower stretches of the creek, where it flows through Hydetown. Much of this lower part of Thompson Creek has been channelized, making the stream wider and shallower than it should be.

SR 1013 parallels Thompson Creek upstream from Route 8. From Route 8 up to the first bridge, access is made difficult by houses lining the road. There is some parking at the SR 1013 bridge, and upstream from this bridge the creek flows through an eroded cow pasture. If you walk up above the pasture, a little bit beyond the mouth of McLaughlin Creek, you will find Thompson Creek flowing through a brushy, wooded area. There are deep holes here amid a tangle of tree roots, downed logs, undercut banks and overhanging branches. It's the sort of place that makes a fly fisherman wish he had brought some worms along.

At the next bridge up, on T599 (Finney Road), there is good parking, and you can fish up or downstream in pleasant woods. At the bridge above this, on SR 2031, you can park and fish downstream only. Thompson Creek is posted against trespassing from the SR 2031 bridge upstream to its origin, the confluence of Shirley Run and Hummer Creek at Shelmandine Springs.

McLaughlin Creek - Crawford County
(map: page 197)

McLaughlin Creek is a small tributary to Thompson Creek, in the Oil Creek drainage. If you are willing to deal with some irritating access problems, you can find decent fishing here for both stocked and wild trout. McLaughlin Creek is stocked from its mouth upstream about 3 miles to the upper bridge on T890 (Gilson Ridge Road). The Fish Commission stocks trout preseason and once inseason, around the third week in April.

At the lower end of the creek, you can park at the SR 1013 bridge, which crosses the creek a short distance above the mouth. From here up to the lower bridge on T890, there is a scattering of houses and trailers along the creek. This lower bridge on T890 is closed, but just before the bridge there is a pulloff on the right. A ferocious border collie attacked me a short distance downstream from here.

A good place to fish McLaughlin Creek is above T639 (Bogg Hollow Road). The creek is posted below this bridge, but upstream from the bridge there is pleasant fishing in the shade of tall trees, far from the madding crowd, and far from mad dogs too. The stream flows here through an undeveloped wooded area. In this upper part of the creek, there are fair numbers of wild brown and brook trout.

Shirley Run - Crawford County
(map: page 197)

This small tributary to Thompson Creek is no longer stocked, but it has a good population of wild brown trout and also some native brook trout in its upper stretches. Shirley Run flows through a rural area of dairy farms and woodlots. The lower part of the creek, from the mouth on Thompson Creek at Shelmandine Springs upstream to the Route 89 bridge, is posted.

A good place to park is at the Route 89 bridge. The short stretch of stream from here up to T669 (Cloverdale Road) flows under the shade of tall trees. Above T669 the creek flows through a cow pasture. The banks here are lined with brushy willows, which make casting a little tricky, but there are plenty of wild brown trout in this part of the stream. Upstream from this pasture, Shirley Run becomes very small and nearly choked off by brush.

Pine Creek - Warren and Crawford Counties
(map: page 197)

There are many Pine Creeks in Pennsylvania, three of which are described in this book. This particular Pine Creek is the largest tributary to Oil Creek. The two streams are of about equal size when they meet near the Drake Oil Well museum, just south of Titusville. Pine Creek is stocked from its mouth upstream 12 miles to the bridge on T313 (Swede Road). The Fish Commission stocks trout preseason and twice inseason, with the last stocking coming around mid-May.

In addition to stocked trout, Pine Creek has a fair population of wild brown trout, although water quality problems from oil and gas operations, logging, and road building have hurt the stream somewhat. Pine Creek flows through an area of rolling, forested hills with scattered houses and a few small farms.

The lower part of the creek, from the influx of Caldwell Creek to the mouth, is big water. The creek is wide here and flows at a moderate pace through gentle riffles and long, flat pools. This openness allows for easy fly casting, but water temperatures get pretty high in the summer months and fishing slows.

You can reach the lowest part of Pine Creek by parking along T602 a short distance upstream from the Drake Well Museum. Another good spot can be found by following SR 3002 upstream from Route 27 for about a half-mile, then turning left onto Messeral Road (T993), a dirt road that leads to a nice pool at an abandoned bridge.

There is also good access at the bridge on T926 (Dotyville Road) and at the bridge on T928 (Duncan Road). A trail leads from the T928 bridge to the junction of Pine and Caldwell Creeks. Local anglers report that large browns are sometimes caught here during the spawning season in October and November.

Above the confluence with Caldwell Creek, Pine Creek becomes considerably smaller. Upstream from T928, the stream flows through alternating riffles and pools that are well shaded by overhanging branches. There is a private campground near the bridge on T306 (Mount Hope Road).

Just above the SR 3002 bridge at Enterprise, the stream flows along the wide lawns of a large home. A sign here reads, "Fishing permitted, walk in only." Parking is available along the shoulder of SR 3002.

If you like getting away from it all, fish up or down from the bridge on T309. The stream flows through scenic woods here, and there are few signs of civilization other than some old oil pipe lying around.

Pine Creek is still a fair-sized brook at T313 (Swede Road), but a short distance up from here some tributaries branch off, and above this Pine Creek is tiny. Brook trout are common in these headwaters.

Caldwell Creek - Warren County
(delayed harvest, fly fishing only, 1.4 miles)
(map: page 197)

Caldwell Creek and its tributary, the West Branch of Caldwell Creek, offer fine trout fishing. Both streams flow through forested areas and both have clean, clear water. Special regulations stretches on both creeks allow many stocked trout to survive the early-season onslaught, and both streams carry a good population of wild brown trout.

Caldwell Creek is a tributary to Pine Creek, which is a tributary to Oil Creek. Stocking on Caldwell Creek extends from the mouth upstream about 5 miles to the confluence of the West Branch. Above this point Caldwell Creek is very small, brushy, and slow moving, and seems to hold few trout. Where the West Branch and upper Caldwell Creek meet, the West Branch is by far the larger stream.

Most of Caldwell Creek is slow moving, but excellent shade from surrounding trees and brush moderates summer water temperatures. Roots, fallen trees, undercut banks, and deep pools provide good cover. The stream flows through a sparsely populated wooded area with only occasional dwellings.

A delayed-harvest, fly-fishing-only area begins at the bridge on SR 3004 (Selkirk Road) and extends downstream 1.4 miles. A parking lot is located just east of this bridge, and a rough road follows the creek downstream along the east bank.

Caldwell Creek has good fly hatches, including Blue Quills and Hendricksons early in the year, followed by March Browns, Grey Foxes, and Light Cahills. Various caddis hatch all through the season.

Not many people fish this stream in midsummer. The clear, slow-flowing water makes fooling the trout difficult. It is worth a try, though, because Caldwell Creek holds many trout through the summer, not only in the fly area, but in the lower stretches as well. Water temperatures remain much cooler here in the summer months than in larger streams such as nearby Oil Creek.

West Branch Caldwell Creek - Warren County
(catch and release, 3.6 miles)
(map: page 197)

The catch-and-release area on West Branch Caldwell Creek starts at the bridge on T304 (Flat Road), just above the junction with Caldwell Creek, and extends upstream approximately 3.6 miles to the confluence of Three Bridge Run. Parking is available at the T304 bridge at the bottom of the stretch, and at the T357 bridge in the upper part of the stretch. Only artificial lures or flies may be used and all hooks must be barbless.

The West Branch flows through an undeveloped forest area owned by the Hammermill Paper Company. This is a remote area, and fishing pressure is not very heavy, even though the creek has a good wild brown trout population. Trees and thick brush surround the West Bank, making it difficult to walk along the banks. The stream moves slowly in the

Caldwell Creek.   (Thad Bukowski photo)

lower reaches, but farther upstream it flows more quickly over rocky riffles.

The Fish Commission stocks trout preseason and once inseason, usually around the third week in May. The West Branch also holds good numbers of wild and holdover brown trout, including some large ones. This is a good stream for summer fishing because water temperatures stay cool.

West Branch Caldwell Creek is also stocked above the special regulations stretch, upstream as far as the village of Sanford. (The uppermost reaches are not shown on the map.) The stream is very small in this upper water, and fewer trout remain here after the opening weeks of the season than downstream in the catch-and-release area.

Three Bridge Run, which flows into the West Branch at the upper end of the catch-and-release area, is a very small stream, but it is worth a try for native brookies.

Middle Branch Caldwell Creek is also a very small creek, but it holds many small wild brown and brook trout. Expect to battle some very thick brush along the banks of this stream.

Pithole Creek - Venango County
(map: page 197)

Pithole Creek flows through the forested northeast corner of Venango County before meeting the Allegheny River east of Oil City. There is little development along the stream other than oil and gas drilling and logging. The stream has several road crossings, but long stretches can be reached only on foot.

Above the junction with West Pithole Creek, Pithole Creek is fairly small and mostly shallow and slow moving. There have been some water quality problems in this upper water. The fishing depends on stocked trout here, and few wild trout are found. The Fish Commission stocks Pithole Creek preseason and once inseason, in late May.

Below the junction with West Pithole Creek, Pithole Creek increases in size, and its gradient steepens as the stream begins its drop toward the Allegheny River. The lower part of the creek has deep pools and fast, rocky rapids, which swirl past Volkswagen-sized boulders. Most of this section is accessible only to walk-in fishing. SR 1004, which runs east from Plumer, crosses the creek at the Stone Arch Bridge. Beautiful water can be found up or downstream from this bridge. Pithole Creek holds many wild brown trout in this area, including quite a few in the 12- to 15-inch range. Occasionally, trophy trout over 20 inches are caught near the mouth. These fish apparently move into the lower end of the creek from the Allegheny River.

To reach the mouth of Pithole Creek, take SR 1005 to Oleopolis, a small village of houses and cabins. Park your car where the road ends and walk east along the old railroad grade for about a quarter-mile.

West Pithole Creek - Venango County
(map: page 197)

This small tributary to Pithole Creek flows through a forested area and offers fishing of the put-and-take variety. The Fish Commission stocks trout preseason and once inseason, around mid-May. There are few wild trout in the stream, and there have been water quality problems caused by sewage effluent. The lower part of the creek, which is paralleled by T614, flows swiftly through rocky riffles and pockets

and is surrounded by scenic woodlands. The upper stretch of the creek flows more slowly.

Little Sandy Creek - Venango County
(delayed harvest, fly fishing only, 1.3 miles)
(map: page 201)

The fly area on Little Sandy Creek is very popular with the fly fishers of northwestern Pennsylvania; some travel from as far as Erie to fish it. The fly area extends from the SR 3024 bridge upstream to a pumphouse on the grounds of Polk Center, which is a large state psychiatric hospital. The regulations have been changed recently from the previous fly-fishing-only regulations to delayed-harvest, fly-fishing-only regulations.

At the lower end of the fly stretch, there isn't much parking available right at the SR 3024 bridge, but there is a parking area nearby at the intersection of SR 3024 and Route 62. In the lower part of the fly area, the stream flows through a dense stand of mature hardwood trees.

Long guardrails prevent parking right at the Route 62 bridge, but you can park not far from the bridge on the shoulder of Route 62. Little Sandy Creek is about 35 feet wide at the Route 62 bridge and narrower in most places.

Above Route 62, Little Sandy Creek flows past tall trees and thick underbrush. Stream improvement

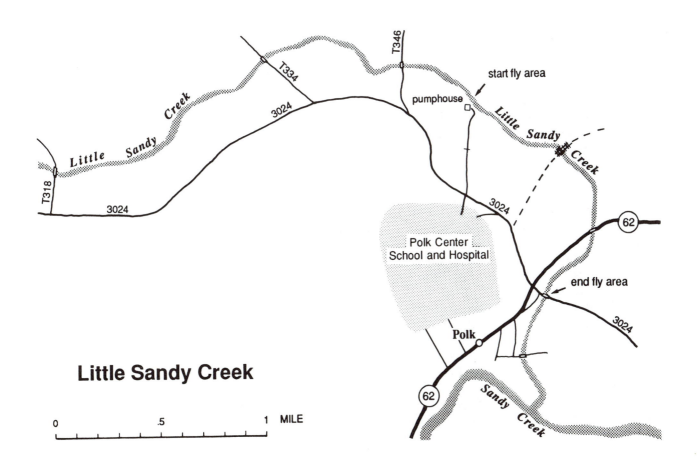

Little Sandy Creek

0   .5   1   MILE

Little Sandy Creek at the old railroad bridge.

devices built in this stretch provide good cover and blend in well with the natural features of the stream. Tree roots and downed timber also provide good cover. There is a large pool at a picturesque old railroad bridge about a half-mile upstream from Route 62.

To reach the upper end of the fly stretch, drive north on SR 3024. You will notice a large barn on the Polk Center grounds to your left. At this point, turn right off SR 3024 onto a narrow paved road, which is lined with tall pine trees. This road leads over a hill to a pumphouse at the upper end of the fly area. If the road is chained off, you may have to walk down to the stream.

The Fish Commission stocks Little Sandy Creek preseason and three times inseason, with the last stocking coming in late May or early June. Trout are stocked from the mouth upstream nearly 5 miles, to the bridge on T304. (The T304 bridge is upstream of the area shown on the map.)

Little Sandy Creek becomes low and clear in the summer months, but the skilled and persistent angler can catch trout here year around. The fly area holds stocked trout and wild browns into the summer and fall, and wild browns are found in fair numbers in other parts of the creek as well.

The Penns Woods and Oil Creek Chapters of Trout Unlimited, the Franklin Chapter of the Izaak Walton League, and the Boy Scouts of America have all worked on projects to improve the fishing on Little Sandy Creek.

Neshannock Creek - Mercer and Lawrence Counties
(delayed harvest, artificial lures, 1.1 miles)
(map: page 203)

Neshannock Creek is a large trout stream that is stocked over a distance of 20 miles, from Mercer, where the stream originates at the confluence of Cool Spring and Otter Creeks, downstream to New Castle. Between these two towns, the creek flows through a rural area of rolling hills, woods, farms, and small villages. There is little or no posting along the stream, and just about every bridge crossing provides access.

There are few wild trout in Neshannock Creek, but some big holdover brown trout are caught each year. Trout are stocked pretty heavily, and because the stream is large and many stretches are far from road access, the trout are not all quickly removed. Fishing is usually good from opening day through the month of June, but fishing becomes difficult in July and August, after the water has warmed.

A delayed-harvest, artificial-lures-only stretch has been approved for Neshannock Creek, beginning with

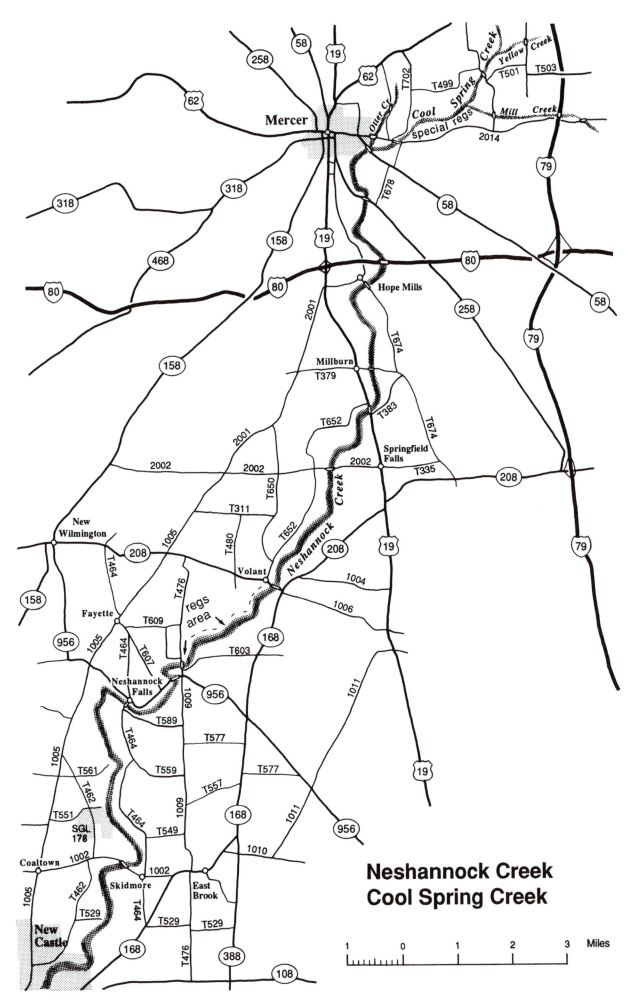

**Neshannock Creek
Cool Spring Creek**

the 1991 season. This stretch extends from the first bridge below Volant (it's a covered bridge) upstream 1.1 miles.

Caddis hatches provide much of the fly fishing action on Neshannock Creek, and imitations with cream, tan, and olive bodies will cover most of these. March Browns are the best mayfly hatch, and sparser hatches of Grey Foxes, Brown Drakes, and Green Drakes also bring trout to the surface.

Fly fishing tackle can be found at Neshannock Outfitters in the small village of Volant. Many old buildings in Volant have been restored and now house craft shops. A railroad grade that has been converted into a wide hiking trail extends from the train station in Volant down along the creek. This provides access to the 2.5 mile stretch of Neshannock Creek that lies between Volant and the next bridge crossing. This roadless stretch is float stocked to better distribute the trout along the length of the creek.

Cool Spring Creek - Mercer County
(delayed harvest, artificial lures only, 1.25 miles)
(map: page 203)

The best fishing on Cool Spring Creek is found in the delayed-harvest, artificial-lures-only area near Mercer. To find this stretch, take Route 58 east from the majestic courthouse on the square in Mercer. In 0.4 miles, Route 58 turns to the right, but continue driving straight onto SR 2014 (East Market Street). In another 0.3 miles, you will cross over Otter Creek (which is not a stocked stream), and in another 0.3 miles past Otter Creek you will cross a bridge over Cool Spring Creek.

The delayed-harvest regulations are in effect from the SR 2014 bridge upstream 1.25 miles to an old railroad grade. There is little parking available near the SR 2014 bridge, but there is a developed parking area and also several pulloffs along T702 (Dump Road), which parallels the lower part of the special regulations stretch.

Cool Spring Creek is a medium-sized stream, approximately 40 feet wide, and it flows at a moderate pace, with gentle riffles and glides. It drains a rural area of woods, meadows, and farms. The trout fishing on Cool Spring Creek is dependent on hatchery fish, as there are few wild trout. The Fish Commission stocks trout preseason and twice inseason, with the last stocking coming in early to mid-May. Trout can be found in the delayed-harvest section late into the season, when the rest of the stream has few trout remaining.

Caddis hatches are the mainstay of the fly fishing on Cool Spring Creek, and the Olive Caddis, which hatch in May, are particularly important. Mayfly hatches to be prepared for include March Browns, Grey Foxes, and Light Cahills.

Slippery Rock Creek - Lawrence and Butler Counties
(delayed harvest, fly fishing only, 0.5 mile)
(map: page 205)

Slippery Rock Creek is well known for its beautiful gorge in McConnells Mill State Park. This very scenic spot is well worth a visit for anyone who enjoys the outdoors. Rock walls and tall trees rise up from the streamside, and small tributary streams create waterfalls as they spill over the lip of the gorge.

Slippery Rock Creek is big compared to most Pennsylvania trout streams, about 100 feet wide, and it rushes through numerous boulder-strewn rapids, which alternate with swift, deep glides. The white water attracts many kayakers and rafters, but only the experienced should attempt running this stream. Several hiking trails can be followed to explore the gorge. McConnels Mill, a restored gristmill, and an old covered bridge just below the mill are interesting historical features of the park.

The steepest part of the gorge and the swiftest white water extend from Route 422 near Rose Point downstream 2.5 miles to Eckert Bridge. From Eckert Bridge downstream 4 miles to Harris Bridge, the walls of the gorge begin to recede, and the water, while still swift, loses some of its ferociousness.

Near the lower end of the park, there is a 0.5 mile delayed-harvest, fly-fishing-only section, which is a very popular fishing spot. About half of this stretch is above the Armstrong Bridge and half below. Fly fishers come here not only from Pennsylvania, but also from Ohio and West Virginia. Because this stretch is open to fishing year around, it is particularly busy on the weekends leading up to opening day. The first stocking is usually made in mid-March.

The trout fishing in Slippery Rock Creek relies almost entirely on stocked trout; there is little natural reproduction. The Fish Commission stocks trout preseason and once inseason, usually around the third week in May.

In the 1960's Slippery Rock Creek was badly polluted by acid mine drainage, but a water treatment plant in the headwaters has greatly improved water quality. Recently the Fish Commission has stocked fingerling trout in addition to the usual legal-size trout. Even though the stream holds few wild trout, some stocked fish can be found late into the season, particularly in the fly area, but also in some of the remote stretches away from the bridges. Fishing pressure outside the fly area is generally light after the opening week of the season.

The 4 miles of water from Eckert Bridge down to Harris Bridge is a good section for walk-in fishing. You can also find solitude in the stretch between Eckert Bridge and Route 422, but the wading is more hazardous in this area. Watch out for slippery rocks!

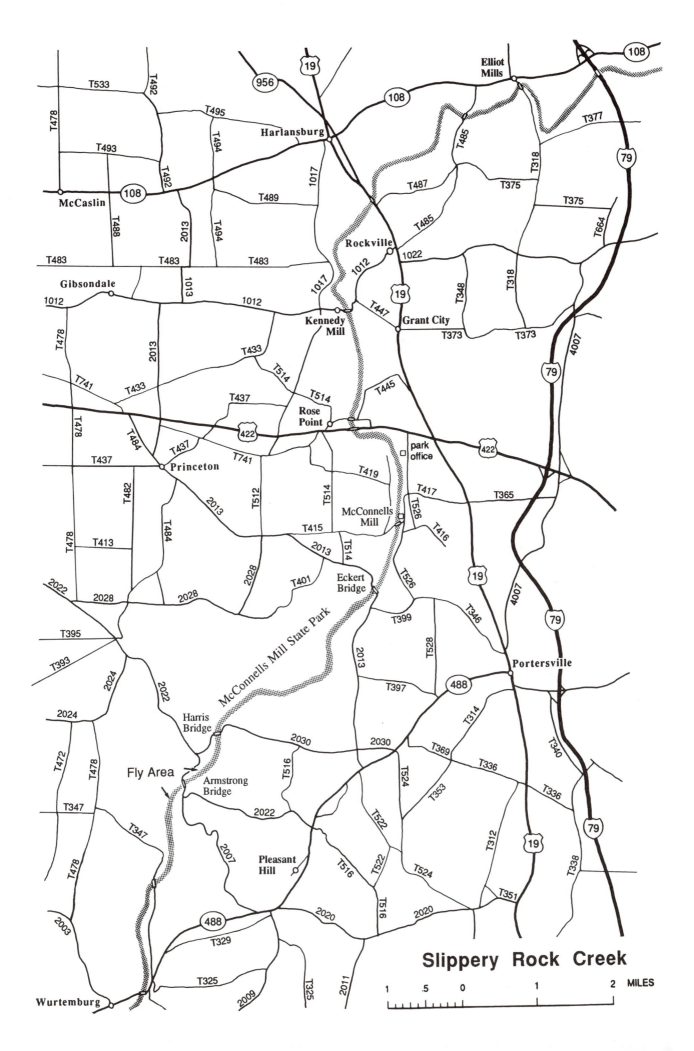

Slippery Rock Creek

Caddis hatches provide most of the fly fishing action on Slippery Rock Creek, and there are also scattered hatches of March Browns, Grey Foxes, and Brown Drakes.

Erie County Salmon and Steelhead Streams
(maps: pages 208 and 210)

The introduction of salmon and steelhead into the Great Lakes has produced some terrific fishing in the states bordering the lakes. Pennsylvania only has about 45 miles of shoreline bordering Lake Erie, so it doesn't have as extensive a salmon and steelhead fishery as some other states, such as New York and Michigan, but some good fishing can be found here.

The Fish Commission and local sportsmen's cooperative hatcheries stock fingerling steelhead and salmon (mostly coho salmon but also a few chinook salmon) and these fish feed in Lake Erie and grow rapidly. When they run up the streams to spawn, they are strong, hefty fish. Fish from 5 to 10 pounds are common, and larger fish are sometimes caught.

As of this writing (1990), the coho salmon runs are undergoing a slump on Lake Erie tributaries and also on the other Great Lakes fisheries. The salmon runs were very good in the late 1970's and early 1980's, but they started dropping off around 1984. The steelhead runs are still going strong.

The most popular and productive waters are Elk Creek, Walnut Creek, and the mouth of Trout Run, all west of Erie; and Twenty Mile Creek, east of Erie. These are usually considered to be the best bets for salmon and steelhead fishing, but numerous other Erie County streams also have salmon and steelhead runs. (Descriptions of individual streams follow this general introduction.) The regulations controlling the salmon and steelhead streams are complex and vary from stream to stream. Check the regulations booklet that comes with your fishing license.

Salmon and steelhead can be found in Lake Erie offshore from the mouths of the streams at all times of the year, and they are pursued there by anglers casting from the beach or fishing from boats. In the fall the fish begin moving up the streams to spawn. Runs are heaviest after the streams receive enough rainfall to raise their water level and make the water cloudy. Salmon begin entering the streams around mid-September, and by early October the runs are usually well under way. Salmon are found in the streams from September through late October and into early November.

Some steelhead enter the streams in late September, but most move into the streams in October and November. Fall steelhead fishing often peaks during the last two weeks in November. Steelhead are found in the streams all winter, but the streams freeze over during cold winter weather. Even when the streams are frozen, their mouths on Lake Erie often remain open. Sometimes warm spells in January and February melt the ice in the streams, and steelhead can be caught at these times. The ice usually melts for good by early March, and rising water temperatures make the fish more active. Spring steelhead fishing usually peaks during the last two weeks of March.

The streams are closed to fishing from April 1 through the opening day of trout season, which always falls on a Saturday in mid-April. Steelhead are sometimes caught in the opening week or two of trout season, but by the end of April most of the fish that haven't been caught have returned to the lake.

Similar tackle is used for both salmon and steelhead fishing. When the water is low and clear, light line is called for and many anglers use 4 to 8 pound test. Some spin fishers use fly rods or 10- to 12-foot "noodle rods" with their spin reels because the flexibility of these rods makes it easier to land big fish on light line.

Egg sacs and single salmon eggs are the preferred baits, and nightcrawlers and grubs are also popular. Roostertails, Mepps, and other popular brands of spinners are effective, as are Little Cleo wobblers. Black and fluorescent colors are the most popular finishes for lures.

Fly fishers constantly experiment with steelhead flies on Erie County streams. Egg flies tied with Glo Bug yarn are the most popular. Fluorescent orange, chartreuse, and white are the top colors. A great variety of streamer patterns are also used, including Skunk, Green Butt Skunk, Orange Comet, Black Wooly Bugger, Yellow Wooly Bugger, Black Leech, Thor, and Silver Hilton. Some anglers have even had success using standard trout-fishing patterns of nymphs and wet flies.

Anglers visiting Erie County for the first time will be pleasantly surprised by the scenic beauty of the Lake Erie shoreline. Sandy beaches line the shore in some places and rocky headlands rise up in others.

In the following stream descriptions, the Lake Erie tributaries have been divided into the West Side streams, which are located west of Erie, and the East Side streams, which are located east of Erie.

Lake Erie Tributaries, West Side

Walnut Creek - Erie County
(map: page 208)

This is one of Pennsylvania's better salmon and steelhead streams. Walnut Creek is not nearly as large as Elk Creek, but it is larger than many of the other Erie County streams, and many fine fish are caught here.

A fisherman lands an 11-pound steelhead at the Walnut Creek pier.   (Thad Bukowski photo)

Traveling west on Route 5 from Erie, you will see the Erie Airport and the Presbyterian Lodge on your left. At the next traffic light, turn right and follow the signs to the public access area and marina located at the mouth of Walnut Creek. Fishing is good along the concrete wall that lines the creek from the marina to the mouth. Fishing is also good in the riffles and pools upstream from the marina.

There is some parking available at the bridge on SR 4007 and along Route 5. There is also parking available farther upstream, near the Route 20 bridge. Traveling west on Route 20 from Erie, turn right just before the bridge. Drive past a rifle club and park at the parking area near the creek bank.

Trout Run - Erie County
(map: page 208)

Trout Run is a small nursery stream. Fishing is not permitted in the stream itself, but fishing is permitted in Lake Erie at the mouth. This is a productive and also a very popular spot. During the peak fishing periods, the mouth of Trout Run is so crowded with anglers that you really can't cast and retrieve lures without tangling other lines, so the accepted procedure is to soak bait and wait.

At the intersection of Route 5 and Route 98, turn right onto SR 4005 and follow it down towards the mouth. Parking is permitted along part of the road; signs indicate where you may not park.

Godfrey Run - Erie County
(map: page 208)

Godfrey Run is another small nursery stream with fishing permitted only at the mouth on Lake Erie. Traveling west from Erie on Route 5, turn right onto Godfrey Road. In about 0.5 mile you will see no-parking signs. Park along the road before you get to these signs and walk the remaining distance down

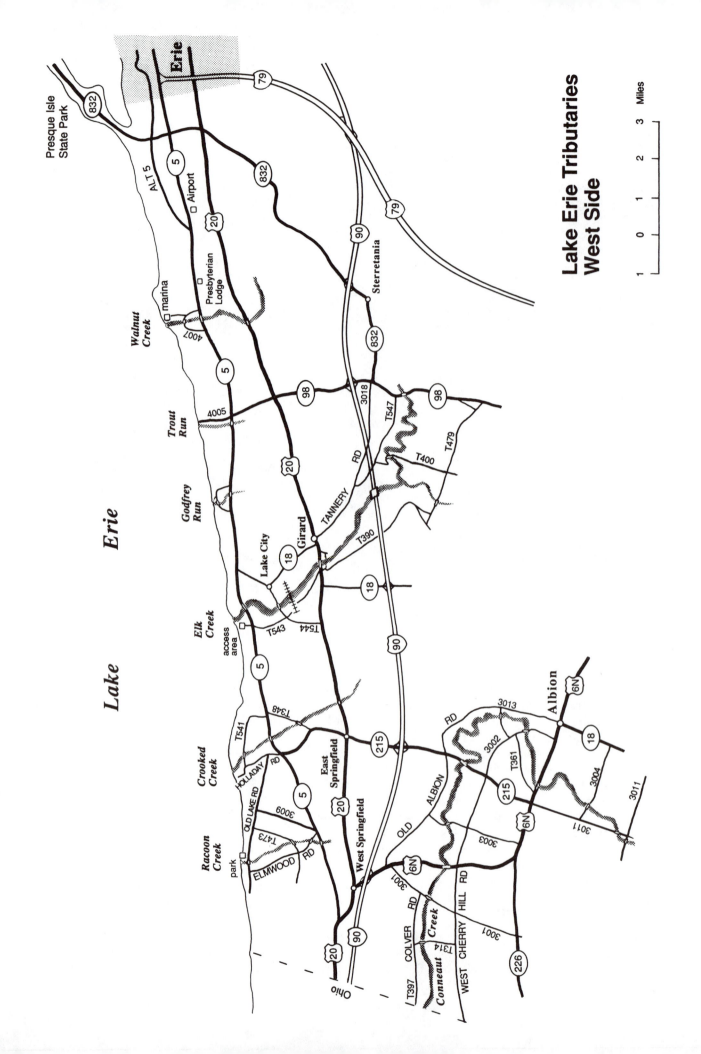

Lake Erie Tributaries
West Side

Presque Isle State Park

Erie

Lake   *Erie*

Walnut Creek

Trout Run

Godfrey Run

Elk Creek

Crooked Creek

Racoon Creek

Conneaut Creek

ALT 5

832

79

5

Airport

20

832

marina

Presbyterian Lodge

4007

5

98

4005

20

3018

T547

98

Girard

TANNERY

RD

T400

T479

T390

Lake City

18

18

90

T544

T543

access area

5

T348

T541

East Springfield

215

OLD ALBION RD

3013

3002

T361

Albion

6N

18

215

3004

3011

HOLLADAY RD

OLD LAKE RD

3009

T473

ELMWOOD RD

park

West Springfield

20

6N

90

20

Ohio

T397

COLVER RD

3001

T314

WEST CHERRY HILL RD

3003

3001

226

6N

3011

Sterretania

90

832

79

Miles

1   0   1   2   3   Miles

the hill to the mouth. This is a scenic spot, with high cliffs rising from the lake shore.

Elk Creek - Erie County
(map: page 208)

This is the largest and probably the best of Pennsylvania's salmon and steelhead streams. Fish run far upstream, at least as far as Route 98. As with the other Lake Erie tributaries, though, the best fishing is usually found in the lower reaches. Driving west from Erie on Route 5, you'll go down a big hill before crossing Elk Creek. A private campground is located on the left, a short distance past the bridge. Some anglers park here on the narrow right shoulder of Route 5. To reach the lower end of Elk Creek, continue west on Route 5 up a hill, then turn right at the sign marking the Elk Creek Access. A large parking area, boat launch, and restrooms are found here.

There is some parking available at the next bridge upstream, on T544 (Elk Park Road), which is near Lake City. There is no access directly at the Route 20 bridge because the bridge crosses high above the creek, but roads on either side of the bridge lead upstream to an old abandoned bridge, where you can park your car.

Access gets tricky upstream from here. The creek flows through a long, inaccessible, wooded stretch, and there is heavy posting at the T400 (Beckman Road) bridge.

Elk Creek offers fishing not only for salmon and steelhead, but also for stocked trout during the regular trout season. The Fish Commission stocks trout preseason and twice inseason, with the last stocking coming in late April or early May. Anglers expecting typical hatchery trout are occasionally surprised when they hook into one of the big steelhead that sometimes remain in the stream through April. Few trout or steelhead remain in Elk Creek during the summer months.

Crooked Creek - Erie County
(map: page 208)

Crooked Creek is not fished as hard as some of the other Erie County streams because of access problems and because of its brushy banks. Some anglers park along Route 5, but the shoulder is very narrow here; Winnebago drivers will have to park elsewhere.

Just past the Route 5 bridge, turn onto SR 3009 (Holladay Road). T541 (Ables Road) turns off from this road and crosses Crooked Creek, but fishing is prohibited above and below this bridge. So, continue on Holladay Road as it winds first left then right and passes by Virginia's Beach Campground. As you near the lakeshore, you will see a few houses and some no-parking signs. Park along the road before you get to these signs and walk down the road to the beach.

Walk to the right along the beach to the mouth of Crooked Creek.

There is plenty of parking along Route 20 near the bridge over Crooked Creek. Even though Crooked Creek is quite small here, fish do run this far upstream when the water is high.

Crooked Creek offers fishing not only for salmon and steelhead, but also for hatchery trout during the regular trout season. Trout are stocked prior to opening day and once inseason, usually in late April.

Raccoon Creek - Erie County
(map: page 208)

Raccoon Creek is a small, brushy stream that is best fished at its mouth on Lake Erie. Traveling west on Route 5 from Erie, cross the creek then turn right on T324 (Elmwood Road). Follow this to a T intersection at Old Lake Road. Turn right here and you will soon arrive at a bridge over Raccoon Creek. A county park and picnic area are located near the mouth.

Conneaut Creek - Erie County
(map: page 208)

The mouth and lower reaches of Conneaut Creek are in Ohio, but steelhead run far upstream into Pennsylvania and are sometimes caught even upstream of the town of Albion. Juvenile steelhead are stocked in both Pennsylvania and Ohio.

Some parts of Conneaut Creek flow through farming areas, so the stream runs high and muddy after heavy rains, and it takes longer to clear than the other Erie County streams. There are some houses near the stream in the Albion area, but much of the stream is wooded and little developed. The upper creek is slow and silted, but downstream from Route 215 the current flows more rapidly, and the bottom is mostly shale and gravel.

Conneaut Creek is stocked with hatchery trout for the regular trout season. The Fish Commission stocks trout preseason and twice inseason, with the last stocking coming around the first week in May. Occasionally wild or holdover brown trout are caught, but they are not common. Conneaut Creek also holds smallmouth bass and muskies.

Lake Erie Tributaries, East Side

Four Mile Creek - Erie County
(map: page 210)

Traveling east from Erie on Route 5, you will cross Four Mile Creek just after passing a huge General Electric factory on the right. Parking is available upstream of the bridge at pulloffs along Lawrence Parkway, which parallels the west side of the creek.

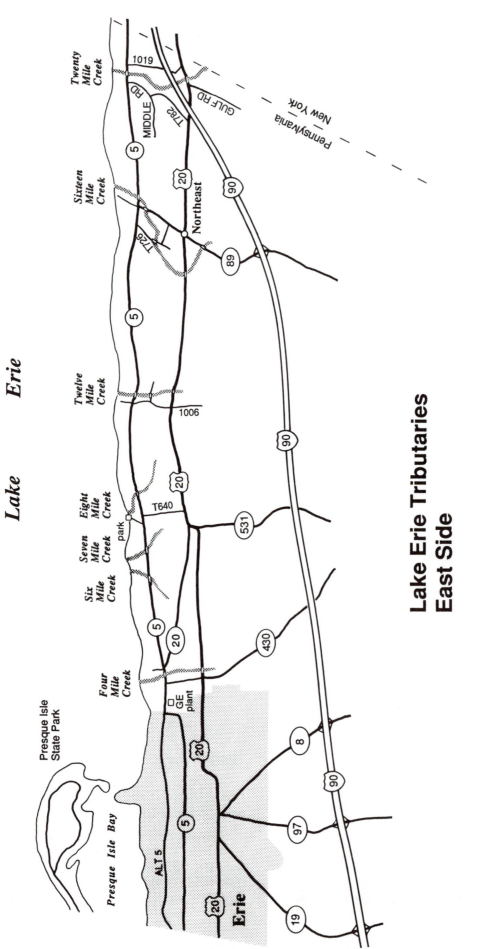

Lake Erie Tributaries East Side

Just past the Route 5 bridge, a road leads to the left, follows downstream along the creek, and ends at a private golf course. There is some parking along the first part of this road, but the golf course property is posted against trespassing. Four Mile Creek is larger than some of the other Lake Erie tributaries, but it is a small, shallow stream, nonetheless.

Six Mile Creek - Erie County
(map: page 210)

This small stream is probably not worth fishing. The landowner on the lower part of the creek does not allow fishing, and rock ledges prevent most fish from moving very far upstream. Also, there is only limited parking available.

Seven Mile Creek - Erie County
(map: page 210)

Seven Mile Creek is quite small. Traveling east on Route 5 from Erie, you will cross the creek soon after passing the grounds of Mount Saint Benedict on the right. Adequate parking is available along Route 5, near the bridge.

Eight Mile Creek - Erie County
(map: page 210)

This small creek is best fished at its mouth on Lake Erie. Traveling east on Route 5 from Erie, turn left at a flashing traffic light and follow the signs to Shades Beach Park. At the park, walk past a group of cottages to the beach. A short walk to the right (east) along the beach will bring you to the mouth of Eight Mile Creek.

Twelve Mile Creek - Erie County
(map: page 210)

Twelve Mile Creek is best fished from its mouth upstream to just above the bridge on Route 5. Just above the bridge, the creek drops over some ledges into a deep, swirling hole, and few fish make it upstream of this barrier. There is some parking along the road that leads from Route 5 to the lakefront, and more parking is available at the lakefront. Moorheadsville Road follows up along the creek from Route 5, but parking here is poor.

Sixteen Mile Creek - Erie County
(map: page 210)

Sixteen Mile Creek is not as large a stream as Twenty Mile Creek, but is is larger than the other streams east of Erie. Traveling east on Route 5 from Erie, turn left at the blinking light at the intersection with Route 89. This leads to a public beach at the mouth. You can also park past the Route 5 bridge, on the right shoulder near a baseball field. Farther upstream, the houses of the town of Northeast make parking difficult.

Twenty Mile Creek - Erie County
(map: page 210)

This is the largest, most productive, and most popular stream on the eastern shore of Lake Erie. There are places to park near the bridge on Route 5. A private lane leads downstream from here and a sign reads, "Fishing permitted, walk in only."

There is also some parking near the Route 20 bridge. Traveling east on Route 20 from Erie, turn right just before the bridge onto SR 1017 (Gulf Road). Drive under a railroad bridge, then park along the shoulder. A trail leads down to the creek.

Twenty Mile Creek originates in New York State, and only the lower 4 miles of the stream flow through Pennsylvania. The creek drains an area with many vineyards and orchards, and its waters run muddy after heavy rains.

Twenty Mile Creek is best known for its salmon and steelhead runs, but it is also stocked with hatchery trout during the regular trout season. The Fish Commission stocks trout preseason and twice inseason, with the last stocking coming in late April.

Other Northwest PA Streams
(no maps)

No maps were included for the following streams and the descriptions were kept brief, but these streams are also well worth fishing.

Potato Creek - Mckean County

Potato Creek is stocked with trout from its origin at the confluence of Havens Run and East Branch Potato Creek downstream 13 miles to where it meets Marvin Creek at Smethport. It flows through a wide, rural valley of farms, woodlots, and scattered houses. The Fish Commission stocks trout preseason and once inseason, usually in late April.

Potato Creek is a large trout stream and it warms quickly in the summer, so fishing is mostly for stocked trout and few people fish here after the early season. Stream surveys indicate that few trout remain in Potato Creek into the summer months, but local anglers report that they sometimes catch large wild or holdover browns.

The following tributaries of Potato Creek are worth a try:

Havens Run is a small, attractive woodland stream that flows through State Game Lands No. 30. The Fish Commission stocks brook trout from the mouth upstream about 2 miles to Pigeon Hollow, and the stream also holds a good population of native brook trout.

East Branch Potato Creek flows through a remote, wooded area. No trout are stocked and the water quality suffers from acid drainage from old coal mines in the headwaters. Local anglers say that despite the mine acid, the East Branch holds some wild brook trout and that its small tributaries are good brook trout streams.

West Branch Potato Creek is stocked from its mouth near the village of Betula upstream 3.2 miles to where the stream forks. The upper stretches flow through a wooded area that can be reached by walking up a gated access road. The West Branch holds some wild brown and brook trout, but they don't seem to be very plentiful, at least in the lower stretches.

Brewer Run is a small tributary to Potato Creek where you can find both hatchery trout and native brook trout.

Hemlock Creek - Venango County

Hemlock Creek flows into the Allegheny River near the village of President, which is along Route 62 about halfway between Oil City and Tionesta. Only the lower 1.1 mile of the stream is stocked with trout, from the mouth upstream to Porcupine Creek. Hemlock Creek holds fair numbers of wild brown trout, and brook trout are found in the headwaters. Big browns from the Allegheny River are sometimes caught in the lower part of Hemlock Creek.

Many of Hemlock Creek's small tributaries also hold wild trout. This whole watershed is a rugged, forested area, and the streams are crossed in only a few places by dirt forest roads.

Allegheny Portage Creek - Mckean and Potter Counties

This stream originates near Keating Summit in Potter County, and flows north to meet the Allegheny River at Port Allegany in Mckean County. Most of the stream has been polluted by acid mine drainage, but good water quality and good trout fishing remain in the upper reaches.

The Fish Commission stocks trout from the mouth of Scaffold Lick Run, at the village of Liberty, upstream 1.6 miles to Brown Hollow. A good population of wild brown trout and brook trout are found in this stretch and up into the unstocked headwaters.

Presently, no trout are stocked below Scaffold Lick Run because of mine acid flowing in from this tributary. The Seneca Chapter of Trout Unlimited is working on a limestone diversion well to neutralize mine acid on Scaffold Lick Run and thereby improve the water quality in the lower sections of Allegheny Portage Creek.

Brokenstraw Creek - Warren County

Brokenstraw Creek and its many tributaries drain most of the northwest corner of Warren County. The main branch of Brokenstraw Creek, often called the Big Brokenstraw, is heavily stocked and heavily fished from the Route 77 bridge at the village of Spring Creek downstream 10.5 miles to Youngsville. This large stream holds few wild trout because water temperatures become too warm during the summer months. Camping is available at Buckaloons Campground, an Allegheny National Forest campground located at the mouth of Brokenstraw Creek.

Little Brokenstraw Creek is stocked with trout from Lottsville downstream to the mouth. The stream holds few wild trout, but fair numbers of stocked trout carry over into the summer months.

Coffee Run, a small tributary to Little Brokenstraw Creek, is also stocked with trout.

If you like woodland streams, give Blue Eye Run a try. This small, brushy trout stream flows most of its length through State Game Land No. 143 before meeting Big Brokenstraw Creek near the village of Garland.

Spring Creek flows into the Big Brokenstraw near the village of Spring Creek. Spring Creek and its tributary, East Branch Spring Creek, are stocked with trout, and these streams also hold fair numbers of wild brown trout.

Sugar Creek - Venango and Crawford Counties

The main branch of Sugar Creek originates near Townville in Crawford County and flows south into Venango County, where it meets French Creek at the village of Sugar Creek. Stocking begins several miles south of Townville at the T549 bridge, which crosses the stream at the edge of State Game Land No. 69. Trout are stocked from here downstream to the mouth, skipping over some posted areas.

Sugar Creek has good water quality and it holds wild and holdover trout in addition to the stocked fish. Wild brown and brook trout are common in the upper stretches near State Game Land No. 69 and brown trout predominate farther downstream. The lower stretches of Sugar Creek become quite warm in the summer months, but Sugar Creek regulars can find trout in certain places throughout the year.

Sugar Creek has some good tributary streams that are easily confused because several of them have the same names. A stream named Little Sugar Creek flows most of its length through Crawford County before crossing into Venango County, where it meets the main branch of Sugar Creek. Trout are stocked by the Fish Commission preseason and once inseason.

A stream named East Branch Sugar Creek originates near Troy Center in Crawford County and flows past the village of Luces Corner before flowing into the main branch of Sugar Creek. This stream is entirely within Crawford County. Trout are stocked from the mouth upstream to the Route 428 bridge. Even though this is a slow moving stream, it has good water quality and holds many wild brown trout.

In Venango County, there is a different East Branch Sugar Creek, which is stocked from its mouth at Cooperstown upstream 5.8 miles to the Route 428 bridge. This stream flows through farms and woodlands and holds fair numbers of wild brown trout. Near the middle of the stream, a long stretch flows through State Game Land No. 96.

This East Branch Sugar Creek has a tributary that is also named Little Sugar Creek. This Little Sugar Creek is stocked from the village of Diamond (Venango County) downstream to its mouth. A long stretch of this stream flows through a different section of State Game Land No. 96.

Prather Run, which flows into Little Sugar Creek south of Wallaceville (Venango County), is also stocked with trout.

North Fork Red Bank Creek - Jefferson County

The North Fork suffers from acid rain and summer warming, but the delayed-harvest, fly-fishing-only stretch at Brookville provides good fishing for hatchery fish until about mid-June. This stretch begins at the Route 322 bridge in Brookville and extends upstream 2 miles. Near the Route 322 bridge, turn onto Water Plant Road, which follows the stream up to a municipal park.

In Brookville, Red Bank Creek is formed by the junction of North Fork Red Bank Creek and Sandy Lick Creek. Red Bank Creek is stocked from Brookville downstream about 20 miles to just below the Jefferson/Armstrong County line. Much of this stretch is away from immediate road access. Float stocking ensures a good distribution of trout all along the length of Redbank Creek.

Red Bank Creek becomes warm in the summer months and holds few wild trout, but it is popular with both spin fishers and fly fishers. Many anglers float the stream in canoes. The lower stretches of Red Bank Creek hold bass, walleyes, pike, and muskies.

Before 1977, Sandy Lick Creek was not stocked with trout because of water quality problems caused by acid mine drainage. Even before stocking began, though, a few savvy anglers caught wild browns in this stream and in some of its small tributaries. The best fishing is found from the mouth at Brookville upstream to Reynoldsville. Above Reynoldsville, the stream flows very slowly and holds few trout. Much of Sandy Lick Creek is inaccessible by road. A long stretch flows through State Game Land No. 244.

Mill Creek flows into Sandy Lick Creek about 1 mile east of Brookville. Summer stream surveys indicate that Mill Creek holds few wild trout, but some local anglers say that native brook trout are found in the remote upper stretches. Much of the stream is accessible only by walking. Sulger Road follows Mill Creek upstream from the mouth for about a mile, and Route 830 crosses the stream in its upper reaches.

Little Mill Creek, a very small, brushy tributary of Mill Creek, is stocked with trout and it also holds native brookies.

Southwest Pennsylvania

Loyalhanna Creek just downstream from the Route 711 bridge, near Ligonier.

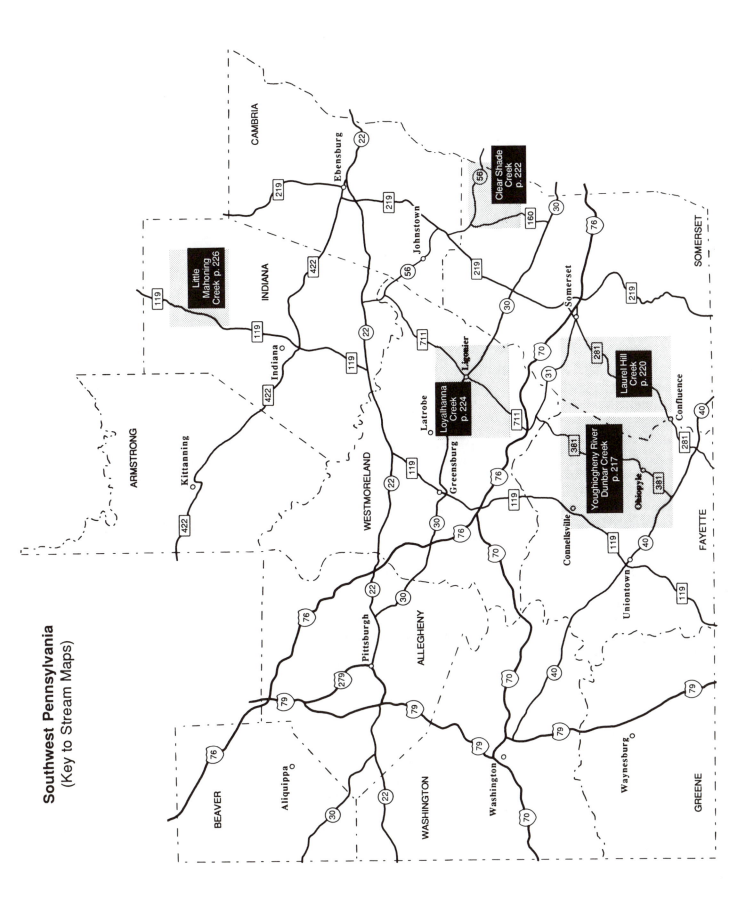

Southwest Pennsylvania
(Key to Stream Maps)

Southwest Pennsylvania

Youghiogheny River - Fayette and Somerset Counties
(map: page 217)

Trout fishing on the Youghiogheny River, often referred to as "The Yough," is made possible by the releases of cold water from the Youghiogheny Reservoir dam, near the town of Confluence. The 26 miles of river between the dam and South Connellsville are managed as trout water by the Fish Commission.

Legal-sized trout are stocked only in the first mile below the outflow of the dam; this stretch is stocked nine times each year, with the last stocking coming in August. An Army Corps of Engineers campground is located beside the outflow of the dam.

The water discharged from the dam outflow is icy cold. The water temperature here measured a chilly 42 degrees on a warm day in early summer. By comparison, nearby Laurel Hill Creek's temperature was 70 degrees two days earlier. There is a deep hole at the dam's outlet, then some swift runs, then some wide, smooth flats near the Route 281 bridge that are popular with dry fly fishers.

Just below the town of Confluence, the Casselman River and Laurel Hill Creek join the Yough, greatly increasing its size. The Casselman River once added a lot of mine acid to the Yough, but its water quality has been much improved. The Casselman River still carries a lot of silt, though, and after heavy rains it muddies the Youghiogheny below Confluence.

Between Confluence and South Connellsville, the Fish Commission annually stocks between 50,000 and 150,000 rainbow and brown trout fingerlings, which range in length from 2 to 5 inches. These fish grow fast in this big river, often reaching a length of 10 inches within a year.

Confluence to Ohiopyle

The 10 miles of river between Confluence and Ohiopyle, often called the Middle Yough, is generally considered to be the best trout stretch on the Youghiogheny. (The Upper Yough is the stretch above the dam, in Maryland.) Some big trout, from 20 to 25 inches, have been caught in the Middle Yough. A bike trail follows the river from the Ramcat Access Area near Confluence downstream to another access area near Ohiopyle. Numerous anglers' paths lead from the bike trail down steep banks to the river.

Wading conditions are challenging on the Middle Yough. This is big, swift water. When river levels are high, it's best to fish between the dam outflow and Confluence, where the Yough is smaller, and leave the big water below Confluence for when river levels are low to moderate. The stretch just upstream from the Ohiopyle access area is perhaps the toughest to fish because the water is so deep even at the water's edge that wading is nearly impossible. The angler is forced to scramble over huge boulders and through thick brush along the shoreline. The stretch below the Ramcat Access Area is easier to wade and the stretch near Bidwell Station is free from heavy rapids.

Probably the best way to fish the Middle Yough is to float it in canoes or rafts. If you don't have your own canoes, you can rent them from River Sport Outfitters, located in Confluence. Their phone number is (814) 395-5744.

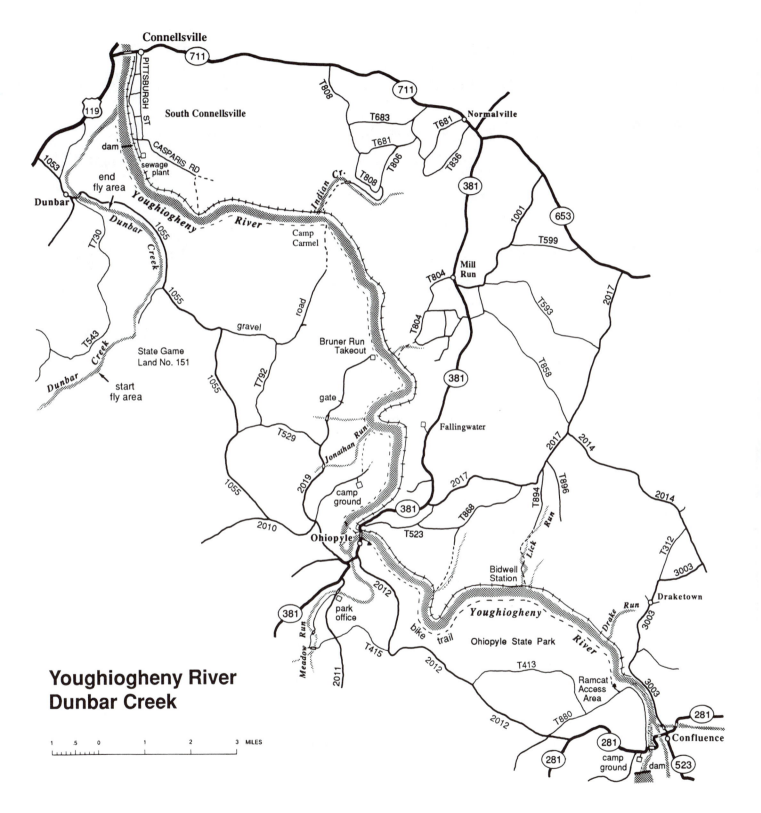

Youghiogheny River
Dunbar Creek

The Youghiogheny River between Confluence and Ohiopyle.

The Confluence-to-Ohiopyle stretch has some challenging Class I-II rapids, so boaters should be experienced at river running, but the river is less rough here than in the famous white water stretch below Ohiopyle. Boaters must take out at the access area upstream from Ohiopyle because the river takes a 40-foot drop over Ohiopyle Falls a short distance downstream from the Route 381 bridge.

One evening I stopped to look at the falls and saw two kayakers paddle over the brink. They disappeared in the foam at the bottom for about five seconds before bobbing to the surface. Running the falls is not only foolish but also illegal. Because several people have drowned here, the authorities have imposed a $1,000 fine for those caught running the falls.

Ohiopyle to Bruner Run Takeout

From Ohiopyle downstream 7 miles to the Bruner Run Takeout, the Yough flows through a series of heavy rapids that attracts white water enthusiasts from all over the eastern United States. Trout are found in this stretch, but it is difficult to fish here because of the heavy raft traffic and because the rugged terrain limits access to the river.

Near the Youth Hostel, across the Route 381 bridge from Ohiopyle, an old railroad grade crosses a bridge over the river, then continues down along the west bank. Plans are underway for turning this grade into a bike trail, which will extend from Ohiopyle to Connellsville. In most places it is a very steep, brushy hike from the railroad grade down to the river.

It is also possible to reach the river by hiking down a trail that begins near the Ohiopyle State Park campground and follows down along Jonathan Run. Here again, the water is so deep and the shoreline is so rugged that it's difficult to move up or downstream along the river.

While you are in the Ohiopyle area, you may wish to take a break from fishing to raft the white water stretch. There are several outfitters in Ohiopyle who run guided trips from Ohiopyle down to the Bruner Run Takeout. Another good diversion from fishing is a visit to Fallingwater, a house designed by Frank Lloyd Wright. It is located about 4 miles north of Ohiopyle, off Route 381.

Bruner Run Takeout to South Connellsville

To fish the lower river, the best bet is to canoe or raft from the Bruner Run Takeout downstream to South Connellsville. The first part of this stretch has some serious rapids, so boaters should be experienced at river running. Fishing pressure and canoe traffic is very light in this remote area. The road to Bruner Run Takeout is gated, and you must make arrangements ahead of time with the Ohiopyle State Park office to have it opened. Call them at (412) 329-8591 at least a day in advance. Shuttling is complicated by the fact that vehicles may not be left at the Bruner

Run Takeout. After floating this stretch, boaters can take out in South Connellsville near the sewage plant or at the Route 711 bridge at Connellsville.

It is also possible to reach the lower river by driving down the gravel and dirt road that leads to Camp Carmel. This road becomes rough and rutted as it nears the river, and high clearance vehicles are recommended. There are some very deep pools upstream from Camp Carmel that produce trout, smallmouth bass, channel catfish, and perch. Just downstream from Camp Carmel, the river widens into knee-deep riffled shallows.

Below South Connellsville, the Yough becomes essentially a warmwater river, although local sportsmen's groups stock trout early in the season as far downstream as West Newton.

Dry fly fishing on the Yough is mainly produced by caddis hatches, including the Olive Caddis, which hatch in May and early June. When flies aren't hatching, which is most of the time, try stonefly nymphs, Wooly Buggers, or crayfish imitations. Spin fishers will find spinners and spoons effective.

The Youghiogheny trout fishery probably has not yet reached its full potential. Presently the river produces lots of small trout and the occasional trophy trout, but fewer 12- to 16-inch fish than you might expect in such a large river. The Youghiogheny is open to trout fishing all year. The daily limit from the opening day of trout season to Labor Day is eight trout, and the daily limit from the day after Labor Day to the succeeding opening day is three trout.

An interesting and detailed account of the Youghiogheny River and its history is found in Tim Palmer's *Youghiogheny, Appalachian River* (Univ. of Pittsburgh Press, 1984).

Meadow Run - Fayette County
(map: page 217)

Meadow Run is a small stream that flows past the office of Ohiopyle State Park and into the Youghiogheny River. The Fish Commission stocks trout before opening day and once inseason, from just below the park office upstream 5 miles to the Route 381 bridge. There are few wild trout found in Meadow Run, but local anglers report occasionally catching big brown trout here. Some anglers say these big fish move up from the Youghiogheny River; others say they come from private stockings in the upper part of Meadow Run.

Dunbar Creek - Fayette County
(fly fishing only, 4.1 miles)
(map: page 217)

Dunbar Creek, which flows into the Youghiogheny River near Connellsville, is very popular with the fly fishers of southwestern Pennsylvania. Most of the stocked water on this pretty woodland stream is within the fly-fishing-only stretch, which extends from a quarry along SR 1055 upstream 4.1 miles to the confluence of Glade Run. The lower part of the creek is paralleled by SR 1055. At a white Game Commission building, SR 1055 and the creek separate, and from there a gravel forest road follows up along the creek into State Game Land No. 51.

Dunbar Creek gets low and clear in the summer months, but it is well shaded and water temperatures stay reasonably cool. The Fish Commission stocks trout prior to opening day and three times inseason, with the last stocking coming in mid to late May. Some native brookies are found in the upper part of the creek, but their abundance is limited by acid rain and acid mine drainage in the headwaters.

Laurel Hill Creek - Somerset County
(delayed harvest, artificial lures only, 2.2 miles)
(map: page 220)

The most consistent fishing on Laurel Hill Creek is found in the 2.2-mile delayed-harvest, artificial lures-only area located in Laurel Hill State Park. This stretch begins at the bridge just above Laurel Hill Lake and extends upstream to a Boy Scout Camp. There is a parking area near the bridge. Upstream from the bridge, you will find a pleasant stretch of riffles and pools flanked by tall trees. The fishing here, as on the rest of the creek, is almost entirely for stocked trout, but the regulations keep good numbers of fish in the stream through the summer. This stretch is well shaded and summer water temperatures remain cooler here than on the rest of the creek.

The Fish Commission stocks virtually the entire length of Laurel Hill Creek. Trout are stocked prior to opening day and three times inseason, with the last stocking coming in early May. Laurel Hill Lake is also stocked with trout.

Below Laurel Hill Lake the creek becomes warm in the summer months, and few people fish here after early June. Several small tributaries, such as Allen Creek and Fall Creek, add some cool water, and trout can sometimes be found below the mouths of these streams in the summer. If you enjoy covered bridges, check out the one at Barronvale and another at the next bridge down, on Route 653.

Between Metzler and Humbert, the creek flows through a remote, roadless forest, some of which is within State Game Land No. 111. From Humbert downstream to the mouth at Confluence, Laurel Hill Creek is wide and mostly shallow. This lower stretch holds more smallmouth bass, rock bass, and crappies than trout in the summer months.

Fly fishing on Laurel Hill Creek is pretty good, with caddis flies providing much of the action. Even

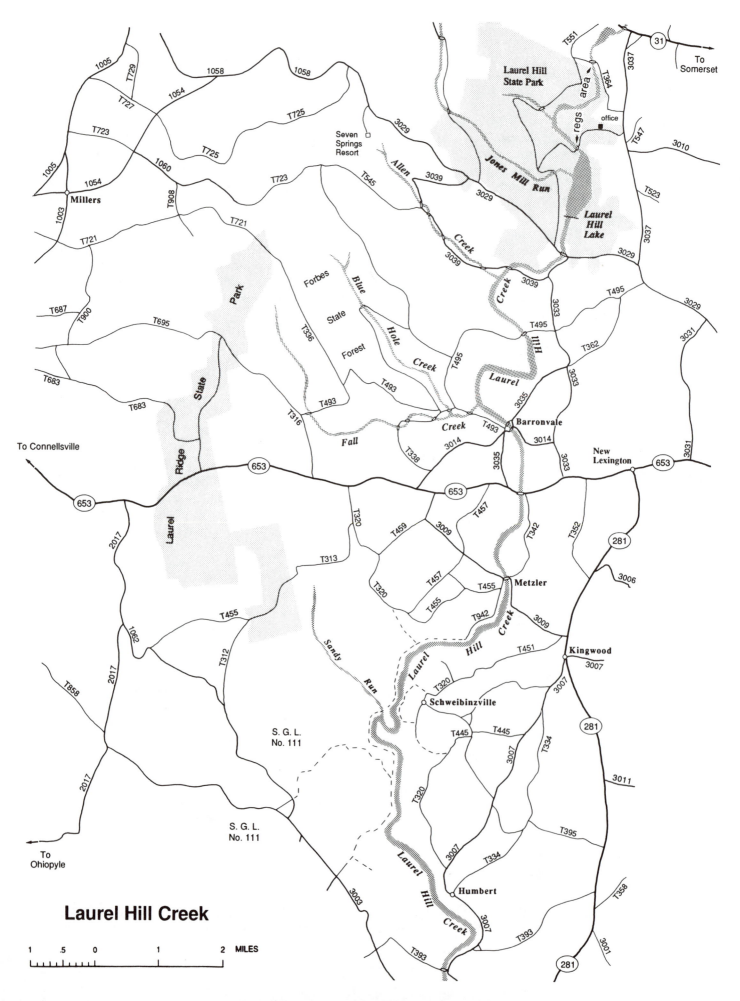

Laurel Hill Creek

1   .5   0   1   2   MILES

Laurel Hill Creek in the delayed-harvest area at Laurel Hill State Park.

when no trout are rising, prospecting with a good general-purpose dry fly pattern, such as an Adams, Grey Fox Variant, Light Cahill, or Elk Hair Caddis, is often rewarding.

Jones Mill Run - Somerset County
(map: page 220)

Jones Mill Run is a well-shaded little brook that flows into Laurel Hill Lake in Laurel Hill State Park. You won't find many big pools here, but it's fun to fish the pocket water with a dry fly. The Fish Commission stocks the whole stretch of the stream that lies within the park boundaries. Stocking takes place before opening day and also three times inseason, with the last stocking coming in late May. In addition to stocked trout, Jones Mill Run also holds a fair number of wild brook and brown trout.

Allen Creek - Somerset County
(map: page 220)

Allen Creek flows into Laurel Hill Creek a short distance south of Laurel Hill State Park. The Fish Commission stocks trout from the mouth upstream

2.3 miles. Finding access is difficult on this stream because there are many cottages along the banks.

Fall Creek - Somerset County
(map: page 220)

Fall Creek is a fast-flowing, rocky stream that adds its cool waters to Laurel Hill Creek upstream from the Barronvale bridge. Because of acid rain problems early in the season, the Fish Commission does not stock trout prior to opening day, but instead stocks trout once inseason. Trout are stocked from the mouth upstream 3.2 miles, to a point a short distance above the T493 bridge. Fall Creek has a fair number of native brook trout, and it flows through a scenic, wooded area.

Blue Hole Creek - Somerset County
(map: page 220)

Blue Hole Creek is a small, rocky tributary to Fall Creek. Like Fall Creek, Blue Hole Creek suffers from acid rain early in the year, so the Fish Commission doesn't stock any trout prior to opening day, but instead stocks trout once inseason, from the mouth upstream 1.4 miles. Much of the stream is shallow and scoured down to bedrock, but the pockets and pools hold some native brook trout.

Blue Hole Creek is well shaded by surrounding trees, which provide a cool oasis from summer heat. Nearly the entire length of the stream lies within the boundaries of Forbes State Forest.

Clear Shade Creek - Somerset County

(fly fishing only, 1 mile)
(map: page 222)

Clear Shade Creek is stocked from Pine Lake, north of Ogletown, downstream to its mouth on Dark Shade Creek. Upstream from the Route 56 bridge at Ogletown, there are some houses near the creek, but the rest of the stream flows through an undeveloped area, some of which is in the Gallitzin State Forest.

From Ogletown down to Crumb Road, the creek flows through a rather remote stretch where you'll find fair numbers of wild brown and brook trout in addition to the stocked fish. Shade Road, a gravel forest road, parallels this stretch of Clear Shade Creek at a distance, and several anglers' trails lead through the woods to the stream. The upper part of this stretch is brushy enough to make casting difficult, and there are some low, boggy areas along the banks. The lower part of this stretch, near the Crumb Road bridge, is lined by mature trees, whose spreading branches create a canopy over the stream.

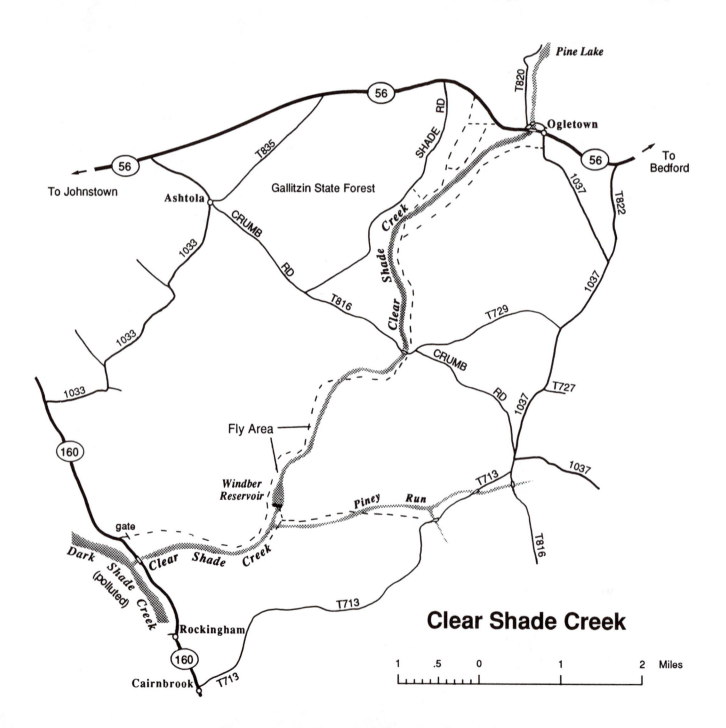

Clear Shade Creek

Clear Shade Creek upstream from Crumb Road.

Below the Crumb Road bridge, the canopy of tall trees continues for a short distance, but then the creek widens and the trees give way to low shrubs that provide little shade. Clear Shade Creek is rather shallow in much of this stretch, and some of the pools are filling in with sand. Occasionally, you will find a deeper pool with good cover for trout. Most of the trout in this part of the creek are stocked fish, but there are also a few wild browns.

A fly-fishing-only stretch extends from the backwaters of Windber Reservoir upstream 1 mile. The fly area is a long walk from any vehicle access. It's about a 2-mile walk down from Crumb Road, and it's also about a 2-mile walk up from the bottom on a gated maintenance road. To find this maintenance road, drive north from the Route 160 bridge about one-half mile. Here you will see a gate with the letters WAA (Windber Water Authority) on it. No motor vehicles are permitted on this road, but bicycles are permitted.

In the summer few trout are found in lower Clear Shade Creek, from Windber Reservoir to the mouth, probably because of the warming effect of the reservoir. Most of Clear Shade Creek flows at a moderate pace, but above the Route 160 bridge, there is a series of swift rapids and deep holes. Below the Route 160 bridge, Clear Shade Creek meets Dark Shade Creek, which is polluted by acid mine drainage.

Clear Shade Creek is stocked for opening day and also three times inseason. Fishing gets pretty tough after mid-June, but the fly area holds good numbers of fish into the summer months, and wild trout can be found year around from Crumb Road up into the headwaters. Fly fishers can expect caddis hatches, and terrestrial patterns are also useful.

Piney Run - Somerset County
(map: page 222)

This small stream flows through a wooded area and meets Clear Shade Creek below the Windber Reservoir. The Fish Commission stocks trout preseason and again in mid-May, from the T816 bridge downstream to the mouth. Even though its water quality suffers from acid rain and possibly some mine drainage, Piney Run holds fair numbers of native brookies and also a few wild browns.

Loyalhanna Creek - Westmoreland County
(delayed harvest, artificial lures only, 1.5 miles)
(map: page 224)

The main attraction of Loyalhanna Creek is the delayed-harvest, artificial-lures-only section, which extends from Route 711 near Ligonier downstream

1.5 miles to about 100 yards above the SR 2045 bridge. The restrictions create good fishing for stocked trout through middle to late June. In most years water temperatures get too warm in midsummer for good fishing, though.

Access is a little tricky at the lower end of the delayed-harvest area because the property on both sides of the SR 2045 bridge is posted. If you drive east on Route 30 about 0.4 mile from the intersection with SR 2045, you will see a large parking pulloff on the right side, next to the creek. Continuing east on Route 30, you will find another parking area past the

bridge over Mill Creek, at the Loyalhanna Nature Trail. There is also parking at the upper end of the delayed-harvest area at the Route 711 bridge.

At the upper end of the delayed-harvest area, the Loyalhanna is a clean-flowing stream of medium size, about 45–50 feet wide. Mill Creek adds a lot of water to the Loyalhanna, approximately doubling its volume. It also adds a lot of silt. If you're fishing soon after a rainstorm, you'll find the water much less murky upstream from the influx of Mill Creek.

The trout fishing on Loyalhanna Creek relies almost entirely on hatchery fish. Above Ligonier the

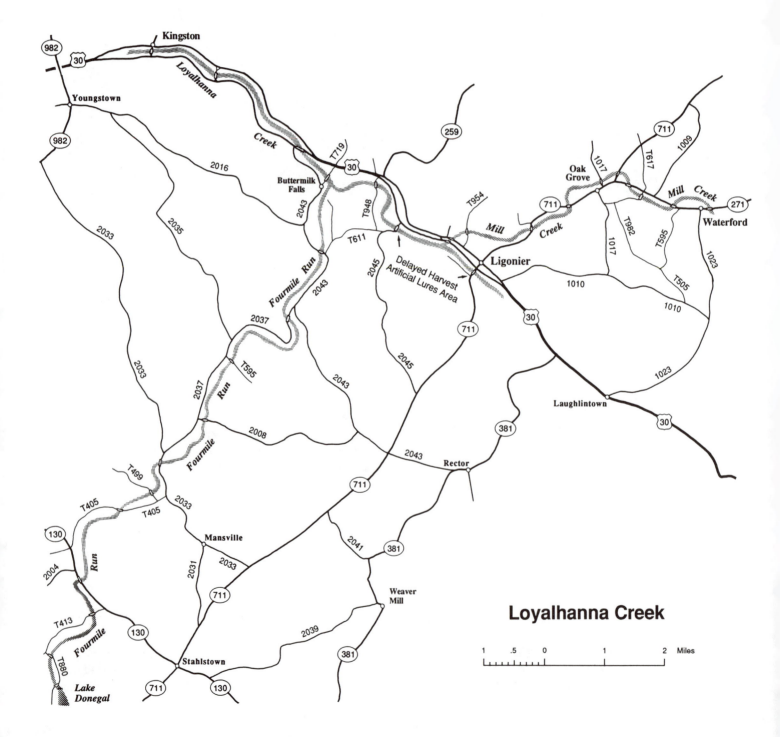

Loyalhanna Creek

creek holds some wild trout, but most of this water is posted. Some sections of Loyalhanna Creek's streambed between Ligonier and Kingston were channelized after flooding in 1972. Members of the Forbes Trail Chapter of Trout Unlimited are making efforts to improve the stream habitat.

The Fish Commission stocks trout from Ligonier downstream to Kingston. Stocking takes place prior to opening day and three times inseason, with the last stocking coming in mid-May.

Fly fishers will find primarily caddis hatches on Loyalhanna Creek. Terrestrial imitations are effective when water levels are low to moderate.

Mill Creek - Westmoreland County
(map: page 224)

This medium-sized tributary of Loyalhanna Creek is stocked with trout from the confluence of its North and South Branches, which join above Waterford, downstream to its mouth near Ligonier. The Fish Commission stocks trout for opening day and once inseason.

The fishing depends mostly on hatchery trout, but a few wild browns and brookies are found from Oak Grove up into the headwaters, and anglers who know the stream well can catch trout here even in midsummer. From Oak Grove down to the mouth, the stream moves more slowly, and the water gets too warm and sluggish in midsummer to hold many trout.

The land along Mill Creek is all privately owned, but there is little posting. The stream flows through a patchwork of woods, open land, and homes. Mill Creek runs very muddy after rainfall.

Fourmile Run - Westmoreland County
(map: page 224)

Fourmile Run is stocked with trout from below the outflow of Lake Donegal downstream 11 miles to its mouth on Loyalhanna Creek. The Fish Commission stocks trout preseason and once inseason, in mid to late May. Few wild trout are found in Fourmile Run, probably because of the warming effect of Lake Donegal. There are many dwellings along the lower part of the creek, and there is some scattered posting. Upstream closer to the dam, Fourmile Run flows through some less-developed wooded areas.

Little Mahoning Creek - Indiana County
(delayed harvest, fly fishing only, 4 miles)
(map: page 226)

Most anglers who travel some distance to fish Little Mahoning Creek are attracted by the delayed-harvest, fly-fishing-only stretch, which begins at the bridge in Rochester Mills and extends upstream 4 miles to Cesna Run. The fishing on Little Mahoning

Creek relies on hatchery trout, and the restrictive regulations keep good numbers of fish here through the summer and into the fall. In the fly area, Little Mahoning Creek flows through a wooded area, and some remote stretches can be reached only by walking. The stream is medium-sized, about 60 feet wide at Rochester Mills, and it flows at a moderate pace through long flats and deep pools.

Trout are also stocked above the fly area, as far upstream as the SR 1020 bridge near Deckers Point. Below the fly area, trout are stocked as far downstream as the Route 954 bridge in Smicksburg. (This lower part of the stream is not shown on the map).

Below Rochester Mills, Little Mahoning Creek slows and widens, and its water temperatures rise quickly in the summer months. This lower stretch of the creek flows through a rural area of farms and woodlots. All of the creek turns muddy after a good rain because of siltation from farmland and strip mines in the watershed.

The Fish Commission stocks trout before opening day and three times inseason, with the last stocking coming in mid-May.

Fly fishers visiting the Little Mahoning will find hatches of caddis and also some mayflies, including Green Drakes.

Little Mahoning Creek at Rochester Mills.

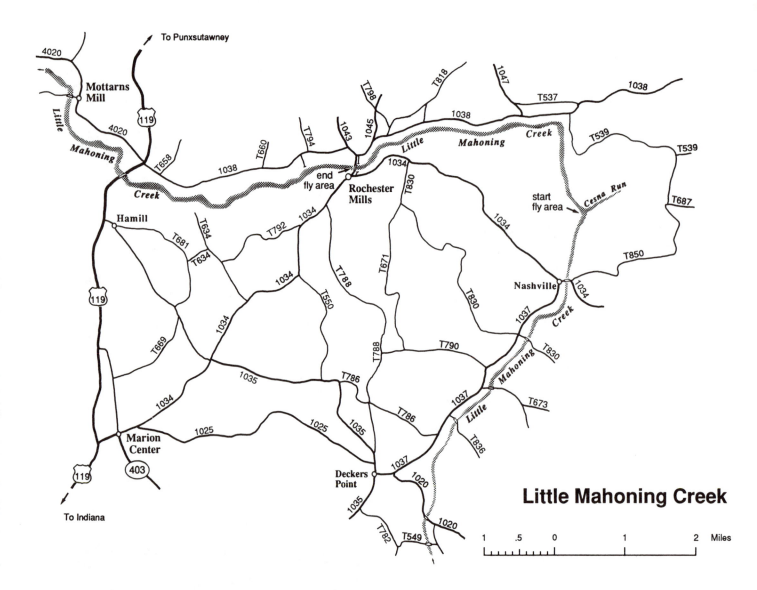

Little Mahoning Creek

Other Southwest PA Streams

(no maps)

No maps were included for the following streams and the descriptions were kept brief, but these streams are also well worth fishing.

Deer Creek - Allegheny County

A 1.6-mile delayed-harvest, artificial-lures-only area was established on Deer Creek beginning in 1990. Deer Creek flows through Indiana and West Deer Townships, just northeast of Pittsburgh.

The special regulations area begins at a bridge that is 0.4 miles upstream of the Route 910 bridge, and extends downstream to the lower boundary of the Rose Ridge Golf Course. This new special regulations area should provide consistent fishing through much of the season for the many dedicated trout anglers who live in the Pittsburgh area.

Yellow Creek - Indiana County

From the dam at Yellow Creek State Park downstream to the Route 954 bridge, Yellow Creek flows through a scenic, semi-remote area, some of which lies within State Game Land No. 273. The fishing here is for stocked trout, but quite a few brown trout carry over into the summer months, especially in the stretches that are a long walk from road access. Route 954 crosses Yellow Creek a few miles south of the town of Indiana.

Cush Creek - Indiana and Clearfield Counties

Cush Creek flows from northeastern Indiana County into Clearfield County, where it joins the upper stretch of the West Branch Susquehanna River. Cush Creek is stocked with trout and also holds good numbers of wild browns. No trout are stocked above the confluence of Horton Run at Glen Campbell, but wild browns are often caught in this upper water.

This headwater stretch may not appeal to everyone, though. Cush Creek is narrow and brushy here, and it flows past mining spoil piles.

Wills Creek - Somerset and Bedford Counties

Wills Creek is a swift, rocky stream that white water boaters enjoy running when water levels are high. Trout are stocked along most of the stream's length in Somerset County and from the county line down to the village of Hyndman in Bedford County. Some of the creek flows through State Game Lands No. 82 and 104, and some stretches are privately owned. The fishing on Wills Creek is mostly for stocked trout, but local anglers report catching some large wild or holdover browns.

Wills Creek's stocked tributaries include Little Wills Creek, Shaffers Run, Brush Creek, and Laurel Run. Laurel Run holds many wild brook trout.

Raystown Branch of the Juniata - Somerset and Bedford Counties

The Raystown Branch is stocked with trout over a distance of about 28 miles in Somerset and Bedford Counties. In Somerset County, trout are stocked from the county line upstream about 7 miles to near the Route 31 bridge. In Bedford County trout are stocked from the county line downstream to near the town of Bedford. The fishing is mostly for stocked trout because the Raystown Branch warms quickly in the summer months, but some brown trout are caught in the late season, and wild brook trout are found in the headwaters.

Breastwork Run is a small tributary that meets the Raystown Branch near the village of New Baltimore in Somerset County. Here you can fish for both hatchery trout and native brook trout.

Stream Index

Additional Copies

Additional copies of *Trout Streams of Pennsylvania* may be ordered directly from the publisher for $18.95 each. Please include $1.50 per order for shipping and handling. Pennsylvania residents add 6% sales tax ($1.23). Prices are subject to change without notice.

Send to:
Hempstead-Lyndell
P.O. Box 69
Bellefonte, PA 16823